New Good Food

New Good Food

Essential Ingredients for Cooking and Eating Well

Margaret M. Wittenberg

TEN SPEED PRESS
Berkeley

Dedicated to the plants, animals, farmers, fishermen,
and producers that provide us food to share,
enjoy, and flourish.

Copyright © 1995, 2007 by Margaret M. Wittenberg

All rights reserved. Published in the United States by Ten Speed Press, an imprint of
the Crown Publishing Group, a division of Random House, Inc., New York.
www.crownpublishing.com
www.tenspeed.com

Ten Speed Press and the Ten Speed Press colophon are registered trademarks of
Random House, Inc.

Library of Congress Cataloging-in-Publication Data
Wittenberg, Margaret M.
  New good food : essential ingredients for cooking and eating well /
Margaret M. Wittenberg.
      p. cm.
  Includes bibliographical references and index.
  1. Food. 2. Nutrition. 3. Cookery. 4. Diet. I. Title.
  TX354.W583 2007
    641.3—dc22   2007016712

ISBN-13: 978-1-58008-750-6

Printed in Korea

Cover and text design by McGuire Barber Design
Cover photos by Ed Anderson

12 11 10 9 8 7 6 5 4

First Revised Edition

Table of Contents

vii   Acknowledgments

ix   Introduction

1   Fruits and Vegetables

29   Grains

69   Whole Grain and Specialty Flours

95   Breads

105   Pasta and Noodles

117   Beans, Peas, and Lentils

141   Nuts and Seeds

167   Culinary Oils

187   Meat, Poultry, and Eggs

197   Dairy Products

209   Seafood

221   Essential Seasonings

241   Sweeteners

263   Bibliography

278   Index

284   About the Author

Acknowledgments

As any author will tell you, books only happen when you have a great support system behind you. Many, many thanks to:

My husband, Terry, for his love and the many years of exploring foods and ideas together, which not only provided much inspiration for this book, but also made life a whole lot of fun.

My parents, Dolores and Merle Moothart, from whom I learned the two big lessons in life: the joy and power of laughter and that food tastes even better when it is shared.

Phil Wood, founder of Ten Speed Press, and Lorena Jones, publisher, for their confidence in me and the honor to be an author for a publishing house I have always held in utmost esteem.

Amanda Berne, my fabulous editor, who not only has been fun to work with but has also been an amazing source of insightful guidance, ideas, and moral support.

Dennis Hayes for his longtime encouragement of me and belief in my writing, as well as for his much appreciated humor that always keeps me smiling.

The entire editorial and design team at Ten Speed Press, including Lily Binns, my original editor, for her help shaping the book in the early days of its development; Ten Speed editorial director Aaron Wehner; Jasmine Star, my very talented, ace copy editor; Karen Levy, the proofreader with extra keen eyes; Patrick Barber for his beautiful cover design and Holly McGuire for the great book layout design.

Friends and colleagues with whom I enjoyed many delicious dinners and stimulating conversations regarding all aspects of food production, cooking, and environmental sustainability throughout the years.

And, last but certainly not least, my cat, "Junior", who has been a true writing companion and teacher, demonstrating to me that life should be enhanced with plenty of naps and just plain silliness.

Introduction

I am an intuitive cook. Put a variety of foods in front of me and I can visualize
how they might fit together, enhancing one another in terms of flavors, textures, and
presentation. Although some of my knack is likely innate, much of it I developed
through experience, by cooking, observing, listening, and reading. In the process, I
have learned a lot about different foods, their history, how they are grown or produced,
their nutritional attributes, and their cooking methods, as well as how various foods
make me feel. Writing this book, then, has stirred up a lot of memories for me. With
each food I describe, I can recall the time and place when I first tried or heard about it
and all the circumstances surrounding that experience.

Nourishing My Interests

My mother's extraordinary cooking served as a backdrop to sharing the day's happenings
at meals with my parents and five siblings. Sunday breakfasts were my father's realm.
Inspired by my parents' talents, I tried my own hand at cooking, following recipes
from my beloved *Better Homes and Gardens Junior Cook Book* and also improvising on
my own.

My interest in cooking reached a new level when, for a 4-H Club meeting food
demonstration project, I was assigned the task of highlighting the visual differences
between two cakes, one made with baking powder and the other without. That a food
could change so dramatically by adding or deleting just one ingredient was utterly
fascinating to me, igniting what would be a lifelong enthusiasm for food science and
the interactions between foods and various ingredients.

When I met my husband, Terry, in 1974, we realized immediately that we shared an
interest in food. Starting with a visit to a local natural foods co-op, Terry introduced
me to many new foods, as well as familiar ones that, to me, were largely unrecognizable

in their raw forms. Take dried beans, for example. Although I had eaten plenty of navy bean soup and pork and beans while growing up, they were purchased precooked in cans. The beautiful, earthy colors and various shapes of uncooked beans amazed me, as did the many bins of whole grains, nuts, and seeds.

Terry was also the catalyst for my fascination with the nutritional aspects of food. Because he's an avid cyclist, using food as a source of functional fuel has been just as important to him as the sensual pleasure of eating.

Fortunately for me, my love of food turned into a career. The start of more than three decades of professional connection with food began with Sunseed Natural Foods, a small natural foods store Terry and I opened in West Bend, Wisconsin, during the fall of 1977. Along with the challenges of introducing natural foods to a small, conservative Midwestern town, we also had to learn the realities about running a business, but we thrived on the experience. From teaching cooking classes to helping customers in the aisles, for us it was all about sharing the great flavors, fun, and health benefits of cooking with natural foods. It also laid a good foundation for what was to come.

After selling our store at the end of 1980, Terry and I happened by the first Whole Foods Market in Austin, Texas, just four months after the store had opened for business. We were hired in January 1981 as two of the company's original twenty-five team members, sharing in the excitement of being part of a new concept in grocery stores, a one-stop shop where all the food was natural and minimally processed. Never in our wildest dreams did we imagine that the first, humble Whole Foods Market would eventually evolve into the world's leading chain of natural and organic foods supermarkets.

I've worked as a cashier, stocker, product specialist, buyer, team leader, and store manager, had roles involving teaching and writing, and now am one of the company's global vice presidents. In the mid-1980s, I also had a one-year part-time stint as the principal cook of the Austin East West Center, where I honed my cooking skills, learning about balancing elements within a meal and the effects food has on body, mind, and spirit.

Most fulfilling of all has been my work at Whole Foods Market as lead coordinator and researcher in the development and maintenance of quality standards. I've had the good fortune to meet a number of extraordinary people—from farmers and producers to scientists, food experts, and activists worldwide—who have contributed to the ongoing growth of my knowledge and appreciation of food.

Deeper Issues

My work has also given me the chance to participate in national and international advisory groups exploring some of the deeper issues about food and how to work together to deal with them. Primary topics have included the short- and long-term effects of pesticides and other pollutants on our food supply, sustainable agriculture, genetic engineering, sustainability of wild seafood, aquaculture, and the welfare of food-producing animals from birth through slaughter.

To me, the most disturbing of all these issues is the genetic engineering of our food supply. Genetic engineering (GE) is the manipulation of an organism's genes by eliminating or rearranging specific genes or by introducing genetic elements from one or more organisms into another organism, including across species boundaries, in order to create new traits in plants and animals that don't occur in nature and probably can't be developed by natural means. In my view, this brings food production schemes to a new low, putting our health, the future of our food supply, and the environment at great risk for the short-term gain of a few.

A result of my work is that I remain fully committed to helping ensure the continued availability of whole foods grown and raised in a responsible, sustainable manner. Although there are several ways of going about it, organic agriculture remains the most effective way in which good food, good health, and support of the environment have a very real opportunity to merge and thrive. Organic is what I always look for when I shop, and it serves as a primary gauge for choosing which foods to buy.

The Intrinsic Value of Whole Foods

Every day, discoveries are being made that underscore that keeping foods whole, not processed or fractionated, is vital to overall health and wellbeing. Increasingly, we are learning that isolated nutrients don't always have the same health benefits as the whole foods from which they were originally isolated. And beyond the familiar vitamins and minerals most of us know about, whole plant foods contain an almost bewildering spectrum of healthful compounds known as phytonutrients (*phyto* means "plant"). Pigments and bitter-tasting components, which we once thought were primarily of benefit to plants, either to better flourish or to protect themselves, have turned out to be powerful antioxidants that can help moderate damage to our own human cells. The vast array of phytonutrients may not be essential for keeping us alive, but their positive effects on health, such as helping prevent cancer and reducing inflammation, certainly make living life that much more enjoyable.

Scientific studies have repeatedly shown the powerful, positive effects of eating a good diet, starting from the maternal nutrition we receive while still in the womb and continuing throughout all stages of life, including our senior years. Good diet and nutrition, along with sufficient exercise, are essential for reducing the incidence of myriad chronic, noncommunicable diseases, such as obesity, cardiovascular disease, hypertension, stroke, diabetes, cancer, dental diseases, and osteoporosis.

The lowest rates of coronary heart disease, certain types of cancers, and other diet-related chronic diseases have been found in cultures where the everyday diet is high in fruits, vegetables, whole grains, whole grain breads and pastas, beans, nuts, seeds, and olive oil, with only low to moderate amounts of eggs, red meat, fish, poultry, and dairy products in the form of cheese and yogurt. Although commonly referred to as the Mediterranean diet, as it reflects the food patterns that were typical of Crete, much of Greece, and southern Italy in the early 1960s, it's not just about a focus on all foods Mediterranean. It's about recognizing the inherent value in using a wide variety of good, basic, natural foods, no matter what the culture or cuisine.

And that is exactly what this book is all about. Rather than being about what food is *not,* it is an introduction to or a reminder of what food *is.* It is a weaving together of descriptions, cooking suggestions, and just enough history, food science, and nutrition to get a glimpse of all the wonders each food has to offer. It is also an appreciation of food for its possibilities, its bringing together of people to the table, its melding of cultures, its nourishment which enriches body and soul, its celebration of the people, plants, and animals that make it all happen, and, of course, its extraordinary flavors.

Each chapter focuses on specific foods and ideas that I personally have found to be essential to an intuitive style of wholesome, delicious cooking. Rather than intending to be a comprehensive reference guide, this book is meant to be a catalyst toward the development of your own natural connection to foods. In the process, your path of discovery will bring not only sheer enjoyment but also better health and well-being.

Go ahead, get out your fork. Explore the possibilities.

Fruits and Vegetables

My mother had a knack for making the simple taste divine. Take cooked carrots, for example. Because she had an aversion to butter, they were merely cooked in water with a little salt, but we couldn't get enough of them. Years later, I learned how unusual it was for fruits and vegetables to play such a central role in family meals. But fresh, frozen, or canned, they were a customary and anticipated component at the table at our house, and they often served as snacks, as well.

That love of fruits and vegetables has stayed with me to this day. When I'm in a well-stocked produce department or farmers' market with a wide variety of produce in all sizes, shapes, flavors, and colors, I genuinely want to eat my way through it, and it takes all the restraint I can muster to hold myself back.

In essence, fruits and vegetables represent one of our closest links to nature—and to life itself. Who doesn't have a sense of wonder that a tiny seed can grow into an entire plant that we can then harvest and eat? Or not marvel at the transformation of small flowers that transform into crisp apples or succulent pears as the season progresses? Fruits and vegetables don't merely appease the pangs of hunger; they nourish us on many levels.

Nutrition

Science has corroborated what we instinctively know: eating plenty of fruits and vegetables enhances overall health and well-being. More specifically, it helps reduce the risk of many diseases and disorders that are largely avoidable, including heart disease, stroke, and cancer, as well as age-related eye diseases, such as macular degeneration and cataracts. Both fruits and vegetables are equally essential in the diet, with each making valuable and unique contributions to health that cannot be completely replaced by the other.

The high vitamin, mineral, and fiber content of fruits and vegetables has long been proclaimed to be the reason why they are so nourishing and beneficial. Now, however, other compounds called phytonutrients, which were originally thought to provide merely color, texture, flavor, or aromatic qualities, have been recognized for their ability to provide extraordinary health benefits.

What's in a Label?

Whether buying fruits and vegetables from a grocery store, from a farmers' market, or directly from the farmer, specific terms are typically used to convey how the product was produced or other special attributes. While some of the claims on these labels may reflect the producer's claims, many represent adherence to specific standards.

For extra assurance, such claims, especially those related to special methods of production or environmentally sound methods, are ideally verified by an inspector not personally affiliated with the producer or a company for whom a farmer may grow products. In most cases, the name of the auditing group is listed on the label. Such inspectors, hired by a private auditing company, governmental agency, or standards-creating organization, are trained and qualified to objectively evaluate the producer's compliance with the standards represented by the label.

BIODYNAMIC

Biodynamic farming, an agricultural method in which the farm is managed as a self-contained, living organism, integrates soil health and nutrient management, not only in conjunction with raising crops and livestock, but also within the context of the subtle rhythms and energies of nature. Biodynamic agricultural methods are based on lectures presented in 1924 by Rudolf Steiner, an Austrian scientist who believed farming should done with both an understanding of the practical, scientific aspects and a spiritual appreciation of nature.

Biodynamic farming is similar to organic agriculture in many regards. It has a focus on building and maintaining soil quality by rotating crops, using cover crops, and composting. And like organic farming, it doesn't make use of genetically engineered seeds or crops, sewage sludge as compost, or toxic pesticides, herbicides, or fungicides. However, biodynamic farming is different than organic agriculture because of its metaphysical underpinnings, which manifest in specific practices used to enhance vital life forces and subtle energetic frequencies on the farm. Planting and harvesting are planned according to certain lunar and astrological cycles, and specific soil treatments are made in a precise manner from minerals, plants, or animal manure extracts and applied to compost in extremely diluted amounts. Research has affirmed that the quality of soil on biodynamic farms is indeed superior, and it may be that food quality and overall nutrition of products from such farms are enhanced far beyond the standard nutritional analysis, which is focused on vitamin and mineral content.

Food and products that have been certified by qualified, independent auditors as meeting the rigorous requirements of biodynamic farming are labeled with the Demeter International trademark. As biodynamic standards include those required by organic standards, many biodynamic products are doubly certified as organic, too.

ECOLOGICALLY GROWN

Also known as biointensive integrated pest management (IPM), ecologically grown fruits and vegetables are produced using methods focused on effectively managing pests and beneficial organisms in an ecological context. The overarching intent is to prevent pest infestations before they happen by monitoring crops closely and treating pests only as needed and using only the amount and duration of treatment needed to get the job done. Preferred pest controls used in biointensive IPM include ladybugs, spiders, wasps, bacteria, and predatory mites that may be natural enemies to a particular pest. Pest-specific synthetic sex pheromones may also be used to reduce insect populations. In essence, these work by confusing male insects, thus disrupting the mating cycle. Chemical pesticides are used as a last resort, with a focus on choosing those that are the least environmentally disruptive.

This style of farming requires a thorough understanding of insects and microbes, both beneficial and potentially destructive varieties, and their interactions with other organisms and the environment. Skill is required to determine which combination of methods to use to prevent or treat pests in the most ecological, integrated manner and restore and enhance natural balances in the ecosystem. These could include crop rotation, companion crops that draw insects away from the main crop, disease-resistant crop varieties, physical barriers against pests, and measures to increase biological diversity within the farm system.

A wide range of labels refer to products as ecologically or sustainably grown in one way or another. Standards for some of these prohibit specific pesticides and the use of genetically modified seeds. Other standards may be crop-specific or cover many types of fruits and vegetables grown within a specific region. Still others may require producers to incorporate sound management of wildlife habitat and soil and water conservation practices to enhance ecosystem health. Look for details about the particular requirements of any given label and, for extra assurance that label claims were met, the name or seal of an independent auditing company on the label itself.

HEIRLOOM VARIETIES

Like family heirlooms, valued possessions passed down from generation to generation, heirloom fruits and vegetables are treasured varieties that have been recognized as symbols of regional pride and a living connection to the past. In general, an heirloom plant is a variety that has been known through historical documentation or folk history for at least fifty years. Most are grown through open pollination, which means their seeds are set naturally, often helped by wind, rain, and insects. One benefit is that the seeds produced by open pollination can be used to grow a new generation of plants, which is not the case with hybrids.

Many heirloom varieties grown in the United States originated from seeds brought by immigrants. Subsequent decades and centuries of adaptation and natural selection have resulted in one-of-a-kind fruit and vegetables varieties, many of which thrive only in certain regions within the country. That's why their names are often as interesting as their characteristics; some are known by the name of the family, farm, or locale where they're grown, while others are tagged with colorful names that attempt to describe flavor or appearance.

Unusual shapes and sizes, flavors that range from familiar to complex and unique, curious colors, and mottled facades—all are typical hallmarks of heirloom fruits and vegetables and allow us to celebrate diversity in a world that is all too often focused on the homogenous. By keeping a wide array of plants in circulation, heirloom varieties help protect the biodiversity that is so vital to the health of our planet and, in particular, to the resilience of our food supply. Many heirloom varieties also demonstrate exceptional tolerance to adverse weather and pests.

If you were to compare the amounts of vitamins and minerals in heirloom varieties and their modern counterparts, they might look much the same. However, the distinctive colors and flavors of some heirloom foods hint at the presence of unique phytonutrients not available in contemporary hybrids, which have been developed by deliberately crossing two or more varieties of plants to achieve certain traits, such as uniformity, prolonged shelf life, higher yield, or specific flavors or cooking properties. Heirloom apples, pears, tomatoes, potatoes, and beans are widely available in many parts of the country. Explore the world of these interesting and flavorful alternatives. Because many of them grow better in small-production systems or certain areas, buying them locally is often the best way to go.

LOCALLY GROWN

There is no single definition of locally grown. It might indicate how many miles or hours away a farm is, or it could be considered in terms of state or regional production. Whatever the criteria, a focus on locally grown produce has the potential to provide fruits and vegetables that are much fresher and, therefore, more flavorful and nutritious, especially considering that produce shipped from outside the local area may already be a couple of days old by the time it arrives in a market.

Buying locally grown produce also increases your opportunity to enjoy the flavors, shapes, sizes, and textures of varieties that are unique to the area. Knowing that a person within your community produced a particular product adds a personal level to the experience, including appreciation of the effort and commitment the farmer took to grow it, given the weather and other conditions in your area. Still, it's important to remember that locally grown produce isn't necessarily grown without agricultural chemicals. Look into a local producer's growing methods, perhaps a certified organic label. Better yet, ask the farmer directly.

ORGANICALLY GROWN

Organic agriculture is a system of production based on enhancing the health of the soil in order to produce crops in a way that fosters the health and harmony of the ecosystem, including the people and animals within it. Certain cultivation practices, such as rotating crops, planting cover crops, and composting, are used to help support soil fertility. Pests, weeds, and diseases are managed primarily through physical, mechanical, and

biological controls, many of them similar to those used in biointensive integrated pest management programs. However, in organic farming, the use of pesticides that persist within the environment or toxic chemicals are not allowed. In the event that more support is needed for a particular crop, only biological, botanical, or specific approved low-risk substances may be used, and these are quickly broken down by oxygen and sunlight.

In the United States, a list of substances allowed or prohibited in organic farming, production, and processing is maintained as part of the national organic standards. All are evaluated for their effects on human health and their short-term and long-term effects on the environment, taking into consideration toxicity and mode of action, availability of gentler alternatives, chances of environmental contamination (during manufacture, use, and disposal), potential for interactions with other substances, and overall compatibility with a system of sustainable agriculture.

Methods that support and enhance biodiversity within the agricultural landscape are also emphasized, including recycling of nutrients, protection of habitat for wildlife and beneficial insects, conservation of soil and water, and protection of soil and water quality. Accordingly, organic standards prohibit use of genetically engineered seeds or crops, sewage sludge as compost, or toxic chemical pesticides and fertilizers. In addition, fruits and vegetables certified as organic must be grown on land that has had no prohibited substances applied to it for at least three years prior to harvest of the crop.

Certification audits are conducted by sanctioned or accredited companies qualified to conduct rigorous reviews of records and thorough on-site inspections of the farm. In the United States, the U.S. Department of Agriculture accredits certifiers who ensure producers are adhering to the country's national organic standards. In other parts of the world, certification may be done by

How Much and How to Choose

At the very least, aim for seven to nine servings of fruits and vegetables per day (five for small children). Given that a serving is relatively small, these minimum amounts are easy to achieve.

One Serving of Fruit
1 medium-size piece of whole fruit
½ cup of freshly chopped, cooked, or
    canned fruit (canned in its own juices),
    including applesauce and fruit cooked
    in baked goods
¾ cup (6 fluid ounces) of 100% fruit juice
    with no added sugar
¼ cup dried fruit

One Serving of Vegetables
1 cup of raw leafy vegetables
½ cup of chopped raw, cooked, or
    canned vegetables
½ cup of cooked, canned, or frozen
    legumes (beans or peas)
¾ cup (6 fluid ounces) of 100% vegetable
    juice

governmental agencies or independent certifying groups. Although different standards exist in different countries, the International Federation of Organic Agriculture Movements (IFOAM), a worldwide umbrella organization for agencies supporting organic agriculture, is working toward creating international standards and methods of assessment and accreditation.

Many people who support organic agriculture—both farmers and consumers—do so out of concern for environmental stewardship and because organic products are a good alternative to conventionally grown products that may have been treated with persistent pesticides and other toxins. More recently, science has begun to confirm many of the benefits of eating organically produced food. For example, consuming organic foods is an excellent way to avoid exposure to organophosphate pesticides. Widely used in conventional agriculture, these pesticides have been associated with increased risk of negative neurological effects in infants and children. Studies of dietary interventions have shown dramatic reductions in organophosphate metabolites within children's bodies when they were switched to a diet consisting pri-

marily of organic foods. Another benefit may be enhanced levels of nutrients. Studies suggest that both organic farming methods and organic food processing techniques may contribute to increased antioxidant content.

PESTICIDE-FREE

Typically, pesticide-free is a self-affirmed producer claim simply stating that no synthetic chemical pesticides were used to grow the fruit or vegetable. Be aware that such a declaration does not mean the produce was organically grown, nor does it necessarily indicate that the crop was grown using any other ecologically friendly methods.

NO DETECTABLE PESTICIDE RESIDUES

Produce designated as having no detectable pesticide residues has generally been tested in a laboratory, via a representative sample, to determine how much or how many pesticides remain on the produce after harvest. Results are based on the specific level of detection deemed possible for a specific pesticide. Fruits and vegetables raised using conventional agricultural methods are generally most likely to be evaluated for such labeling.

Let Color Be Your Guide

The easiest way to experience the diversity of fruits and vegetables and take advantage of the wide range of nutrients they contain is to include selections from all the color groups each day: green, yellow-orange, red, white, and blue or purple.

It's important to eat both raw and cooked fruits and vegetables. Because some phytonutrients and vitamins, such as vitamin C and folic acid, are heat sensitive, be sure to include some raw fruits and vegetables in your diet every day. On the other hand, certain nutritional components of some vegetables, such as tomatoes and carrots, are more bioavailable after cooking. Using only a minimal amount of cooking water will help retain nutrients.

While fresh produce is usually optimal in terms of nutrition, sometimes frozen fruits and vegetables are more nutritious than fresh ones, depending on the length of time since a fresh product was harvested and the conditions under which it was transported and stored. If packed without any additives, including sweeteners, canned products can be healthful options, too.

Although juices can be a good way to consume fruits and vegetables, they usually lack the fiber and phytonutrients found in their whole forms. And because they are low in fiber, their concentrated sugars will be absorbed very rapidly, depending on the amount consumed, its dilution, and whether it's drunk as part of a meal or as a single beverage. Moderation, as always, is the key. Reading labels is particularly important when shopping for juice. Be sure to buy only 100% fruit juice with no added sweeteners.

Another way to enjoy fruit is in its dried, dehydrated state. Grapes become raisins, some plums become prunes, and other fruits reveal sides of themselves that are merely hinted at when they're consumed fresh. Besides concentrating flavors and sugar content, drying fruit also concentrates its nutrients, making it very high in fiber, potassium, and phytonutrients, including carotenoids and other antioxidants. On the other hand, as with cooking, the dehydration process can lower levels of heat-sensitive nutrients, such as vitamin C.

Even though most dried fruits are very sweet, some are sprayed with a honey or sugar solution to keep the fruit soft, balance out acidity, and prevent the dried fruit from turning brown. Avoid dried fruit preserved with sulfites (sulfur dioxide, sodium sulfite, sodium and potassium bisulfite, and sodium and potassium metabisulfite). Although they prevent discoloration in dried fruit and help retain moisture, sulfites are known to cause reactions—sometimes serious—in sensitive individuals. Fortunately, dried fruits processed without sulfites are readily available. Even though some of them may be more leathery in texture and less vibrant in coloring, their flavor remains remarkable. Dried fruit can be softened by steaming or cooking in a small amount of water for a few minutes or by soaking in water for a few hours or overnight. These methods can help plump dried fruit nearly to its original size, and as a side benefit, the soaking water can be used as a cooking liquid or sweet beverage. Soaking the fruit also reduces the tendency to overeat dried fruit; although it's a healthful food, it does contain concentrated sugars.

The high sugar content of dried fruits acts as a preservative, so refrigeration of dried fruits is not necessary. However, they will keep much longer if refrigerated. Store them in airtight jars or plastic containers to keep them from absorbing moisture and becoming infested with insects. Occasionally the natural sugars in the fruit will solidify, forming crystals on the surface of the fruit, particularly prunes and figs, but this is harmless.

Storage and Food Safety Tips

Keep fruits and vegetables separate, as the ethylene gas produced by some fruits can make certain vegetables taste bitter. However, you can put that ethylene gas to work to help fruit ripen more quickly.

The Colors and Peak Seasons for Fruits and Vegetables

GREEN

Fruits	Spring	Summer	Fall	Winter
Apples, Granny Smith	x	x	x	x
Avocados	x	x	x	x
Grapes, green (Thompson or Perlette)	x	x	x	x
Honeydew			x	x
Kiwifruit	x	x	x	x
Limes	x	x	x	x
Pears, Anjou	x		x	x
Pears, Comice			x	x
Pears, Packham	x	x		

Vegetables	Spring	Summer	Fall	Winter
Artichokes	x		x	
Arugula	x	x	x	x
Asparagus	x			
Beans, green		x		
Beet greens		x	x	
Bok choy	x	x	x	x
Broccoflower			x	x
Broccoli	x		x	x
Broccoli raab	x		x	x
Broccoli Romanesco			x	x
Brussels sprouts			x	
Cabbage, Chinese	x	x	x	x
Cabbage, green	x	x	x	x
Celery	x	x	x	x
Chayote squash	x		x	x
Chives	x	x	x	x
Collard greens	x		x	x
Cucumbers		x		
Dandelion greens	x			
Endive, curly	x			x
Herbs, all fresh	x	x	x	x
Kale			x	x
Leeks	x		x	x

GREEN (cont.)

Vegetables (cont.)	Spring	Summer	Fall	Winter
Lettuce, all	x	x	x	x
Mâche	x	x	x	x
Mizuna	x	x	x	x
Mustard greens	x			x
Okra		x		
Onions, green	x	x	x	x
Parsley	x	x	x	x
Peas, fresh	x			
Peas, snow	x	x		
Peas, sugar snap	x	x		
Peppers, green bell	x	x		
Sorrel		x	x	
Spinach	x	x	x	x
Sprouts, alfalfa and sunflower	x	x	x	x
Swiss chard, green		x	x	
Tomatillos	x	x	x	x
Turnip greens	x		x	x
Watercress	x	x	x	x
Zucchini	x	x		

YELLOW and ORANGE

Fruits	Spring	Summer	Fall	Winter
Apricots, dried	x	x	x	x
Apricots, fresh	x	x		
Bananas, red	x	x	x	x
Cantaloupe		x	x	
Carambola (star fruit)		x	x	x
Figs, Calimyrna, dried	x	x	x	x
Figs, Calimyrna, fresh		x		
Grapefruit	x			x
Kumquats	x			x
Lemons	x	x		
Lemons, Meyer			x	x
Mangoes	x	x	x	x

The Colors and Peak Seasons for Fruits and Vegetables (cont.)

YELLOW and ORANGE (cont.)

Fruits (cont.)	Spring	Summer	Fall	Winter
Nectarines	x	x		
Oranges	x		x	x
Papayas	x	x	x	x
Peaches	x	x		
Pears, Bartlett			x	x
Persimmons			x	x
Pineapple	x	x		
Quince			x	x
Tamarind	x	x		
Tangelos				x
Tangerines	x			x
Ugli fruit	x			x
Vegetables				
Carrots	x		x	x
Corn		x	x	
Mushrooms, chanterelle	x	x	x	
Onions, yellow	x	x	x	
Peppers, yellow bell		x	x	
Potatoes, fingerling	x		x	x
Potatoes, Yellow Finn		x	x	
Potatoes, Yukon gold		x	x	
Rutabagas	x		x	x
Summer squash, yellow	x	x		
Sweet potatoes			x	x
Sweet potatoes, Japanese	x		x	x
Tomatoes, yellow		x	x	
Winter squash			x	x
Yams			x	x
Zucchini, golden	x	x		

RED

Fruits	Spring	Summer	Fall	Winter
Apples	x		x	x
Blood oranges	x		x	x
Cherries		x		

RED (cont.)

Fruits (cont.)	Spring	Summer	Fall	Winter
Cranberries			x	x
Grapefruit, pink or red	x			x
Grapes, red (Flame, Tokay)	x	x	x	x
Guava, red-fleshed	x			x
Pears, Red Bartlett			x	x
Plums, El Dorado, Laroda		x	x	
Pomegranates			x	x
Raspberries	x	x		
Strawberries	x	x		
Watermelon		x		
Vegetables				
Beets		x	x	
Onions, red	x	x		
Peppers, red bell		x		
Potatoes, red			x	
Radicchio				x
Radishes	x			
Rhubarb	x	x		
Tomatoes		x	x	

WHITE

Fruits	Spring	Summer	Fall	Winter
Bananas	x	x	x	x
Dates, dried	x	x	x	x
Dates, fresh		x		
Figs, brown Turkey	x			x
Lychees		x	x	
Nectarines, white	x	x		
Peaches, Babcock	x	x		
Pears, Bosc	x		x	x
Plaintains	x	x	x	x
Vegetables				
Burdock	x	x	x	x
Cauliflower			x	x
Celery root	x		x	x

WHITE (cont.)	Spring	Summer	Fall	Winter
Vegetables (cont.)				
Corn, white		x	x	
Daikon			x	x
Endive, Belgian	x			x
Fennel bulb	x		x	x
Garlic	x	x	x	x
Ginger	x	x	x	
Jerusalem artichokes			x	x
Jicama	x		x	x
Kohlrabi		x		
Lotus root		x	x	x
Mushrooms, beech	x	x	x	x
Mushrooms, button	x	x	x	x
Mushrooms, crimini	x	x	x	x
Mushrooms, enoki	x	x	x	x
Mushrooms, portobello	x	x	x	x
Mushrooms, shiitake	x	x	x	x
Onions	x	x	x	
Parsley root				x
Parsnips			x	x
Potatoes, new	x	x		
Potatoes, russet	x		x	x
Shallots	x			
Sprouts, mung bean	x	x	x	x
Taro root	x	x	x	x
Turnips	x		x	x

BLUE or PURPLE	Spring	Summer	Fall	Winter
Fruits				
Blackberries		x	x	
Black currants		x		
Blueberries		x	x	
Elderberries		x	x	
Figs, black Mission, dried	x	x	x	x
Figs, black Mission, fresh	x	x	x	
Grapes, purple (Ribier)	x	x	x	x
Passion fruit		x	x	x
Plums		x		
Prunes	x	x	x	x
Raisins	x	x	x	x
Vegetables				
Cabbage, red or purple	x	x	x	x
Carrots, purple	x	x	x	x
Eggplant		x	x	
Mushrooms, black trumpet			x	x
Mushrooms, morel	x			
Potatoes, purple			x	
Salsify, black			x	x

Adapted from *Fruits & Veggies More Matters*
(www.fruitsandveggiesmorematters.org).

Just place underripe bananas, peaches, plums, nectarines, or apricots in a loosely closed paper sack or a ripening bowl made expressly for that purpose. Within a day or two, some of the fruit's starch will convert to its sweeter form—sugar. Refrigerate fruit after it is fully ripened to slow further ripening. Bananas are an exception; they turn black when refrigerated. Instead, peel and freeze any extra ripe bananas and use them as a flavorful thickener for smoothies.

Some raw vegetables, including whole tomatoes, potatoes, and sweet potatoes, should also never be refrigerated, as cold temperatures can adversely affect flavor and texture. Winter squash need not be refrigerated, either. However, fresh-cut produce should always be sold and stored refrigerated. Likewise, all perishable fresh fruit and vegetables and fresh-pressed juices should be kept at temperatures below 40°F and away from raw meat, poultry, and seafood. Mushrooms should be stored in the refrigerator in paper bags, not plastic. Remove any green tops from root vegetables to prevent moisture from being drawn up and out of the roots.

Treat fresh basil and cilantro like flowers, placing their long stems in water, changing the water daily, and keeping at a cool room temperature for up to a couple of days. Store other fresh herbs in the refrigerator loosely within perforated or partially open plastic bags to provide air flow, inserting a paper towel to absorb excess moisture.

Because berries are very perishable, keep them dry, washing them only right before eating rather than before storing in the refrigerator. It's important to thoroughly wash or rinse all produce before eating, including fruits or vegetables that will be peeled, even if they're organically grown. Firm produce should be scrubbed with a vegetable brush. Damaged or bruised portions of fruits and vegetables should be cut away and discarded before cooking or eating them. Bagged produce can be used without further washing, although it's safest to rinse it thoroughly just prior to use.

Exploring Fruit

Asian Pear

Also known as apple pears, Asian pears have the juicy, sweet flavor of a pear and the crispness of an apple. Not a hybrid, this fruit was brought to the United States by Chinese prospectors during the California Gold Rush. Since Asian pears are picked ripe, they are ready to eat when purchased. Unlike other fruits, they store well for months when refrigerated. Their refreshing flavor and texture are best appreciated when they are eaten out of hand or added to fruit salads.

Carambola

When cut horizontally, carambola slices look like a five-pointed star, accounting for its alternate name, star fruit. Yellow when ripe, it has translucent flesh that can be sweet, very tart, or a combination of both. The texture of carambola is slightly crisp, making it an excellent contrast element in fruit salads composed of soft fruits. It is also terrific eaten out of hand.

Cherimoya

Although its rough, notched exterior may not look too inviting, cherimoya has an unusual, delicious flavor, described as a combination of strawberry, banana, and pineapple, which more than makes up for its first impression. It has a custardlike texture, accounting for its alternate name, custard apple. Cherimoyas are high in vitamin C. Unfortunately, cherimoyas are one of the more expensive fruits available for a couple of reasons: The female cherimoya flowers must be hand-pollinated to produce fruit. And because cherimoyas are so fragile, they must be harvested and sorted by hand. All the more reason to savor every bite. When ripe, their skin turns brownish green and yields to light pressure. A cherimoya can be eaten right out of its own "cup" when halved or quartered, or cut it into chunks and add it to fruit salads. Discard its large black seeds. Don't bother cooking cherimoya; the flavor dissipates with heat.

Guava

Guavas are small, round fruits with skin ranging in color from green to yellow and flesh ranging from white to deep pink. Some guavas taste like pineapple, while others have a flavor reminiscent of strawberries. They are ready to eat when slightly soft. Remove the seeds and eat out of the "half shell," or peel and slice. Firm guavas can also be baked or used to make jellies and preserves.

Kiwifruit

A prime example of how patient marketing can pay off, kiwifruit were once a relatively obscure, exotic fruit but are now widely recognized and appreciated. Originally called the Chinese gooseberry, it was officially renamed kiwifruit in the 1970s in honor of the native bird in New Zealand—and for greater market appeal during the Cold War era. Inside its inauspicious brown, suedelike skin lies bright green flesh, studded with tiny, edible black seeds, with a flavor often described as similar to a combination of strawberries and melon. Kiwis are very high in vitamin C. They are ripe when slightly soft, a state than can be preserved for weeks if they're refrigerated. To prepare kiwis, cut them in half and spoon the flesh out of the skin, or peel them before cutting into slices. Like papaya, kiwi contains an enzyme that breaks down proteins. Accordingly, it can be used as a meat tenderizer. For the same reason, raw kiwi will prevent gelatin from setting unless its enzymes are first deactivated by brief cooking. Likewise, when raw kiwi is added to milk products, such as yogurt, the mixture should be consumed immediately.

Kumquat

Kumquats look like miniature, oblong oranges. Unlike oranges, however, both the skin and the flesh can be consumed, with the sweet skin providing a delicious contrast to the pulp's tart flavor. The seeds aren't edible and should be discarded. Thinly slice kumquats and add them to fruit salads, or take advantage of their high pectin content and use them to make preserves and marmalade.

Lychee

Under the bright red, rough-skinned shell of a lychee fruit is a creamy white pulp with a jellylike texture and a flavor similar to grapes, although more aromatic. In the middle of the golf-ball-size fruit is a large seed, the reason you may sometimes hear it referred to as a lychee nut. To eat a lychee, peel off the shell starting at the stem end and remove the seed. Eat the flesh straight from the shell, or slice it and add to fruit salads. Lychees are high in vitamin C.

Mango

Surprising as it may seem, mangoes are one of the most widely eaten fruits in the world, being highly popular in India, South Africa, Brazil, Mexico, and Central America. The skin of this kidney-shaped fruit ranges from yellow to green to red, and its flesh is golden orange and very sweet and juicy when ripe. In the middle is a long, oval, inedible seed. Mangoes are very high in vitamins A and C. Green, immature mangoes are used for chutneys, relishes, and pickles. Ripe mangoes can be peeled and eaten like a banana or cut into chunks for use in fruit salads or as a garnish. Combined with lime juice, cilantro, red onion, and a variety of other ingredients, mangoes are also commonly made into a salsa to accompany fish and other dishes.

Papaya

Originating in Central America, papayas are large, elongated fruits with a distinctive aroma and taste. There are two main commercial varieties, known as Mexican and Hawaiian papayas. The Mexican variety, which can grow as large as 10 pounds, is less common in the United States. Hawaiian papayas are ripe when their skin changes from green to yellow. The flesh is golden yellow or orange, with round, black seeds in the center, and it has a sweet, mellow taste. Papaya contains a natural enzyme, papain, which aids digestion and can be used to tenderize meat. As with kiwi, raw papaya will prevent gelatin from setting. Papaya is also very high in vitamins A and C. To prepare papayas, slice them lengthwise and scoop out the fruit, separating it from the skin. Fresh lemon or lime juice enhances its flavor. Use papaya in fruit salads or smoothies, or cook it with meat or fish, as is the custom in Caribbean cuisine. The seeds are edible and have a peppery taste and texture that works well in salad dressings and marinades.

Passion Fruit

Passion fruit, also known as granadilla, is an egg-shaped fruit with a thick, purplish red skin. Inside, its juicy, seedy, orange pulp has a sweet yet tart flavor and an alluring aroma reminiscent of jasmine and honey. The orange color provides a hint that it's high in carotenoids, making it a good source of vitamin A. Passion fruit was named as such by early Christian missionaries stationed in South America who thought the flower of the plant resembled the crown of thorns and nails of Christ's crucifixion. Passion fruit is ready to eat when it becomes very wrinkled. If it gets cracked or squishy, you've waited too long. Passion fruit cannot be eaten out of hand. Rather, the pulp is typically scooped out and used as a sauce or flavoring, either as is or lightly sweetened, over fruit salads, cakes, or frozen desserts. Passion fruit is also processed into juice. Its small black seeds are edible, but they can be strained out before using the pulp, if you wish.

Persimmon

Although there is a species of persimmon tree native to the United States, the two varieties most often available commercially—Hachiya and Fuyu—are from a species native to the Orient. The Hachiya persimmon has a bright orange color and is slightly pointed in shape. The Fuyu is also bright orange but flatter, shaped much like a tomato. Both have a very sweet flavor with spicy undertones. They are also very high in vitamins C and A. Only eat persimmons when they are very soft, like jelly in a bag. They can be consumed raw, including the skin, or use a spoon to scoop the flesh out of the skin (use a bowl to catch the juicy pulp). Pureed, they can be used in pies, cakes, and custards.

Plantain

Although they are longer and more pointed at the ends, plantains are unmistakably a member of the banana family. However, unlike bananas, plantains are never eaten raw; they are always cooked and served as a starchy vegetable. Plantains are especially rich in fiber and a fair source of vitamin C. Plantains can be used at any degree of ripeness, from green and starchy to when they're totally ripe, at which point they'll be black, sweeter, and softer. Peel and slice them, and then bake, sauté, broil, grill, deep-fry, or simmer as you would any other vegetable. You can also bake them whole in their peel. Bake at 350°F for 45 to 60 minutes, or until they are easily pierced with a fork. Remove the skin and season them with butter or a flavorful oil, if you wish.

Pomegranate

Inside the hard, red, leathery rind of the pomegranate lie many seeds surrounded by translucent sacks bursting with red, tart, juicy pulp. Larger pomegranates are best, containing the plumpest, juiciest kernels. While the results are worth it in the long run, a pomegranate is a fruit you probably wouldn't want to eat on a first date, due to its inevitable spurting of juice in every direction. Try cutting away the top one-fourth and scooping out the seeds with a spoon. The seeds within the pulp are also edible, although some people prefer to discard them. Don't eat the white membranes surrounding the clusters, which is very bitter. The juice can also be extracted from the pomegranate by briefly pureeing the pulp in a food processor or blender and then straining out the seeds.

Quince

Although the quince looks similar to an apple, it is never eaten raw because of its acidic flavor and very hard texture. Instead, it is most valued for its high pectin content, making it a perfect candidate for jams, preserves, and chutneys. They're also good baked, either whole or in pies and crisps, as well as stewed or poached, providing they're adequately sweetened. They are ready to use when they become pale yellow in color. Perfumed quince and pineapple quince are the two varieties most commonly marketed, and larger fruits are a better buy.

Tamarind

Tamarinds are an unusual fruit in every regard. The fuzzy, brown pods, ranging from 2 to 8 inches long, grow on a tropical evergreen tree. Within the pods are seeds surrounded by a sticky pulp that has a tart flavor reminiscent of apricots and dates. Although the pulp can be eaten raw, it is generally used in marinades or to flavor chutneys and curries. When sweetened and diluted with water, it makes a refreshing drink. Tamarind can be used when the pods are green or when they're brown and brittle. Crack and peel the pods to access the pulp. To make tamarind concentrate, soak the pulp from 6 tamarind pods in 1 cup of hot water for 2 hours. Then strain the pulp, pressing the pulp to extract as much of the flavorful juice as possible. Use the concentrate to flavor grains, beans, and vegetables, or dilute and sweeten it for a beverage.

Ugli Fruit

This citrus fruit originated in Jamaica as a cross between a grapefruit and a tangerine. Although its thick, bumpy, greenish yellow mottled skin and odd shape may not seem very attractive, the fruit itself is very juicy and delicious, with a sweet, orangelike flavor. Peel Ugli fruit and eat it out of hand, or add sections to fruit salads.

White Sapote

White sapote, also known as Mexican custard apple, is a fruit native to Central America and Mexico. It looks like a green apple without any indentation on the bottom. When ripe, it becomes soft and creamy textured with a unique flavor similar to banana and papaya. Sapote can be eaten out of hand as you would a peach. No peeling is necessary. They can also be eaten like persimmons, spooning the pulp out of the skin. Add sapote to fruit salads or smoothies for a special treat.

Exploring Vegetables

Leafy Greens

The greens category encompasses a wide variety of leafy vegetables, from delicate to hardy. Many of the latter are classified as cruciferous vegetables, described below, and are typically eaten steamed, braised, or sautéed rather than raw. The nutrients in greens are best absorbed when they're served or cooked with oil, particularly olive oil. Beyond the more familiar selection of lettuces, there are many other interesting greens available that are great to add to your repertoire.

Varieties and Cooking Guidelines

Belgian endive looks like a cigar made from pale yellow leaves. Its bitter flavor contrasts nicely with milder lettuces in a salad. Braise in vegetable or chicken broth for 5 to 10 minutes for a delicious hot vegetable.

Endive (also called chicory) has curly, frilly, coarse leaves with dark green edges and pale yellow stems. Use it raw in salads for a bitter accent or cook it briefly for a milder flavor.

Escarole has broad, coarse, flat leaves that are slightly bitter. Use it raw in salads or cook it briefly to mellow the bitter flavor.

Mâche, an exquisite lettuce with small, soft, tender, rounded leaves, is generally sold with its rootlets still attached. Its flavor has a faint floral essence, making salads and sandwiches made with mâche seem like a delicacy, whether it's used as the sole type of lettuce or as an accent amidst other varieties. An old variety, mâche has gone by several names in the past, including corn salad and lamb's lettuce.

Sorrel, which has a sour lemony flavor and bright green color, resembles young spinach leaves. Use it sparingly in salads, cooked vegetable medleys, and soups.

Cabbage Family

The cabbage family, also known as cruciferous vegetables, includes a wide variety of vegetables that would outwardly seem to be in different categories. Arugula, bok choy, Chinese cabbage, collard greens, kale, and mustard greens have dual citizenship in the leafy greens category. Although daikon, radishes, rutabagas, and turnips are generally classified as roots, they're cruciferous vegetables, too. The final catch-all category includes "flowers" and round vegetables, such as broccoli, brussels sprouts, cauliflower, green and red cabbages, and a few more, mentioned below, with which you may not be as familiar.

Varieties and Cooking Guidelines

Arugula, also known as rocket, has tender, dark green, jagged leaves and a somewhat bitter, pungent flavor. Use arugula raw in salads and sandwiches, as a substitute for basil in pesto, cooked briefly with other vegetables, or in soups.

Bok choy has soft, dark green leaves; long, thick, white stalks; and a sweet, milky flavor. Best known for its use in stir-fries, bok choy remains crisp even when cooked to a tender stage. Because the stalks require a longer cooking time, cut the leaves from the stalks and add the stalks first, stirring in the leaves during the last few minutes of preparation to prevent overcooking. Since *baby bok choy* is picked when less mature, it is much more delicate than regular bok choy, requiring less cooking time. Its miniature size also provides the opportunity to cook it whole. Both regular and baby bok choy can be used raw in salads, cooked in soups, stir-fried, or simply steamed.

Broccoflower looks like a green cauliflower, which is exactly what it is, despite the fact its name implies it's a cross between broccoli and cauliflower. Originating in Italy, broccoflower has a milder flavor than cauliflower but a hint of green vegetable flavors. Steam broccoflower whole for a special treat, cooking only until just tender to maintain its pleasant flavor.

Broccoli raab looks more like kale or turnip greens than broccoli. As it turns out, turnip is, indeed, its closest relative. Bitter with pizzazz is likely the best way to describe its flavor, which provides a special spark when combined with other foods. Unlike other hardy greens, the stems of broccoli raab are generally tender enough to eat. Braise or simmer, watching closely not to overcook the leaves.

Broccoli Romanesco, another type of green-colored cauliflower, has a beautiful shape and form, with swirled geometric patterns of turrets or cones. Its flavor, which matches its exotic look and texture, is lighter and nuttier than that of broccoflower or white varieties of cauliflower. Steam broccoli Romanesco in chunks or whole until just tender, making sure to avoid overcooking.

Cabbage, whether green or red, is very versatile and because it stores well, refrigerated, for up to a couple of weeks, it's a great staple to keep on hand. Grate it raw for use in salads, sandwiches, and wraps. Chunks or strips of cabbage may be steamed or simmered with carrots and peas or added to soups. Or remove whole leaves, steam them until tender, and, while still warm, use them as a wrap to encase savory fillings to eat on the spot or to bake in a sauce. If cooking in fairly alkaline, hard water, adding a splash of vinegar or wine will help prevent red cabbage from turning blue.

Chinese cabbage, also known as napa cabbage, is a tall, elongated cabbage with pale green, crinkled leaves and broad-ribbed stalks. A favorite for stir-fries, its mild, delicate flavor and crisp texture also make it a good choice in salads and soups. For a different way to serve Chinese cabbage, steam whole Chinese cabbage leaves with herbs, such as basil, and wrap them around cooked julienned carrots, beets, or green beans.

Collard greens have leathery, gray-green leaves. For optimum flavor and tenderness, buy them during fall and winter and choose a bunch with small to medium leaves. Steam, braise with onions, or sauté in a fragrant cooking oil and serve topped with a finishing salt like Portuguese flor de sal.

Dandelion greens are pungent and have deeply notched leaves. While young leaves can be used in salads, older, larger leaves are best cooked in stews.

Kale has dark bluish green, finely curled, plume-like leaves and a subtle cabbagelike flavor. Braising it with a little liquid helps to tenderize tougher leaves. It is especially good sautéed with olive oil or sesame oil or braised with onions and mushrooms. There are several varieties of kale, including *Tuscan kale,* more popularly known as dinosaur kale for its puckered leaves, and *Russian red kale,* which looks like large oak leaves. While all varieties of kale are chewy, each has a different texture, and any of them can range from quite tender to very fibrous, depending on their age when picked or sold.

Mizuna is a leafy green with a pungent, exotic flavor that adds a nice accent when mixed with other greens in a salad. It is also good briefly steamed or braised.

Mustard greens have curly edges, a texture that's more tender but more rough than that of collard greens, and a spicy, peppery, sometimes pungent flavor. Steam, braise, or sauté them.

Radicchio looks like a small, ruby red cabbage with thick, white-veined leaves. Slightly bitter, radicchio provides an interesting flavor contrast in salads. It can also be cooked like other cabbages: steamed, braised, or stir-fried. It is especially good cut into wedges and grilled with olive oil, herbs, and a splash of tamari or shoyu.

Savoy cabbage is a version of green cabbage with crinkled leaves, a milder flavor, and a more tender texture. Use it raw or cooked, as you would regular cabbage.

Fresh Herbs

Fresh herbs are valued for their exceptional flavor, texture, shape, and style, which can make even the simplest salad or sandwich a masterpiece. They're also a rich source of nutrients. Even when used as a garnish, an edible one at that, they make an irreplaceable contribution. A whole sprig or chopped leaves arranged on an entrée or as an accent on a plate can help whet the appetite and create a harmonious mood. Herbs are generally easy to raise, and because many of them can be grown in pots, even someone without a garden or backyard can have a personal culinary herb garden.

As a general rule, use three times as much fresh herb as dried. Except for the more hardy herbs such as rosemary, thyme, and winter savory, fresh herbs should be added only during the last 10 to 15 minutes of cooking—just long enough to lose their volatile oils without losing flavor or becoming bitter. Sometimes it's best to add especially tender herbs, such as cilantro and chervil, at the end of the cooking time, when you turn off the heat. On the other hand, when making dips, herb butters, and cheese spreads, fresh herbs should be added several hours before serving to allow the flavor to fully develop.

Varieties and Cooking Guidelines

While basil, chives, cilantro, dill, oregano, parsley, rosemary, and sage will always remain cherished favorites, explore the fresh herbs described below for a new twist in cooking.

Chervil is an herb with lacy, green, fernlike leaves and a delicate flavor and fragrance reminiscent of anise and parsley. Although it is most frequently found in traditional fines herbes mixtures, it is delicious in its own right, finely minced or used as sprigs as you would parsley, in salads, or as a garnish. Also try it adding it to soups, potato dishes, cooked beans, and egg dishes just before serving.

Curry leaves are small, soft-textured, shiny, pointed leaves with a mild, lemony, bitter taste and spicy, citruslike aroma. They grow on a tree native to India and Sri Lanka, where they contribute their distinctive flavor to curries and other dishes. They are typically fried briefly in butter or oil before being added to a dish. Look for them sold fresh and still on the branch, detach the leaves right before using them.

Fennel has feathery bluish green leaves with a mild aniselike flavor and fragrance. Mince the leaves and sprinkle them sparingly on salads or use them to garnish soups, beans, cabbage, fish, egg dishes, and rice. It is also delicious when added to gently heating oil for a vegetable sauté. Fennel seeds are equally important as a seasoning; I always add them to spaghetti sauce and even include a few when preparing oatmeal.

Kaffir lime leaves are dark green, glossy, fragrant leaves from a Southeast Asian tree that also produces a small, wrinkled, green citrus fruit. An essential ingredient in Thai soups, stir-fries, and curries, kaffir lime leaves have a refreshing and unique lemonlike flavor and aroma. The leaves are very distinctive, as they grow in doubles, with one leaf connecting directly to the end of another. Use kaffir lime leaves whole when making soups and curries (but, as with bay leaves, don't eat them), or finely shred them to add to salads or sprinkle over curries.

Lemongrass has long, fibrous stalks with a decidedly lemon flavor that is so characteristic of soups, stir-fries, and noodle dishes from Thailand and Southeast Asia. When intended as an ingredient within a dish, only the tender inner stalk is minced. For use as a flavoring agent, cut a large piece from the whole stalk that will be easy to remove once the dish is cooked.

Mint is available in many varieties beyond the more familiar peppermint and spearmint, several with names that suggest their heavenly scents and flavors. Use *chocolate mint* in tea (2 tablespoons fresh mint per 1 cup hot water) or as a garnish on desserts, or just rub the leaf between your thumb and index finger to enjoy its marvelous aroma. *Pineapple mint,* with just a hint of pineapple taste, also makes a wonderful tea and works well as a garnish for sweet beverages, fruit salads, and desserts. Finely chopped, it's a delicious addition to cooked rice or other grains; stir it in just before serving. *Ginger mint,* another must-try fruity-flavored variety, is delicious in salads or when stirred into steamed carrots or cooked rice just before serving.

Rau ram, also referred to as Vietnamese coriander, has narrow, pointed leaves with a spicy taste and aroma similar to those of lemon and coriander. Commonly served with Vietnamese spring rolls, it's also used fresh in salads or as a garnish for many foods in Vietnam, Malaysia, and Singapore.

Summer savory has small, narrow, grayish green leaves with a peppery flavor and aroma. It's similar to winter savory but milder. Best used fresh, summer savory is most celebrated as a seasoning for cooked beans, but it's also very good in salads, served with cheeses, and cooked in soups, sauces, and poultry dishes, as well as with sweet vegetables like carrots, winter squash, or parsnips.

Tarragon has narrow, delicate, grayish green leaves that are at their best when used fresh. The preferred variety, French tarragon, has an assertive but sweet flavor and an aroma reminiscent of anise and fennel. It's a familiar component in culinary blends such as herbes de Provence, fines herbes, and bouquet garni, and sprigs of tarragon are often used to flavor vinegar. On its own, it's a good seasoning for beans, vegetables, sauces, poultry, eggs, and fish dishes, but use a light hand when adding it.

Thai sweet basil is an Asian variety of basil with dark green leaves, thick purple stems, and an anise scent and flavor, making it quite different from typical Italian basil varieties. Add it to soups, curries, and stir-fries, or use it whole or shredded as a garnish.

Thyme is an all-purpose herb that, like mint, is available in a wide range of flavors. Some have a lemony taste; others, a hint of orange or caraway. Use all varieties in salads, as a garnish, or cooked with vegetables, especially sautéed or grilled mushrooms, as well as in soups and stews and to season poultry, meat, or fish dishes.

Edible Flowers

Although it may seem unusual to eat a salad that contains flowers we normally admire in gardens or arrange in vases, when you think about it, it's no stranger than eating leaves such as greens or lettuce, or other flowers, such as broccoli and cauliflower. Beyond providing flavor and color, edible flowers add drama to salads, soups, entrées, and desserts. As they are eaten in such minute amounts, they are nutritionally negligible in the standard vitamin and minerals framework. Nonetheless, they supply a range of beneficial phytonutrients, and beyond that the beauty and sense of adventure they contribute to a meal can lift the spirits and make a significant contribution to overall well-being.

However, it is very important to eat only those flowers known to be nontoxic. Never experiment; always make sure you can identify the flower as one that is safe to eat. When purchasing edible flowers, only buy those grown specifically for consumption. Avoid flowers from florists and, in many cases, even wildflowers. They may be treated with pesticides, herbicides, or fungicides. Even better, grow your own organically.

Home gardeners growing any kind of squash, both summer and winter varieties, will have a ready source of squash blossoms as the plants produce new squash, particularly with zucchini. They are best gathered in the morning before the sun causes them to wilt. It's best to harvest the female blossoms, which have an immature squash at their base. Male flowers end at the stem and are needed for pollination, to ensure a steady stream of vegetables for the rest of the season.

Varieties and Cooking Guidelines

Since edible flowers are very delicate, wash them by gently immersing them in a bowl of water to remove any dirt and insects, then dry them on a towel. Use edible flowers raw in salads, on sandwiches, or as a colorful garnish on pasta, cooked rice and other grains, or on any dish in the meal. Go easy; only a few petals are needed per portion. Although only the petals of some flowers should be eaten, other flowers, such as violets, nasturtiums, and Johnny-jump-ups, can be eaten in their entirety, including the stems and leaves.

Many of the heartier flowers, such as squash blossoms, calendula, chive blossoms, and chrysanthemums, can be cooked, too. Add them to creamy soups or sauces, omelets, scrambled eggs, or mashed and sautéed tofu, or sauté them with any vegetable. Squash blossoms are substantial enough that they can be stuffed with cheese or other savoring fillings and baked; for this purpose, be sure to keep the stem on the blossom so it will retain its shape.

Common, edible flowers and their respective flavors include the following:

Begonias: sweet, lemony

Borage: cucumber-like

Calendula: slightly tangy, bitter

Chive blossoms: like mild sweet onions

Chrysanthemums: mildly to strongly bitter

Geraniums: lemony

Johnny-jump-ups and pansies: mild, lettucelike

Lavender: strong, lemony, perfumelike

Marigolds: lemony, tangy

Nasturtiums: sweet, mustardlike

Rose petals: strong, fragrant

Squash blossoms: sweet, nectarlike

Tulip petals: sweet, lettucelike

Violets: sweet, floral

Sprouts

Sprouts are the very young shoots from the germinated seeds of vegetables, beans, or grains. Almost any seed, bean, or grain will sprout. Red clover, alfalfa, cabbage, radish, sunflower, and buckwheat seeds will sprout into leafy greens. Starchy beans and grains can also grow edible shoots and roots.

Sprouts have long been hailed as a good source of vitamin C, fiber, folic acid, and phytonutrients. Sprouting beans and grains can also improve their digestibility. As they are easy to grow and generally locally produced, sprouts are also likely to be one of the fresher selections in the produce section. However, as with other vegetables, each day after harvest brings reductions in nutrient levels, so they should be used as soon after purchase as possible.

When buying sprouts, it is very important to buy only from certified growers who follow stringent food safety standards for growing and handling sprouts. To guard against potential bacterial contamination, only sanitized, uncontaminated seeds should be used. The conditions that promote sprouting of the seeds, including temperature and humidity, can increase the potential for growth of pathogens, making raw sprouts a potentially risky choice for children, the elderly, and people with compromised immune systems. Improper handling of sprouts after they are purchased can also be an issue. They should be kept cold—at temperatures no higher than 40°F—at all times, whether purchased from the produce section or from a salad bar. Thoroughly cooking sprouts can help reduce the risks, and although some sprouts are so delicate that they are intended to be eaten raw, all bean and grain sprouts can and should be cooked.

You can also grow sprouts at home, but again, it's important to use sanitized seeds, exceptionally clean equipment, and proper sprouting procedures to ensure the best quality and, most critical of all, food safety. Equipment can be as simple as a sterile wide-mouth glass jar covered with a piece of cheesecloth affixed with a rubber band, or as elaborate as sprouting devices with multiple vessels or trays. Screw-on plastic or stainless steel screen lids that fit on wide-mouth 1-quart jars are also available.

The amount of seed needed depends on the size of the seed. For alfalfa seeds and other similarly small seeds, use 1 tablespoon of seeds to grow a volume of sprouts that will fill a quart jar. For beans and other large seeds, you may need to use as much as ¼ cup. To initiate the sprouting process, soak the seeds in cool water, generally for 8 to 12 hours, depending on the type of seed. After soaking, rinse and drain them thoroughly a couple times or more per day. Most sprouts will be ready to eat within 2 to 6 days, depending on the type of seed and the ambient temperature.

In general, alfalfa sprouts are done in 6 or 7 days when their sprouts are 1 inch long. Exposing the jar to the natural light after the fourth day will help them turn green.

Grain sprouts take only about 1 to 3 days, until their sprouts grow as long as the length of the grain itself. Mung bean sprouts are ready when they are 2 inches long, about 4 to 5 days, while, for best flavor, other beans that are sprouted are grown until ½ to 1 inch in length. Sprouts should be stored in a clean, perforated container that allows air circulation or loosely packed in a plastic bag; they should keep for 3 to 7 days.

Peppers, Fresh and Dried

There is a type of pepper for everyone. Sweet peppers, like bell peppers and pimentos, are a mild haven for those adverse to heat. They can be served raw, cooked, or roasted, and used like many other vegetables as a side dish or flavorful adjunct to a recipe. Hot peppers, on the other hand, more frequently referred as chiles, are generally used for flavoring, to provide depth, character, and extra pizzazz to foods, rather than standing on their own.

Paradoxically, chile peppers can also help cool us off, which explains why they are so commonly used in the cuisines originating in hot climates. The sweating that occurs from eating spicy food and its subsequent evaporation creates a cooling effect on the skin. And then there is the stimulant effect of hot peppers, thanks to capsaicin, a natural chemical component found in the seeds and the whitish ribs within the pepper. When capsaicin produces its trademark heat, it triggers the brain to produce endorphins, which transforms the painful burning sensation into pleasure.

Classifying the heat of chile peppers is done in a variety of ways. The simplest is by just looking at the size: the smaller the chile, the higher the heat. In 1912, pharmacologist Wilbur Scoville created the Scoville Units scale for rating the heat of chiles by measuring the number of grams of water required to cancel the heat of 1 gram of chile. The scale ranges from 0 for green and red bell peppers and sweet banana peppers to as much as 500,000 heat units for red habanero peppers, and even higher for a few obscure varieties. However, as chiles grown on the same plant can vary in their heat, the Scoville Units claimed for one type of pepper can vary widely from source to source. Accordingly, simple subjective heat ratings tend to prevail; some use numbers, while others use creative visual icons.

That's all well and good, but how do you quell the heat? Cooking, roasting, drying, or freezing won't do the trick. The answer is to remove some or all of the seeds and inner membranes inside the chiles. At the table, drinking milk or eating yogurt, sour cream, rice, or bread can help provide a welcome cooling sensation.

Varieties and Cooking Guidelines

Chiles are available fresh, freshly roasted, dried, and dried and roasted or smoked, and each form provides distinctive flavors. Take jalapeños, for example: These medium-hot chiles are slightly bitter

Peppers from Mild to Very Hot

Fresh Peppers	Relative Heat	Appearance	Flavor	Suggested Use
Bell pepper	0	Green, red, yellow, orange, purple, or white; rounded, cubic shape; about 4 inches long, 3 inches wide, but size varies widely.	Very mild. Green: vegetable-like flavor. Red, orange, and yellow: sweet. Purple and white: less sweet than red.	Raw in salads, stir-fried, stuffed, roasted, grilled, and cooked in sauces and stews.
Pimento	1	Dark red, smooth, heart-shaped, 3 to 4 inches long, 2 to 3 inches wide.	Sweet and succulent.	Raw in salads, dips, spreads. Cooked in vegetable and pasta dishes, stuffed with cheese, and roasted. Pickled.
Hungarian cherry	1 to 3	Deep red, round, about 1¾ inches in diameter.	Mild, medium sweetness.	In salads and pickled.
Anaheim	2 to 3	Related to New Mexico pepper. Green, red when ripe, about 6 inches long, 2 inches in diameter, tapered.	Mild. Green has vegetable-like flavor. Red is sweeter.	Generally used cooked or roasted. Leave whole and stuff with cheese. Dice or cut into strips and add to cornbread batter, omelets, stews, dips, and sauces.
Poblano	3	Dark green or reddish brown when ripe, 4 inches long and 3 inches in diameter, tapered, thick fleshed and shiny surface gloss.	Deep, rich, green bell pepper-like flavor	Best roasted or cooked. A favorite for chiles rellenos and in sauces, moles, and stews.
New Mexico	red: 2 to 4; green: 3 to 5	Related to Anaheim peppers. Green, red when ripe, and sometimes brown, orange, or yellow.	Red is sweeter; green has a vegetable-like flavor.	Use like Anaheim peppers.
Hungarian wax	3 to 4	Yellow, 6 inches long and 1½ inches wide, tapered, waxy surface texture.	Mild to medium heat; subtle, slightly lemony flavor.	Salads, soups, stews, dips, and pickled.
Jalapeño	5.5	Green, red when ripe, 2 to 3 inches long and 1½ inches in diameter.	Green: slightly bitter, vegetable-like flavor. Red: sweet.	Raw: diced as a topping and in nachos and dips. Cooked in salsas, stews, and sauces. Roasted, pickled, and stuffed with cheese.
Serrano	7	Green, red when ripe, 2 to 3 inches long and ¾ inch diameter.	Clean, biting heat, pleasant acidity. Red is sweeter.	Raw: a favorite for making salsa, pico de gallo, and guacamole. Pickled or roasted.

Fresh Peppers (cont.)	Relative Heat	Appearance	Flavor	Suggested Use
Thai	7 to 8	Green, red when ripe, thin, 1½ inches long, ¼ inch in diameter, thin wall, tapered.	Grassy, vegetable-like flavor. Green are hotter than red.	Sauces and Thai and Southeast Asian cooking. Red provide a decorative accent.
Rocotillo	7 to 8	Related to habanero and Scotch bonnet. Orange-yellow or red, rounded with vertical furrows, 1 inch long, 1½ inches in diameter.	Very hot, mildly fruity.	Ceviche and salsas and pickled.
Scotch bonnet	9 to 10	Close cousin to habanero and rocotillo. Light yellow, orange, or red, 1½ inches long and in diameter, some furrows.	Very hot, fruity, smoky.	Jamaican jerk sauce, Caribbean curries, and used in condiment sauces.
Habanero	10	Green, orange, or red, lantern-shaped, 2 inches long, 1½ inches in diameter.	Very hot; tropical fruit and apricot tones in flavor and aroma.	Salsas, chutneys, marinades, and sauces.

Dried Peppers	Relative Heat	Appearance	Flavor	Suggested Use
Hungarian cherry	1 to 3	Dark red, round and wrinkled, 2 inches long and in diameter.	Lightly fruity and peppery.	Stews and sauces.
Guajillo	2 to 4	Orangish red to brown, 5 inches long, 1 inch wide, tapered.	Notes of green tea, pine, tannins, and berry.	Salsas, sauces, soups, and stews.
New Mexico	red: 2 to 4; green: 3 to 5	Olive to dark green or bright red; 5 inches long, 1 inch wide.	Red: dried cherry, earthy. Green: light, smoky, fruity, with herbal undertones.	Red: sold as crushed flakes and ground; also decoratively in ristras. Green: beef jerky seasoning, soups, and stews.
Ancho	3 to 5	The dried form of poblano peppers. Large, flat, mahogany-colored, wrinkled, 4 inches long, 3 inches wide at the "shoulders."	Sweet, faintly reminiscent of raisins and coffee.	Widely used in Mexican cuisine, including mole and adobo. Often sold as ristras (many anchos strung together) and hung in the kitchen for easy access.
Pasilla	3 to 5	Very dark brown, wrinkled, about 5 to 6 inches long, 1 inch wide, tapered.	Mild; flavor similar to Spanish meaning of its name: "little raisin."	Sauces, including mole.

Peppers from Mild to Very Hot *(cont.)*

Dried Peppers (cont.)	Relative Heat	Appearance	Flavor	Suggested Use
Cascabel	4	Reddish to brown, round, smooth, 1½ inches in diameter. Rattles when shaken.	Rich, smoky, woodsy.	Salsas, stews, soups, and sauces.
Pepperoncini	5	Orangish red, 2 inches long, ½ inch wide, tapered and curved.	Sweet.	Southern European seafood dishes and tomato sauces.
Chipotle	5 to 6	The dried, smoked form of jalapeño pepper. Brown, ridged, 2 to 4 inches long, 1 inch wide.	Subtle heat, smoky, sweet, slightly chocolatey.	Mexican and South-western cooking; sauces, salsas, soups, and cooked in adobo.
De árbol	7.5	Brick red, 2 inches long, ¼ inch wide.	Hot, tannic, smoky, grassy.	Sauces, soups, and stews.
Serrano seco	7.5	Dried form of serrano pepper. Orangish red, 2 inches long, ½ inch wide, tapered.	Very hot, fruity.	Sauces.
Cayenne	8	Red, crinkled, 2 to 4 inches long, ½ inch wide.	Very hot, tart, smoky.	Sauces, soups, and seasoning; African and Cajun cooking.
Pequín	8.5	Orangish red, ¾ inch long, ¼ inch wide.	Very hot, sweet, smoky, with citrus and nutty tones.	Salsas, soups, and vinegars.
Habanero	10	Yellow-orange, lantern-shaped, 1½ to 2 inches long, 1 inch wide.	Very hot, tropical fruit flavor.	Sauces.

Relative heat data from Mark Miller's *The Great Chile Book*. Berkeley, CA: Ten Speed Press, 1991.

when dark green but become more sweet if left to ripen until red. In contrast, ripe jalapeño peppers that are dried and smoked, called chipotle peppers, are known for their rich, slightly chocolaty flavor.

Roast fresh peppers in a 450°F oven for 4 to 5 minutes (turning them a time or two) or campfire style, on a grilling fork about 4 inches above a gas flame, until the skin turns black. Place them in a covered pot to steam and cool. Then peel them and remove the stems, seeds, and all or part of the inner membranes, as desired, before proceeding with your recipe.

Always use caution when working with hot chiles. To avoid potential burning, protect your hands by wearing rubber gloves, and be sure not to touch your eyes, any part of your face, or any sensitive skin at any time when working with chiles, fresh or dried. Afterward, wash your hands thoroughly with soap and warm water to ensure all traces of capsaicin are removed.

Because peppers readily cross-pollinate, there are hundreds of varieties of chile peppers. Check out some of the more commonly available fresh and dried varieties listed in the previous chart to whet your appetite for exploring the rest.

Mushrooms

Wild, cultivated, fresh, or dried, mushrooms are both center-stage performers and potent flavor enhancers that can accentuate and bring together all of the flavors in a dish. While a few cultivated varieties, such as white button, crimini, portobello, and enoki, can be eaten raw, most wild varieties should be cooked to ensure food safety. Besides, most mushrooms taste better, when sautéed, grilled, or baked, and many are also more easily digested and even more nutritious once they're cooked.

Nutrient-wise, mushrooms have been recognized for their mineral content, especially potassium, copper, and selenium, as well as being a good source of certain B vitamins. But recently, knowledge about their powerful phytonutrient potential has begun to emerge. In Asia, varieties such as shiitake, oyster mushrooms, maitake, and enoki mushrooms have long been valued for their immune-enhancing properties, but even common white button mushrooms and criminis contain healthful antioxidants that help protect our bodies against cancer and other diseases.

Choose only whole and dry mushrooms with spongy, firm, plump caps. Certain varieties of cultivated mushrooms, such as beech and enoki mushrooms, will be sold as a clump with their stems still attached to the growing medium.

Unlike most other vegetables, mushrooms should be stored in the refrigerator in paper bags rather than plastic. Transfer mushrooms purchased in shrink-wrapped or vacuum-sealed containers into a paper bag, with the exception of delicate beech and enoki mushrooms, which can be refrigerated in their original containers, if provided.

To clean fresh mushrooms, wipe them with a damp cloth or soft vegetable brush, using minimal water to prevent loss of nutrients and a change in texture. Some mushrooms, such as chanterelles and morels, may need to be briefly rinsed in running water to remove dirt embedded within crevices.

To reconstitute dried mushrooms, pour hot water over them to cover and let them soak for about 30 minutes. The flavorful soaking liquid is wonderful in soups or sauces. Strain it through a paper coffee filter to remove any grit. Much of the flavor of dried mushrooms will be lost to the liquid, but when chopped or sliced, the reconstituted mushroom provide a chewy texture to dishes. Risotto and tomato sauce, in particular, benefit from the addition of dried mushrooms, especially porcini.

Varieties and Cooking Guidelines

Beech mushrooms, also known as hon shimeji, are a cultivated variety that grows in clusters. Each small mushroom has a 1- to 2-inch stem and sports a small cap. Brown varieties may be referred to as brown clamshell mushrooms, while white types are sometimes called alba or white clamshell mushrooms. They have a somewhat crunchy texture and a flavor that's mild, nutty, and somewhat herbaceous. The individual mushrooms should be separated from the thick base before cooking. They can then be sautéed, stir-fried, braised, or roasted in the oven. They require a much shorter cooking time than most other mushrooms.

Bluefoot mushrooms are the cultivated variety of blewits. Both varieties are dense-fleshed and whitish, with a blue tint throughout. When cooked, their flavor is deep and earthy, and unlike many mushrooms, they remain firm, becoming tender but not watery. As such, they can add a lot of texture and body to a dish. Cook them like any other mushroom—sautéed, roasted, or braised—whether alone or in a dish.

Chanterelles, a beautiful trumpet-shaped, forest mushroom, grow widely throughout western North America. Golden-colored chanterelles have a light, delicate, almost fruity, apricot-like flavor and aroma and a texture that's slightly chewy and dry but meaty. Dramatic black varieties have an earthier flavor. Use chanterelles quickly after purchase.

While they are expensive, you owe it to yourself to experience, at least once, their incredible flavor. They can be sautéed or braised, or combine both techniques, first sautéing, and then braising. They make a wonderful addition to pastas, sauces, soups, or virtually any savory dish. Dried chanterelles are available, but they are not nearly as tasty as fresh.

Crimini mushrooms, also known as Italian brown mushrooms, are closely related to the common button mushroom. In fact, they are variants of the same species, *Agaricus bisporus,* but criminis are much richer in flavor and meatier in texture, primarily due to their lower moisture content. Use them as you would white button mushrooms, raw or cooked.

Enoki mushrooms are mild-flavored, creamy white mushrooms with long slender stems and very small round caps. Originally grown on stumps of the enoki tree in the mountains of Japan, enoki mushrooms are commercially produced on a growing medium of moist sawdust and rice bran packed into plastic containers to yield a more leggy appearance. Their crisp, tender texture makes them a delicious raw addition to salads. If using them in a stir-fry or other cooked dish, stir them in just before serving to preserve their exceptional texture.

Hedgehog mushrooms are wild orange-gold mushrooms with a cap that has a depression in the middle. They are characterized by tiny spindles on the underside of the cap. Their wonderful flavor and dry texture is reminiscent of chanterelles, for which they can be substituted. Braise, roast, or sauté them, and because they're a bit dry, cover the pan so they can simmer in their own juices.

Maitake, also known as hen-of-the-woods, is a smoky brown color and looks somewhat like a head of curly lettuce or—with a little imagination and a nod to its nickname—perhaps feathers. Maitake can grow to immense sizes—over 50 pounds! Its texture, when cooked, is tender but firm, and its flavor is somewhat earthy and nutty. Cut maitake as you would a cauliflower, break-

ing it into wedges or clumps and cleaning them thoroughly before cooking—a task more critical for wild varieties than cultivated. Indigenous to both North America and Japan, it is very good in Japanese-inspired soups and dishes. Although it's best braised, stewed, or cooked in a sauce, it can also be roasted. Or sauté it with onions, covering the pan for a few minutes in the middle of the process to allow the mushroom to become tender and absorb juices and flavors.

Morels, which look like elongated sponges or honeycombs with stems, can be yellow, brown, or black. Gathered from woodland areas during the spring, particularly within recently burned forests, morels have a deep, earthy, nutty flavor and a crisp, chewy texture that is terrific with creamy sauces, pasta, rice dishes, fish, or poultry. For optimum flavor and texture, use them quickly after purchase. Dried morels are also available.

Oyster mushrooms are fan-shaped mushrooms that grow on the trunks and limbs of trees. True to their name, they look like oyster shells, and they even have a similar taste to oysters. Lightly sauté them and add to sauces, soups, pasta, and rice. *French horn mushrooms,* also known as **king trumpet,** are a particularly large variety of oyster mushrooms. Long and conical in shape, French horns have a thick, meaty texture and a taste reminiscent of nutty-flavored porcini. They are delicious sautéed, braised, or roasted.

Pom-pom mushrooms, also called bear's head or lion's mane, look like small heads of cauliflower with a slightly furry texture. Their delicate flavor is enhanced when baked whole or sliced and sautéed.

Porcini mushrooms, or king boletes, or cèpes as they are known in France, are woodland mushrooms gathered during late summer to late fall. Light brown in color with flat, very large caps and chunky stems, they are prized for their rich, meaty, nutty, assertive flavor. Instead of gills underneath the cap, as found in many other mushrooms, this variety of mushroom has a spongy layer consisting of pores and tubelike crevices. Grill the caps, or slice them and braise or sauté for adding to sauces or pasta and grain dishes. Dried porcinis are also highly valued.

Portobello mushrooms are very flavorful, meaty-textured, dark brown Italian mushrooms whose caps range from 3 to 8 inches in diameter. Unlike their cousins, criminis and common button mushrooms, which are picked while their gills are still enclosed, portobello mushrooms are picked when their gills are fully exposed. Sometimes referred to as "vegetarian steak," portobellos are exceptional when marinated and grilled. They can also be sliced and sautéed with olive oil or butter and seasonings such as tamari or rosemary. Serve the slices with a thick piece of crusty bread or as a side dish.

Shiitake mushrooms have a woodsy, almost smoky flavor and meatlike texture, making them a favorite in both Oriental and Western dishes. They are named from their origins in Japan, where they're grown on the wood of the shii tree; in other parts of the world they are grown on wood from other varieties of oak. Just a few shiitakes will impart a delicious flavor to soups, stews, stir-fries, and pasta dishes. Because they have a tendency to dry out and burn more easily, for maximum flavor and meatiness, keep the caps whole or cut them in bite-size chunks rather than slicing them. When cooking, first lightly sauté them, then simmer in a little liquid until dry. Eat the caps only, and use the tough, woody stems for stock. Herbs and spices such as rosemary, thyme, and ginger are exceptional with shiitakes, as is a splash of tamari added during cooking. Dried shiitakes are also available.

Straw mushrooms are typically sold dried, canned, or in jars, and only rarely fresh. Their interesting name relates less to their appearance than to the fact that they are produced on a growing medium of soaked rice. Use them in stir-fries and soups.

White button mushrooms are the white, mild-flavored mushrooms commonly sold in supermarkets. Although this type of mushroom, *Agaricus bisporous,* has been commercially cultivated since 1650 in France, the white variety to which we are so accustomed was unknown until its discovery by a Pennsylvania farmer in 1926. Button mushrooms are harvested when the gills on the underside of the cap are tightly enclosed. However, they are most flavorful when they are allowed to "ripen" in the refrigerator until their gills are exposed. While white button mushrooms can be eaten raw, sautéing, steaming, or baking will enhance their flavor.

Wood ear mushrooms are grown on logs and are indeed shaped like an ear when fresh. Firm yet gelatinous, wood ear mushrooms add an interesting texture to stir-fries, pasta, and rice dishes. Dried wood ear mushrooms are also available.

Roots and Tubers

Roots and tubers are hearty vegetables that impart a grounding, comforting quality to meals, in keeping with their belowground origins. Potatoes and carrots are most familiar, but many other roots and tubers of all shapes, sizes, and colors deserve equal attention. Some are quite surprising, changing character and flavor significantly depending on whether they're left raw or cooked to different levels of tenderness. In general, roasting will provide the most depth and concentration of flavor. For a special treat, roast a medley of root vegetables with rosemary and a splash of oil and tamari.

Varieties and Cooking Guidelines

Beets are rich, sweet roots that come in a variety of sizes and several colors. Small, baby beets, typically sold along with their tender, delicious leaves, cook more quickly than do the hearty-flavored and mature medium-size versions. Red beets, which are most familiar, have their own natural deep magenta dye that can impart its color to everything else in the dish. To avoid this effect, steam or bake the whole root with 1 inch of the stem still attached and the root end intact. Once the beet is tender, its tougher outer skin will slip off easily. Then slice or cube and serve alone as a side dish or in a salad. Red and white candy-striped chioggia (kee-OH-ja) beets should be prepared similarly. They are also delicious grated raw in a salad or cooked into borscht, a traditional Russian beet-based soup finished with a dollop of yogurt, crème fraîche, or sour cream. Golden beets have a milder flavor and cook to a deep yellow color.

Burdock, most familiar in Japanese cuisine, is a long, slender root vegetable with an earthy flavor that is a perfect complement to sweet-tasting vegetables such as carrots, winter squash, and onions. To prepare burdock, scrub it but don't peel it. As it can be somewhat tough, burdock often is simmered 10 minutes before adding other vegetables. In addition to cutting burdock into slices, try shaving it with a knife, as if you were manually sharpening a pencil.

Celery root, or celeriac, is a tough, knobby root derived from a different variety of celery than the one raised for its stalks. Since its rough-textured skin is difficult to clean, it is generally peeled before use. It has a subtle celery flavor and can be cooked like carrots. It can also be grated and used raw as a component or basis for a salad with a creamy salad dressing. If using it raw, tenderize the grated root by adding 1½ teaspoons of salt and 1½ teaspoons of lemon juice or vinegar per pound of celery root. Refrigerate for 30 minutes, rinse thoroughly, and use a towel or paper towel to squeeze out any excess moisture. Then add a salad dressing and marinate for an additional 2 hours.

Daikon is a long, cucumber-shaped white radish native to Asia that's actually a member of the cabbage family. Used raw, it has a hot, spicy flavor that's a nice addition to salads, or it can be grated and served on its own as a delicious condiment for fried or oily foods. When cooked in soups, stews, or alone, daikon becomes surprisingly sweet.

Elephant garlic, true to its name, looks like a giant bulb of garlic. Although it is much milder in flavor than regular garlic, it can be used in any recipe that calls for garlic. Elephant garlic is especially good when roasted. Drizzle it with oil while it's still in its papery wrapper and bake it at 350°F for 30 to 45 minutes. Once it's soft, the flesh can be squeezed out and spread on bread or baked potatoes, or enjoyed on its own.

Fennel is not so much a root as the bulbous base of a stalk. The compact greenish white bulb has a licorice flavor and can be used raw or cooked. Try it in casseroles, salads, soups, stews, or stuffings, or, equally delicious, by itself. Its feathery tops can be used as an herb for seasoning.

Jerusalem artichokes, also known as sunchokes, certainly bear no resemblance to an artichoke. Rather, they are a brown-skinned tuber that can be cooked like potatoes—sautéed, boiled, baked, or simmered in soups. They can also be eaten raw in salads or used as a substitute for water chestnuts.

Jicama (HEE-cah-mah) is the light brown root of a plant native to Central America. It can be sautéed, boiled, or used raw in salads or for dips. Because the skin is tough, it must be peeled before use. When raw, it has a texture similar to that of an apple and a refreshing, somewhat sweet flavor. It stays crisp when cooked.

Lotus root is the mild-flavored, ivory-fleshed underwater stem of a water lily. On the outside, it looks like lengths of sausage. Inside, several tunnels run the length of the root and form an attractive pattern when the root is sliced crosswise. Soak lotus root in lemon juice and water after cutting to avoid discoloration. It can be baked, steamed, boiled, or added to soups and vegetable dishes both for flavor and for its visual interest.

Parsnips, which look like white carrots, are indeed related to carrots, but they have a quite different flavor. Usually cooked rather than eaten raw, their distinctive sweet and nutty flavor complements bean dishes, soups, hearty stews, and curries.

Rutabagas are round and have yellow-brown skin and yellow flesh. They're thought to be an accidental cross of a turnip with a cabbage that occurred sometime in the Middle Ages. When eaten raw, they have a more cabbagelike flavor, but when they're cooked, a distinctive nutty, sweet flavor emerges, becoming even sweeter the longer they're cooked.

Taro root is a vegetable most familiar to people living in Japan, Egypt, Syria, New Zealand, Hawaii, and other islands in the Pacific Ocean. Technically a corm, not a root, it resembles a hairy potato and can indeed be cooked like a potato—baked, steamed, boiled, or used in soup. It generally can't be eaten raw because of bitter, irritating compounds in the sap. The tough skin should be removed; this is most easily accomplished after cooking. If you're determined to peel raw taro and you have sensitive skin, wear rubber gloves.

Squash

Squashes can be divided into two primary categories, summer and winter, denoting the time of year each is at its peak in flavor, the differences in thickness of the skin, the density of the flesh, and the relative water content.

As any home gardener knows, summer squash, including cucumbers, are prolific warm-weather crops, and as a result, they have found their way into a variety of recipes, from basic salads, vegetable side dishes, and fritters to muffins, cookies, cakes, and even cobblers. It's a good thing this sometimes overabundant vegetable is so versatile. Many varieties have been developed over the years, in a wide range of shapes and colors.

Winter squash, more correctly stated as fall and early winter squash, have hard rinds, are sweeter in flavor, and contain high levels of beta-carotene, as evidenced by the color of their flesh—usually yellow to orange. Most types of winter squash can be steamed, braised, or baked.

Summer Squash Varieties and Cooking Guidelines

Chayote, once a principal food of the Aztecs and Mayas, is a squash with a pale green rind, a flavor somewhat similar to cucumber, and a fibrous texture like that of winter squash. Chayote can be steamed or baked; try it stuffed. If peeled, it can be eaten raw in salads or sautéed.

Cucumbers represent a mini spectrum within the broader category of summer squash. *Pickling cucumbers* are grown primarily for pickling purposes, although they can also be eaten raw, if desired. They are fairly small, about 2 to 4 inches long, with a crisp texture, light flavor, and bumpier skin than that of slicing cucumbers. Slicing cucumbers have a crisp interior, a refreshing, mild taste, and vary in size, number of seeds, and flavor depending on the type. Regular *Green Market cucumbers* are dark green, have smooth skin, and are about 8 inches long and 1½ inches in diameter. *English cucumbers*, also known as European cucumbers, are dark green, 8 to 16 inches long, thinner, less bitter in flavor, and seedless. *Armenian cucumbers* are long and coiled, with ridged skin and crisp, pale flesh. Although slicing cucumbers are delicious raw, they can also be cooked as you would any other summer squash.

Pattypan squash are yellow or a very pale green, round, and about 2 to 4 inches in diameter, and have scalloped edges. The smaller pattypans are more tender and are delicious steamed whole. Larger pattypans can be sliced or quartered before steaming, sautéing, or baking.

Scallopini squash, shaped like pattypan squash but with a dark green color like a classic zucchini, are the result of a cross between the two. Prepare them just like pattypan squash.

Yellow squash, also known as summer squash, are about the same size as zucchini, and may have either a curved neck, as found in the sweeter, more flavorful *yellow crookneck varieties,* or a straight neck, like zucchini.

Zucchini, also known as courgettes, are typically sold when between 4 to 6 inches long, as this is when they're at their peak in flavor and texture. Although they're typically green or sometimes striped, *golden zucchini* are also available. When allowed to continue to grow, they can become quite large, longer than 1 foot—at which point they are best stuffed and baked.

Winter Squash Varieties and Cooking Guidelines

Acorn squash is somewhat stringy and also has one of the mildest and least sweet flavors of all the squash. As such, it serves as an excellent backdrop, ready to be accented with other seasonings or a flavorful stuffing. Its outer skin is ridged, somewhat thick, and typically dark green, although it sometimes has splashes of orange, and other color varieties do exist. Cut it in half or in wedges and steam, or bake with a splash of oil, a favorite seasoning, and salt or tamari.

Banana squash is a very large, pink to orange banana-shaped squash that can grow to immense sizes—larger than a small child! As such, it is often sold precut into smaller, more reasonably sized pieces. It can be steamed or baked, resulting in a mildly sweet and fruity flavor.

Blue Hubbard squash is a blue-gray, thick-skinned squash that can be quite large in size, which is one reason it is sometimes stuffed with a bread or rice dressing and baked, similarly to a stuffed turkey. Its flavor is sweet and its pulp has a dry texture.

Buttercup squash looks like a dark green globe with a light green crown. It has a dry, smooth pulp and a very sweet flavor reminiscent of a dry-textured sweet potato. Bake, braise, or steam and season with a splash of oil and tamari.

Butternut squash is a light brown, bottle-shaped squash with a sweet, fruity flavor. When cooked, its firm flesh turns creamy, which accounts for its frequent use in soup. Unlike other varieties of squash, its seeds are located toward the bottom end of the squash, rather than in the middle. In addition to being an excellent basis for a classic butternut squash soup or a welcome addition to stews, it can be baked or steamed.

Delicata squash is an elongated, thin-skinned squash. Its skin is usually yellow or beige, with green stripes. Best when baked, it is moist and has a very mild, sweet flavor.

Golden Hubbard squash is a smaller variety of Hubbard squash with orange skin and sweet flesh. It is delicious baked or steamed, and each half is the perfect size for an individual portion.

Golden nugget squash is a small, round squash with a very thick, hard orange skin and a sweet, nutty flavor. Cut it in half before baking or steaming.

Kobocha squash, with its dark-green skin and pumpkin shape, is the sweetest of all the squashes and has a delicious smooth and dense pulp. Baked, braised, or steamed, it's perfectly complemented by sautéed and braised kale cooked with onions and seasoned with tamari.

Pumpkins are available in two basic types: the less flavorful *jack-o'-lantern* variety and the *sugar pumpkin,* which is used for cooking and baking. Pumpkins are not as sweet as other winter squashes and generally need additional sweetening, particularly when they're used in pies or sweet breads. Still, they can be cooked and used as you would any other type of winter squash.

Red kuri squash is a medium to large, reddish or golden squash with sweet, golden flesh and a high ratio of seeds. Cut in half, or into wedges or chunks, and bake or steam.

Spaghetti squash, as its name implies, can be a vegetable substitute for spaghetti. Cut this yellow-skinned, oblong squash in half and bake or steam until tender, and then use a fork to separate the fibers and produce the mildly sweet-flavored "noodles."

Grains

"What grain would you like for dinner?" It's a frequent question at my house. For many people, however, the concept of grain starts and ends with rice. Not until you've experienced the extensive variety of grains from around the world does the question of which grain to choose for a meal even begin to make sense. Because my husband and I have been exploring the world of whole foods for decades, our answer could range from a specific variety of rice, such as Bhutanese red rice, to quinoa, Kamut, millet, or farro. Then again, it could be bulgur, spelt, wild rice, or barley. My husband may choose corn while I might go for rye.

Fortunately, there's rising interest in the wide variety of grains used in traditional cuisines, in part due to their excellent health benefits. This has propelled a whole world of grains from humble fare to trendy and almost exalted status. Relatively obscure varieties, such as quinoa, now commonly appear in recipes in the food section of local newspapers, and they're also frequently featured on menus in restaurants and delis.

When it comes down to it, their extraordinary flavors and pleasing textures is the clincher. And because several kinds of grains can be cooked in less than half an hour, they can easily be incorporated into a busy lifestyle.

What Is a Whole Grain?

The definition of a whole grain is as simple as this: A whole grain contains all of the components that are naturally present in the seed of a cereal grass plant, and thus all the nutrients. And because grains are packed with nutrients to support the growth of the seed when it sprouts, they're a compact source of nutrition—both for the sprout and for us. Some of the foods we typically think of as grains are actually the seeds of plants other than cereal grasses: buckwheat and quinoa, for example. However, they are very similar to grains from cereal grasses, both functionally and nutritionally, so they are included in this category. There are three major structural components of a whole grain—the bran, germ, and endosperm:

- The **bran,** the outer covering of the grain, contains the highest concentration of fiber and is also rich in B vitamins, trace minerals, and potent antioxidants, including lignans. The role of bran is to protect the contents of the seed prior to germination. This is beneficial to humans, too, helping preserve the quality and nutrients of whole grains during storage.
- The **germ** is the life force of the grain, the small part of the seed that sprouts to form a new plant. It contains vitamin E, trace minerals, unsaturated fats, B vitamins, minerals and protein—all the nutrients needed to get the sprout going during its initial growth phase.
- The **endosperm,** the largest part of the seed, consists of starchy carbohydrates, protein, and small amounts of vitamins and minerals, stored as fuel to nourish the sprouted grain during its early growth.

There is a lot to be said about the extraordinary benefits of whole grains and the foundational role they play in a healthy diet. Their complement of fiber, vitamins, minerals, and health-promoting phytonutrients has been shown to reduce cholesterol levels, improve intestinal health, stabilize blood sugar levels, and decrease the incidence of heart disease, diabetes, and some forms of cancer. Eating whole grains can also reduce the risk of diabetes, obesity, and stroke; epidemiological studies even indicate that it reduces early mortality rates.

Whole grains in their intact seed form are the most nourishing option. However, grains that are processed in ways that preserve most or all of the major components—bran, germ, and endosperm—are still considered whole grain products. This includes grains that are cracked, rolled, ground, flaked, extruded (pasta), or minimally pearled to remove only a tough, inedible outer hull.

In contrast, refined grains (and refined carbohydrates) are grains that have been processed to remove the bran, the germ, or both, leaving primarily the starchy endosperm. Refining results in a significant loss of valuable dietary fiber, as well as vitamins, minerals, antioxidants, lignans, phytosterols, and a wide variety of other phytonutrients, compounds found in plants that are critical for optimum health.

Refining was once a difficult and costly process, and as a result, products made with white flour were primarily consumed by the upper classes. During the Industrial Revolution, it became more economical to produce white flour, so items such as white bread became more affordable. For a long time thereafter, many regarded them as superior because they were a symbol of privilege. There are other reasons for the prevalence of refined grain products, and as is often the case, a big one is that it's beneficial for manufacturers. Because the germ contains more oils, which can go rancid, whole grain products generally have a shorter shelf life. There's even at least one nutritional benefit. Bran contains phytic acid, which can bind with minerals and prevent them from being absorbed in the body. However, this is primarily a concern among populations whose diets are low in minerals, or if bran is consumed in excessive amounts.

Overall, the health benefits of whole grains greatly outweigh any benefits of refined grains. Recognizing this, many manufacturers add nutrients back into their flours to replace those lost during processing. However, this is no panacea. Generally, only five of the missing vitamins and minerals are replaced, leaving refined grains deficient in many important nutrients and, of course, fiber.

Is there any room for refined grains in a good diet? While there is no question that whole grains are significantly more nutritious and flavorful, as long as at least half of your daily intake of grains consists of whole grains it's acceptable to consume some refined grains. And depending on the recipe or occasion, the lightness of refined grains may be appropriate in certain situations.

Nonetheless, it's easy to incorporate more whole grains into your diet. Breakfast is a good place to start—in part because that's one meal where we do tend to eat more whole grains. They've long been at the top of the list as a good, satisfying, nutrient-dense choice for supplying sustained energy throughout the day. Even if you have a busy schedule, it doesn't take long to make a delicious hot cereal from any type of whole grain, perhaps with some fresh or dried fruit. Rolled, coarsely cracked, or finely ground grains all cook in less than 20 minutes. Or you can let whole grains cook overnight in a slow cooker. When choosing dry, ready-to-eat cereals, your best choices are shredded whole grain cereals, muesli, low-fat granola that's only lightly sweetened, or whole grain flakes free of preservatives and artificial colors, flavors, and sweeteners.

When it comes to lunch and dinner, any type of grain can be topped with stir-fried or grilled vegetables. Or serve grains as a side dish alongside beans, tofu, tempeh, meat, or poultry. They are a wonderful basis for casseroles, croquettes, salads, and stuffings. Or you can simply add them to soups to lend a chewy texture and act as a thickening agent.

How to Buy and Store Whole Grains

Look for plump, unbroken grains with uniform size and color. Whether you're buying packaged or bulk grains, you'll be assured of the best quality and freshest flavor if you buy them from businesses that specialize in selling grains and know how to store them properly. They're also likely to have a faster turnover, so their products are likely to be fresher. While buying grains in bulk is usually less expensive, make sure the bins are tightly covered and constructed to allow for easy rotation of the bulk goods.

Grain pests such as weevils and mealworm moths can be avoided by storing grains in clean, airtight containers—plastic and paper bags don't qualify. Instead, use glass jars or rigid plastic containers with good seals. Whole grains are best stored at a cool room temperature (below 70°F), and will generally keep for up to six months. Warmer conditions will significantly reduce shelf life. If you have room in your refrigerator, that's a good option, too. Since refined grains such as white rice and white flour lack the natural oils found in the bran and germ, they can be stored at room temperature much longer, often as much as a year.

Cooking Guidelines

Though the amount will vary depending on appetites and what else is being served, 1 cup of uncooked whole grain typically yields enough cooked grain to serve 2 to 4 people.

All whole grains should be rinsed prior to cooking to remove any dirt and dust. For best results, place the grain in its cooking pot, add approximately twice the amount of cool water, then swish the grain to allow the debris to rise to the top. Carefully pour off most of the water to remove the grit, then repeat the process one or two more times to ensure that all the dirt is washed away.

Depending on the type of grain and the cooking method, preparation time can be as little as ten minutes or as long as several hours. Although refined grains generally cook more quickly than do their whole versions, there are many whole grains that require only minimal cooking time. Even hearty whole grains that typically need longer cooking can be prepared more quickly if cooked in a pressure cooker or soaked for several hours before cooking. Or a slow cooker can also do all the work while you sleep or while

Quick-Cooking Grains

10 minutes or less
Couscous, whole wheat and white
Rice, kalijira (white)
Wheat, farina

15 minutes or less
Oats, rolled
Quinoa
Rice, white (basmati, jasmine, long-grain, short-grain)

20 minutes or less
Buckwheat
Bulgur
Kamut flakes
Rice, Arborio, Carnaroli, Vialone Nano
Rice, Bhutanese red rice
Rice, kalijira brown

Rice, parboiled (converted)
Spelt flakes
Teff
Triticale flakes
Wheat, cracked

30 minutes or less
Amaranth
Corn grits, whole
Farro, semipearled
Grano
Millet
Oats, steel-cut
Rice, Camargue red
Rye flakes
Wheat flakes

you're away from home. Although cooking on the stovetop in a saucepan using the absorption method is the most familiar way of preparing grains, other cooking methods bring out unique qualities, flavors, and textures.

ABSORPTION METHOD

Depending on the amount of water added, the texture of grain cooked in a saucepan can range from somewhat dry and dense to moist and even soupy. To use the absorption method, bring the liquid to a boil in the pot, then add the grain and a pinch of salt. Occasionally, a recipe will specify that the grain, liquid, and salt be combined in the pot first and then brought to a boil together. Either way, allow the liquid to return to a boil, then cover, lower the heat, and simmer gently until the grain is tender and the liquid is absorbed. To prevent a sticky texture, avoid stirring or removing the lid during cooking. Let the pot stand, undisturbed, for 5 to 10 minutes before fluffing with a fork to separate the grains.

Toasting the grain in a dry skillet over medium heat before cooking enhances flavor and provides a light and fluffy texture. In contrast, sautéing the grain in a bit of oil or butter results in a fluffier texture with more separate, individual grains; this method is often used when making pilafs. With either method, stir constantly until the grain is slightly browned and fragrant, being careful not to burn the grain. Then add the toasted grain and a pinch of salt to boiling water and cook as above.

PRESSURE-COOKING

Long gone are the days of pressure cookers prone to blowing their lid—and the cooker's contents. Newer pressure cookers incorporate built-in safety mechanisms and are extremely easy to use. In addition to reducing cooking time, they also help retain the distinctiveness of each grain while creating a softer texture and sweeter taste. Even quick-cooking grains, including millet, quinoa, and white rice, can be pressure-cooked for variety in texture. Risotto can be cooked more quickly in a pressure cooker, too, taking only 4 to 5 minutes under pressure and 3 to 5 minutes of stirring.

In general, use ½ cup less water per cup of dry grain than required for the absorption method unless a softer consistency is desired. Add the water, rinsed grain, salt, and any herbs or spices to the pressure cooker and bring to full pressure, then lower the heat to medium-low. A heat diffuser or "flame tamer" is optional, but it can help distribute the heat evenly and prevent scorching or burning. Pressure-cooking typically shaves 5 to 10 minutes off time required to cook the grain using the absorption method. At the end of that time, remove the pressure cooker from the heat and let the pressure come down naturally. If you're pressed for time, place the pressure cooker in the sink and run cold water over the lid until the pressure comes down. Either way, allow the grain to rest, undisturbed, in the unopened pressure cooker for 5 to 10 minutes before serving.

SLOW-COOKING

A slow cooker makes it effortless to prepare hot cereal and long-cooking whole grains such as wheat, Kamut, oat groats, and corn. All you have to do is add the ingredients—water, grains, salt, and other seasonings you wish-—then plug in the slow cooker, put on the lid, and cook at low heat. Eight hours later, you'll have the basis for a great meal ready to eat. If you're planning on a cooked grain for dinner and your time away from home will be longer than 8 hours, you can cook the grain in the slow cooker overnight, refrigerate it the next morning, and then warm it up that evening. If you use the high setting, the grains will be ready in half the time—3½ to 4 hours.

The amount of water needed depends on the final texture desired. To make pilafs in a slow cooker, only use hearty kinds of whole grains, and use 3½ to 4 cups of water per cup of grain. Parboiled or converted rice and rice varieties specifically used to make risotto are the only kinds of white

rice suitable for cooking in a slow cooker. For hot breakfast cereals, the proportion of water to grain is typically 4 to 5 cups of water per cup of grain. Congee, a thin, soupy rice porridge traditionally served at breakfast in China, is an ideal, easily digested, nourishing, and even centering way to start the day. This hot breakfast cereal is made by slow-cooking rice or any other whole grain with a bit of salt and approximately six times as much water as grain. It's easily made in a slow cooker; cook at low heat for 4 to 8 hours. Other ingredients can be added, as well, such as walnuts or almonds, raisins or dates, fennel or cinnamon, or even vegetables, such as fresh ginger, carrots, sweet potatoes, leeks, or celery.

RICE COOKER

An automatic rice cooker is specifically designed for steaming rice. It shuts off automatically when it senses the water has been absorbed and keeps the rice warm until ready to eat. The original rice cookers were made for cooking medium and short-grain white rice, but most of them are now adaptable to cooking other types of rice, including brown rice, as well as other whole grains. The current machines vary in complexity. Some just have a basic on-off switch, whereas others are multipurpose machines that use advanced technology to automatically adjust the cooking time depending on the weight of rice put into the machine. Some also include options like a programmable timer to start the cooking process while you're away or a special lower-temperature porridge cycle to prepare hot cereals, polenta, and risotto.

BAKING

Cooking grains in a covered baking dish in the oven is a handy method when all the burners on your stove are in use. To prepare grain for baking, first sauté it in 1 tablespoon of oil or butter per cup of grain, making sure all of the grains are evenly coated with the oil. Although this step is optional, it enhances the flavor of the grain and helps prevent it from drying out. Then combine the grain, any desired seasonings, and water in a baking dish, using the same amount of water as you would for that grain with the stovetop absorption method. Cover tightly with a lid or foil and bake at 350°F until the water is absorbed and the grain is tender. Most grains require longer cooking time when baked than they do when using the stovetop absorption method, usually about one-third longer. For example, white rice will be done in about 30 minutes and brown rice will take about 1 hour.

SPROUTING

Whole grains can also be sprouted, becoming more nutritious in the process. Protein and vitamin content increases, minerals are made more available and easier to absorb, and some of the carbohydrates are converted into more easily digested simple sugars. Consequently, grain sprouts can taste quite sweet.

From start to finish, most grain sprouts can be ready to harvest in about two or three days and some, like quinoa, require only one day. They're ready when the length of the sprouting "tail" has extended between just beginning to sprout to longer than the length of the seed. The longer the sprout, the more alpha-amylase, an enzyme that breaks down some of the complex starches in flour into sugar, will be developed. For instructions on how to sprout grains, see page 18. Larger grains, such as wheat, rye, barley, and spelt, begin to develop into grass when grown longer than three days. The grass can then be processed into a nutrient-dense beverage using a specialized wheatgrass juicer. These larger sprouts also make good nibbling for cats, especially those who don't have the opportunity to graze on naturally growing grasses outside. Grain sprouts and grain grass will keep for about a week in the refrigerator.

Grain sprouts can be eaten raw as you would eat cold cereal, topped with milk or yogurt. Most sprouts are also good steamed, and in this form they can be used like hot breakfast cereal. For lunch or dinner, try them in a stir-fry or sautéed in oil or butter. Or add them, either raw or cooked, to soups and salads. Up to 1 cup of whole fresh grain sprouts or ¼ cup of chopped grain sprouts can be added to bread dough for extra flavor and to provide additional enzymes to help convert some of the flour into fuel for the yeast. Grain sprouts can also be ground, shaped, and baked into a dense and chewy loaf.

Drying sprouts gives them an even sweeter flavor, which is not a surprise given that dried and ground sprouted barley is also known as barley malt. Very low temperature drying, around 125°F, will retain the enzymatic activity of grain sprouts that were grown long enough (about the length of the grain) to develop alpha-amylase enzyme, creating what is referred to as diastatic malt. Higher drying temperatures, between 140°F and 160°F, will inactivate the enzyme in the sprouts. Also known as non-diastatic malt, it is used as an ingredient in baked goods to contribute a sweet flavor and darker color.

To dry grain sprouts, preheat an oven or a food dehydrator to 125°F or between 140° and 160°F, depending on the final purpose for drying the grain sprouts. Spread them out on a baking sheet or tray and dry them for 8 to 12 hours or until the sprouts are completely dehydrated and brittle. Similar to fresh grain sprouts, they can be used as the basis of a delicious, ready-to-eat breakfast cereal. When finely ground, dried grain sprouts can be used as a 100% sprouted grain flour for baked goods. Due their high level of enzymatic activity, grain sprouts dried into diastatic malt should be used sparingly when making bread, only about ¼ teaspoon per loaf, as too much can make sticky-textured loaves. On the other hand, flour made from other sprouted grains dried at higher temperatures can be substituted freely in recipes that call for traditional flour.

Seasoning Grains

Although optional, adding a pinch of salt per cup of grain during cooking deepens the flavor and also boosts the grain's natural sweetness. It can also reduce the tendency to add excessive salt or salty condiments at the table, adjusting for what should have been accomplished during the cooking process. Cooking grain with salt may also improve its digestibility. Chlorine, one of the main components of salt (sodium chloride), plays an important role in digestion in the form of hydrochloric acid, a primary constituent of the body's digestive juices.

Fresh or dried herbs and spices can also enhance the flavor of grains, cutting down on the need for salt while providing variety and interesting flavor accents. Add dried herbs and spices at the start of the cooking process. Due to their delicacy, fresh herbs should be added only during the last few minutes of cooking or right before serving. Another way to season grains is to cook them with liquids other than water, such as vegetable or meat broth or diluted fruit or vegetable juice.

Gluten-Free and Wheat-Free Grains at a Glance

Grains are categorized in two primary ways:
- The presence or absence of gluten, the protein complex that affects the texture of baked goods and helps give bread the structure to rise.
- Whether or not it is wheat.

While the search for gluten-free grains can simply be due to an interest in exploring a wide variety of tastes and textures, some individuals must avoid all grains that contain gluten, specifically the gliadin fractions found in wheat. Other gluten-containing grains include Kamut, spelt, rye, barley, and triticale. Strict avoidance of gluten-containing grains is a lifelong obligation for individuals with celiac disease or dermatitis herpetiformis. Celiac disease, also known as gluten intolerance, is a

Gluten-Free Grains

Amaranth	Quinoa
Buckwheat	Rice
Corn	Sorghum
Job's tears	Teff
Millet	Wild rice
Oats*	

Grains That Contain Gluten

Barley	Rye
Farro	Spelt
Grano	Triticale
Kamut	Wheat

*Although oats don't contain gluten, in North America they are often listed as inappropriate for gluten-free diets because of concerns that they could have been grown or processed in the vicinity of wheat.

hereditary disorder in which the body responds to gluten by damaging the lining of the small intestine, which blocks the body's ability to absorb nutrients from food. While symptoms will vary, they can include difficulty gaining or losing weight, fatigue, bloating, abdominal pain, diarrhea, constipation, and anorexia. Dermatitis herpertiformis is another form of celiac disease that manifests in severe, itchy, blistering skin, usually on the elbows, knees, and buttocks.

Wheat allergy and wheat intolerance are entirely different conditions from gluten intolerance, and from each other. A wheat allergy is a condition in which eating even a small amount of wheat can trigger the body's immune system to produce immunoglobulin E (IgE), which causes the release of histamine. Swelling, inflammation, nausea, diarrhea, and other symptoms may occur as a reaction, including hives or even life-threatening anaphylactic shock. A wheat allergy requires strict lifelong avoidance of wheat and triticale, a grain that is a hybrid of wheat and rye. Although Kamut and spelt are related to wheat, their gluten components are unique. Still, any experimentation with Kamut or spelt for anyone with a wheat allergy should always be done under the guidance of a health professional.

In contrast, wheat intolerance is a condition in which the body does not adequately digest wheat, although the reaction remains a metabolic disorder and does not involve the immune system. Symptoms are milder, although not particularly comfortable, and include bloating, flatulence, cramping, diarrhea, rashes, and fatigue. Some individuals with wheat intolerance may still be able to eat wheat occasionally or in small servings.

Exploring Grains

Amaranth

Gluten free

Sometimes referred to as "the grain of the future," amaranth is actually a rediscovered ancient Aztec crop harvested from a broad-leaved plant, not a cereal grass. Although difficult to plant and harvest, amaranth is naturally resistant to weeds and can grow in poor soil and dry conditions, making it a promising crop for otherwise unproductive areas. It is also a high-yield crop, with each plant producing up to half a million tiny seeds, about the size of poppy seeds.

Amaranth is high in fiber and rich in calcium, iron, and phosphorus. It is especially noted for its high concentration of lysine, the amino acid usually found in only limited amounts in grains. This extra lysine gives it a better amino acid profile, in terms of complete protein, than any other grain except quinoa.

Varieties and Cooking Guidelines

Flavor enhancers: Onions, garlic, parsley, walnuts, almonds, lemon, and olive oil. Sweet flavor enhancers include apples, apple juice, raisins, and orange peel.

Various types of amaranth range from purple-black to buff yellow. The golden variety is most commonly available, with black amaranth more limited in supply. Different colors of amaranth also have different textures when cooked. While buff-colored amaranth thickens like cornmeal as it cooks, the seeds of black amaranth remain more separate.

With its nutty, mildly spicy flavor, whole amaranth is delicious whether eaten on its own, cooked with other grains for a breakfast cereal or pilaf, or used to make an alternative version of thick polenta. Or try adding a small amount of amaranth to stews and soups to make them heartier and thicker. For extra crunch and variety in cookies, muffins, pancakes, and quick breads, use raw amaranth as a substitute for poppy seeds in the batter. Amaranth also blends well with brown rice, buckwheat, or millet, making for an interesting texture and a better nutritional profile. Use one part amaranth to three parts other grains and cook according to the predominant grain's instructions.

To prepare amaranth as a side dish, use one part amaranth to two parts liquid and cook for 15 to 20 minutes. When making a hot breakfast cereal, go with one part amaranth to three to four parts liquid and simmer for 20 to 30 minutes. In either case, the method is the same: Bring the amaranth and water to a boil, add a pinch of salt per cup of amaranth, then lower the heat, cover, and simmer. Plain cooked amaranth congeals as it cools, so eat it immediately or keep it warm until ready to serve.

Amaranth can also be popped; the result looks

like a miniature version of popcorn. Since it turns rancid quickly, prepare only as much as you'll use immediately. In addition to being a great snack, popped amaranth can be sprinkled on top of cereal, used as a substitute for bread crumbs, or added to soups, stews, and cakes for additional flavor and texture. To prepare popped amaranth, heat a wok or deep, heavy skillet until very hot. Start with just 1 tablespoon of amaranth and move the seeds constantly with tongs or a heat-resistant spatula to prevent them from burning. Transfer the popped amaranth into a bowl, and if more is desired, add another tablespoon of amaranth to the skillet and continue popping until each grain has popped and expanded. Each tablespoon of whole amaranth makes ¼ cup of popped amaranth.

Barley

Contains gluten

As one of the first grains cultivated for food, for both humans and animals, barley is an old soul. After falling out of favor because it was perceived as peasant fare, it has recently become more popular again because of its beta-glucans, a form of soluble fiber. When beta-glucans (and all forms of soluble fiber) mix with liquids in the digestive tract, they develop a gelatinous consistency that can bind with fatty substances and remove them from the body, thus helping to reduce low-density lipoprotein (LDL, or bad cholesterol) and total cholesterol. Fortunately, the beta-glucans are found throughout the entire barley kernel, so even pearled barley provides this benefit. And because soluble fiber helps slow the release of sugars into the bloodstream, eating barley with other foods helps moderate blood sugar levels and provide steady, sustained fuel for the body

Varieties and Cooking Guidelines

Flavor enhancers: Onions, mushrooms, parsley, thyme, garlic, chives, cilantro, basil, dill, and peas, and especially miso, shoyu, and black olives.

When it comes to flavor and texture, barley is well known for its role in making hearty soups and stews. But that is just a hint of what barley can bring to a menu. It is also excellent as a hot breakfast cereal or as a basis for warming pilafs or cooling summer salads. Since barley readily absorbs flavors, it's a chameleon among grains, reflecting the flavors of other ingredients it's cooked with: water, broth, or fruit juices used as the cooking liquid; seasonings such as herbs and spices; dried fruits or sun-dried tomatoes; or flavorful culinary oils, salad dressings, and marinades.

Two main types of barley are grown, and their names can be a little confusing. Hulled barley refers to barley that grows with an inedible hull that adheres tightly to the grain. Hull-less varieties do have a hull, but it is only loosely attached to the grain and generally falls off during harvesting.

■ HULLED BARLEY

The tightly attached tough outer husk of hulled barley varieties must be mechanically removed for the grain to be cooked and eaten. The process, known as pearling, is comparable to sanding. The term *pearled* is very fitting, as barley looks very much like a small pearl when all of the husk and bran layers are removed. Use this as a visual guide when buying barley: the browner the barley, the less it has been pearled.

Whole barley has only the hull removed, leaving the bran in place. This form has the most fiber, protein, vitamins, and minerals, making it the most nutritious, but it also requires the longest cooking time.

- Whole barley will cook more quickly if it's presoaked for 2 to 6 hours. To retain nutrients, soak it in its cooking water, using 3 cups of water per cup of barley. If the ambient temperature is warm (above 75°F), soak it in the refrigerator.
- For the absorption method, use 3 cups of water per cup of barley. Bring the barley

Other Forms of Barley

Barley flakes are produced from barley kernels that have been rolled flat and dried. Use them as you would oatmeal, in cookies, breads, and casseroles, or as a thickening agent in soups and stews. To make a hot cereal, add 1 cup of barley flakes and a pinch of salt to 3 cups of boiling water, then lower the heat, cover, and simmer until the water is absorbed, about 25 minutes.

Barley grits are made from barley kernels cracked into tiny pieces, which reduces cooking time to about 20 minutes. Use barley grits as a hot cereal or to thicken soup.

Buckwheat

Gluten free

Despite its name, buckwheat isn't related to wheat, and in fact, it isn't even truly a grain. Rather than being produced by a cereal grass, it is the seeds of a plant related to rhubarb that was brought to the United States by Dutch and German settlers. The name buckwheat is a variation on its Dutch name, *bockweit* and the German *buche weisen* (beechwheat). Both of those names arose because the three-cornered buckwheat kernels resemble the triangular nuts of the beechnut tree, and because buckwheat has nutritional qualities similar to those of wheat. Buckwheat is rarely grown with agricultural chemicals. Fertilizer tends to encourage too much leaf growth, and pesticides harm or kill the bees needed for pollination.

Because it contains all of the essential amino acids, including lysine, in proportions close to those that are ideal, buckwheat can almost be considered a complete protein. It also contains good amounts of calcium, iron, and B vitamins.

Varieties and Cooking Guidelines

Flavor enhancers: Onions, parsley, sage, poultry seasoning, garlic, red bell peppers, roasted walnuts, thyme, mushrooms, black pepper, and especially potatoes. Sweet flavor enhancers include maple syrup, honey, roasted walnuts, almond butter, and raisins.

Though the hard, black hulls of buckwheat may be retained when buckwheat is ground into flour, they must be removed to make whole forms of buckwheat edible. Hulled whole buckwheat kernels, known as buckwheat groats, are white and have a mild flavor and soft texture, making them a nice accompaniment to delicately flavored foods.

To cook buckwheat groats using the absorption method, use 2 cups of water and a pinch of salt per cup of buckwheat. Bring the water to a boil, stir in the buckwheat and salt, then lower the heat, cover, and simmer until tender, about 15 to 20 minutes. For a nuttier flavor, toast the buckwheat groats before cooking, either dry-roasting them or sautéing in butter or oil, and stirring constantly for 2 to 3 minutes. Buckwheat groats don't require or benefit from the egg treatment described below for kasha. Potatoes are a great companion to buckwheat.

To make anyone an instant fan of buckwheat, sauté 1 cup of uncooked buckwheat with an onion in olive oil or butter, then add 2 cups of boiling water, along with a couple of cubed potatoes, celery sliced on the diagonal, and ½ teaspoon of thyme. You might serve it topped with a sprinkling of Parmesan cheese. This pilaf is a good side dish for fish or tofu, or for a quick and easy take on knishes, wrap some of the pilaf in a tortilla.

To make a buckwheat version of polenta, combine 1½ cups of buckwheat groats, plain or toasted, with 4 cups of water. Bring to a boil, then lower the heat, cover, and simmer until the buckwheat becomes very thick, about 25 minutes. Spoon the cooked buckwheat into an oiled baking dish in an even layer, then allow it to cool. Cut it into strips, slices, or cubes and serve with your favorite sauce. For an interesting breakfast dish, warm the polenta in a skillet and serve with maple syrup, applesauce, or apple butter.

Buckwheat croquettes are another way to serve cooked buckwheat groats. Cook 1 cup of buckwheat groats, then mix in 2 tablespoons of flour as soon as you turn off the heat, stirring until thoroughly combined. Allow the mixture to cool just until it is easy to handle, then form it into patties or golf-ball shapes. Bake the croquettes on an oiled cookie sheet at 375°F for 20 minutes. They're delicious with either savory or sweet accompaniments; try them with your favorite sauce or topped with nut butter and maple syrup.

Kasha is simply white buckwheat that has been pretoasted, giving it an assertive flavor and drier texture when cooked. Traditional foods such as kasha varnishkes (kasha mixed with bowtie pasta), stuffed cabbage rolls, and dumplings are based on kasha. To prepare kasha the traditional way, coat 1 cup of kasha with one beaten egg, allowing any excess egg to drain off as you transfer the mixture to a saucepan. Over medium heat, stir the kasha constantly until toasted. The egg coating seals each individual buckwheat groat, preventing the kasha from becoming mushy. Once the kasha is toasted, add 2 cups of boiling water and a pinch of salt. Lower the heat, cover, and simmer until the water is absorbed, about 15 to 20 minutes.

Buckwheat grits, sometimes called cream of buckwheat, are a finely ground form of untoasted white buckwheat. They cook in just 10 to 12 minutes, making a delicious, very digestible hot cereal with a texture similar to that of wheat farina. To cook ½ cup of buckwheat grits, bring 2½ cups of water to a boil. Add a pinch of salt and the grits, then lower the heat, cover, and simmer for 10 to 12 minutes.

Corn

Gluten free

Corn is one of the few grains native to the western hemisphere and the only grain that contains appreciable amounts of vitamin A, with the highest levels in yellow corn. In its whole, dried form, complete with the bran and germ, corn is also a good source of B vitamins, vitamin C, potassium,

and fiber. However, unless corn is pretreated with an alkaline substance, eating too much corn can cause significant nutritional deficiencies. Besides being low in two essential amino acids, tryptophan and lysine, most of its niacin is bound by another molecule, making it unavailable to the body.

In the past, entire regions and cultures with a corn-based diet, including the southern United States, South America, and Africa, have suffered devastating epidemics of pellagra, a serious disease resulting from niacin deficiency. Fortunately, many native cultures instinctively cooked whole corn with various alkali substances, such as slaked lime (calcium hydroxide created from the thermal decomposition of materials such as limestone), wood ashes (potassium hydroxide), or lye (sodium hydroxide). Today, slaked lime (sometimes sold as "cal") is most often used. Not only does this alkalinizing treatment, also known as nixtamalization, help remove the corn's tough outer hull for easier eating and processing, it also improves the amino acid balance, liberates the bound niacin, and, when slaked lime is used, provides bonus calcium. The distinctive slightly sour flavor of corn tortillas, corn chips, hominy, and masa harina are a result of their manufacture from alkaline-treated corn.

Varieties and Cooking Guidelines

Flavor enhancers: Onions, chives, tomatoes, cilantro, cumin, cheese, garlic, hot and sweet peppers, oregano, epazote, chili powder, and parsley.

The sweet corn eaten as a vegetable is a relatively new variety in which the sugars in the kernel don't turn into starch as the corn matures. In terms of grain forms of corn, popcorn is a distinct variety. There are two other primary varieties of corn—dent corn and flint corn—each with a distinctive flavor and texture. Dent corn has hard, smooth sides and a soft inner core of starch that collapses during drying, causing a dent at the top and explaining its name. There are yellow and white versions of dent corn; the yellow has a deeper, richer corn flavor. Flint corn has a hard outer shell and kernels in a variety of colors. It has recently become more popular, especially in the form of blue and red corn used for cornmeal and chips, after decades of being thought of primarily as a decorative item. However, it has a long history of use as a staple food among native peoples in the southwestern United States, Mexico, and Central and South America. Flint corn has a hard, starchy interior (though not as hard as flint!)—so much so that it is gritty rather than powdery when ground. Blue and red corn are known for their sweet, nutlike flavor. They are also higher in protein, iron, potassium, and zinc than typical yellow or white varieties of dent corn.

POPCORN

Popcorn, which is probably the most widely consumed whole grain form of corn, is a specific variety of corn that has a hard outer protein layer protecting the inner starch layers and a moisture content between 11% and 14%, factors that combine to make it especially poppable. When subjected to high heat, pressure builds up in the interior starch layers until the protein layer explodes. Yellow popcorn, with its corny flavor and crunchy, firm texture, pops up the most, expanding up to forty times its original size. In contrast, white popcorn has a slightly sweet taste, is crisp yet tender, and expands up to thirty-five times its original size.

Store dry popcorn in a tightly sealed jar or plastic container, preferably in the refrigerator, to retain the moisture inside the kernels. Just ¼ cup of popcorn kernels will yield about 8 cups of popped corn. With 2 grams of fiber and only 69 calories in 3 cups of popcorn, it can be a very nutritious whole grain snack if popped using a good-quality, nonhydrogenated oil specifically designated for high-heat applications and served without butter or even salt. If plain popcorn isn't enough for you, dust it with any of your favorite seasonings such as garlic granules, cayenne pepper or paprika, basil,

cinnamon, ginger, granulated sea vegetables, or, nutritional yeast.

HOMINY AND POSOLE

Hominy, also known as posole (or samp when coarsely ground), is whole dent or flint corn that has been treated with an alkali agent. When cooked, the whole kernels are very chewy and have a slightly sweet, slightly sour flavor that, surprisingly, is not very cornlike. Hominy is used whole in soups and stews or as a side dish, or it may be ground to make fresh masa. Slaking corn with lime at home to make hominy takes about 2½ hours, but the flavor is significantly better than canned, precooked whole hominy. However, there is a time-saving alternative: Buy dried corn labeled "posole," which means it has already been slaked with lime, had its hulls removed, and then been dried again. After soaking the dried posole for 6 to 8 hours or overnight, all you need to do is the final cooking step. The posole is done when the kernels have bloomed open and become soft.

- To cook posole using the absorption method, put the dried posole in a pot and add water to cover. Bring to a boil, then lower the heat, cover, and simmer until tender, about 3 to 4 hours.
- To pressure-cook, put the dried posole in the pressure cooker and add water to cover. Cook at pressure for 1 hour and then simmer for an additional hour.
- To slow-cook, use 6 cups of water per cup of posole. Cook on the high setting for 1 hour and then on the low setting for 9 to 12 hours.

OTHER FORMS OF CORN

Hominy grits, made by grinding dried hominy, are available in coarse, medium, or fine grind. Most often served as a hot cereal or simple side dish in Southern-style cooking, they can also be used as the basis for soufflés and puddings. To cook hominy grits, use four parts water to one part grits. Bring the water to a boil, then gradually pour in the grits, whisking all the while. Lower the heat, cover, and simmer for 25 to 30 minutes. Quick-cooking grits are very finely ground and will cook in 5 minutes.

Masa, also called *nixtamal,* is a dough made from ground, freshly cooked hominy. It's typically used to make tamales, tortillas, and dumplings, but it can also be served like mashed potatoes, topped with butter or cheese. When dried and finely ground, it is called masa harina.

Corn grits are made by coarsely grinding whole or degerminated corn. Look for stone-ground whole corn grits, processed to retain the bran and germ. Unlike true hominy grits, corn grits are not processed with lime. To cook corn grits, use four parts salted water to one part grits. Bring the water to a boil, then slowly pour in the grits, whisking all the while. Lower the heat, cover, and simmer for 25 to 30 minutes.

Farro

Contains gluten

Although farro and spelt are often confused with one another or considered to be the same, they are, in fact, two different species. Plant taxonomy isn't always set in stone or universally agreed upon, but the current thinking classifies farro as *Triticum diococcum,* whereas spelt is *Triticum spelta.* Also known as emmer, farro (FAHR-oh) is an unhybridized and ancient type of wheat that was common throughout Europe, northern Africa, and the Near East well before the early days of the Roman empire, and it is said to be the grain that fueled the Roman legions. Farro ultimately fell from favor as other types of wheat were developed that had higher yields and were easier to produce, such as durum wheat. Like spelt and hulled barley, farro has a tough outer hull that must be removed prior to cooking or further processing. Still, its cultivation survived in Ethiopia and some areas of northern and central Italy, especially in Tuscany, Umbria, and areas around Rome. After languishing in obscurity for centuries, it is becoming popular once again.

Farro has a chewy texture and delicious flavor reminiscent of a cross between wheat and barley. The whole grain has a shape and color similar to that of short-grain brown rice, but is a bit darker. Nutritionally, it is rich in fiber, magnesium, and vitamin A, vitamin E, and various B vitamins. Because it is distinct from modern hybridized wheat and is lower in gluten, many people who are allergic to wheat find that they can tolerate farro. Still, anyone with severe allergies or sensitivity to wheat should consult a medical professional before experimenting with farro.

Varieties and Cooking Guidelines

Flavor enhancers: Basil, garlic, rosemary, thyme, mushrooms, olives, and red bell peppers.

In Italy, where farro continued to be grown and appreciated after its popularity waned elsewhere, farro is often made into a risotto-like dish called farrotto. It is also added to soups and stews for thickening and texture, with the added bonus of making the final dish especially delicious, since farro captures the flavors foods it's cooked with. In salads, it adds both a complementary chewy texture and a satisfying depth of flavor.

Whole farro takes a long time to cook—2 to 3 hours. However, you can reduce that time to about an hour by presoaking it for 6 to 12 hours. When adding presoaked farro to soups or stews, add it 1 hour before the soup or stew will be done.

- To retain nutrients, soak in its cooking water, using 3 cups of water per cup of farro. If the ambient temperature is warm (above 75°F), soak it in the refrigerator.
- For the absorption method, bring the farro and its soaking water to a boil, then lower the heat, cover, and simmer until tender, about 50 to 60 minutes.

- To pressure-cook, use 3 cups of water per cup of farro and, if time permits, soak for 30 minutes before cooking at pressure for 45 minutes.
- To slow-cook, use 4 to 5 cups of water per cup of farro and cook on the high setting for 3½ hours or on low for 8 hours.

To make farrotto, use 5 cups of hot broth per cup of farro and cook as you would regular risotto. However, farrotto requires 1 hour of stirring and cooking time to achieve a tender, slightly chewy texture, rather than the 20 minutes it takes with Arborio and similar Italian rices. You can shorten that time to about 25 minutes by using semi-pearled farro, in which case only about 4 cups of hot broth will be needed.

Semi-pearled farro has been slightly pearled to reduce cooking time to 30 minutes or less without presoaking. For the absorption method, use 2 cups of water per cup of semi-pearled farro.

Cracked farro, made by coarsely cracking whole farro, cooks in about 30 minutes with no presoaking. Use 3 cups of water per cup of cracked farro. Use it as a hot cereal for breakfast, in pilafs, or in salads, such as tabbouleh.

Grano

Contains gluten

Durum wheat is typically used to make pasta and semolina flour, but for many centuries, before pasta was even on the menu, durum wheat was eaten as a grain in the Apulia region in Italy and in Sicily. In fact, its name, *grano* (gra-NO), is the Italian word for "grain." Starting with whole durum wheat, grano is lightly pearled to remove the thick outer casing. With only a small amount of the bran sacrificed in the process, grano remains a very nutritious grain, especially in comparison to pasta, which is typically derived from durum wheat that is further refined.

Cooking Guidelines

Flavor enhancers: Onions, chives, dill, mushrooms, black pepper, garlic, curry powder, parsley, cilantro, and mint.

Golden in color like semolina flour, grano tastes like pasta and is cooked like pasta, albeit for a bit longer. Traditional recipes featured the pleasant chewiness of grano in soups, pilafs, and entrées, but it's also a natural served cold in salads, where it provides added flavor, texture, and nutrition. When cooked with extra water, grano also makes a delicious hot breakfast cereal. Grano contains gluten, so it is inappropriate for gluten-free diets.

To cook grano, use 8 cups of water per cup of grano. Bring the water to a boil, salt it as you would for pasta, then add the grano. After it returns to a boil, lower the heat to medium and cook, stirring frequently, until the grano is tender but still chewy, about 35 minutes. Then, just as with cooking pasta, drain the grano and serve it with a sauce or as an accompaniment to meat, seafood, tofu, tempeh, or beans.

Grano can also be cooked in soups such as minestrone. Use 1 cup of grano for 2 quarts of soup, allowing at least 30 minutes of cooking after the grano is added. For a hot breakfast cereal, use a proportion of 4 cups of water per cup of grano. Bring to a boil, then lower the heat, cover, and, ideally, simmer for about 4 hours so it will become soft and creamy. Alternatively, a delicious, chewy version can be ready within 2 hours.

Job's Tears

Gluten free

Also known as *hato mugi* and *adlay,* Job's tears is a grain with a teardrop shape that somewhat resembles barley. Sometimes it is said to be a type of barley, but the two are in different genuses. The seed of a wild grass cultivated for over four thousand years in China, it has been used extensively in traditional Chinese medicine. It's also often used in macrobiotic cooking, where it has a reputation for being strengthening to the body. Since only the outer husk is removed, it serves as a good source of dietary fiber. Its pleasant nutlike flavor permeates any dish in which it is cooked.

Cooking Guidelines

Flavor enhancers: Ginger, parsley, onions, and chives.

Job's tears are generally cooked along with other grains or in soups or stews. For a good balance of flavor and texture, use one part Job's tears to four parts other grains, and use two parts water for each part Job's tears. Cook until all the grains are tender, typically about 10 minutes longer than the primary grain would require. Job's tears can also be cooked and eaten on their own.

- For the absorption method, use 2 cups of water per cup of Job's tears. Bring the water to a boil, stir in the Job's tears, then lower the heat, cover, and simmer until tender, about 50 to 60 minutes.
- To pressure-cook, use 2 cups of water per cup of Job's tears and cook at pressure for 45 minutes.
- To slow-cook, use 4 cups of water per cup of Job's tears and cook on the low setting for 6 to 8 hours.

Kamut

Contains gluten

Kamut is a registered trademark for a type of durum wheat said to have originated in Egypt, and the name Kamut is derived from the ancient Egyptian word for wheat. The grains have a humpbacked shape and are much larger than a typical kernel of wheat—nearly two or three times as large.

Its flavor is rich, sweet, and buttery and the texture of the cooked whole grain is pleasantly chewy. In comparison to conventional wheat, Kamut has 20% to 40% more protein, more fatty acids, 30% more vitamin E, and more magnesium, selenium, and zinc. By virtue of the attributes included in its trademark registration, Kamut also has the distinction of always being grown organically. This nutritious and healthful grain's increasing popularity is reflected in an expanding variety of food products made with Kamut, ranging from flakes, couscous, and bulgur to pasta and ready-to-eat cereals.

Since it is a type of wheat, Kamut does contain gluten. However, because it has never been hybridized, Kamut isn't entirely like modern-day wheat. Because of that, some people who are sensitive to wheat can eat Kamut and products made from it. Still, anyone with severe allergies or sensitivity to wheat should consult with a medical professional before experimenting with Kamut.

Varieties and Cooking Guidelines

Flavor enhancers: Onions, garlic, Parmesan cheese, parsley, basil, black pepper, mushrooms, raisins, and lemon.

Whether hot or cold, whole Kamut makes a terrific breakfast cereal. With a texture and shape similar to that of pine nuts (although larger in size), cooked whole Kamut is excellent in baked goods, salads, cereals, and pilafs. It is also a good addition to soups, stews, and chili, providing both texture and thickening. Or try adding it to pancakes and muffins, where it will enhance both flavor and texture. For an appealing texture contrast in side dishes and grain-based salads, combine cooked Kamut with rice, barley, or quinoa.

Whole Kamut takes 1½ to 2 hours to cook, but presoaking will shorten that time. No matter which of the following cooking methods you use, instead of it absorbing all its cooking liquid, the proportion of water called for in the recipe is purposely greater than needed, in order to enhance and maintain the suppleness of the cooked grain. In fact, leftover cooked Kamut is best stored in the refrigerator submerged in its own cooking liquid to help keep it hydrated and soft. Excess liquid can be reserved for broth.

- For quicker cooking, presoak whole Kamut

for 6 to 12 hours or overnight. To retain nutrients, soak it in its cooking water, using 3 cups of water per cup of Kamut. If the ambient temperature is warm (above 75°F), soak it in the refrigerator.

- To cook on the stove, use 3 cups of water per cup of Kamut. Bring the Kamut and its soaking water to a boil, then lower the heat, cover, and simmer until the grains are plumped and a few have burst, about 1 hour if presoaked and 1½ to 2 hours if not.
- To pressure-cook, use 3 cups of water per cup of Kamut and cook at pressure for 35 minutes if presoaked, or 45 minutes minutes if not.
- For slow-cooking, presoaking is optional. Use 4 cups of water per cup of Kamut and cook on the high setting for 3½ to 4 hours or on low for 7 to 8 hours.

Kamut bulgur is cooked similarly to its wheat-based counterpart. Use 2 cups of water per cup of Kamut bulgur. Bring the water to a boil, stir in the bulgur, then lower the heat, cover, and simmer for 25 minutes. Remove it from the heat and allow it to stand, covered, for another 10 minutes before serving or using in a recipe.

Kamut couscous is also cooked similarly to its wheat-based counterpart. Use 1½ cups of water or broth per cup of Kamut couscous. Bring the water to a boil, then stir in the couscous, lower the heat, cover, and simmer for 5 minutes. Remove from the heat and allow it to stand, covered, for another 5 minutes. Stir to fluff before serving or using in a recipe.

Kamut flakes are made like oatmeal. Whole Kamut is steamed, dried, then flattened between rollers. Use them as you would oatmeal in cookies, other baked goods, and casseroles. For hot breakfast cereal, use 2 cups of water per cup of Kamut flakes. Bring the water to a boil, stir in the Kamut flakes, then lower the heat, cover, and sim-

mer for 15 to 18 minutes. It's especially delicious when cooked with vanilla extract and dried apples and served topped with roasted pecans.

Millet

Gluten free

Its delicious, delicate flavor and soft, cohesive texture make millet perfect for basic side dishes, stuffings, burgers, and casseroles. Although this quick-cooking grain is most often associated with birdseed in the United States, it's a sacred grain in China, where it has a long history of use, and is a staple crop for about one-third of the world's population. The word *millet* is actually applied to at least five different unrelated species of varying colors and palatability. The variety of millet used in the United States is yellow proso millet, and the tiny grain is always hulled or pearled, but the bran remains intact. In addition to being a good source of dietary iron, millet is also rich in lysine, making it a higher-quality protein than most grains. It is also very alkaline, making it easy to digest and a soothing comfort food.

Varieties and Cooking Guidelines

Flavor enhancers: Curry powder, chili powder, orange, rosemary, onion, chives, parsley, black pepper, bay leaf, thyme, garlic, ginger, roasted walnuts, and roasted pecans.

Try adding a couple of tablespoons of uncooked millet to breads and baked goods for a nutlike crunch, or stir some uncooked millet into stews and soups about 20 minutes before the end of cooking to provide body. To enhance millet's nutty flavor and ensure the grains cook up light and dry, toast it in a dry skillet, stirring constantly, for 3 to 4 minutes *before* rinsing it and cooking it. However, untoasted millet is equally good; it just has a milder flavor and softer texture.

- For the absorption method, use 2 cups of water per cup of millet. Combine the water and millet, bring to a boil, then lower the heat, cover, and simmer for 15 minutes. Remove from the heat and let stand, covered, for 20 minutes before fluffing.

- To pressure-cook, use 2 cups of water per cup of millet and cook at pressure for 10 to 15 minutes.
- To slow-cook, use 4 cups of water and cook on the low setting for 6 to 8 hours. For a hot breakfast cereal, consider replacing some of the water with juice, and add some fresh or dried fruit.

For a softer texture, similar to mashed potatoes, cook using the absorption method and increase the water to 3 or even 3½ cups per cup of millet. Simmer, covered, until the water is absorbed, about 45 minutes to an hour. Adding 1 cup of coarsely chopped cauliflower per cup of millet enhances the flavor and texture. Or, for a rich, creamy hot breakfast cereal, use 5 cups of water or a combination of water and apple juice per cup of millet and cook using the absorption method.

For a savory vegetable stew with millet, use 3 cups of water or broth per cup of millet and add any chopped vegetables and seasonings you wish. Bring to a boil, reduce the heat, and simmer for 45 minutes.

To use it as you would polenta, press cooked millet into an oiled baking dish while it's still warm. Allow it to cool, then cut it into squares or strips. You can also press warm millet into oiled muffin cups to make millet timbales. Leftover millet splashed with your favorite dressing is an exceptional basis for a grain and vegetable salad.

Oats

Gluten free

Of all the grains, oats are the ultimate comfort food, bringing soothing warmth whether cooked into a bowl of steaming hot oatmeal, a chewy raisin-studded oatmeal cookie, or a hearty pilaf made from steel-cut oats or whole oat groats. Processing oats is a two-step operation: First the outer hull is removed to expose the inner kernel, called the groat, then the groats are steamed to inactivate enzymes that would otherwise cause them to go rancid very quickly. Thanks to this process, oats have a shelf life of up to one year when stored at a moderate room temperature, and even longer if kept in cooler conditions. The steaming also partially cooks the oats and enhances their nutty flavor. From there, the groats may be left whole, rolled into thick old-fashioned flakes, or chopped into small, coarse pieces, called steel-cut oats. Steel-cut oats can also be made into flakes, yielding the small, thin flakes of quick-cooking oatmeal or the even smaller and thinner flakes of instant oatmeal.

Besides having great flavor and texture, oats have extensive nutritional benefits. Because only the outer, indigestible husk is removed during processing, leaving the bran and germ intact, all forms of oats are considered to be whole grain, no matter what size or shape they're processed into. In addition, all forms of oats contain beta-glucan, the viscous soluble fiber that helps lower both total cholesterol and LDL, or bad, cholesterol. Their beta-glucan content means that oats, like barley, digest more slowly, which helps stabilize blood sugar levels and keeps you going longer, feeling more satisfied and energized. This type of fiber is also responsible for the smooth, thick texture of cooked oats and their moistening and tenderizing effect in baked goods.

While still fairly low in fat, oats contain more fats than most grains, mostly in the form of unsaturated fat, and particularly linoleic acid. This essential fatty acid plays an important role in the synthesis of prostaglandins, hormonelike compounds that help regulate vital body functions, including supporting a strong nervous system and healthy skin. Oats are also a good source of vitamin E, including tocotrienols, a component of vitamin E that helps reduce serum cholesterol by preventing the synthesis of cholesterol in the liver.

Oats are gluten free and studies have shown that oats do not trigger the symptoms associated with grains that contain gluten. In North America they are often listed as being inappropriate for a gluten-free diet, but this is only out of concern that they may be contaminated by wheat during harvest and processing.

Varieties and Cooking Guidelines

Flavor enhancers: Dried fruits, cinnamon, fennel seed, honey, and maple syrup. Savory flavor enhancers include sage, Parmesan cheese, dill, nutmeg, parsley, and celery.

Oat groats have only their inedible outer chaff removed, so they have the most full-bodied flavor and provide the most nutrition. They make an exceptional hearty breakfast cereal. Because they retain their shape and have a soft but chewy texture when cooked, they can also be served in place of rice or used as the basis for pilafs and stuffings. For any of the methods below, you can make a sweet dish by adding a bit of cinnamon and some raisins or other dried fruit during cooking. For a savory twist, add chopped onion, celery, salt to taste, and a sprinkling of your favorite herb.

- For the absorption method, use 3 cups of water per cup of oats. Combine the water and oats, bring to a boil, then lower the heat, cover, and simmer until tender, about 90 minutes, adding more water if necessary.
- To pressure-cook, use 3 cups of water per cup of oats and cook at pressure for 30 minutes.
- To slow-cook, use 4 cups of water per cup of oats and cook on the low setting for 8 to 12 hours.

Steel-cut oats, also known as Scotch oats, Scottish oats, or Irish oats, are oat groats that have been cut into small, coarse pieces. As a result, cooking time is reduced to 30 minutes, and you can further reduce that time to 15 minutes by soaking the oats in their cooking water overnight; you may need to increase the amount of water a bit. Another way to reduce the cooking time to about 15 minutes is to toast steel-cut oats in a pan over medium heat for 3 minutes before cooking. Because steel-cut oats have virtually all of the flavor and chewy texture of oat groats, they make a remarkable hot cereal, a great base for a pilaf, or a flavorful addition to breads. They can even be used to make an oat-based risotto. Sauté a small onion in 1 tablespoon of oil or butter. Then stir in 1 cup of steel-cut oats and continue to stir and sauté for 5 minutes. Add ½ cup of hot broth, stirring constantly until the liquid is absorbed, then add another ½ cup of broth and continue in the same manner until you've added 3 cups of broth and the dish has the rich, creamy texture but slightly al dente quality as traditional risotto.

- For the absorption method, use 2 to 2½ cups of water per cup of oats. Bring the water to a boil, stir in the oats, then lower the heat, cover, and simmer until tender—about 15 minutes if the oats were pre-soaked or toasted, and about 30 minutes otherwise.
- Pressure-cooking isn't recommended because of the tendency for steel-cut oats to plug up the steam vent.
- To slow-cook, use 4 cups of water per cup of oats and cook on the low setting for 7 to 8 hours.

Rolled oats or oat flakes are the largest, thickest, and most flavorful kind of "oatmeal." While they require more cooking time than any other type of oatmeal, it's only 15 minutes tops—hardly anything to consider lengthy, making them a quick and easy way to get more whole grains in your diet. In baking, they can be added to bread, cookies, and muffins, or add them to pancakes or casseroles for extra flavor, texture, and nutrition. Rolled oats also make a delicious creamy base for dairy-free soups. Just add a small amount while the soup is cooking—about ¼ cup of oats per 3 cups of broth.

In most recipes, rolled oats and quick-cooking oatmeal are interchangeable, though you may need to add a bit more water when substituting rolled oats for quick-cooking oatmeal.

- To cook rolled oats in the traditional way, use 2 cups of water per cup of oats. Combine the water and oats, bring to a boil, then lower the heat, partially cover the pot with a lid, and simmer for 10 to 15 minutes. However, some people swear by adding the rolled oats to boiling water, preferring its more chewy, less creamy texture.
- Pressure-cooking isn't recommended because the rolled oats could clog the steam vent.
- To slow-cook, use 2½ cups of water per cup of oats and cook on the low setting for 8 hours.

Quick-cooking oatmeal is about half the thickness of oat flakes and smaller, making a flake that can cook in just 5 minutes. Their texture doesn't stand up as well as do regular rolled oats, making oatmeal cookies that are less chewy. And because the flakes are smaller and sliced more thinly, they're digested more quickly; they don't seem to keep hunger at bay as long as the thicker rolled oats.

Instant oatmeal, an extremely thin form of oat flakes, cook in a snap. Just pour boiling water over them, let stand for 1 minute, and they're ready. Although convenient, they are the least flavorful. And because they are the most processed, they have a higher glycemic index value. This means their starch is converted into sugar and released into the bloodstream more quickly; as a result, you're likely to get hungry sooner than if you eat a thicker form of oatmeal. Also, most of the instant oatmeal sold is highly sweetened—and laden with artificial flavorings—making it more like a very sweet snack than a healthful, satisfying breakfast. Instead of reaching for a presweetened variety, choose plain instant oatmeal and add your own

fresh or dried fruit or, better yet, use quick-cooking oatmeal or rolled oats. Instant oatmeal cannot be substituted for rolled oats or quick-cooking oatmeal in recipes.

Oat bran is the outer covering of hulled oat groats. It has a light color and texture and a pleasant oat flavor when cooked. It can be added to muffins, hot cereals, breads, casseroles, and soups for its beneficial soluble fiber, as well as its tenderizing and moistening effects. As the health benefits of oat bran are a function of it forming gels or viscous solutions in water, oat bran should be cooked with plenty of water or added as an ingredient within food that will be cooked rather than simply sprinkled on foods. Oat bran can be cooked up into a delicious hot cereal that is ready to eat in just a few minutes. For one serving, slowly pour ⅓ cup of oat bran into 1 cup of boiling water, stirring all the while, then add a pinch of salt if you wish, lower the heat, and simmer for a total of 2 minutes.

Quinoa

Gluten free

Quinoa (KEEN-wah) has been cultivated for several thousand years in the high Andes of Peru, Bolivia, Ecuador, and Chile, as were potatoes. Because both can be cultivated at high altitudes, they were critical elements in the native diet. Although prepared as a grain, quinoa is actually the small dried seed of a plant in the same botanical family as beets and spinach. The seed is disk-shaped with a white band around its outside edges. During cooking, this band becomes more visually apparent, retaining its curved shape—and also giving quinoa its slightly crunchy texture. Quinoa is very quick cooking and versatile; within only 15 minutes, it can be transformed into an outstanding entrée or side dish, a hot breakfast cereal, or even a dessert.

Quinoa is the Spanish spelling of the Quechua name for the grain, which translates to "mother grain"—a befitting name not only because quinoa was a source of sustenance in the harsh, cold, dry climate, but also as a tribute to its amazing nutritional profile. Unlike most grains, quinoa is considered a complete protein, containing all the essential amino acids in a nearly perfect balance. Combining quinoa with other grains or beans can help compensate for any amino acids they lack or are low in. Quinoa is also a good source of fiber and, compared to other grains, a relatively good source of iron, magnesium, calcium, vitamin A, and vitamin E. It is easily digested, but it has a relatively low glycemic index value, meaning its sugars are released into the bloodstream slowly, allowing it to provide sustained energy over many hours.

Quinoa seeds are coated with saponins, a bitter, inedible substance that serves to repel insects. This is removed after harvest either by soaking the seeds or through a mechanical polishing process. As with the pearling process for barley, mechanical polishing also removes some of the grain's dietary fiber and nutritional value; the extent depends on how much polishing the grain receives. Although hybrid, saponin-free varieties of quinoa have been developed, they are more vulnerable to insects and thus more likely to be grown with pesticides.

Most quinoa is imported from South America, but cultivation has been attempted in higher-elevation areas of the United States, such as Colorado. Over the many centuries of its use and cultivation, many different varieties evolved, and they vary in color and richness in flavor. While the seeds can be black, purple, orange, red, pink, or white, most of the commonly available quinoa is either light tan or dark red. The tan version has a delicate nutty flavor when cooked, while red quinoa tastes somewhat like roasted walnuts and is crunchier in texture.

Varieties and Cooking Guidelines
Flavor enhancers: Curry powder, onions, parsley, cilantro, cumin, coriander, and orange.

Although most commercial quinoa has been prewashed or mechanically processed to remove the bitter-tasting saponins on its seed coat, play it safe and always rinse quinoa thoroughly, until the water runs clear, before cooking. Quinoa is so small that it can slip through the mesh of many strainers. To help with this, and to help remove the sticks and debris sometimes found in quinoa, wash it in a bowl rather than rinsing it in a strainer under a faucet. Put the quinoa in a bowl, cover with water, then swish it around to help the debris float to the top. Carefully pour off the water and debris, then repeat the process two more times.

Neither pressure-cooking nor slow-cooking is recommended. To cook quinoa using the absorption method, use 2 cups of water or broth per cup of quinoa. Combine the quinoa, water, and any seasonings in a pot, bring to a boil, then lower the heat to medium, cover, and cook for 15 minutes. For a richer flavor, toast quinoa in a dry or an oiled skilled before cooking. To use quinoa to thicken soup, add a small amount of uncooked quinoa during the last 15 minutes of cooking. For a unique breakfast or dessert, cook leftover plain quinoa with a bit of apple juice, dried fruit, nuts, and vanilla.

For more variety in color, flavor, and texture, combine equal amounts of tan and red quinoa, or try cooking quinoa with grains that have a similar cooking time and grain-to-water proportion, such as millet, white basmati rice, bulgur, and buckwheat. Leftover quinoa is an excellent basis for a quick main dish salad. Just add chopped vegetables, a cooked protein source (beans, tofu, tempeh, or chicken), fresh herbs if available, and your favorite salad dressing. This is a light but nutritious meal that can keep you going for hours.

Rice
Gluten free

More than forty thousand varieties of rice are grown throughout the world. While only a small percentage of these types are commercially available, interest in ethnic cooking has introduced us to the wide array of colors, flavors, and textures of rice—and shattered the common belief that there are only two main types of rice: white and brown.

When it comes to nutrition, the clear winners are whole grain varieties, easily distinguished by their medium to dark colors, including brown, red, purple, and black. With only its inedible hull removed, whole grain rice is a good source of fiber, vitamin E, and trace minerals. However, when it's milled into white rice by machines that remove the bran layer and germ, leaving only the starchy endosperm, nutrient levels decrease significantly. In an effort to try to replace at least some, but certainly not all, of the nutrients lost during processing, several brands of white rice have thiamin (vitamin B_1), niacin, folic acid, and iron added as a coating. This is why cooking instructions on packages of enriched rice discourage rinsing before cooking.

Varieties and Cooking Guidelines

Flavor enhancers: Onions, sautéed mushrooms, garlic, curry powder, bay leaf, raisins, dill, roasted red bell peppers, parsley, basil, thyme, lemon thyme, ginger, and grated lemon zest. Cooking with a cinnamon stick and a few whole cloves and cardamom seeds is a nice touch.

The primary differences among the various types of rice can be attributed to the predominant type of starch found in the grain, and specifically the proportion of amylose to amylopectin. Amylose, the straight-chained starch characteristic of long-grain rice, expands when cooked to form drier, firmer, more separate grains of rice. In contrast, amylopectin, the branched-chain starch in short-grain rice, absorbs more moisture, which helps generate moister, softer, clingy grains. Medium-grain rice occupies the middle ground in terms of amylose and amylopectin content and, consequently, cooks up with some properties of both but is unique in its ability to develop a creamy texture. Let's explore

just a few of the many varieties of rice within each of these broad categories.

■ LONG-GRAIN RICE

Long-grain rice has slender grains that are 4 to 5 times longer than their width. Due to its relatively high proportion of amylose, its grains cook up light, fluffy, and separate. Since it becomes hard when it's cold, it is typically used for rice-based dishes that will be served warm: as a simple side dish, as a pilaf, or to be served with stir-fries and curries. Beyond the familiar brown and white versions, there are many aromatic varieties, each with its own unique flavor and qualities.

While the absorption method is the most common way to cook long-grain rice, its firmness allows it to be pressure-cooked if a moist, slightly sticky texture is desired. Thai black sticky rice is an exception. It is best cooked in a special steaming apparatus. Slow-cooking is only suitable for parboiled or converted white rice.

Long-grain brown rice adds plenty of fiber and nutrition, and a distinctively nutty flavor, to any dish. Unlike white rice, which depends on seasonings or a flavorful accompaniment to make up for its blandness, brown rice can easily stand on its own.

- For the absorption method, use 2¼ cups of water per cup of long-grain brown rice. Combine the water and rice, bring to a boil, then lower the heat, cover, and simmer for 45 minutes. Don't peek until the rice is completely done.
- For variety, cook equal parts of brown rice with barley or with presoaked and drained Kamut, farro, wheat, or spelt, using 2½ cups of water per cup of mixed grains, and proceeding as for the absorption method.
- To pressure-cook, use 2 cups of water per cup of rice and cook at pressure for 40 to 50 minutes. Experiment with cooking times to find the texture you most prefer.

Parboiled or converted rice is the result of a process in which unhulled brown rice is soaked in water and then steamed and dried before it is milled. As a result, nutrients from the bran and germ are driven into the center of the grain, making it a more nutritious type of white rice. Flavor and texture are also affected by the process. Parboiled rice has a mild nutty flavor and a texture that is less clingy and has more separate grains than that of ordinary white rice. Although this process has been used in Pakistan and India for more than two thousand years, it wasn't until World War II that parboiled rice was introduced in the United States. The U.S. military recognized it as a relatively nutritious option with a long shelf life, and also appreciated its resilience in food service applications, such as standing up for long periods in steam tables.

- For the absorption method, use 2 cups of water per cup of rice. Combine the water and rice, bring to a boil, then lower the heat, cover, and simmer for 20 to 25 minutes.
- To slow-cook, use 2 cups of water per cup of rice and cook on the high setting for 1½ hours or on low for 2½ hours.

Long-grain white rice, or polished white rice, which is milled to remove its bran and germ without first being steamed, has a dry, fluffy texture and a mild, plain flavor. To cook using the absorption method, use 1½ to 1¾ cups of water per cup of rice. Bring the water to a boil, stir in the rice, then lower the heat, cover, and simmer for 15 minutes.

Long-grain instant white rice is partially cooked and dried, creating a porous structure that allows for rapid rehydration. Although it's quick, the flavor, texture, and nutritional value suffer a great deal in the process. Instant white rice is often enriched.

Thai black sticky rice, also known as black sticky rice or black glutinous rice, is a whole grain, long-grain rice that looks similar to wild rice. Although its name implies otherwise, it is a whole grain with its bran layers retained, and it doesn't stick together when cooked. While there are many savory side dish recipes that use Thai black sticky rice, in Thailand this variety of rice is traditionally used for snacks or desserts. Its purplish black color readily discolors anything cooked with it. Therefore, if combining it with other grains in a mixed pilaf, it should be cooked separately so that each grain retains its distinctive color. The best way to prepare Thai black sticky rice is to soak the rice in water for 6 to 12 hours, then drain it and steam in a woven bamboo steamer or Thai sticky rice steaming basket over a pot of boiling water until tender, about 45 minutes.

Basmati rice is an aromatic rice with a wonderful flavor and aroma, as suggested by its name, which means "fragrant." Authentic basmati rice is only grown in northern India and Pakistan, where naturally cool conditions contribute to its exceptional qualities. After harvest, basmati rice is aged for at least a year to develop its flavor and decrease its moisture content so it will cook more evenly. A distinctive characteristic of basmati rice is that it doubles in length during cooking. Although it's usually sold in its white form, with the bran and germ removed, brown basmati is also available. As with other varieties of brown rice, brown basmati takes almost three times longer to cook and has a chewier texture and nuttier flavor. Rinse either variety of basmati rice several times prior to cooking to release excess starch, which would otherwise make for very sticky rice.

- To cook white basmati rice, use 1½ cups of water per cup of rice. To help retain some of the natural components within the grain that are responsible for its nutty, floral aroma, presoak basmati in its cooking water for 20 to 30 minutes after rinsing. Bring the rice and its soaking water to a boil, then lower the heat, cover, and simmer for 15 minutes. Remove from the heat and let stand, covered, for 10 minutes before fluffing.

- White basmati is a perfect grain to cook with other grains with a short cooking time, such as millet, quinoa, bulgur, and buckwheat. Use less water based on the proportion of white rice to other grains, since white basmati requires ½ cup less water per cup of grain than these other grains.
- To cook brown basmati rice, use 2 cups of water per cup of rice and presoak and cook it as described for white basmati. The cooking time for brown basmati is 45 to 50 minutes, whether on the stove or in a pressure cooker.

Jasmine rice, an aromatic rice named after the sweet-perfumed jasmine flower, is traditionally grown in Thailand, where the climate and soil are perfect for creating this fragrant rice. Delicately flavored and very white in color, jasmine rice is known for its soft, slightly sticky texture; unlike other long-grain rices, it doesn't harden when it cools. That's because it has a high percentage of amylopectin rather than amylase starch. As a result, its sugars are released into the bloodstream more quickly, so it doesn't provide as much sustained energy as other long-grain varieties do. This also accounts for its stickier texture. To distinguish authentic jasmine rice from Thailand from varieties grown in other parts of the world, Thailand's Department of Foreign Trade developed an authenticity certificate for use on packaging. Look for a round seal with an image of rice grains and rice plants that includes the statement "Thai Hom Mali Rice—Originated in Thailand—Department of Foreign Trade." In contrast, jasmine rice grown in the United States has a different flavor and aroma profile, with a taste and aroma more like that of popcorn.

Although steaming jasmine rice in an Asian-style stacked steamer is often recommended, both to deal with its slightly sticky texture and to better retain its fragrance, an effective way to cook it using the absorption method is to presoak it as described for basmati rice, using 1¾ cups of water per cup of rice. Bring the soaked rice and its water to a boil, then lower the heat, cover, and simmer for 15 minutes. For best results and to prevent the rice from sticking to the pot, allow it to stand, covered, for 15 minutes before fluffing.

Kalijira rice, an heirloom variety of aromatic long-grain rice grown solely in Bangladesh, is traditionally used for certain holidays and religious festivals. It has a wonderful and delicate aroma, taste, and texture and looks like a miniature version of basmati rice. Both white and brown kalijira rice are available; the whole grain version has a nuttier flavor, although still remains delicate.

- To cook white kalijira rice, use 1½ cups of water per cup of rice. Presoak the rice in its cooking water for 20 to 30 minutes after rinsing, then bring to a boil. Lower the heat, cover, and simmer for 10 minutes. Remove from the heat and let stand, covered, for 10 minutes before fluffing.
- To cook brown kalijira rice, use 2 cups of water per cup of rice and presoak and cook it as described for white kalijira, but increase the cooking time to 20 to 25 minutes.

Texmati rice was developed to provide a less expensive, albeit less aromatic, alternative to basmati that could be grown in the United States. It's a variation of a strain developed by crossbreeding basmati rice with long-grain American rice. As its name implies, Texmati is grown primarily in Texas. While similar to basmati, Texmati rice is milder in flavor, making it a more all-purpose type of aromatic rice. Although it's most widely marketed in its refined, white form, as with basmati, a whole grain brown version is also available. It has a richer, nuttier flavor and is more nutritious.

- To cook white Texmati, use 1¾ cups of water per cup of rice. Combine the water and rice, bring to a boil, then lower the heat, cover, and simmer for 15 minutes. Remove from the heat and let stand, covered, for 5 to 10 minutes before fluffing.

- To cook brown Texmati, use 2 cups of water per cup of rice. Combine the water and rice, bring to a boil, then lower the heat, cover, and simmer or pressure-cook for 50 minutes. Remove from the heat and let stand, covered, for 5 to 10 minutes before fluffing.

Wild pecan rice is closely related to Texmati rice. Although it neither contains pecans nor is related to wild rice, it does have a very nutty flavor and aroma. Grown in Louisiana, wild pecan rice is only lightly milled, leaving it with 80% of the bran and a pleasing amber color. To cook wild pecan rice, use 1¾ cups of water per cup of rice. Combine the water and rice, bring to a boil, then lower the heat, cover, and simmer for 15 minutes. Remover from the heat and let stand, covered, for 5 to 10 minutes before fluffing.

■ MEDIUM-GRAIN RICE

Medium-grain rice is two to three times as long as it is wide. Because it has less amylose and more amylopectin, it cooks up slightly soft and sticky, with a creamy texture when certain preparation techniques are used, but it also retains some of the individual separateness of the grains, as long-grain rice does. This explains its use in risotto, paella, and rice pudding. And because it has less amylose, medium-grain rice doesn't become hard as it cools, making it the best choice for rice salads.

The absorption method is the most common way to cook medium-grain rice, but a pressure cooker may also be used. For pressure-cooking, use the same proportion of water to rice, and experiment with the cooking time to determine what amount of time yields the texture you prefer. If pressure-cooked for the same amount of time as required for the absorption method, the texture will be softer; or try cooking it for 10 minutes less time, for a firmer, chewier texture. Although part of the experience of preparing risotto is watching the rice transform as you stir in small amounts of broth, it can also be prepared less dramatically in a pressure cooker with similar results.

Many strains of rice either originating in Asia or complementary to Asian-based fare are included in this category, as are many varieties used in Italian and Spanish cuisines. Because there are so many varieties of rice for risotto and paella, we'll explore them separately at the end of this section. Be aware that sometimes varieties of rice in the medium-grain category are classified as short-grain, since some countries use only a two-tiered, long-grain and short-grain classification system.

Bhutanese red rice, an heirloom variety of rice grown high in the Himalayas of Bhutan, is irrigated with glacial meltwater rich in trace minerals. Being only lightly milled to remove the husk, it retains much of its brownish red bran, but the shade lightens somewhat after cooking. Remarkably, it cooks in only 20 minutes. With a texture that is both chewy and soft, it is also exceptionally flavorful, far surpassing in complexity the flavor of most whole grain rice varieties. It is delicious whether used as a side dish, as the foundation for a stir-fry, or in salads or stuffings for vegetables or poultry. To cook Bhutanese red rice, use 1¾ cups of water per cup of rice. Combine the water and rice, bring to a boil, then lower the heat, cover, and simmer for 20 minutes. Remove from the heat and let stand, covered, for 10 minutes before fluffing.

Black forbidden rice, which originated in China, takes its name from the fact that only the ruling class was considered worthy to eat it. This whole grain rice has a somewhat sweet flavor and a dark purple color when cooked. Its grains remain separate after cooking, making it a good choice for rice salads and pilafs. It is delicious and striking on its own, especially when paired with white or red protein foods such as halibut, tofu, or salmon, but it also makes for a nice color contrast when combined with other cooked varieties of rice. Cook them separately to ensure that the unique color of each variety is retained. To cook black forbidden rice, use 1¾ cups of water per cup of rice. Combine the water and rice, bring to a boil, then lower the heat, cover, and simmer for 30 minutes for a chewy texture or for 40 to 45 minutes for a soft texture.

Calrose rice, an all-purpose medium-grain white rice, accounts for about 85% of the rice grown in California. With its soft, slightly clingy texture and mild flavor, it can be used as an everyday rice or in Asian or Mediterranean cuisine. To cook calrose rice, use 1½ cups of water per cup of rice. Combine the water and rice, bring to a boil, then lower the heat, cover, and simmer for 12 to 15 minutes. Remove from the heat and let stand, covered, for 5 to 10 minutes before fluffing.

Camargue red rice hails from the Camargue region of Provence, located along the Rhône River, which has the distinction of being the northernmost area where rice is grown in Europe. Snowmelt from the Alps supplies the water used to flood the fields. Camargue red rice is a hybrid of the area's native red rice and a short-grain rice variety. Its delicious nutty flavor and texture are similar to those of Bhutanese red rice, but its color is deeper and the grains are oval shaped and somewhat longer. It's delicious in pilafs and salads, or when prepared simply, by mixing in some freshly chopped thyme or oregano and a splash of olive oil once it's cooked. To cook Camargue red rice, use 2½ cups of water per cup of rice. Combine the water and rice, bring to a boil, then lower the heat, cover, and simmer for 40 minutes. Remove from the heat and let stand, uncovered, for 10 minutes before fluffing.

■ ITALIAN RISOTTO RICE

Risotto is a celebrated Italian rice dish made using a method that defies all the rules for cooking rice: Hot liquid is added to the rice in small increments, the pot is never covered, the rice is stirred constantly, and more liquid is used than normal—usually 3½ cups of hot broth or other liquid per cup of rice. The result is rice that is infused with flavor and an unusual and pleasing texture that combines a rich, creamy consistency and an al dente firmness. Risotto can be the highlight of a meal or an extraordinary accompaniment that further accentuates the main course.

Successful results depend not only on technique but also on using the proper type of rice. Arborio rice is most commonly used to make risotto, but three other varieties of medium-grain rice are also recommended, including Vialone Nano, Baldo, and especially Carnaroli. All of these, and any other variety of rice suitable for risotto, are derived from the japonica family of rice, which is distinguished by a low percentage of amylose, allowing for the al dente texture within each grain of rice in the finished risotto. Japonica rices also have a high percentage of amylopectin, which is responsible for the creamy texture. Both types of starch are actually visually apparent in the grains. Within the translucent amylopectin that makes up the bulk of the kernel, you can see an amylose-rich "pearl" in the middle of the kernel.

Recipes for risotto are created based on using polished white rice rather than brown whole grain versions. The best quality risotto results from using rice aged in the husk up to a year before being hulled and polished. Because drying reduces the moisture content of the rice, the longer it's dried, the more broth it can absorb, yielding a more flavorful risotto. For optimum flavor and freshness, look for rice that is vacuum-packed.

Although since 1992 Italian law has not required packaging to state the grade of rice, rice used for risotto is still often described or marketed according to its grade. These grades are not a gauge of quality; they're simply used to differentiate the rice according to size and rate of absorption. This information helps you determine which rice is best for a particular application. Three primary grades of Italian rice are used for making risotto: *super-fino*, *fino,* and *semifino*. *Superfino*, considered to be best, has the largest, most pearly white grains. It is longer and more tapered than round. Arborio, Baldo, and Carnaroli are three *superfino* varieties to choose from when making risotto, and each brings a unique quality to the dish. *Fino* is the next best grade; its grains are somewhat shorter and rounder than *superfino*. *Semifino*, which is yet rounder and shorter in length, is the least preferred for risotto. A fourth grade of Italian rice, *originario* (*comune* grade) is used for making desserts and dishes that will be cooked for a long time, such as soups and baked rice casseroles made with sauces—applications where using a rice with high absorbency works well to capture flavors.

Arborio (ar-BOH-ree-oh) is the most commonly used *superfino* rice in the United States, but it has less amylose and therefore absorbs less liquid than Baldo or Carnaroli does, making it somewhat more starchy and sticky. Beyond risotto, Arborio rice makes a good rice pudding.

Baldo (BAL-doh), a long, slim, golden-colored *superfino* rice, is a good choice for rice salads, rice pudding, and risotto. It has less amylose than do Vialone Nano and Carnaroli and therefore cooks up softer and much like Arborio.

Carnaroli (car-nah-ROW-lee), a *superfino* rice, has the highest amylose content of any risotto rice, which allows it to absorb the most liquid while still having firm, distinct grains and a creamy but not sticky texture. Accordingly, many chefs consider it to be the rice of choice when making risotto.

Vialone Nano (Vee-ah-LO-nay NAH-no), a *semifino* rice, is grown in the northeastern part of Italy. This hybrid of traditional Vialone rice and a smaller Nano (dwarf) variety is a favorite for traditional Venetian rice dishes and soup. In risotto, it provides a good amount of starch, creating a creamy but wavy consistency—a characteristic of a well-made risotto in which the rice and sauce move as one rather than as separate layers when tossed in the pan. With almost as much amylose as Carnaroli, it cooks up firmer than Arborio rice. Since it can absorb twice its own weight in liquid, it also absorbs flavors particularly well.

Although rice from Italy usually springs to mind when choosing rice for risotto, American Arborio rice is also available. The flavor is good, but the results aren't as creamy. Whatever variety of rice you use to make risotto, don't rinse it before cooking, as this will wash away some of the rice's amylopectin layer and cause the rice's internal starch to release too soon, disrupting the gradual cooking process needed to coax out the creaminess.

Cooking risotto is a process that never ceases to be amazing as, seemingly in an instant, the separate, translucent kernels of rice become creamy—something everyone needs to experience at least once.

Medium-grain Italian rices are also good in rice-based salads. Try mixing it with tomatoes, olives, fresh herbs, and pesto or your favorite salad dressing. To cook any of these rices for salad, use 4 cups of water per cup of rice. Bring the water to a boil, then stir in the rice, lower the heat, and cook uncovered until the rice is firm but tender, about 15 minutes. Drain the rice and spread it on a clean kitchen towel to cool.

■ SPANISH RICE OR PAELLA RICE

While Italian rice brings to mind risotto, rice from Spain conjures up visions of paella, a native dish of Valencia, a city on Spain's Mediterranean coast. Authentic paella is made with foods that were commonly found or grown in the area, including beans, snails, rabbit or chicken, shellfish, fresh vegetables, and saffron, traditionally cooked outside over a fire using a wide, shallow pan specially shaped to cook rice in a thin layer. These days, many recipes for paella call for seafood of all kinds.

Regardless of the specific ingredients used, it is the rice that is the real key to exceptional paella. You can't use just any rice; it must be medium-grain rice that, like rice for risotto, has the *perla*—the amylose-rich pearl in the middle of the kernel. This allows for both proper al dente texture and maximum ability to absorb liquid and soak up the essence of this flavorful dish. Paella differs from risotto in that the rice should ultimately be dry and separate rather than creamy. There are some basic similarities in how the two are prepared, including not rinsing the rice before cooking and cooking the rice uncovered for 18 to 20 minutes. However, there is a major distinction: Paella is not stirred after the rice is distributed evenly in the pan. Crusty, caramelized rice that sticks to the bottom, called the *socarrat* (soh-kah-RAHT), is considered the delicious prize of the paella. Paella is covered for just the last 5 to 10 minutes of cooking, allowing all the flavors to meld fully.

Spanish medium-grain rice for paella is designated primarily by where it is grown, and then is usually further defined by the variety of rice. Choosing among them is a matter of carefully reading the label to make sure you're getting the real thing—and then determining how much you're willing to spend. There are three primary paella rice-producing regions in Spain: Ebro, Valencia, and Calasparra.

The Ebro delta in northeastern Spain is distinctive in that the rice is grown within a protected bird sanctuary, with the rice fields providing a good habitat for aquatic birds such as herons, egrets, ducks, gulls, and flamingos during much of the year. Rice from the other two regions, Valencia and Calasparra, is identified by Denominación de origen (DO) labeling. This designation guarantees that that the rice is truly grown in that area, that it is from a pure strain unique to the region, and that it was grown according to certain standards.

The three varieties of DO-labeled medium-grain paella-type rice grown in Valencia are Bahia, Senia, and Bomba. Valencia, the birthplace of paella, is Spain's major rice-producing region. Located within the marshy wetlands of the protected Al-bufera nature preserve, the rice fields here, like those in the Ebro delta, provide habitat and forage for many species of birds, including cranes, herons, and terns.

The two varieties of DO-labeled rice grown in the Calasparra region are Balilla Sollana and Bomba. Located in the mountains of Murcia in southeastern Spain, the Calasparra region is known for the exceptional quality of its rice. This is largely due to both the cooler weather at high altitude and the irrigation with cold mountain water, which extend the time required for the rice to mature, making for a harder grain with less moisture and thereby increasing the rice's ability to absorb liquid. Both varieties of Calasparra rice will be more expensive than their counterparts from other regions, but they're well worth it for special occasions.

Any of the varieties of rice from these three regions will work well in paella. However, Bomba is the preferred choice, as it can absorb as much as six parts liquid to one part rice—two to three times more than the other varieties. Because Bomba is harder to grow and has lower yields, it is more expensive. So top honors for quality and flavor—and top price—goes to Calasparra Bomba.

Spanish rice need not be used only for paella. They are also good in rice salads, soups, and stews. To cook Spanish varieties of rice using the absorption method, use 1¾ cups of water per cup of rice. Combine the water and rice, bring to a boil, then lower the heat, cover, and simmer for 15 to 18 minutes. Remove from the heat and let stand, covered, for 10 to 15 minutes before fluffing.

■ SHORT-GRAIN RICES

Short-grain rice is almost round; it's only slightly longer than it is wide. Because it has more amylopectin and less amylose than does long-grain or medium-grain rice, it has a moist, soft, sticky texture when cooked. It's perfect for Asian cuisine, rice puddings, croquettes, and casseroles, as well as for rice dishes prepared during colder weather, when its inherent warming nature feels especially welcome. Short-grain rice is often cooked using the absorption method, but there are several techniques and special types of cooking apparatus that can give better results for certain types of short-grain rice. Short-grain brown rice and sweet brown rice can also be pressure-cooked.

Short-grain brown rice is a hearty, somewhat sticky, rice that's particularly appealing during the colder months. Pressure-cooking enhances its sweet flavor and compact texture. It's also a great whole grain alternative for making sushi or nori maki.

- For the absorption method, use 2¼ cups of water per cup of short-grain brown rice. Combine the water and rice, bring to a boil, then lower the heat, cover, and simmer for 50 minutes.
- To pressure-cook, use 2 cups of water per cup of rice and cook at pressure for 40 to 50 minutes. Experiment with the amount of time to find the texture you most prefer.

Short-grain white rice is milled to remove its bran layer and germ. It has a soft, sticky texture and mild, plain flavor. To cook short-grain white rice, use 1¼ cups of water per cup of rice. Combine the water and rice, bring to a boil, then lower the heat, cover, and simmer for 15 minutes.

Sushi rice is a semipolished, white, very sticky short-grain rice traditionally used to make nori-wrapped sushi rolls. Before cooking it, rinse and drain the rice several times until the rinse water is almost clear, then allow it to drain for 30 to 60 minutes. Combine equal amounts of water and sushi rice, bring to a boil over medium heat, cover, and cook for 1 minute. Then turn down the heat to low and cook for 8 to 10 minutes. Turn down the heat once again, to very low, and cook 10 minutes longer, being sure to keep the cover on at all times during cooking. Remove from the heat and let stand, covered, for 10 minutes before fluffing the rice.

Sticky rice, also known as sweet rice or glutinous rice, is very high in amylopectin, making it very sticky when cooked and therefore easy to form into bite-size pieces for dipping into sauce. This increased starchiness also makes the uncooked kernels look chalky white when raw but translucent after cooking. Sticky rice is used to make traditional Asian desserts, amasake (a beverage), rice wine, and mochi (a delicious food that puffs up like a biscuit when cooked). For more nutrients and flavor, choose the brown version, known as sweet brown rice, over the more refined white version. Sticky rice can be cooked using the standard absorption method, but it will turn out mushier than if steamed.

- The best way to prepare sticky rice is to first soak it in water for 6 to 12 hours, then drain it and steam it in a woven bamboo steamer or Thai sticky rice steaming basket over a pot of boiling water. Steam white sticky rice for about 30 minutes and sweet brown rice for 40 to 45 minutes.
- For the absorption method, use 1½ cups of water per cup of sticky rice. Combine the water and rice, bring to a boil, then lower the heat, cover, and simmer for 30 minutes for white sticky rice, or 50 minutes for sweet brown rice.
- To pressure-cook sweet brown rice, use 1 cup of water per cup of rice and cook at pressure for 45 minutes. A combination of ¼ cup of sweet brown rice and ¾ cup of short-grain brown rice pressure-cooked with 1½ cups of water for 50 minutes makes a delicious cool-weather rice blend.

Rye

Contains gluten

Rye berries are bluish brown kernels that are longer and thinner than wheat. Although primarily ground into flour and eaten in the form of breads and crispbreads, rye's delicious, hearty flavor is equally as good when it's cooked as a whole, cracked, or flaked grain. Rye is grown predominately in Eastern Europe, where it's long been a staple in part because it grows well in poor soil and cool, moist conditions, and is more often used in cuisines of that region, but its popularity continues to increase throughout the world due to its exceptional nutritional profile.

Rye is particularly recognized for a unique type of soluble fiber it contains: long chains of polysaccharides called pentosans, and specifically arabinoxylans. Present throughout the entire kernel of rye, pentosans act much like the beta-glucan fiber in oats and barley, helping to decrease absorption of cholesterol and also making rye digest more slowly, so it keeps blood sugar levels stable and provides a steady source of energy. Lignans, compounds thought to help reduce the risk of cancer, are present in rye's bran layer.

Varieties and Cooking Guidelines

Flavor enhancers: Caraway seeds, fennel, anise, orange zest, raisins, maple syrup, roasted pecans, roasted walnuts, roasted sunflower seeds, onions, potatoes, parsley, peas, red bell peppers, and cabbage.

Whole rye berries have only their outer hull removed. They can be cooked alone or with other grains, such as brown rice or barley. They make a nice addition to soups, salads, and breads.

- It's best to presoak rye berries before cooking. To retain nutrients, soak them in their cooking water, using 3 cups of water per cup of rye berries. If the ambient temperature is warm (above 75°F), soak it in the refrigerator.
- For the absorption method, use 3 cups of water per cup of rye berries. Bring the rye berries and their soaking water to a boil, then lower the heat, cover, and simmer until tender, about 60 minutes if presoaked or 1½ to 2 hours if not. With further cooking,

the rye berries will split open, making for an even softer, more cereal-like texture.

- To pressure-cook, use 3 cups of water per cup of rye berries and cook for 40 minutes if presoaked, or 50 minutes if not.
- For slow-cooking, presoaking is optional. Use 4 cups of water per cup of rye berries and cook on the high setting for 3½ to 4 hours or on low for 8 hours.

Rye grits, or steel-cut rye, is whole rye cracked into small pieces. It is ideal as a hot cereal or for adding to casseroles. To cook rye grits, use 3½ cups of water per cup of grits. Bring the water to a boil, then gradually pour in the grits, whisking all the while. Lower the heat, cover, and simmer for 35 to 40 minutes.

Rye flakes are made from whole rye that is steamed, pressed, and rolled into thick flakes. Add them to breads for flavor and texture, or use them to make a hot breakfast cereal. Even better, combine them with other flaked grains, such as oats, Kamut, or spelt, to make a breakfast cereal medley. To cook rye flakes, use 3 cups of water per cup of flakes. Bring the water to a boil, stir in the flakes, then lower the heat, cover, and simmer for 25 to 30 minutes.

Sorghum

Gluten free

Whole grain sorghum has a round shape similar to that of millet but is significantly larger. Native to the tropical areas of Africa, the plant itself looks somewhat like corn, and the grain is nutritionally similar to white corn. Not too surprisingly, in western Africa it is known as great millet, Kaffir corn, or Guinea corn. Due to sorghum's ability to adapt to and grow in a variety of environments, including arid as well as tropical and subtropical conditions, it is widely cultivated for both food and fodder. There are many varieties of sorghum with just as many colors. Although both sweet sorghum and grain sorghum are grown for human consumption, sweet sorghum is only used to make a sweet syrup (see page 259).

Traditionally, grain sorghum is fermented and used to make beer, porridge, and flatbread—including Ethiopia's injera bread—where it serves as an alternative to the grain teff. Not only does the lactic acid bacteria in the fermented sorghum create a slightly sour taste that's appreciated in the areas of Africa where it is a staple, but it also helps to naturally preserve the food and protect against harmful bacteria. Sorghum is high in dietary fiber, and its protein and starch components digest more slowly than those of other grains, which helps stabilize blood sugar levels and provides steady energy for several hours.

Varieties and Cooking Guidelines

Flavor enhancers: Curry powder, orange, rosemary, onions, chives, parsley, black pepper, bay leaf, thyme, garlic, ginger, sun-dried tomatoes marinated in olive oil, and miso-tahini sauce.

To provide a more versatile grain and appeal to prospective cooks, a white sorghum hybrid that is low in tannins has been developed. Its lighter color and neutral flavor make it a natural for cooking with more assertive seasonings or serving with a flavorful sauce. When cooked, whole sorghum has a taste and texture similar to that of untoasted buckwheat groats. It is an excellent grain to use for a main dish pilaf or breakfast cereal. It's also a good alternative to pearled barley, bulgur, or couscous in salads. Or for variety and more well-rounded nutrition, cook it along with other grains with a similar cooking time, such as brown rice and barley.

- For the absorption method, use 3 cups of water per cup of sorghum. Combine the sorghum and water, bring to a boil, then lower the heat, cover, and simmer until the water is absorbed and the grains are tender, about 60 minutes.
- To pressure-cook, use 3 cups of water per cup of sorghum and cook at pressure for 45 minutes.
- To slow-cook, use 4 cups of water per cup of sorghum and cook on the high setting for 3½ to 4 hours or on low for 8 hours.

Spelt

Contains gluten

Spelt, a distant cousin of modern varieties of wheat, is an ancient grain originating in the Middle East at least 6,000 years ago. Over the millennia, it became popular in parts of Germany, Switzerland, Austria, France, and Spain as a major variety of bread wheat. Known as *dinkel* in Germany, spelt was so significant that they named several towns in its honor, including Dinkelhausen and Dinkelsbühl. Hildegard of Bingen, a twelfth-century herbalist, mystic, and abbess of a convent in Germany, further popularized spelt through her teachings on using natural remedies to create a healthy balance in body, mind, and spirit. Hildegard considered spelt to be the best, most digestible grain one could eat for overall good health, and it remains a fundamental food in German health clinics that follow her teachings even today.

European immigrants established spelt in the United States, and it was a commonly grown grain until 1900, when it was largely replaced by newer, hull-less hybrids of wheat that produced higher yields and were easier to harvest and process. Recently, however, it has become valued once again for its unique nutritional properties and superior flavor, which is sweeter and nuttier than wheat. And, although its sturdy hull makes spelt harder to process, it also makes it naturally resistant to insects, so it typically is grown without any pesticides.

Although spelt is higher in protein than conventional wheat and does contain gluten, it has proportionally less gliadin, the component of gluten's protein complex that appears to be most responsible for adverse reactions to gluten. What this means is that some people who are sensitive to wheat may find spelt's gluten easier to digest. Nonetheless, anyone with severe allergies should consult with a medical professional before experimenting with spelt.

Spelt is more water-soluble than wheat is, leading some people to believe that it is more easily digested and its nutrients more easily absorbed. This also means that when substituting spelt for conventional wheat, it's generally a good idea to use less water to compensate for spelt's greater solubility. However, this is more of an issue when cooking with spelt flour.

Varieties and Cooking Guidelines

Flavor enhancers: Onions, chives, dill, mushrooms, black pepper, garlic, curry powder, parsley, and cilantro. Sweet flavor enhancers include cinnamon, ginger, and allspice.

Whole spelt isn't nearly as familiar as spelt flour, but it's easy to cook and very versatile. It's terrific for cooked cereal, makes a great foundation for a pilaf or salad, and is a delicious, chewy addition to casseroles, soups, and breads. It takes a long time to cook, but you can reduce the amount of time by presoaking it. If you use the cooking times recommended below, the kernels will still be whole and somewhat chewy. Further cooking will cause the kernels to split open, making the spelt softer and more like a cereal. To add texture to other cooked whole grains in a pilaf, soup, or cereal, combine cooked whole spelt with cooked quinoa, bulgur, millet, barley, or any variety of rice.

- It's best to presoak whole spelt for 6 to 12 hours. To retain nutrients, soak it in its cooking water, using 3 cups of water per cup of spelt. If the ambient temperature is warm (above 75°F), soak it in the refrigerator.
- For the absorption method, use 3 cups of water per cup of spelt. Bring the spelt and its soaking water to a boil, then lower the heat, cover, and simmer until tender, about 50 minutes to 1 hour if presoaked and 1½ to 2 hours if not.
- To pressure-cook, use 3 cups of water per cup of spelt and cook at pressure for 40 minutes if presoaked, or 50 minutes if not.
- For slow-cooking, presoaking is optional. Use 4 cups of water per cup of spelt and cook on the high setting for 3½ to 4 hours or on low for 8 hours.

Spelt bulgur is whole spelt that has been steamed, dried, and cracked, making it a delicious and quick-cooking foundation for pilafs, salads, and stuffings. Use 2 cups of water or broth per cup of spelt bulgur. Bring the water to a boil, then stir in the bulgur, season with salt and any herbs or spices you like, then lower the heat, cover, and simmer for 25 minutes. Remove from the heat and let stand undisturbed for 10 minutes before serving or using in a recipe.

Spelt flakes are made from whole spelt that has been steamed, dried, and flattened. It can be used like any other flaked grain for hot cereals, granolas, cookies, and casseroles. For a hot cereal, use 2 cups of water per cup of spelt flakes. Combine the water and spelt in a pot, bring to a boil, then lower the heat, cover, and simmer for 15 to 18 minutes. Spelt flakes can also be combined in any proportion with other flaked grains for variety in flavor.

Teff

Gluten free

Teff's name means "lost," an appropriate moniker considering its seeds are so tiny that if they were dropped on the ground, you'd be hard-pressed to find them. Introduced to the United States during the 1980s, teff is the most commonly cultivated grain in Ethiopia. It is traditionally used to make soup, porridge, beer, and especially *injera*, the crepelike Ethiopian bread that is used as plate, fork, and food during the meal.

Teff is only available in whole grain forms because it would be impossible to refine away the bran or germ on each tiny seed. While its protein content is similar to other grains, teff is particularly high in fiber, calcium, and iron. The grain itself is often accompanied by a symbiotic yeast that easily ferments when moisture is added, resulting in a sweet, slightly molasses-like, malty taste.

Varieties and Cooking Guidelines

Flavor enhancers: Chives, onions, thyme, and parsley. Sweet flavor enhancers include cinnamon, allspice, raisins, dates, pecans, walnuts, and maple syrup.

White teff has the most delicate and mild flavor, while red and brown teff have a nuttier flavor. To add flavor and texture to familiar grains, include 2 tablespoons of teff when cooking 1 cup of rice, millet, or barley. Uncooked whole teff can also be added to soups and stews, casseroles, and puddings as a thickener and for variety in texture and flavor. As it needs only about 20 minutes of cooking time, whole teff is a good choice for making hot cereal, side dishes, or polenta. Its cooked texture is similar to that of wheat farina, although slightly crunchy. For the absorption method, use 2 cups of water per ½ cup of teff. Bring the water to a boil, stir in the teff, then cover, lower the heat, and simmer until all of the liquid is absorbed, about 15 to 20 minutes. For extra flavor, toast the teff in a pan before adding boiling water. Pressure-cooking and slow-cooking are neither recommended nor necessary.

Triticale

Contains gluten

Triticale (trit-i-KAY-lee) has grayish brown, oval-shaped kernels that are larger than wheat and plumper than rye. Its name is a combination of the genus names of wheat (*Triticum*) and rye (*Secale*), and indeed, it's a hybrid of the two. It was first developed in the late 1800s but didn't become commercially viable until the 1950s. This nutritious grain combines the nutty flavor and higher yields of wheat with the better balance of amino acids and hardiness of rye. Still a newcomer in the history of grains, it remains a relatively obscure grain with high hopes for increased recognition and use. Look for it in natural foods and specialty stores.

Varieties and Cooking Guidelines

Flavor enhancers: Onions, sage, black pepper, garlic, dill, basil, oregano, and thyme. Sweet flavor enhancers include cinnamon, ginger, raisins, and dates.

Whole triticale can be used as wheat berries: for breakfast cereal, as a foundation for pilafs or salads, or in bread dough, for texture. It takes a long time to cook, but presoaking will shorten that time. If you use the cooking times recommended below, the kernels will still be whole and somewhat chewy. Further cooking will cause the kernels to split open, making the triticale softer and more like a cereal. For variety, cook whole triticale along with long-cooking grains such as brown rice and barley. If adding triticale to quinoa, millet, or shorter-cooking grains, cook it separately and then add it to the other grain during the last few minutes of cooking.

- It's best to presoak whole triticale for 6 to 8 hours or overnight. To retain nutrients, soak it in its cooking water, using 3 cups of water per cup of triticale. If the ambient temperature is warm (above 75°F), soak it in the refrigerator.
- For the absorption method, use 3 cups of water per cup of triticale. Bring the triticale and its soaking water to a boil, then lower the heat, cover, and simmer until tender, about 50 to 60 minutes if presoaked, and 1½ to 2 hours if not.
- To pressure-cook, use 3 cups of water per cup of triticale and cook at pressure for 40 minutes if presoaked, or 50 minutes if not.

• For slow-cooking, presoaking is optional. Use 4 cups of water per cup of triticale and cook on the high setting for 3½ to 4 hours or on low for 8 hours.

Triticale flakes can be used like other flakes: in granolas, cookies, and meat loaf or a vegetarian version of it. To make a hot cereal, use 2 cups of water per cup of triticale flakes. Bring the water to a boil, stir in the triticale flakes, then lower the heat, cover, and simmer for 15 to 20 minutes. For variety and more well-rounded nutrition, combine triticale flakes with barley flakes, oatmeal, or rice flakes for a hot cereal medley.

Wheat

Contains gluten

Wheat is the most commonly used grain throughout the world. What we know as wheat today has been hybridized throughout the years for higher yields, easier harvesting, and specific baking and cooking properties. Heirloom forms of wheat that are still produced include farro (emmer wheat), Kamut, and spelt. While wheat may be most familiar and often used in the form of flour for pasta, bread, and other baked goods, it has tremendous versatility as a whole grain. Ironically, both wheat bran and wheat germ, the very components of wheat that are removed during refining, are often added to foods to boost levels of fiber and other nutrients.

Varieties and Cooking Guidelines

Flavor enhancers: Onions, chives, dill, mushrooms, black pepper, garlic, curry powder, parsley, cilantro, and mint. Sweet flavor enhancers include dried fruits, cinnamon, pumpkin pie spices, apple pie spices, ginger, and allspice; another option is to replace the water with fruit juice when cooking.

Whether in the form of whole wheat berries or cracked, wheat serves as the basis for chewy breakfast cereals, pilafs, salads, stuffings, and casseroles,

and both are also often added to breads for texture. Wheat berries also make excellent sprouts. Though couscous is technically a pasta, it's used much like cracked wheat and bulgur are, especially in salads and side dishes. Wheat flakes are as versatile as any other grain flake, and when wheat is coarsely ground into farina and cooked, it makes for soft and creamy comfort food. Wheat bran and wheat germ also see wide use in a variety of applications, particularly cereals and baked goods.

■ WHEAT BERRIES

Wheat berries are short, round kernels of varying shades of brown. They take a long time to cook, but you can shorten that time if you presoak them. Cooked whole wheat berries are delicious when combined with cooked rice or barley. If you use the cooking times recommended below, the kernels will still be whole and somewhat chewy. Further cooking will cause the kernels to split open, making the wheat berries softer and more like a cereal.

• It's best to soak wheat berries for 6 to 8 hours or overnight. To retain nutrients, soak them in their cooking water, using 3 cups of water per cup of wheat berries. If the ambient temperature is warm (above 75°F), soak them in the refrigerator.

• For the absorption method, bring the wheat berries and their soaking water to a boil. Lower the heat, cover, and simmer until tender, about 1 hour if presoaked, and 1½ to 2 hours if not.

• To pressure-cook, use 3 cups of water per cup of wheat berries and cook at pressure for 40 minutes if presoaked, or 50 minutes if not.

• For slow-cooking, presoaking is optional. Use 4 cups of water per cup of wheat berries and cook on the high setting for 3½ to 4 hours or on low for 8 hours.

■ WHEAT FLAKES

Wheat flakes are made from whole wheat berries that have been steamed, dried, and flattened. Use them as an alternative to oat flakes for hot cereal, in baking, or in meat loaf or a vegetarian version of meat loaf. If you make granola, try substituting ½ cup of wheat flakes for oatmeal next time you make it. To cook wheat flakes, use 3 cups of water per cup of dry flakes. Bring the water to a boil, stir in the wheat flakes, then lower the heat, cover, and simmer for 15 to 20 minutes.

■ CRACKED WHEAT AND BULGUR

Cracked wheat is made by coarsely cracking wheat berries between rollers. It cooks much more quickly than do wheat berries and is more versatile. It has many uses beyond tabbouleh: Use it as a cereal, a substitute for rice, or in casseroles and stuffings. To cook cracked wheat, use 2 cups of water per cup of cracked wheat. Bring the water to a boil, then stir in the cracked wheat, lower the heat, cover, and simmer for 20 minutes. For best texture, remove from the heat and let stand, covered, for 5 minutes before serving or using in a recipe.

Bulgur is similar to cracked wheat, but the wheat berries are parboiled and dried before being cracked into one of three granulations, each with its own cooking properties and preferred uses.

- Fine granulation is best for making tabouli, hot cereal, Lebanese kibbe, and desserts.
- Medium granulation bulgur, the type most widely available, is considered all-purpose, appropriate for a wide range of dishes, including tabouli, pilafs, and stuffings.
- Coarsely granulated bulgur is used like medium bulgur, but it will have a chewier texture.

A mainstay of traditional cuisines for thousands of years, bulgur remains a popular ingredient because it's so quick and easy to prepare. As a bonus, the process of creating bulgur from wheat berries also yields a product that's more tender than cracked wheat and also has a longer shelf life. Since bulgur is partially cooked, it has a nuttier and richer flavor than that of cracked wheat. Further differences in flavor and aroma depend on the type of wheat used to make the bulgur and the skill of the processor. Bulgur made from red wheat is more commonly available. It has a mild flavor, nutlike aroma, and soft texture. Golden or tan bulgur made from white wheat has a sweeter flavor and coarser texture. Whichever variety you choose, look for uniform-size particles to ensure more even cooking results.

Bulgur can be prepared using the absorption method or by soaking it in hot water. The soaking method results in a coarser, chewier texture.

- For the absorption method, use 2 cups of water per cup of bulgur. Bring the water to a boil, stir in the bulgur, lower the heat, cover, and simmer for 20 to 25 minutes. For best results, remove from the heat and let stand, covered, for 10 minutes before serving or using in a recipe.
- For the soaking method, use 2½ cups of boiling water per cup of bulgur. Pour the boiling water over the bulgur, cover, and let stand for 1 hour. Drain the bulgur in a colander lined with cheesecloth, then squeeze out the excess moisture.

Bulgur is handy for adding texture to soups and stews. For example, to give chili a texture reminiscent of ground beef, add ½ cup of bulgur per 4 to 5 cups of chili during the last half hour of cooking. Because bulgur absorbs a lot of liquid, you may need to add extra water or tomato sauce to get the final consistency you desire. For variety, experiment with cooking bulgur with vegetable broth or chicken broth instead of water. Or for breakfast fare, use fruit juice for the liquid. To further broaden the possibilities, try a different herb or spice each time you make bulgur.

■ FARINA

Farina is a hot cereal made from wheat that has been ground to a medium-fine consistency. Although when cooked it's often generically referred to as Cream of Wheat, that's just one specific brand name. The more accurate term is *farina*, a word originating from the Latin (and current Italian) word for "flour." True to its roots, farina can be substituted for some of the flour in some recipes. It can also be cooked like polenta.

For optimum nutrition and the best flavor, look for products labeled "whole wheat farina" (you may have to check the ingredient listing). Products labeled as simply "wheat farina" are made from refined wheat, processed to remove the fiber-rich bran layer and nutrient-rich wheat germ. Disodium phosphate is added to some brands of refined farina to help speed cooking by causing the grains to swell and gelatinize faster. Proteolytic enzymes may also be added to decrease cooking time by weakening the grain to facilitate the penetration of water. While these timesavers are not harmful, neither are they essential, especially when you consider it only takes 10 minutes to cook farina without these additives.

To cook whole wheat farina, use 3 cups of water or milk per cup of farina. Bring the liquid to a boil, then slowly pour in the farina, stirring all the while to prevent clumping. Continue stirring until it returns to a boil, then lower the heat, cover, and simmer for about 10 minutes, stirring occasionally. Serve with fresh or dried fruit, nuts, milk, or soymilk.

■ COUSCOUS

Although technically a pasta, couscous is more commonly regarded as a grain due to its use in a wide variety of recipes spanning the range of breakfast, lunch, dinner, and dessert. There are four varieties of couscous—Moroccan couscous, fregola, Israeli couscous, and Lebanese couscous—each unique in size and cooking method. With the exception of Moroccan couscous, which is also available in a whole wheat version, couscous is typically made with refined wheat.

Moroccan couscous is the smallest and most familiar variety. A staple food in northern African nations, especially Morocco, Algeria, and Tunisia, couscous is traditionally made using a labor-intensive process in which refined durum wheat flour is sprinkled with water, rolled into small pellets by hand (between the palms), steamed and cooled (twice), and then dried.

In these countries, couscous is typically steamed over a hearty meat and vegetable stew in a special two-tiered steaming pot called a *couscousiere*. The couscous is first moistened, then after steaming a bit, it's removed to break up any clumps, and then replaced over the stew to steam again. The result is couscous that is very light and fluffy, with each grain soft and separate—and saturated with flavors and aroma absorbed from the stew. Even though the process takes about an hour from start to finish, it is very easy and needs only minimal hands-on cooking during that time. If you don't have a *couscousiere*, you can improvise with a heat-proof colander that fits snugly into a stockpot. The steaming method also yields delicious couscous even if it's just cooked over plain water. It's well worth the extra effort if you have the time.

On the other hand, Moroccan couscous can easily be prepared and enjoyed in just a matter of minutes, including whole wheat varieties, which cook in the same amount of time but have more flavor and nutrients. It's one of the fastest-cooking grains around, not to mention a real lifesaver when extra guests show up unexpectedly for a meal. Just add it to boiling water and let it stand for 5 to 10 minutes. Although couscous made this way tends to be drier and clump together more, it is still very good. Try different brands of couscous until you discover your favorite, as they can vary quite a bit in flavor and texture.

To steam 1 cup of couscous, you'll need either

a *couscousiere* or a fine-mesh stainless steel colander that fits snugly over a large stockpot with at least 4 inches between the bottom of the colander and the water needed for steaming. First, place the couscous in a 9 by 13-inch baking pan, cover with water to moisten, then immediately drain through the colander. Return the couscous to the baking pan, spread the grains out evenly, and set aside for 10 to 15 minutes to let the grains begin to swell.

Meanwhile, put water in the lower half of the *couscousiere* or in the stockpot and bring it to a boil. Put the couscous into the steamer basket of the *couscousiere* or in the colander, rubbing the grains to break up any clumps. Reduce the heat to moderately high and steam the couscous, uncovered, for 15 minutes, being sure to maintain the water level so it doesn't boil away. (If steam is coming out through any gaps between the rim of the stockpot and the colander, seal it with a damp dishtowel or cheesecloth.) After 15 minutes, return the couscous to the baking dish and sprinkle ½ cup of cold water and ½ teaspoon of salt over it. Break up any clumps and let the couscous sit for 10 to 30 minutes (or up to 4 hours if covered with a paper towel). In the interim, fill the bottom of the *couscousiere* or stockpot with water (or stew) and heat until steam begins to rise. Return the couscous to the colander and steam again, uncovered, for 20 to 25 minutes. Transfer the couscous to a platter or bowl and serve with stew or as an accompaniment to any meal.

For faster cooking, use 1½ cups of boiling water per 1 cup of couscous. Stir the couscous into the boiling water, then cover and remove from the heat. Let it stand undisturbed until all the liquid is absorbed, about 5 to 10 minutes. Then, stir to fluff before serving or using in a recipe. Use broth or fruit juice instead of water to infuse the couscous with more flavor, and experiment with a variety of herbs and spices. However it's prepared, couscous can be served plain as a side dish, topped with a sauce or stew, or cooled and used as a basis for a salad.

Couscous is especially good when cooked with fruit juice, cinnamon or other sweet spices, raisins or dates, and chopped nuts. The mixture can then be pressed into a baking dish that has been quickly rinsed with water but not dried. Once cooled, the couscous can be cut into squares for a sweet snack or dessert. If cooked with vegetable broth, pressed and cooled couscous is transformed into a wheat-based polenta.

Fregola or fregula (the Sardinian spelling) is a traditional version of couscous from Sardinia. It is coarser and rougher than Moroccan couscous, and since it is toasted, it has a nuttier flavor. Traditional uses include adding fregola to soups and stews for thickening and texture, serving it with clams and tomatoes, or baking it topped with tomato sauce, herbs, and Pecorino Romano.

Israeli couscous, which is the size of tapioca pearls, is a delicious and versatile food that bears little resemblance to Moroccan couscous. It is truly more akin to pasta. Created in Israel in the 1950s, it is made from a semolina that's extruded into shape and then dried by toasting. It's much larger than Moroccan couscous and has a nutty flavor and different texture. It's also prepared differently.

Like pasta, Israeli couscous can be used as the basis of a pasta salad or in any recipe that calls for pasta. It's cooked like pasta, too: Add it to boiling salted water and cook for 7 to 8 minutes, then rinse it briefly under cold water to stop the cooking and remove some of the sticky starch. It can also be added to soups during the last 10 minutes of cooking. Or use it to make a creamy risotto-like dish, substituting Israeli couscous for the rice and stirring until the broth is absorbed, about 12 minutes altogether. Use 2 cups of broth for each cup of Israeli couscous.

For a texture suitable for pilafs, with separate rather than sticky grains, first sauté 1 cup of Israeli couscous in oil or butter for a few minutes, then add 1¾ cups of water and a bit of salt. Bring to a boil, then lower the heat, cover, and simmer until the water is absorbed, about 15 minutes. The cooked couscous can be served immediately as a side dish or cooled for use as the basis for a salad.

Lebanese couscous, also known as *moghra-bieh*, is even larger, the size of small peas. It, too, can be cooked like risotto or as an addition to soups or stews to provide a chewy texture, but the more traditional method is to cook it on its own and serve it topped with stew. First soak 2 cups of Lebanese couscous by pouring boiling water over it. Cover and let stand for 45 minutes. Drain the couscous, then cook it in 4 cups of broth for about 30 minutes until the liquid is absorbed and the couscous is tender.

For cooking it directly within soups or stews as a textural additon, use ¼ cup of Lebanese couscous for about 12 cups of soup, adding it about 30 minutes before the soup is done. Then cover the pot and cook the Lebanese couscous until tender.

■ WHEAT BRAN

Wheat bran is the outer protective covering of the wheat berry, sometimes called miller's bran or unprocessed bran. If you're already eating whole wheat cereals and other whole grain products, you're automatically getting bran in your diet and really don't need to supplement it. But if you choose to do so, perhaps sprinkling it on cereals, soups, or salads or adding it to muffins and other baked goods, limit the amount of bran to no more than 2 tablespoons per serving. Too much bran can have a negative effect of binding up minerals such as copper, iron, and zinc, preventing their absorption. And because it readily absorbs water, it is important to always drink plenty of liquids for digestive ease when consuming bran.

■ WHEAT GERM

The germ is the embryo of the grain, and as such it is particularly rich in nutrients, including fiber, protein, vitamin E, thiamin, folic acid, iron, zinc,

magnesium, and healthful fats. As with bran, if your diet already includes whole wheat products, you're automatically getting the benefits of wheat germ. Still, its nutty flavor and crumblike texture make it a popular addition to recipes for pancakes and other baked goods. It also makes a nice topping for smoothies, cereals, entrées, and desserts and can be used as a substitute for bread crumbs for coating a variety of foods.

Because it is so high in natural oils and thus very prone to rancidity, wheat germ should never be purchased in bulk. Instead, look for it in shelf-stable nitrogen-flushed packages or vacuum-packed jars or packages. Once opened, wheat germ should always be refrigerated or stored in the freezer to help stave off rancidity. It is time to throw it away when it has that telltale unpleasant aroma and bitter flavor. As with all rancid foods, any health benefits are more than outweighed by the rancidity. Really fresh raw wheat germ that is only a few days old would undoubtedly be the most nutritious choice, but for most of us, this is impossible to procure. If you're going to use raw wheat germ, buy it in a nitrogen-flushed package, use it within a week, and then discard the rest.

Toasted wheat germ is a better option. Because heat inactivates enzymes that can accelerate rancidity, toasted wheat germ retains its freshness longer than raw wheat germ does. It will keep up to three months if stored in an airtight container in the freezer or refrigerator. It also imparts a delicious flavor that's even nuttier than regular wheat germ. Stabilized wheat germ is also available, in which a specialized heat treatment is used to kill bacteria and mold, extending storage time for up to six months if refrigerated and even longer if stored in the freezer. And finally, the most stable (although least nutritious) type of wheat germ is defatted. Since all the oils are removed (along with their nutrient value), it is not as essential to store defatted wheat germ in the refrigerator or freezer.

Wild Rice

Gluten free

Wild rice is neither a rice nor a grain. Rather, its long, dark brown kernel is the seed of an aquatic grass that grows primarily in marshy areas of northern Minnesota, Wisconsin, and southern Canada. Early North American inhabitants called it *manoomin*, meaning "good berry"; early English explorers came up with the name "wild rice." Nutritionally, wild rice is a good source of protein, containing more than common rice, and it's rich in lysine, the amino acid that's usually limited in grains. Its texture is chewy and its flavor is often described as nutty, earthy, and somewhat reminiscent of green tea.

Laws in Minnesota, Wisconsin, and Canada regulate wild rice harvesting, both to protect the rights of the Native American communities considered to be the official harvesters of wild rice, and to preserve the native wild rice beds. A limited number of wild rice harvesting permits are issued, and they require strict adherence to the season, harvesting methods, and hours of harvesting allowed per day. Traditional harvesting is done manually, using only a canoe and two ricing sticks, called "knockers." While one person guides the canoe, another person uses one stick to pull the head of rice into the boat. The other stick is used to knock the ripe seeds loose.

However, most of what is sold as wild rice is actually one of several hybrid versions cultivated and mechanically harvested in rice paddies in California and Minnesota—a practice that started years ago when the demand for wild rice exceeded the wild supply. While nontraditional growing and harvesting methods make "wild rice" less expensive, the flavor of these varieties is not as robust or nutty as that of authentic wild rice. Also, cultivated wild rice is more likely to be grown with fertilizers, herbicides, and insecticides.

Whether harvested in the wild or cultivated, wild rice is cured for a couple weeks to further develop its flavor and to make it easier to husk. The rice is then parched, traditionally over a fire, or commercially within a large rotating drum to reduce its moisture content and enhance its characteristic flavor. As a final process, the chaff is removed in a thresher and fanning mill. Since the specific techniques used vary from producer to producer, each brand of wild rice is unique in flavor.

Varieites and Cooking Guidelines

Flavor enhancers: Onions, chives, leeks, dill, mushrooms, parsley, sage, thyme, celery, and red bell peppers.

Only cultivated hybrid "wild rice" is graded according to its size. Giant wild rice features uniform 1-inch-long grains. Extra fancy wild rice is medium in length. The least expensive type, select wild rice, generally includes uneven lengths and sizes of kernels and broken kernels. It can be used in muffins, pancakes, soups, stuffings, and anywhere uniform appearance doesn't matter.

Wild rice is excellent for pilafs or as an ingredient in pancakes, breads, salads, soups, and stuffings. When cooked, it expands to three or four times its dry volume. To cook it, use 3 cups of water per cup of wild rice. Bring the water to a boil, stir in the wild rice, then lower the heat, cover, and cook for 50 to 60 minutes, or until the grains begin to split open and become tender but not mushy. However, some wild rice is mechanically scarified, meaning its hard black bran layer is scratched to reduce cooking time, so be sure to consult the instructions for the variety you purchase. It can be cooked together with brown rice without sacrificing its hearty flavor. Or it can be cooked separately and mixed with other cooked grains, where it will provide a striking color contrast and chewy texture.

Whole Grain and Specialty Flours

All whole grains can be ground into flour, as can some other foods, but using them in cooking and baking is seldom just a matter of substituting them for wheat flour. Each contributes its own unique flavor and texture. Some are mildly flavored, while others are downright assertive. Textures range from silken to sandy. Some have gluten and others don't, which can significantly affect the texture and volume of baked goods, particularly breads that are kneaded. And even within the category of wheat flours, protein content can vary widely, making them perform quite differently in baking. Some types of wheat flour are more appropriate for certain types of baking than others. Recognizing the characteristics of each type of flour can not only make experimentation fun and interesting but also yield delicious baked goods as a reward for all your efforts.

Grinding Methods

Flour can be ground in several ways: stone ground, hammer milled, or roller milled. Whole grain flours are typically stone ground or hammer milled. Refined flours, from grains stripped of their bran and germ, must be milled with rollers.

Stone-ground flour is ground between two flat millstones that rub against each other, the most traditional way of grinding flour. The stones slowly crush the entire grain, distributing its bran and nutrient-rich germ throughout the flour, something many bakers feel is an essential component for making excellent whole grain breads. Since this slower method of grinding generates less heat than hammer milling or roller milling does, the flavors and nutrients within the grain are better retained. Also, since stone grinding creates larger particles of flour, products made with stone-ground flour will be digested and absorbed more slowly by the body. This keeps blood sugar levels more stable and, consequently, helps maintain a steady energy level. Since stone grinding can be just one part of the process, look for products labeled "100% stone-ground."

Hammer-milled flour is ground in a mill in which bars swinging on an axle rotate inside a steel cylinder, crushing the grain against the inner surface. A faster way to grind grains, hammer milling also yields a more consistent grade of finely ground flour. However, the speed of the process generates higher temperatures, which can destroy some nutrients within the flour.

Roller-milled flour is ground in a machine that features several rollers with different surfaces, ranging from smooth to coarse, set various widths apart. Unlike stone grinding and hammer milling, grinding flour in a roller mill makes it possible to quickly separate the bran and germ from the endosperm and completely control the particle size of the flour through various stages of grinding and sifting. The miller can then analyze each grinding, or stream, to assess many characteristics, including the quality of the starch, the type of gluten, and the amount of protein. This also allows millers to create customized flour blends geared for various purposes, such as commercial bread baking or home use, and specific products, such as specialty breads, cakes, crackers, pastries, and pasta. Because roller milling, like hammer milling, generates more heat, some oxidation and damage to the nutrients within the flour can occur.

There are significant and surprising differences in quality and overall performance among the many brands of flour. Some of the key factors involved in this variation include the type of grain, growing conditions, quality control measures during processing, conditions in which the flour is stored (including in any warehouse along the way as well as the grocery store), and how old the flour is by the time you buy it—and actually use it. But it doesn't stop there: humidity and other factors in your home at the time of baking can also affect how flours perform, and different brands work better in different situations. It's definitely worth the time and investment to experiment with various brands of flour to discover which provides the best results.

You can also grind flour at home, which guarantees it's as fresh as possible. Several home manual and electric flour mills are available, some with grinding stones and others with metal burrs. Flour-grinding attachments are also available for some juicers, food processors, and electric mixers. Certain grains, such as rice, millet, oats, and quinoa, can be ground in a blender, but too much grinding could burn out the motor unless your blender is particularly heavy-duty. Also, a blender tends to grind flour unevenly. A small electric coffee grinder does a good job if only small amounts of flour are needed.

Processing Methods

Refined wheat flour may also be subjected to further processing, including the addition of bleaching and maturing agents, dough conditioners, and enzymes, as well as vitamins for enrichment. Artificial bleaching agents began to see use in the United States in the early 1900s as a quicker, cheaper way to mature refined flour and condition the gluten. Traditionally, refined flour was stored for two to three months to allow oxygen to naturally bleach the flour's yellow tint to a creamy white color. It also oxidized the protein, making the gluten stronger and more elastic for better baking results.

Since storage involves some expense and the flour has to be rotated to make sure all of it is exposed to oxygen, artificial measures to get the job done in less than a couple days, discovered in the early 1900s, were enthusiastically accepted by many millers. Either benzoyl peroxide or chlorine dioxide can be used to chemically mature and condition flour depending on what type of flour is being produced. Benzoyl peroxide is used in some all-purpose flours and some bread flours. Chlorine dioxide yields a whiter color, as well as a more acidic flour, which makes for finer texture, so it's used in cake flour and also sometimes in all-purpose flours.

However, artisan and high-quality scratch bakers insist on using only unbleached wheat flour, finding that it far surpasses bleached wheat flour in every regard. Not only do the yellow carotenoids make for a pleasing creamy white tint in baked goods, but they also contribute to the overall taste and fragrant aroma of products baked with wheat. And since natural aging also oxidizes the flour's protein for stronger gluten and better baking results, there is simply no good reason why anyone should use bleached flour.

In addition to bleaching agents, refined flour is often subjected to oxidizing agents, such as potassium bromate and azodicarbonamide, to more quickly mature the flour and strengthen its gluten. Even whole wheat flour sometimes contains these additives to create a higher-rising bread. Although potassium bromate is allowed in the United States, it is banned in several countries, including the United Kingdom, Canada, Mexico, and Japan, as a potential carcinogen. Since remarkable bread is made in countries that have banned potassium bromate, it is clear that it is an unnecessary additive, and the alternatives, including azodicarbonamide, are equally unnecessary. While these additives significantly reduce the time and labor required for mass-production bakeries to develop dough, they don't make any contribution to crafting bread that is as tasty as it is nourishing.

The only additive that can truly enhance flour is alpha-amylase, an enzyme that helps break down some of the complex starches in flour into sugar. This helps provide readily available fuel for yeast, which in turn helps dough rise properly when making bread. Grains naturally contain some alpha-amylase, but the amount increases dramatically during sprouting. The source for supplemental alpha-amylase is often sprouted barley that's been ground into flour, which is generally known as barley malt powder or diastatic malt powder. Flour is typically tested at the mill to determine how much alpha-amylase is naturally present, as the level can

vary depending on the variety of wheat, the weather during growing and harvest, and the storage conditions. If the level is too low, a small amount of diastatic malt powder may be added, and the precise amount is very important. Too much will produce breads with a sticky texture, but too little will yield bread with a dry, crumbly texture.

Alpha-amylase can also be derived from *Aspergillus oryzae*, which synthesizes the enzyme during its growth. This is the same type of mold that is cultured to inoculate soybeans in the production of miso. Because fungal alpha-amylase is inactivated earlier in the baking process than diastatic barley malt is, the amount added need not be so precisely calibrated, as there isn't the same potential for sticky bread if too much is added. However, since fungal enzymes may be genetically engineered, it's best to stick with flour supplemented only with diastatic barley malt unless you're sure that the specific brand of fungal alpha-amylase used is derived from a natural source.

Enrichment

Enrichment of refined wheat flour and other grain products, including breads, pastas, cornmeal, and white rice emerged as a result of health surveys in the late 1930s that revealed alarming nutritional deficiencies in B vitamins, iron, and iodine. The American Medical Association, National Research Council, National Academy of Sciences, and several public health authorities decided a good strategy to remedy the situation would be to fortify commonly consumed refined foods.

In 1941, the U.S. Food and Drug Administration set standards for the use of the term *enriched* on grain products. To use this term products must be supplemented with iron and three B vitamins: thiamin (B_1), riboflavin (B_2), and niacin (B_3). In response to research showing that adequate intake of folic acid prior to conception dramatically reduces the incidence of neural tube defects (spina bifida and anencephaly), folic acid was added to the

How to Store Flour

The shelf life of flour depends on the type of flour, how it was processed, how long it was stored before you purchased it, and the conditions under which it was stored. In general, the cooler and drier the storage conditions, both before and after purchase, the longer it will retain its optimum flavor and performance.

Keep flour in moisture-proof packaging. Transferring it to an airtight plastic or glass container is a good idea, both for prolonging shelf life and for deterring weevils and mealy moths. Whole grain flours should be stored at cool temperatures: below 70°F, and preferably between 40°F and 60°F, to prevent the natural oils in the bran and germ from going rancid. You can store them in your refrigerator, or even your freezer, if you have space available. Although at its peak when used within six weeks of being ground, whole grain flour that has been kept cool will perform well for up to three months.

Refined flour has a longer shelf life since most of the oils in the grain are removed during refinement. It can be stored in an airtight container at temperatures up to 75°F (no hotter!) for a couple months; refrigerating or freezing will extend its shelf life for up to a year. For better results when baking, warm any flour stored in a refrigerator or freezer to room temperature before using it.

Regardless of whether it's refined, the sooner flour is used, the better. Old flour just can't perform at the same level. Off odors, dampness, or excessive dryness indicate that flour is far beyond its prime, as do off flavors or poor volume in baked goods. But don't wait for these obvious clues that it is time to toss out old flour. Rather, buy only the amount of flour you think you'll use within a couple of months. Many brands print expiration dates on the package, so consult these to ensure you're buying the freshest possible flour, and use the flour by that date.

enrichment list in 1993. Although enrichment isn't federally mandated, most states have accepted the enrichment standards, in part because of interstate commerce. Manufacturers want to ensure their products receive wide distribution.

Considering that only five out of the nutrients depleted during refinement are replaced, enrichment is just a drop in the bucket. As many as thirty nutrients are significantly depleted, including magnesium, potassium, calcium, zinc, selenium, vitamin B_6, and vitamin E.

Gluten and Its Role in Baking

Gluten is a protein complex comprised of two types of protein, gliadin and glutenin, which are responsible for giving dough flexibility, strength, and elasticity. When liquids are added to flour and the dough is manipulated, gliadin and glutenin combine to form gluten. The gentle stretching and folding of the dough during kneading helps develop quite a bit of gluten in breads. In cookie dough and cake and quick bread batters, where a lesser amount of gluten is desirable, stirring suffices. In either case, the gluten then captures the carbon dioxide produced by the yeast, sourdough starter, baking powder, or baking soda, leavening the dough and creating baked goods with a lighter texture and more volume.

The gliadin component of gluten gives dough its ability to be stretched and shaped, referred to as plasticity, as well as the ability to expand to accommodate the gases produced by the yeast or other leavening agents. Glutenin, on the other hand, is responsible for the dough's elasticity, letting it hold its original shape and spring back when stretched, which helps improve the dough's ability to capture and contain gas bubbles.

The quantity and proportion of these two proteins in any given flour will determine the overall density, tenderness, and volume of products baked with that flour. With too little gliadin, the dough would be difficult to stretch and shape, springing back too readily and resulting in heavy-textured bread, since the gases produced by the yeast would accumulate in only a few pockets. And without the benefit of glutenin's elasticity, the dough could continue to stretch to the point of bursting, allowing the gases to escape, resulting in a flat bread without volume.

Of all the grains, wheat has the best quality and quantity of both gliadin and glutenin. However, the proportions of these proteins vary significantly depending on the variety of wheat. For instance, the gluten in durum wheat is very strong—good for pasta but too rigid for bread. The amount of gluten in hard wheat is perfect for breads, while soft wheat has much less, but just enough to produce quick breads, muffins, and other baked goods that are intended to be lighter and more airy than bread. Because flour may not be labeled to indicate whether it's made from soft or hard wheat or a combination of the two, here are some guidelines to help you make more informed choices: Flour designated as best for making bread or pasta will be made from hard varieties of wheat, while flour labeled as pastry flour will be from soft wheat. True to its name, all-purpose flour is formulated from a combination of both hard and soft wheat, making it suitable for a wider variety of needs.

Although spelt, Kamut, and wheat are related to one another, they vary in their levels of specific proteins and gluten quality. The impact this has on baking will be discussed in the entries for each type of flour. But their variations in protein content also mean that some people who are sensitive to wheat may be able to eat baked goods and other foods made with spelt and Kamut. Still, anyone with a serious wheat or gluten allergy should check with a medical professional before experimenting with these alternative grains and their flours.

Baking with Nonwheat Flour

Flours made from grains other than wheat can be used for baking, but because each grain has its own unique protein profile and some lack gluten, each type of flour will perform differently. While flour with little or no gluten will generally result in sandy, crumbly, or densely textured products, recipes can be modified to yield better results. If the final product need not be gluten free, you can combine flours with low or no gluten with higher-gluten flours. Unfortunately, some people are sensitive or allergic to gluten and must avoid anything that contains it—that means anything made with wheat, barley, or rye, as well as some less familiar grains, such as farro, grano, Kamut, spelt, and triticale. The gliadin part of the gluten protein complex is considered to be the primary cause of the problem. Other people are allergic or sensitive solely to wheat and can tolerate other grains that contain gluten.

If wheat is still an option, a good starting point for becoming familiar with the characteristics of a wide variety of flours is to experiment by substituting any nonwheat flour for 25% of the whole wheat or wheat flour called for in a recipe. But when it's necessary to use only gluten-free flour, it's important to first learn about the characteristics of various gluten-free flours so that you'll know how to capitalize on their strengths and compensate for their weaknesses, allowing you to create baked goods with a satisfactory texture and mouthfeel. For example, a product made solely with brown rice flour or white rice flour will yield a dry, crisp, sandy texture quite different from the large crumb and chewy texture that result from using whole

Flours at a Glance

Flour	Gluten Free?	Flavor	Baked Texture	Best Used In
Amaranth	yes	spicy, nutty, woody	moist, fine crumb; smooth crisp crust	protein and flavor booster in tortillas, breads, muffins, pancakes, and cookies
Arrowroot	yes	neutral	lightens heavy textures; smooth, crisp crust	sauces and gluten-free baking aid
Barley	no	sweet, malty	moist, cakelike crumb; firm, chewy crust	breads, muffins, pancakes, cakes, quick breads, and gravies
Buckwheat	yes	hearty, earthy	moist, fine crumb; soft crust	pancakes, crepes, and Asian noodles
Carob	yes	chocolaty	dry, light crumb	brownies, cakes, desserts, candy, and beverages
Chestnut	yes	sweet, nutty	silky texture	pastries, breads, muffins, gnocchi, and pancakes
Cocoa	yes	chocolate	dry, light crumb	brownies, cakes, desserts, candy, and beverages
Cornmeal, blue or red	yes	sweet, nutlike	grainy, more dense crumb	tortillas, cornbread, muffins, and pancakes
Cornmeal, white	yes	delicate corn flavor	grainy, slightly dry crumb	cornbread, tortillas, and porridge
Cornmeal, yellow	yes	deep, rich corn flavor	grainy, slightly dry crumb	cornbread, tortillas, polenta, tamales, muffins, pancakes, and porridge
Cornstarch	yes	neutral	lightens heavy textures; smooth, crisp crust	sauces, gluten-free baking aid, and thickener in fruit pies
Garbanzo	yes	sweet, rich	dry, delicate crumb	flatbreads, fritters, breads, sauces, soups, gravies, vegetarian burgers, and for added protein
Garbanzo-fava	yes	nutty, somewhat sweet	moist, tender crumb with added volume	flatbreads, fritters, breads, muffins, quick breads, cookies, cakes sauces, and gravies
Gluten flour	no	tangy	fine, chewy crumb; crisp, thin crust	breads (as a rising aid and for added protein)
Kamut	no	sweet, rich, buttery	dense, heavy crumb	pasta, breads, and flatbreads
Kudzu	yes	neutral	not used in baking	sauces, soups, and dairy-free puddings and pies
Mesquite	yes	sweet, with molasses and mocha tones	dry crumb	seasoning savory or sweet foods, boosting nutrition and flavor in breads, muffins, and cookies
Millet	yes	mildly sweet to bitter, depending on age of the flour	dry, delicate crumb; smooth, thin crust	breads, muffins, quick breads, and cookies
Montina	yes	hearty, nutty	chewy texture	gluten-free baking blends, breads, and quick breads

Flour	Gluten Free?	Flavor	Baked Texture	Best Used In
Oat	yes*	sweet	moist, cakelike crumb; firm crust	breads, cakes, cookies, pancakes, crackers, sauces, and gravies
Potato flour	yes	sweet, strong potato flavor	moist, chewy crumb; soft, dry crust	soup thickener and gluten-free baking blends
Potato starch	yes	neutral, mild potato flavor	moist crumb; lightens heavy textures	sauces and gluten-free baking aid
Quinoa	yes	nutty, earthy	delicate, cakelike crumb	quick breads, pancakes, and cookies
Rice, brown	yes	nutty	dry, fine crumb; soft crust	breads, muffins, and pancakes
Rice, sweet	yes	sweet	supple crumb	sauces and piecrusts
Rice, white	yes	neutral	dry, fine crumb; soft crust	gravies, sauces, breads, quick breads, and muffins
Rye	no	tangy	moist crumb; smooth, hard crust	breads, pancakes, waffles, and crackers
Sorghum	yes	sweet	fine crumb; crisp crust	injera breads, cookies, cakes, muffins, and quick breads
Soy	yes	pungent, slightly bitter, nutty	moist, fine crumb; smooth, hard crust	protein booster in breads, muffins, and quick breads
Spelt	no	sweet, nutty	moderate crumb; supple crust	breads, muffins, quick breads, crackers, and piecrusts
Sprouted grain flour	no**	sweet	lighter, springy crumb; darker crust	breads, muffins, and quick breads
Tapioca	yes	slightly sweet	chewy, springy texture; smooth, crisp crust	sauces and gluten-free baking aid
Teff	yes	sweet, with malty molasses tones	light, delicate crumb	injera, pancakes, waffles, muffins, and cookies
Triticale	no	nutty, tangy	dense crumb; semifirm crust	breads, quick breads, and muffins
Wheat, durum	no	sweet, somewhat buttery	fine, delicate, dense crumb; crunchy crust	pasta
Wheat, semolina	no	sweet, somewhat buttery	fine, delicate, firm crumb; crunchy crust	breads and pasta
Wheat, refined white and all-purpose	no	sweet to neutral	fine, tender crumb	breads, cookies, muffins, quick breads, piecrusts, crackers, gravies, and sauces
Wheat, white whole	no	sweet, nutty	coarse, large crumb	breads, cookies, cakes, muffins, quick breads, piecrusts, crackers, gravies, and sauces
Wheat, whole	no	slightly bitter, nutty	coarse, large crumb	breads, muffins, quick breads, piecrusts, crackers, gravies, and sauces
Wild rice	yes	earthy, nutty	dry, fine crumb	pancakes, quick breads, gravies, and coating fish, poultry, and wild game

*Although oats do not contain gluten, in North America they are often listed as being inappropriate for a gluten-free diet, but this is only out of concern that they may be contaminated by wheat during harvest and processing.
**Sprouted grain flour typically contains wheat.

Does Organic Flour Make a Difference?

Certified organic grain is grown on healthy soil without risky pesticides, herbicides, or fungicides that can persist in the environment, and genetic engineering is never involved. While it only makes sense that food grown without potentially harmful chemicals is better for the earth and for us, does flour from organically grown grain make a difference in baking?

Because professional artisan bakers work directly with flour on an everyday basis, they have the opportunity to notice all of the nuances in the performance of different flours. Many of them report that organic flour—from good-quality grain and properly stored, of course—makes a significant difference, providing a richer flavor. And organic flour is a must for creating sourdough starters, which rely on wild yeast. Because they're never subjected to toxic pesticides, organic grains have a variety of wild yeasts growing on them, resulting in starters that are more vital and active, thus providing better leavening and yielding bread with superior texture and flavor.

wheat flour. To remedy the situation without resorting to wheat, you could balance the rice flour by combining it with another flour that contributes to a moist finished texture, such as buckwheat, millet, or soy flour.

That's just a starting point. Better results are possible when other ingredients are added to try to make up for the absence of gluten. Since gluten-free flour doesn't contribute the proteins needed to capture the carbon dioxide from leavening agents and thereby help bread rise, doughs made with these flours will look like thick cake batter rather than an expanded ball of dough. However, xanthan gum or guar gum can help provide volume and viscosity in the final product. In baked goods that should be chewy, you can compensate for the absence of gluten by adding some starchy root flour, such as tapioca or arrowroot flour.

Ingredients other than flour can also help compensate for the absence of gluten. For example, adding dairy products or eggs can help provide a lighter, more tender texture. Variations in method can also be helpful. For instance, with little or no gluten, piecrusts won't hold together well, but they can be pressed into shape instead of being rolled. For other types of baked goods, it can be helpful to use an electric mixer. This will help create more air pockets in the dough, making for lighter baked goods that rise higher.

You can use the "Flours at Glance" chart (see pages 74–75) to see the highlights and main characteristics of each type of flour. The detailed descriptions in the rest of the chapter will help you further explore the possibilities by providing detailed information about each type of flour, including baking and cooking tips. Fortunately, there are also many recipes for gluten-free baking. In addition to indicating the exact amounts of unusual ingredients like xanthan gum and arrowroot flour, many of them also offer detailed information on gluten-free baking techniques.

Exploring Flours

Amaranth Flour

Gluten free

Amaranth flour adds an unusual nutty, spicy flavor and a moist texture to cookies, muffins, pancakes, waffles, and breads, along with a smooth, crisp crust. Widely used in early Mexican and Central American cultures in traditional breads, it is valued these days for its high-quality protein, which can boost the nutritional content of any recipe. Although rich in protein, it's gluten free, so it can't be used on its own in baked goods intended to rise. Rather than using it as the sole or primary flour in recipes, amaranth flour should be combined in small amounts with other flours to create the right balance in flavor and texture. While too much may result in dense baked goods with a strong flavor, a small amount can add an extra spark that accentuates without overwhelming. A good rule of thumb is to substitute amaranth flour for up to 25% of the flour called for in a recipe. Substituting amaranth flour in a recipe may require a slightly extended baking time.

Arrowroot Flour and Starch

Gluten free

Obtained from a narrow, 6-inch-long root that hails from the West Indies, arrowroot is true to its name, having been used by Indians to draw poison from arrow wounds. These days it's used in dried and powdered form for more peaceful purposes, serving as an easily digested thickener and flour substitute. Arrowroot is sometimes used in teething biscuits and cookies for toddlers, for its velvety consistency and because its starch is in a form that makes these foods easier to chew, swallow, and digest.

Arrowroot has several things going for it as a thickener. Unlike flour, which makes sauces that are cloudy and opaque, arrowroot yields clear sauces with a beautiful glazed appearance. As it is virtually neutral in taste, arrowroot also allows the true flavors of the sauce to come through, and it doesn't require precooking, as flour does, to eliminate unpleasant, raw, floury flavors. Because it starts to thicken more quickly and at lower temperatures than flour does, arrowroot is perfect for delicate sauces and also good to use for last-minute corrections to consistency. While it is the best choice for thickening foods that will be frozen after cooking and when thickening acidic liquids like fruit juices, it doesn't work well in dairy-based sauces, where it develops a slimy texture. Substitute an equal amount of arrowroot powder for either cornstarch or potato starch; if using it as a thickener in place of flour, use half the amount.

Use approximately 1 tablespoon of arrowroot to thicken 1 cup of liquid. To prevent clumping, first dissolve the arrowroot in a bit of cold water, then slowly pour it into hot, not boiling, liquid, stirring or whisking all the while, and continue to stir just until thickened. Lower the heat immediately and serve the sauce within 15 minutes. With prolonged cooking, sauces thickened with arrowroot will start to break down. Like other root-based starches, it isn't particularly heat-stable. For the same reason, sauces made with arrowroot don't reheat well.

Arrowroot is also used as a baking starch in some gluten-free recipes, helping to complement other, more sandy-textured flours that lack the binding properties gluten would provide. It makes for a smoother texture and contributes to a crisper crust. It's particularly useful for lightening the texture of wheat-free baked goods made with amaranth, brown rice, or millet flour. You can use up to 50% arrowroot flour in a flour blend. If stored in an airtight, moisture-proof container, arrowroot will keep almost indefinitely. For those who are allergic to corn, arrowroot can be substituted for cornstarch on a one-to-one basis in any recipe.

Barley Flour

Contains gluten

Ground from whole barley, barley flour contributes a sweet, malty flavor, a moist, cakelike crumb, and a firm, chewy crust to baked goods. It is a delicious addition to breads, cakes, cookies, muffins, pancakes, and quick breads. For optimum flavor, lightly toast barley flour in a dry skillet before adding it to recipes. Although barley contains some gluten, bread made solely with barley flour won't have enough gluten to rise properly. Limit the amount of barley flour to 25% in these breads.

While it can be substituted equally for wheat flour in most baked goods leavened with baking powder or baking soda, some recipes may benefit from decreasing the amount of barley flour and adding in other types of flour to achieve a drier, less moist crumb. For cakes, cookies, muffins, pancakes, and quick breads, a good place to start is to substitute barley flour for up to 25% of the flour called for in the recipe. If that goes well, experiment with a higher proportion of barley flour the next time to explore the possible variations in both flavor and texture. On its own, barley flour performs well in unleavened flatbreads and even piecrusts, though crusts made with barley flour will be more hearty and less flaky. It also makes for an interesting flavor twist in flour-thickened gravies and other cooked sauces.

Bean-Based Flours

Gluten free

Flour ground from dried beans can be combined with other flours to boost levels of protein, soluble fiber, B vitamins, and minerals in baked goods. Because beans are high in methionine, an amino acid that is lacking in most grains, adding some bean flour will also improve the quality of the protein.

Soy flour and garbanzo flour are the most familiar forms of bean flour, and each of these is described below, in its own listing. However, a wide variety of bean flours is available, typically categorized by the color of the bean. For any recipe calling for light bean flour, possibilities include fava bean flour, garbanzo flour, garbanzo-fava flour, white bean flour, and navy bean flour. Dark bean flour options include pinto bean flour, black bean flour, and Romano bean flour (made with cranberry beans). Light bean flours are generally more mild in flavor than dark bean flours. For best digestibility, look for the products described as "micronized," "processed," "precooked," or "toasted."

Bean flour contributes body, flavor, and a moist, fine crumb to baked goods. Because it is gluten free, bean flour must be combined with flours that contain gluten when making baked goods that are intended to rise, using up to 25% bean flour. Alternatively, it can be included as a component within gluten-free baking blends with added xanthan or guar gum and emulsifers to enhance the structure of breads and enable the leaveners to do their job. Bean flour can similarly be used when making cakes and cookies.

Buckwheat Flour

Gluten free

Buckwheat flour, with its robust, somewhat musty flavor, is the basis for Japanese soba noodles, and it also lends its distinctive flavor and functional qualities, including a soft crust, to hearty pancakes and traditional Russian *blini*, paper-thin crepes classically served with sour cream. Light buckwheat flour is made from hulled buckwheat, while stronger-flavored dark buckwheat flour includes some of the hull. As usual, the darker, more whole grain form is more nutritional. For a drier texture and mellower flavor, you can grind white, untoasted buckwheat groats into flour in a blender or electric coffee grinder. Due to its gummy texture when cooked, buckwheat flour is not a good choice when thickening sauces and gravies.

Because buckwheat is gluten free, it must be combined with a high-gluten flour, such as whole wheat, to make breads leavened with yeast. Even then it should be used in only limited amounts because its flavor is so strong and it can create a gummy texture. Don't use more than ⅓ cup of buckwheat flour per loaf of bread. Pancakes, muffins, and crepes can handle a higher proportion of buckwheat flour—up to 50%. It all depends on just how robust you'd like the flavor to be. However, the higher the proportion of buckwheat flour, the more leavening assistance the recipe will need from ingredients such as eggs or yogurt.

Carob Flour

Gluten free

Carob is the dried, roasted, and pulverized pod of a tree that grows primarily in countries surrounding the Mediterranean. Easily digested and rich in pectin, carob is a traditional remedy for soothing an upset stomach. With a flavor similar to that of chocolate but milder, carob is generally used as a substitute for cocoa. But unlike chocolate, carob is naturally sweet, high in fiber and calcium, very low in fat, and free of caffeine-like stimulants.

Substitute carob equally for cocoa in cookies, cakes, candies, and beverages. Because of its high fiber content which, in baking, lends to a dry, light crumb, use a blender when making carob drinks, otherwise it will settle at the bottom of the glass. To replace 1 square of baking chocolate in a recipe, use 3 tablespoons of carob flour plus 1 tablespoon of milk. Since carob is sweeter than cocoa and contains less fat, it's usually a good idea to decrease the amount of sweetener and increase the amount of fat when substituting it for cocoa. It is also sometimes added to bread dough to make loaves with a deep, rich color. For this purpose, add 1 to 2 tablespoons of carob powder per loaf of bread.

Chestnut Flour

Gluten free

Even though chestnuts are classified as a nut, a glance at their nutritional profile, especially when dried and ground into flour—high in carbohydrates (78%) and low in fat (less than 4%)—makes it seem they could just as easily be classified as a grain. Flour made from dried chestnuts can be used like any other gluten-free grain flour.

For many centuries, chestnuts have been an important seasonal staple food in Italian mountain communities, where chestnut trees flourish. In fact, chestnut flour, not cornmeal, was the original basis of polenta. Now considered a specialty item for both gourmet and gluten-free cooking, chestnut flour has a silky texture and sweet flavor that make it perfect for use in breads, muffins, pancakes, and pastries, as well as savory dishes, including chestnut gnocchi.

Chestnut flour can be substituted for up to 25% of the flour in yeasted bread recipes and up to 50% of the flour in recipes leavened with baking powder or baking soda. It can be substituted for cornmeal or oat flour on a one-to-one basis. Since it is very low in fat, chestnut flour will keep for twelve to eighteen months without going rancid.

Cocoa Powder

Gluten free

Unsweetened cocoa powder has more to offer than just its rich, delicious flavor. It also performs similarly to a grain flour or root-based starch, providing structure, absorbing moisture, and serving as a thickening agent in desserts, baked goods, frostings, and fillings.

Cocoa powder is derived from cocoa beans, which grow within large pods on the cacao tree, a tall understory species that grows in humid tropical forests. The beans are fermented to help develop the flavor we associate with chocolate, and then dried and roasted for further expansion of flavor. They are cracked into small pieces known as nibs, which are then crushed to produce a thick, dark paste. Called chocolate liquor, this paste is hydraulically pressed to separate most of the cocoa butter from the cocoa particles. The extracted cocoa butter is utilized as a key ingredient in a wide variety of chocolate products.

The remaining cocoa particles are pulverized to make cocoa powder, which has a strong, complex, bitter chocolate flavor. Depending on how much cocoa butter is separated from the solids, as much as 24% cocoa butter can remain in the cocoa powder. This is one of the primary factors distinguishing the many brands of cocoa powder; the higher the fat, the richer the flavor.

Another key distinguishing factor is whether the cocoa is treated with an alkali. Cocoa powder is naturally acidic, which contributes to its bitter flavor and affects its performance in baking. In 1828, a Dutch chocolatier developed a method for treating cocoa powder with a solution of potassium carbonate, a harmless alkaline chemical substance, to neutralize its acidity and produce cocoa with a milder, less bitter flavor and a darker brown color. As a salute to its developer, cocoa that has been alkalized is referred to as Dutch process cocoa or Dutch cocoa. The process also makes cocoa powder more absorbent, so it's easier to mix with liquids.

Whether to use natural, nonalkalized cocoa powder or Dutch process cocoa is sometimes just a matter of personal flavor preference, but in some recipes the distinction is important, as the degree of acidity can affect the final outcome. Many recipes will specify which form of cocoa to use, but to help you decide in other situations, it often comes down to whether the recipe is leavened with baking powder or baking soda. Baking soda must react with an acidic ingredient to produce its leavening effect, so natural, nonalkalized cocoa powder is generally used with baking soda. In recipes that use baking powder or contain other acidic ingredients, Dutched process cocoa is the better choice. In situations where neither baking powder nor baking soda is used, either type of cocoa should work well.

Cornmeal

Gluten free

Because it is mildly sweet and nutty and has a granular and slightly dry texture, even a small amount of cornmeal makes a wonderful contribution to muffins, pancakes, and breads. Often used to prevent breads and pizza crusts from sticking to pans, it also adds a delicious flavor and texture to the crust. Stone-ground cornmeal from whole corn is the best option in terms of flavor, texture, and nutrition, but because the oil-rich germ is present in whole cornmeal, it should be refrigerated and used within three months. Degerminated cornmeal, made by grinding the corn between massive steel rollers that separate out the fiber and germ, is more shelf stable because most of the natural oils are removed in the process. But as usual, this comes at a cost in terms of valuable nutrients and flavor.

Cornmeal is available in a variety of grinds, from very fine to very coarse. In some cases, a specific grind is important to the outcome of the recipe, but in other cases it's just a matter of personal preference. It's also available in an assortment of colors, each with its own unique flavor. Whether yellow, white, blue, or red, they can be used interchangeably in recipes as long as you are open to the possibilities.

Yellow cornmeal, rich in beta-carotene, has a deep, rich corn flavor. Use medium or coarsely ground yellow cornmeal for cornbread. Use coarsely ground for polenta or better yet, look for cornmeal expressly for polenta. Made from the flint variety of corn, which is harder, it yields polenta that's soft but not mushy.

White cornmeal has a less pronounced, more delicate corn flavor. It's considered to be essential for true Southern-style cornbread, as well as for genuine johnnycakes, a northern specialty.

Blue cornmeal, ground from corn with deep purplish blue kernels, is pale gray but develops a lavender hue when mixed with water. Sweet and nutlike in flavor, blue cornmeal generally has a coarser, grittier texture than yellow or white cornmeal, since it is ground from flint corn, a type of corn with tough outer starchy layers that are harder to grind. Tortillas made with blue cornmeal will be denser than those made with white or yellow corn. Blue corn contains more protein than yellow or white corn, and more of the amino acid lysine, giving it a more complete amino acid profile. It is also higher in minerals, including iron, potassium, and zinc.

Red cornmeal, which can be difficult to come by, is ground from a type of flint corn that has a beautiful red color. It is similar to blue cornmeal in its sweet, intense flavor and in its nutritional profile. It can be used like any other cornmeal in baking or as a coating for fish.

High-lysine cornmeal is made from a hybrid strain of yellow corn that contains up to 70% more lysine than ordinary corn, along with higher levels of tryptophan, isoleucine, threonine, and other amino acids, resulting in a more complete protein profile. It was developed as a way to prevent protein deficiency among populations that depend on corn in their diets. Although not as easy to locate as cornmeal from regular yellow corn, it's worth seeking out, as it has an exceptionally delicious nutty, sweet flavor.

Masa harina is made from corn masa, also known as nixtamal, a dough made by treating whole corn with alkali to improve its nutritional properties (see page 42 for more information on masa). To make masa harina, the wet dough is dried and finely ground into a flour. Typically used for tortillas, corn chips, and tamales, masa harina provides a characteristic subtly sour flavor. Although fresh masa is ready to use and has a better flavor, masa harina is easier to store and keep on hand.

Corn flour is ground to a finer consistency than cornmeal. Use it in breads, pancakes, or waffles if you'd like a smoother, less grainy texture than that of cornmeal. It can also be used in cakes and cookies. If you have trouble finding corn flour, make your own by grinding regular cornmeal (not whole corn!) in a blender or coffee grinder until it's more flourlike. In the United Kingdom, Australia, and New Zealand, the term *cornflour* means "cornstarch."

Great-tasting cornbreads can be made solely from cornmeal, or blend it with whole wheat or white flour for a lighter, softer texture. Suggested proportions vary, but three parts cornmeal to one part wheat flour is a good place to start. Fold in cooked fresh corn kernels for added sweetness and texture.

To cook cornmeal as a breakfast cereal, use four parts water to one part cornmeal. Bring the water to a boil, then slowly pour in the cornmeal, whisking all the while to prevent clumping. Turn down the heat as low as possible, cover, and simmer for 25 to 30 minutes.

For polenta, use 3 cups of water and about ¾ teaspoon of salt for each cup of cornmeal, which should be coarsely ground. Bring the water to a boil, add the salt, and then slowly pour in the cornmeal, whisking all the while to prevent clumping. Lower the heat to medium and continue to cook, stirring constantly, until the polenta thickens and stiffens, about 20 to 30 minutes. Spoon onto plates or onto an oiled platter and serve topped with your favorite sauce. Or transfer it to an oiled baking dish, smooth it to an even layer, and allow it to cool. To serve, cut it into slices or other shapes and bake, broil, or pan-fry the slices.

Cornstarch

Gluten free

Next to wheat flour, cornstarch (known as cornflour in the United Kingdom, Australia, and New Zealand) is the second most commonly used thickener. To be transformed into cornstarch, corn kernels go through a rather extensive refining process. After the hull and germ are removed, the corn is further processed to separate out any remaining protein, resulting in pure starch that is then washed, dried, and ground into a fine powder. On account of the high level of processing it undergoes, and because it has little nutritional value, many people prefer to use arrowroot powder instead. Another good reason to choose an alternative thickener is that much of today's conventionally raised corn is genetically modified, and organic cornstarch can be difficult to come by.

Although it has a fairly neutral flavor, the taste of cornstarch is somewhat more apparent than that of arrowroot. Unlike sauces thickened with flour, those thickened with cornstarch have a smooth texture and are clear, though not as glossy as sauces made with arrowroot or tapioca. Cornstarch is an excellent thickener for dairy-based recipes, but it doesn't work in acidic liquids, nor should it be used in sauces or gravies that will be frozen and used later. Like root-based starches such as arrowroot, cornstarch thickens at lower temperatures than flour does, but if it's overcooked, it will break down, causing the sauce to become thin. For thickening, substitute cornstarch equally for arrowroot powder or potato starch; use only half the amount if substituting for flour. As with other thickeners, dissolve the cornstarch in a bit of cold water before adding it to the liquid to be thickened. Stir the mixture constantly until thickened, then lower the heat and serve as soon as possible.

In baking, adding some cornstarch will help smooth the crust of gluten-free baked goods, and it will lighten the crumb without adding a flavor of its own.

Garbanzo Flour

Gluten free

Like the garbanzo beans, or chickpeas, from which it is ground, garbanzo flour is rich in protein and has a sweet, rich flavor. Unroasted garbanzo flour, also called besan or chana flour, is used to make batter for deep-fried Indian fritters called *pakoras*, a French flatbread known as *socca*, and an old Italian form of polenta called *panissa*. Roasted garbanzo flour makes it a snap to prepare falafel or hummus; just mix 1 cup of roasted garbanzo flour with ⅔ cup of cold water to equal 1½ cups of cooked, mashed garbanzo beans. This also works for other dips, spreads, and patties, and even casseroles. Either unroasted or roasted garbanzo flour can be used to thicken soups, stews, and sauces, and to bind ingredients together to make bean or grain burgers.

Because it's high in protein, garbanzo flour is especially suitable as a substitute for soy flour in many recipes. In baked goods it contributes a dry, delicate crumb. Another consideration is that bean-derived flours have a more pronounced flavor than flour ground from grain, so it's often best to use them in moderation, or in recipes that contain ingredients with stronger flavors and aromas, such as chocolate, cocoa, carob, applesauce, maple syrup, honey, and cinnamon. Since garbanzo flour contains no gluten, when making breads leavened with yeast or sourdough, it should be combined with wheat or spelt flour and should comprise no more than 25% of the total flour in the recipe. It can also be combined up to 25% with other gluten-free flours and starches, such as sorghum flour, cornstarch, and tapioca flour to make gluten-free breads. For best digestion of foods made with bean flour, look for products described as "micronized," "processed," "precooked," or "toasted."

Garbanzo-Fava Flour

Gluten free

This flour blend, made from a combination of garbanzo beans and fava beans, is a good substitute for rice flour in recipes for gluten-free baked goods, providing more volume, tenderness, and moisture. It is tan in color and its flavor is somewhat sweeter than that of rice flour. Garbanzo-fava flour has long been used in international cooking and baking, and small amounts of fava flour (2% or less) are often added to wheat flour in France to provide a subtle, sweet, buttery flavor and promote better rising.

Garbanzo-fava flour adds extra protein and fiber, which are often low in the flours typically used in gluten-free baking.

It's usually best to use no more than 25% garbanzo-fava flour in a flour blend. As it provides a better flavor and lighter texture in baked goods than garbanzo flour alone, try it in muffins, pancakes, cakes, cookies, and quick breads, as well as in bread recipes. Like garbanzo flour, it can also be used as a binding agent or to thicken gravies and sauces. For best digestion of foods made with bean flour, look for products described as "micronized," "processed," "precooked," or "toasted."

Gluten Flour and Vital Wheat Gluten

Contains gluten

Gluten is extracted from wheat flour in a process similar to how seitan, or "wheat meat," is made. The flour is formed into a dough that's kneaded to help develop the gluten, then allowed to rest to further develop the gluten, and finally rinsed under water to separate the starch and bran from the gluten.

There are distinct differences between gluten flour and vital wheat gluten. Gluten flour is white flour with concentrated wheat gluten added to it; it contains up to 14.5% protein. In contrast, vital wheat gluten is pure gluten that's been dried and ground; it contains about 75% protein. Adding either to dough will increase the amount of protein in the bread. However, since gluten is very deficient in lysine, one of the essential amino acids, it isn't a high-quality protein.

The addition of small amounts of gluten—about 5% to 10% of the total amount of flour for gluten flour, and only 2% to 3% for vital wheat gluten—

will help dough rise higher and more quickly, creating a lightly textured bread with a fine, chewy crumb that doesn't crumble when sliced. It is especially useful when baking with flours that contain little or no gluten. Quick breads leavened with baking powder can also benefit from the addition of a bit of gluten flour or vital wheat gluten. It will improve the shape and texture of quick breads, but they won't necessarily rise higher.

While it may sound like a dream come true, adding gluten flour or vital wheat gluten to dough has its drawbacks. Because the dough has more gluten than normal, it requires more kneading to allow the gluten to fully develop. Gluten also imparts a distinctive flavor and chewy texture to breads that isn't universally appreciated. On top of that, breads made with extra gluten stale more quickly. But the biggest problem with using gluten flour or vital wheat gluten is that, because it is so concentrated, some people who don't usually have an adverse reaction to wheat may find breads made with gluten difficult to digest. Clearly, anyone who is allergic to wheat or gluten will also experience a problem if gluten flour is added. Accordingly, those on wheat-free or gluten-free diets shouldn't eat breads made with these products, even if the bread is otherwise free of both wheat and gluten.

Use up to 2 tablespoons of gluten flour per cup of flour in whole grain breads. Since white flour lacks the bran and germ, cup for cup it contains more gluten than whole wheat flour. Therefore, less gluten flour is needed when making breads with white flour; use up to 4 teaspoons per cup. When adding vital wheat gluten to bread doughs, use up to 1½ teaspoons per cup of flour in whole grain breads and up to 1 teaspoon per cup of flour in white breads. Breads that contain bran, nuts, raisins, or seeds may need slightly more gluten flour or vital wheat gluten to compensate for the increased bulk.

Kamut Flour

Contains gluten

Ground from an ancient Egyptian variety of durum wheat with giant kernels and a sweet, buttery flavor, Kamut flour (kuh-MOOT) lends a terrific flavor and beautiful amber color to baked goods. The name Kamut is a registered trademark for this variety of wheat, which is always grown organically. Nutritionally, Kamut flour is higher in protein, minerals, and essential fatty acids than typical wheat flour. Another benefit is that Kamut is always grown organically, by virtue of trademark restrictions.

Although Kamut is a type of wheat, it has a different protein profile than conventional wheat, so some people who are sensitive to wheat but not gluten may be able to eat products made from Kamut with few or no symptoms. Still, anyone who is severely allergic to wheat should consult with a medical professional before experimenting with Kamut.

Since Kamut is related to durum wheat, its gluten is strong, making it an excellent choice for pasta. However, compared to conventional wheat it has less glutenin, the protein that lends elasticity to dough and helps bread rise better by expanding to capture the gases created by the yeast. Therefore, breads made with Kamut flour will have a denser texture than those made with conventional wheat flour. Still, just a few tricks can help produce bread with a lighter, satisfying crumb, albeit still more hearty, and the exceptional flavor of bread made with Kamut is definitely worth the effort. Keeping the dough moist, kneading it a few minutes longer, and allowing it to rest longer will all help create lighter baked products with Kamut flour. Accordingly, the longer leavening times involved in sourdough baking make it a perfect method for baking with Kamut flour.

Because the gluten isn't as springy as is in modern varieties of wheat, it is best to use Kamut flour for loaves that are intended to be smaller. This helps minimize the volume of dough to be leavened, ensuring loaves as voluminous as possible. Baked goods that are intentionally lower in height, such as flatbreads, crackers, cookies, pizza crusts, and pancakes, are also good choices when using Kamut flour.

Kudzu

Gluten free

Kudzu powder (KOOD-zoo) is made from the huge, white root of the kudzu plant. It is indigenous to Japan and China, where it grows vigorously in the mountains and is valued both as a cooking starch and as a traditional remedy for digestive disorders. Scientific research on kudzu's phytonutrients has confirmed that it has a number of positive effects on the body. However, in some parts of the southeastern United States, where it was originally planted to control soil erosion, kudzu is a noxious weed. Its vines are capable of overtaking anything—including roads, bridges, and power lines. Ironically, despite this overabundance, for use as a cooking starch and medicinal herb, it is imported from Japan.

Despite its fearsome reputation as a weed, kudzu is a remarkable thickening agent. Because the dried, pulverized powder sticks together when exposed to the slightest moisture, it's sold in small chalky-looking chunks—an indication that it is best stored in a tightly sealed jar. Like arrowroot, it has a neutral flavor, thickens quickly, and yields sauces and desserts that are smooth and transparent. As an added bonus, foods thickened with kudzu remain set after cooling, making even creamy-textured dairy-free pies and puddings a delicious possibility.

Before measuring kudzu, crush any chunks with the back of a spoon or in a mortar and pestle. Dissolve the kudzu powder in cold water and add it at the end of the recipe's cooking time, stirring constantly for 2 or 3 minutes until the desired thickness is achieved. Use about 1 to 1½ table-spoons per cup of liquid in sauces or soups. To create a thicker, puddinglike consistency, use 2 to 2½ tablespoons per cup of liquid.

Mesquite Flour

Gluten free

Until the sixteenth century, mesquite flour was a principal food for Native Americans in what is now Mexico and the southwestern United States, who valued the tree for many other reasons, including for fuel, tools, and medicinal purposes. Today, the tree is considered infamous or renowned, depending on whom you ask. For ranchers in the southwestern United States who would prefer to see grass growing on their land to feed their cattle, the mesquite tree is a hardy, pesky, prolific plant with a very deep root system, making it hard to eradicate. However, the tree is highly respected in many parts of the world, and many gourmet cooks prefer mesquite when grilling because of the smoky sweet flavor it imparts.

Although mesquite flour slipped into oblivion for several centuries, it has recently regained its reputation as a valuable food, most notably as a gluten-free flour that can boost nutrition and flavor to flour blends. Ground from the ripened pods of the mesquite tree, this high-protein flour has a sweet flavor reminiscent of molasses and mocha. Even just a bit makes a delicious statement.

To further accentuate its high protein content (11% to 17%), mesquite flour is a good source of lysine, an essential amino acid typically lacking in grain flour. It is also rich in minerals, namely calcium, magnesium, potassium, iron, and zinc. It derives its sweetness primarily from the simple sugar fructose, a form of sugar that's metabolized more slowly and without insulin, so it doesn't have much effect on blood sugar levels. Additionally, its high fiber content is largely from galactomannan, a soluble fiber that slows digestion. This also helps stabilize blood sugar levels.

You can use up to 25% mesquite flour in flour blends for baking muffins, cakes, breads, and cookies, whether with wheat flour or with other gluten-free flours. It contributes to a dry crumb. Since the flavor is strong, you may want to start with just 2 tablespoons of mesquite flour in each cup of flour in a recipe. While mesquite flour doesn't contribute any specific structural characteristics beyond fiber, its natural sweetness can boost the flavors of baked goods and dessert sauces while also providing the opportunity to cut down on sugar in the recipe or at the table. Use a couple of tablespoons in a recipe or just a sprinkle, depending on your mood. As a seasoning, it works well on protein-based foods, imparting a wonderful mesquite flavor. Sprinkle it on fish, meat, poultry, tofu, or tempeh before cooking for added flavor. If using it to season beans, add it after cooking.

Millet Flour

Gluten free

Baked goods made with millet flour have a mildly sweet and nutty taste, a dry, delicate, crumb, and a smooth, thin crust, as well as a slight yellow color. It is particularly important for millet flour to be freshly ground. At its prime, it has an appealing sweet flavor, but when even slightly old, it makes anything baked with it taste bitter. For optimum freshness, grind your own millet flour at home in a blender, electric coffee grinder, or flour mill. Store any unused flour in the freezer and use it as soon as possible.

You can use up to 50% millet flour in cookies and muffins. Combine it with whole wheat flour, brown rice flour, or a combination of brown rice flour and tapioca flour to enhance millet's sweet flavor and to balance its texture. Because it contains no gluten, it must be combined with a high proportion of wheat or spelt flour when making yeasted or sourdough breads. For best flavor and texture, limit the millet flour to ½ to ¾ cup per loaf.

Montina Flour

Gluten free

Montina is the registered trade name for flour milled from the seeds of Indian ricegrass (*Achnatherum hymenoides*), a perennial grass native to Montana that grows in poor, sandy soils. Seed production of Indian ricegrass began in the 1980s, as the grass proved to be a valuable management tool for grassland reclamation and soil conservation after wildfires. Research into the value of Indian ricegrass as a food began in the early 1990s at Montana State University as part of an exploration of the economic value of native plants. Researchers discovered that Indian ricegrass is high in protein and fiber and free of gluten, and that its flour can be used in baked goods.

The flour is dark in color and lends baked goods a hearty, chewy texture. Since Montina has no gluten and its nutty flavor is quite strong, it should be combined with other flours for best results. Use up to 20% Montina in a blend with lighter flours. A ready-made, all-purpose Montina baking flour blend is available; it's a blend of Montina, white rice flour, and tapioca flour. Montina representatives claim the blend can be used in a bread machine, but that the yeast should be reduced to 1½ teaspoons and the baking cycle should be set for sweet bread or quick bread.

Oat Flour

Gluten free

Baked goods with a high proportion of oat flour are especially moist and flavorful, with a cakelike, somewhat crumbly texture and firm crust. Its characteristics are primarily due to its bran, which is much higher in soluble fiber than is wheat bran. An added benefit with oat flour is that baked goods made with it remain fresher longer, thanks to its natural antioxidants. Before chemical preservatives were available, bakers often added a small amount of oats to their products to prevent them from going stale too quickly.

Although oats do not contain gluten, North American gluten-free diet associations often list it as a grain to avoid because of concern that oats sometimes may not always be adequately segregated from wheat during growing and processing.

Oat flour is readily available in natural foods stores, but it can also be ground fresh at home in a blender; 1¼ cups of rolled oats will make 1 cup of oat flour. Because oats are gluten free, don't use more than 25% oat flour in breads leavened with yeast or sourdough. Muffins, cakes, cookies, and pancakes can be made with up to 50% oat flour. Oat flour is also a good thickener in sauces, soups, and stews.

Potato Flour

Gluten free

Potato flour is made from cooked potatoes that have been dried and ground. Used primarily as a thickener and binder, it yields sauces that are translucent and glossy. To thicken sauces, substitute potato flour equally for arrowroot and cornstarch, but when substituting it for flour, use only about half as much. It can also be added to cakes and cookies to provide a moist, chewy texture. In gluten-free baked goods, it will help harden the crust. Only use a very small amount of potato flour, about 1 teaspoon per cup, in flour mixes, as it has a much stronger flavor than potato starch.

Potato Starch

Gluten free

Rather than being made from the whole potato, as is the case with potato flour, potato starch is a fine-textured flour made from only the starch of the potato. Because it has a very bland flavor and is free of gluten, potato starch is often used in gluten-free flours and baking blends. It contributes a moist, light, and airy texture to baked goods. Use up to one-third potato starch in flour blends. Potato starch can also be used as a thickener in soups, sauces, and stews. It is unstable at high heat and shouldn't be boiled or cooked for prolonged periods of time. When using potato starch as a thickener, mix it with cold water before adding it to a hot liquid. To thicken sauces, substitute potato starch equally for arrowroot and cornstarch, but when substituting it for flour, use only about half as much.

Quinoa Flour

Gluten free

Baked goods made with quinoa flour have a delicate crumb, making it a nice addition to muffins and breads. It provides the same delicious, earthy, nutty flavor of cooked whole quinoa. Depending on how much is used in a recipe and what other flours it is paired with, it may lend baked goods a light yellow color, almost the color of cornbread. Quinoa flour is an effective nutrient booster, contributing high-quality, complete protein because it contains the amino acid lysine, which is usually deficient in grains. It's also high in minerals, particularly calcium, magnesium, potassium, iron, and zinc.

While the quinoa flour you purchase has a more consistent grind, you can easily grind your own in a blender or an electric coffee grinder, which makes for fresher and tastier flour; ¾ cup of whole quinoa will yield 1 cup of flour with a texture similar to that of finely ground cornmeal. Dry-roasting the flour will enhance its flavor. Because quinoa flour is gluten free, don't use more than 25% quinoa flour when making yeasted or sourdough breads. For best flavor and texture, use up to 30% quinoa flour in quick breads, cookies, and pancakes. Quinoa flour can be used to thicken sauces and gravies, too.

Rice Flour

Gluten free

For a long time, rice flour was the primary flour used in gluten-free baking. It has a fine, somewhat sandy texture that, in turn, creates finely textured but crumbly baked goods. Now, thanks to the increasing variety of alternative grains available, rice flour can be balanced with other gluten-free flours, such as arrowroot flour, potato starch, tapioca flour, and quinoa flour, that complement what rice flour has to offer. As a result, it's now possible to create baked goods with rice flour that have a more pleasing texture and flavor.

To compensate for its lack of gluten, xanthan gum or guar gum is typically added to help bind the dough together and provide some structure to capture the gas bubbles created by leavening agents. Because guar gum has laxative properties, xanthan gum is typically preferred. The general rule of thumb is to use about 1½ teaspoons of xanthan gum or guar gum per 2 cups of flour, but if guar gum is used, mix it with some of the liquid called for before adding it to the recipe.

Brown rice flour is more nutritious since it is ground from whole brown rice, which also gives it the nutty flavor, slightly more grain, dry fine crumb, and light brown color one would expect from brown rice. Because its natural oils are prone to rancidity, purchase the freshest brown rice flour possible and store it in the refrigerator or freezer. Although it's readily available in stores, you can grind your own at home in a blender or an electric coffee grinder using short-grain or medium-grain rice.

White rice flour has a neutral flavor and is less gritty than brown rice flour since it lacks the bran. In baked goods, it helps provide a light, delicate, somewhat springy texture. White rice flour shines in thickening soups, sauces, and gravies, where its blandness and white color allow the primary flavors and colors of the recipe to come through.

Sweet rice flour, which is the least gritty, is ground from short-grain sticky white rice, which makes it starchier than the other rice flours and a better binder. Sweet rice flour is good for thickening sauces that are refrigerated or ones that will be frozen, since it helps keep liquids from separating.

In baking, it can be added to piecrust dough to help make it more pliable.

Use up to 50% rice flour in cookies, flatbreads, and muffins. To minimize crumbling, add eggs, an egg substitute, or xanthan gum to the recipe and allow baked goods to cool for 5 minutes before transferring them to a flat surface, rather than a wire rack, to cool.

Rye Flour

Contains gluten

Rye flour has interesting but sometimes challenging characteristics. Because of its low gluten content and high levels of pentosans (a type of soluble fiber), breads and other baked goods made with 100% rye flour have the potential to be very moist, compact, and heavy.

The gluten in rye contains primarily the glutenin part of the complex rather than gliadin, which means products made from rye flour will be heavier in texture than those made with wheat, since its gluten complex will have less capacity to to stretch to accommodate pockets of carbon dioxide gas formed during leavening.

Pentosans are long chains of five-carbon sugars that have a very high capacity to bind water. In contrast to the carbohydrates in wheat flour, which don't absorb liquids as easily, pentosans become gummy as they absorb water, which accounts for the moistness of most rye breads. Pentosans are also responsible for rye flour's sticky consistency during kneading. Plus, rye is particularly high in amylase enzymes, which break down starches, so even after the structure of the bread is created during the rising process, the amylase enzymes continue to break it down. Fortunately, changing the pH of the dough by making it more acidic or sour can slow the amylase enzymes. This is why most 100% rye loaves are typically leavened with sourdough, which is acidic. Although such loaves aren't lofty in height, they are outstanding in flavor and more

digestible, and they have a pleasing texture that isn't too heavy.

However, most rye breads are made only partially with rye flour—enough to get the rye flavor but not so much that it significantly affects the texture. Even so, delicious, authentic German pumpernickel rye bread, slowly baked in steam-heated ovens and served thinly sliced, reveals how the density and moistness contributed by rye flour can be made into a virtue. Traditional rye crispbreads also show how 100% rye flour can be used successfully.

When used in small amounts, rye flour can also help balance flour with a grainier texture, such as cornmeal or rice flour, yielding a final product that is more moist and has a more pleasing crumb. In fact, in France rye flour is an approved additive for improving bread flour because it makes doughs easier to work, improves texture, accentuates flavor, provides richer color, and increases the shelf life of the baked bread.

Rye flour is classified by grind and by how much of the bran has been removed. The darkest type, coarsely ground from the entire kernel, is pumpernickel rye flour. Rye meal also indicates flour ground from the entire grain, but it may be of a medium or fine grind in addition to coarse. The type most commonly used in rye bread recipes is medium grind. At the opposite end of the spectrum, white rye flour is ground milled rye that lacks the germ and bran. Occupying the middle ground are medium rye, which contains some of the bran, and dark rye, which is typically ground from the entire kernel or at least retains most of the bran.

If you're new to making rye bread and want to start simply, combine rye flour with wheat flour at a ratio of about one part rye to three parts wheat. Knead the dough gently and for less time, just until it starts to get gummy, to minimize developing a sticky texture. Adding extra flour won't compensate for the gummy texture. Cookies, pancakes, and waffles can also be made with rye flour. Try balancing its texture by combining it with flours that have a more grainy texture. The flavor and texture of cornmeal is a perfect complement for rye flour.

Sorghum Flour

Gluten free

Of all the gluten-free flours, sorghum flour, with its slightly sweet flavor and light tan color, tastes and looks most like wheat flour. In Africa and Asia, it has traditionally been used to create flatbreads, including a variety of injera in Ethiopia and dosas in India. In gluten-free baking, it's a nice substitute for rice flour because it contains more protein and fiber and is more flavorful. It can also be used in conjunction with bean-based flours to help counter their somewhat bitter flavor. For best results in baking, use about 25% to 30% sorghum flour in a blend with potato starch and tapioca flour, which will help provide a smoother crust and lighter texture. Xanthan gum is also typically added to help compensate for sorghum's lack of gluten; add about ½ teaspoon per cup of sorghum flour.

Soy Flour

Gluten free

Like amaranth flour and garbanzo flour, soy flour is used primarily to boost protein content. It also makes baked goods moister and contributes a smooth, hard crust. However, it has a strong flavor, so only small amounts should be added to recipes. Look for full-fat soy flour, lightly toasted for better flavor and digestibility. Low-fat and defatted soy flours are by-products of soy oil production, which generally involves use of chemical solvents.

Use no more than 25% soy flour in quick breads, cookies, and cakes. It should be used even more sparingly in yeasted breads—no more than 10% of the total flour—since too much can overcondition the dough and make the bread rise too soon. When substituting soy flour for other flours, lower the oven temperature by 25°F to compensate for its tendency to brown prematurely. Save your taste buds and don't even bother trying to use it as a thickener for sauces and gravies.

Spelt Flour

Contains gluten

A distant cousin of conventional wheat, spelt has good baking characteristics but also possesses traits that make it different than typical wheat flour. It has a sweeter and nuttier flavor, more protein, and a different type of gluten, along with contributing a moderate crumb. Spelt was commonly grown in the United States until 1900, when other varieties of wheat emerged that were easier to grow and harvest. However, it made a comeback in the 1980s not only because of its superior flavor, but also because some people who are sensitive to wheat find that spelt doesn't cause the same reactions that conventional wheat does. Still, anyone with severe allergies to wheat or gluten should consult with a medical professional before experimenting with spelt.

From breads to piecrusts, the richer flavor of spelt flour yields remarkable results. However, its gluten is quite fragile, so some special handling is required. Specifically, spelt is lower in the gliadin component of the gluten protein complex, which means it doesn't as readily develop air pockets to capture gases created by leavening agents. Accordingly, products made with spelt flour need to be handled minimally and more gently. The sponge method, preferably using a sourdough-type culture, will give the best results when making bread, particularly in regard to volume and structure. Spelt flour is also more water-soluble than conventional wheat flour, so it's usually a good idea to reduce the amount of liquids when substituting spelt flour for wheat flour.

Spelt flour can be substituted equally for wheat flour in any recipe. To compensate for its greater solubility, start by reducing the recipe's liquids by 25%. Add more liquid only if it seems necessary to obtain the optimum consistency of batter or dough for a particular recipe. Too much water will make the dough weak and sticky, undermining its ability to rise or, in the case of piecrusts, to roll out properly. While whole grain spelt flour is the most flavorful and nutritious, white spelt flour, which has the bran and germ removed, is also available and can be used for lighter breads or in pastries.

Sprouted Grain Flour

Contains gluten (typically contains wheat)

Some of the lightest and most nutritious whole grain breads are made by bakeries using sprouted grain flour. While many of them create their own sprouted grain flour for in-house use, varieties of sprouted grain flour, including wheat, rye, and spelt, have become available for home bakers. To make the flour, the grain is cleaned and sterilized before it is sprouted. The sprouts are rinsed with hot water to kill any surface bacteria they may harbor. After the sprouts are dried at a low temperature, they are stone ground into flour.

The conversion of some of the grain's starch into maltose during the sprouting process makes for a sweeter flavor and a darker color in the crust. As such, these flours provide more sugar in the dough, which yeasts use to fuel their activity. Additionally, sprouting breaks down phytic acid, a compound found in the bran, that binds minerals and prevents their absorption. So, among the whole grain flours, the minerals in sprouted grain flours are most available to the body. The sprouting process is stopped at an early stage before alpha-amylase, an enzyme naturally found in many grains that helps break down the grain's starch into more easily usable sugars, is allowed to fully develop. This means sprouted flour can be substituted, cup for cup, for some or all of the wheat flour in a recipe without having to worry about gooey-textured baked goods, as can occur with alpha-amylase rich diastatic malt when too much is added to bread dough as a supplemental fuel for yeast.

Sprouted flour is also good in combination with other flours to help create lighter baked goods. Since sprouted flour is much drier than flour ground directly from the grain, modify recipes by either adding more liquid ingredients or using less flour. For optimum flavor, store sprouted flour in the refrigerator or freezer.

Tapioca Flour

Gluten free

Tapioca flour is a gluten-free, grain-free, slightly sweet powdered starch made from the root of the cassava plant, which is cultivated in South America and Florida. Don't confuse it with pearl or quick-cooking tapioca, which would be inappropriate for a sauce. Tapioca flour's thickening and baking properties are very similar to those of arrowroot. Sauces, glazes, and pie fillings thickened with tapioca flour will be translucent and shiny, and have a thick, soft consistency when cool that's not unlike puddings made with pearl tapioca. Like arrowroot, tapioca flour is a good thickener for foods that will likely be frozen after cooking. Like other root-based thickeners, it can be added to sauces at low heat, whereas flour requires higher temperatures to thicken. To use it as a thickener, first mix it with a bit of cold water before adding it to hot liquids. Cook just until thickened; like most root-based thickeners, it isn't heat stable and doesn't stand up well to prolonged cooking. Tapioca flour adds a chewy texture, smooth, crisp crust, and elasticity or springiness to baked goods, making them lighter in texture. It can be substituted equally for arrowroot flour. Use up to 33% tapioca flour in flour blends.

Teff Flour

Gluten free

Teff flour is ground from seeds of a grass indigenous to Ethiopia, which has been cultivated in the United States since the 1980s. It is a seed so small that its very name means "lost." As there would be no way to refine such small kernels, teff flour is only available in whole grain form. Most famous as the preferred grain for making *injera,* the spongy-textured traditional Ethiopian flatbread, teff comes with its own naturally occurring wild yeast living on the grain itself, which helps ferment the batter. In addition to being gluten free, it is also high in potassium, calcium, iron, protein, and fiber.

Brown and white teff flour are ground from two different varieties of teff, each with a distinctive flavor. Brown teff flour, the type most commonly available, gives baked goods a rich, molasses-like flavor, while results with white teff flour are more subtle. The sweet, malty flavor of teff and the light, delicate crumb it contributes to baked goods make it an interesting flour to experiment with in muffins and other quick breads, unyeasted flatbreads, piecrusts, cookies, pancakes, and waffles. Substitute up to 20% teff flour in your favorite recipe, and if substituting for wheat flour, feel free to experiment with more. However, because of its naturally occurring wild yeast, teff should never be added to yeasted breads, as it would be too much of a good thing, overwhelming the dough with yeast.

Teff flour can also be used to make a delicious, creamy breakfast cereal. Toast ½ cup of flour in a dry pan over low heat, stirring constantly for just about 3 minutes, teasing out its malty aroma. Slowly pour in 1½ cups of water, whisking all the while, and season with salt. While continuing to stir constantly, bring to a boil, then lower the heat, cover, and simmer for 5 minutes. For an unusual twist on polenta, spread the cooked teff in an 8-by-8-inch baking dish that's been rinsed in cold water but not dried. Set aside for about an hour to cool and solidify.

Triticale Flour

Contains gluten

Triticale, a cross between wheat and rye, is slightly higher in protein than wheat and has a better amino acid balance than many other grains. Baked goods made with triticale flour have a delicious nutty, ryelike flavor. Its gluten is delicate, specifically lower in the gliadin than it is in wheat, and it is about as tricky a flour to work with as rye, so its popularity has been limited. Although triticale flour is not commonly found in retail markets, it is available through specialty and mail order suppliers.

When making yeasted breads, use up to 50% triticale flour in combination with wheat flour. Since its gluten is weak, knead the dough with a gentle hand. Only allow the dough to rise once, otherwise the loaves will be overly dense. Triticale flour can generally be substituted for some or most of the wheat flour in recipes for quick breads, drop biscuits, cookies, and pancakes.

Wheat Flour

Contains gluten

It's no wonder that flour made from wheat reigns in baking. With its high quality and quantity of both gliadin and glutenin, the components of the gluten protein complex, wheat can respond to all types of leavening to yield a wide variety of textures, from flaky pastries to dense, hearty breads. The different varieties of wheat flour are categorized according to the color, the season in which it's grown, the relative hardness of its kernels, and whether it is refined or a whole grain.

Wheat can be red, white, or amber, depending on the color of the bran on the outside of the kernel. Flavor varies, too, depending on the color of bran. Red wheat's outer bran layer contains somewhat bitter-tasting tannins and phenolic acid, whereas white wheat's bran contributes a sweeter flavor. Red wheat is the type most often grown in the United States. However, there is increased interest in white wheat, primarily because of its color, as breads baked with it look like they're made with white flour.

Spring wheat is planted in the spring and harvested in late summer. It is better suited for machine production of bread, where its higher gluten levels (12% to 14%) are up to the demands the mixers put on the dough. Bread flour, purposely formulated to be higher in gluten, is often made from spring wheat. Winter wheat is planted in fall and harvested in early summer. It is preferred by artisan and home bakers for its moderate gluten content (10% to 12%), which allows the dough to be more easily stretched and worked by hand. Flour sold to consumers may be made from spring wheat, winter wheat, or a combination. Some brands indicate this on the package to help people choose the best flour for the intended use.

Wheat flour is also classified by the ratio of protein to starch in the endosperm—an indication of how much gluten is present and the best application for the flour. Wheat ranges from very hard to soft, and the harder the kernel, the higher the protein content and the stronger the gluten. This factor is most responsible for differences in baking performance among the various types of wheat flour.

Whole wheat flour is labeled as such only when the entire grain has been ground into flour. Refined white flour is usually bleached to remove its natural beta-carotene pigments. Unbleached white flour is the only type of refined flour worth buying. Not only is it the least processed and free of unnecessary additives, but it also provides baked goods that taste better and are more aromatic than those made with bleached white flour.

All of these variables combine to create a wide array of wheat flours, only some of which are described below. Professional bakers have access to even more specialized types of flour, including custom blends they may request directly from flour mills and specialty baking suppliers. While it's always a good idea to explore alternatives to wheat, there are times and applications where only wheat will do. In those cases, it helps to understand the qualities of the different types of wheat flour and how that affect their performance so you can choose the right one for the job.

■ DURUM FLOUR

Durum wheat, referred to as very hard wheat, contains the most protein and the least starch of any variety of wheat. It is available as flour in three forms: whole durum flour, durum flour, and semolina flour.

Whole durum flour is the flour of choice for making pasta, as gliadin is the more predominant component in its gluten complex, making for strong dough that can stretch into various shapes when extruded and expanded without disintegrating during cooking. (Think of the word *durable*.) Whole wheat pastas and whole wheat couscous are made from unrefined durum wheat.

Durum flour, also called fancy durum flour, is refined durum wheat that is finely ground. Unlike most refined wheat flours, durum flour is never bleached, since its buttery yellow color is generally valued in pasta and breads. The refined version of couscous is also made from refined durum wheat.

Semolina is coarsely ground refined durum wheat. Famous for its yellow hue, it is commonly added to bread to provide extra flavor and texture. It can also be used instead of cornmeal to prevent dough from sticking to surfaces during rising. Bread labeled as "semolina bread" may be made with a high percentage of finely milled durum wheat or, more frequently, it may have some coarse semolina added along with other types of wheat flour. It contributes a fine, delicate crumb and crunchy crust. High-quality dry pasta is made from finely ground semolina flour, which is higher in protein than other refined wheat flours, making it less starchy when cooked.

■ FLOURS MADE FROM HARD WHEAT

Whole wheat flour, ground from the entire kernel—bran, endosperm, and germ—is hearty, flavorful, and significantly higher in fiber and nutrients than refined flour is. Products sold simply as whole wheat flour will be ground from hard

International Flour Labeling

British equivalents for U.S. flour classifications:

Soft flour—cake and pastry flour
Plain flour—all-purpose flour
Strong flour or hard flour—bread flour
Self-raising flour—self-rising flour
Wholemeal flour—whole wheat flour

Italian flour specifications

The classifications "1," "0," and "00" refer to how fine the flour is ground and how much of the bran and germ have been removed. "00" is the most highly refined and is talcum-powder soft.

red wheat. Although it is high in protein, its bran cuts into the gluten strands, resulting in bread that doesn't rise as much as those made with refined flour. It also contributes a coarse, large crumb. Nonetheless, whole wheat breads have a full-bodied flavor and coarser texture that make them satisfying and delicious. Whole wheat flour can also be used in quick breads, cookies, and cakes, although their texture will be denser. While these textural qualities are enjoyed by many, if you're looking for a lighter texture, use whole wheat pastry flour instead, or combine whole wheat flour with white flour.

Use less whole wheat flour when substituting for white flour. Initially, try replacing each cup of white flour with about ¾ cup of whole wheat flour to compensate for the fact that the bran in whole wheat flour absorbs liquid more readily than the bran in white flour. Alternatively, you can increase the liquid in the recipe. Store whole wheat flour in the refrigerator or freezer and use it within three months, since it contains the natural oils from the wheat germ.

White whole wheat flour is a pale golden, mild-flavored flour ground from whole grain, hard white wheat. In contrast to whole wheat flour ground from hard red wheat, it produces baked goods that look as though they were made with white flour. Accordingly, when baking for people who object to the more pronounced nutty flavor and brownish color of products made with regular whole wheat flour, white wheat flour may appease without sacrificing nutrition.

Use white whole wheat flour for bread or as an all-purpose type of flour. Even though it contains the bran and germ, which are often assumed to contribute to less voluminous baking results, white whole wheat actually creates breads that rise better due to its high levels of gluten-forming proteins. And because of its subdued flavor and subtle color, white whole wheat flour works very well for cookies, quick breads, muffins, and cakes, despite being less light in texture than pastry flour. Store white whole wheat flour in the refrigerator or freezer and use it within three months, since it contains the natural oils from the wheat germ.

Bread flour, which is generally ground from hard spring wheat, is high in protein and has strong gluten that is ideal for baking light, airy loaves. Bread flour is sold in both whole wheat and refined white versions. Check the label to avoid additives such as potassium bromate, used to artificially age the flour.

Graham flour is another name for coarsely ground hard whole wheat flour. It is named after Sylvester Graham, who promoted the use of whole grain flour as a healthful practice in the 1830s to counter the growing popularity of refined white flour. It's most famous as the flour in graham crackers, but it can be used for other baked goods, too, where it lends a coarse and chewy texture.

■ FLOURS MADE FROM SOFT WHEAT

Compared to durum and hard wheat, soft wheat is higher in starch and lower in gluten (containing only 10% to 11%), making it most appropriate for cakes, cookies, piecrusts, quick breads, and any application where a lighter, less dense texture is desired. It's also the best type of wheat flour to use when making gravies, thickening quicker than those with more gluten. Soft wheat flours, ground primarily from winter wheat, are available in both refined and whole form.

Whole wheat pastry flour, ground from the whole kernel of soft wheat, contains the bran, germ, and endosperm. Like regular whole wheat flour, it provides more nutrients and fiber than refined pastry flour. Because it contains less gluten than regular whole wheat flour, it's less appropriate for breads and better for lighter-textured cookies, piecrusts, and quick breads and muffins leavened with baking powder or baking soda. It may take a little practice to make piecrusts with it, but once you've mastered the technique, the results are delicious, although not flaky. You might want to start by using a combination of whole wheat pastry flour and unbleached all-purpose flour.

Unbleached pastry flour, made from soft wheat with the bran and germ removed, is designed to provide light-textured pastries. However, this functionality comes at a high price in terms of nutrition. Still, it is neither bleached nor treated with chlorine gas, giving it an edge over cake flour.

Cake flour is made from soft wheat with the bran and germ removed. It is ground finer than whole wheat pastry flour and chemically bleached with chlorine gas, not just to whiten the flour, but also to make it slightly acidic so the cake will set more quickly and have a finer texture. In the interest of nutrition, whole wheat pastry flour remains a better bet. If you prefer light-colored, feathery-light baked goods, use unbleached pastry flour or a combination of whole wheat pastry flour and unbleached pastry flour. In most cases, 100% unbleached all-purpose flour can work satisfactorily, too.

■ ALL-PURPOSE WHEAT FLOURS

All-purpose flour is a blend of hard wheat and soft wheat. Its protein content depends on the specific brand's product specifications. True to its name, all-purpose flour works satisfactorily for breads and rolls leavened with yeast and sourdough and also performs well in cookies, cakes, muffins, and pies. If a recipe doesn't specify a particular type of flour, all-purpose flour is a safe bet. However, all-purpose flour often contains bleaching and maturing agents and dough conditioners, so read labels carefully before purchasing.

Self-rising flour is all-purpose flour with salt and baking powder added for convenience. If a recipe calls for self-rising flour, for each cup use 1 cup all-purpose flour and add 1 to 1¼ teaspoons baking powder and ½ teaspoon of salt. Should you choose to buy self-rising flour, try to find a brand that uses aluminum-free baking powder.

Wild Rice Flour

Gluten free

Wild rice flour, which is ground from whole wild rice, provides a rich, hearty, nutty flavor and dry, fine crumb to pancakes, quick breads, muffins, and cookies. It can be difficult to come by, but you can easily grind your own in a blender or an electric coffee grinder. Since wild rice flour is gluten free, it needs to be blended with other flours for best baking results. Use up to 25% wild rice flour in flour blends. Try using it as a flavorful substitute for wheat flour when coating fish, poultry, or wild game before cooking. It can also be used to thicken gravies, stews, and sauces.

Breads

⟋⟍

Throughout civilization bread has provided sustenance and comfort, has symbolized community and sharing, and has even been used as currency. The recent renaissance for remarkable bread can be attributed to the appreciation for good, wholesome ingredients that developed out of the natural foods movement starting in the 1960s along with renewed respect for traditional foods and the craftsmanship of artisanal bakers.

Visiting local bakeries is one of the first things I do upon arrival when traveling. Each country and culture has its own traditional form and variety of bread that has been developed over the centuries to complement its unique climate, local grain, and mode of cooking and baking.

Both the skill of the baker and the type of leavening agent used to make bread can distinguish one bread from another in terms of optimum flavor, texture, nutrition, and overall digestibility. The way breads are made can also help predict which ones will naturally stay fresh longer.

Sourdough

Sourdough breads, also known as naturally leavened, depend on the interaction of microorganisms ever-present in our natural environment. Considered the oldest form of leavening agent, a sourdough culture or starter is a mixture of flour and water that has been cultured from a variety of wild yeasts and bacteria found naturally in the air as well as on the grain and the flour itself. These various strains of wild yeasts in sourdough culture are predominantly of the genus and species *Saccharomyces exiguous*.

In the process of making sourdough bread, a pre-prepared starter culture is added to flour, water, and salt to make dough that is allowed to ferment and rise for several hours before baking. Because the wild yeasts and lactobacilli bacteria vary according to the environment in which the bread is made, sourdough bread made within each bakery and household will truly be unique. In a well-known example, the bacteria found exclusively within San Francisco, conveniently called *Lactobacillus sanfrancisco*, is responsible for the distinctive sour-like flavor and even thicker crust than can be found in sourdough breads made from other cultures developed in different geographical areas throughout the country.

The enhanced depth and complexity of flavors of sourdough breads occur when lactobacilli, "friendly" bacteria originating from the environment that grow in the dough along with the wild yeasts, are given enough time to do their magic. The longer the dough ferments during its rising time, the more opportunity for the natural lactobacillus bacteria within the environment to come into play, creating both lactic acid and acetic acid as by-products as it feeds off sugars in the dough. As the acids slowly accumulate, their flavor permeates the dough. While lactic acid produces rich, sweet, mellow flavors, acetic acid is responsible for a tart tang that increases with time. The increased acidity of the dough also improves overall digestibility of the final loaf, including slower and more sustained absorption of nutrients.

The extended rising time also allows for better availability of minerals, such as magnesium, iron, copper, and zinc. Otherwise bound by phytic acid, a substance found in the bran layers of whole grains, these minerals are released when phytic acid is broken down as the dough ferments. Although the fermentation process for yeasted bread can also help break down some of the phytic acid, the longer the fermentation time as required with naturally leavened breads, the more fully the minerals can be liberated and made available to the body.

Baking yeast is also often included as an ingredient in sourdough breads purchased from a bakery. Even though baking yeast is not necessary to make sourdough, some bakers add a small amount to reduce rising time, lighten the texture of the bread, and create more consistent flavor results. However, since baking yeast grows best in neutral or alkaline dough, the natural bacteria, which require a more acidic environment, are not given the full opportunity to do their work within the bread dough, reducing some complexity of flavor. Shelf life will also be affected. Since the acidic conditions in the dough help hinder mold growth and staling, yeast-assisted sourdough bread won't last as long.

Baking Yeast

Modern baking of yeast-leavened breads has its roots in antiquity. Around 300 BCE, Egyptian bakers made bread by combining the yeasty froth from beer with flour and water and allowing the dough to ferment. Even through the nineteenth century, breweries were the source for packaged cakes of yeast made from starch, water, and the yeast skimmed off the top of their beer-brewing vats. Modern-day yeast is derived from a pure culture of a specific strain of yeast (*Saccharomyces cerevisiae*, meaning "brewer's sugar fungus") that is grown in large fermentation vessels and fed with molasses supplemented with nitrogen, phosphate, vitamins, and minerals. The yeast broth is then concentrated in a centrifuge to create a cream yeast, and from there it is made into three types of baking yeast: cake yeast, active dry yeast, and instant yeast. They differ primarily in duration of shelf life and ease of use, and choosing between them is mostly a matter of personal preference. They can easily be substituted for one another as follows: 0.6 ounce cake yeast = 0.25 ounce (2¼ teaspoons) active dry yeast = 2 teaspoons instant yeast.

In bread machines, both cake yeast and active dry yeast can be used in regular cycles, but not in cycles of less than an hour. Instant yeast can be used in cycles of any length. Yeast specially labeled for use in bread machines is essentially instant yeast with some ascorbic acid added to help the dough stretch easily and enhance volume and structure in the final loaf. Nutritional yeast and brewer's yeast cannot be substituted for baker's yeast. Used for their nutritional value rather than for leavening, both are inactivated forms of yeast.

Cake yeast, also known as compressed yeast, is made by filtering cream yeast to remove water and further concentrate the yeast. Used by many commercial bakers, cake yeast is sold for home use in the form of small squares wrapped in foil. Since it is fresh and not dried, cake yeast is ready to use without having to doing anything extra to activate the yeast cells beyond dissolving it in warm liquid (90°F to 95°F) before baking. On the other hand, it is more perishable, requiring constant refrigeration. It must be used within ten to fourteen days, or by the date indicated on the package. It can also be frozen for up to three months.

Active dry yeast was developed during World War II to provide a low-moisture product with a longer shelf life. Going a step beyond cake yeast, active dry yeast is dried at controlled temperatures to further reduce its moisture content, making it less perishable than cake yeast. Although it need not be refrigerated, it will keep longer if stored at cool temperatures in an airtight container: three months in the refrigerator or up to six months in the freezer. To give the yeast a good jump-start, it must be dissolved in lukewarm water (105°F to 115°F) before use, a process known as proofing.

Instant yeast, sometimes referred to as rapid-rise yeast, is a special strain of yeast developed in the late 1960s, and it's also processed with an improved drying method. Not only does it have more viable yeast cells than active dry yeast, but it can also be added directly to flour without first being proofed in water. However, do avoid combining it with cold liquids and even cold dry ingredients. Another advantage of instant yeast is its long shelf life—one to two years—thanks in part to its protective vacuum packaging. Still, once the package is opened, any unused instant yeast should be refrigerated and used within one week or frozen for up to three months.

Chemical Leavening Agents

Baking soda, ammonium carbonate, ammonium bicarbonate, and baking powder are all chemical leavening agents. Although the word *chemical* may sound disconcerting, it merely describes the process that takes place when a leavening agent is mixed with wet ingredients and reacts to create gas, typically carbon dioxide. The bubbles of gas are trapped in the dough or batter, and during baking they expand, causing the dough to rise. The optimum reaction and rise depends on a proper proportion of acidic to alkaline ingredients.

Baking soda (sodium bicarbonate) is the most common chemical leavening agent. Being an alkaline substance, it is the only chemical leavening agent needed when the batter includes acidic ingredients such as sour milk, buttermilk, sour cream, yogurt, vinegar, honey, barley malt, molasses, rice syrup, lemon juice, or fruit juice.

Baking powder is a combination of an alkali (baking soda) and one or two acids (such as cream of tartar, calcium phosphate, or sodium aluminum sulfate), along with an inert filler (such as cornstarch or calcium carbonate), which serves as a buffer to prevent the alkali and acid substances from reacting with one another during storage. Since baking powder is a properly proportioned blend of alkaline and acidic ingredients, baking powder can be used in recipes that don't contain acidic ingredients.

Originally, baking powder was single-acting, meaning it reacted as soon as it was moistened—more often than not before the pan even made it into the oven. These days, most baking powder is double-acting, reacting twice to give off carbon dioxide—first when moistened during mixing, and then a second time when heated. Beyond that, the primary distinction between types of baking powder is whether they contain aluminum compounds.

Products that contain sodium aluminum sulfate as an acid release most of the carbon dioxide gas when the product is heated, not just moistened, making it less critical to get baked goods into the oven as quickly as possible. However, if too much is used it can create a bitter aftertaste. On the other hand, baking powders that contain monocalcium phosphate or cream of tartar react very quickly, with most of the reaction happening when the baking powder is moistened.

Although there are some differences in how the products may work, the bigger issue has been whether using products with aluminum compounds is linked in some way to Alzheimer's disease. Whether this disease or others can be caused by accumulation of aluminum remains controversial. Until the verdict is in, nonaluminum baking powder remains a good option, especially if you get baked goods into the oven quickly.

Low-sodium baking powders are made with potassium bicarbonate instead of sodium bicarbonate (baking soda) to reduce the amount of sodium in baked goods. For best results, use one and a half to two times more low-sodium baking powder than the amount of regular baking powder called for. Another way to reduce sodium, unless your doctor recommends against it, is to use regular baking powder but cut back on the amount of salt in the recipe.

Exploring Breads

Bagels

Bagels can be dense and chewy when poached in a traditional kettle-boiled process, or, if made in steam-injected rack ovens, soft and doughy. No matter which type of bagel one chooses, the list of ingredients should be simple—flour, fresh yeast, water, barley malt syrup, and salt. And, true to their reputation for being low in fat, no authentic bagel should ever contain oil.

Bialy (bee-AH-lee)

Named after a town in Poland, the bialy is a flat, round, savory roll with curved edges, a flour-dusted crust, and an indentation in the middle that is filled with a paste of sautéed chopped onions. With a very short shelf life of only about six hours, these chewy, dense rolls are best eaten when warm and spread with cream cheese or butter, either on the top or the bottom of the roll. While eating a bialy fresh is definitely better, they can be frozen and then warmed right before eating.

Bolillo (bow-LEE-yoh)

Introduced by the French to Mexico in the nineteenth century, these torpedo-shaped rolls have a crusty exterior and a soft interior. They are typically eaten plain at breakfast, used for sandwiches, or served with entrées.

Brioche (BREE-ohsh)

A light, but rich, somewhat sweet-tasting bread made from a dough enriched with butter and eggs, brioche is traditionally shaped into a fluted round with a small cap. The dough can also be baked in loaf pans and sliced (great for making French toast) or formed into small rolls.

Challah (HAH-lah)

Traditionally used as a Sabbath and special bread for Jewish holidays, challah is sweet, rich, and light. Its golden color is a result of the many eggs used when making the bread. Most often sold as braided, it is customary to break off knobs of the bread while at the table rather than preslicing. Try leftover challah for exceptional toast and French toast.

Ciabatta (chah-BAH-tah)

With some imagination, one can envision why this fairly flat, relatively shapeless bread was called *ciabatta*, the Italian word for "slipper." The bread's crunchy, crisp crust looks dusted with flour as a result of the additional flour needed to shape the very moist dough characteristic for ciabatta and other rustic breads. The interior crumb is moist, nutty tasting, and shiny, with a wide-open honeycomb of holes and tunnels. Ciabatta is best when consumed within a few hours of baking. It is unparalleled for dipping into olive oil or mopping up savory sauces.

Croissants (krwah-SAHN)

The French translation for the word "crescent," croissants originally developed as a pastry to honor the defeat of the Turkish army by the Austrians in the seventeenth century. By shaping the pastry in the form of a crescent as featured on the Turkish flag, the Austrians were able to symbolically relive "consuming" their enemy. Although now made by folding layers of buttery yeasted dough, this rich, flaky roll retains the original crescent shape. Plain or filled, croissants are still most commonly and traditionally served at breakfast.

Crumpet (KRUM-pit)

Similar in size and shape to an English muffin, crumpets are also baked on a griddle. What's different is that they are toasted whole and spread with butter or clotted cream, rather than split. The yeast makes them light and spongy and creates the characteristic little holes on the top.

English Muffin

Like a crumpet, the English muffin is a yeasted muffin that is baked on a griddle. The secret to enjoying an English muffin is to toast it after splitting it in half with a fork—not a knife—in order to create the characteristic nooks and crannies that trap and hold butter and jam. Good-quality English muffins contain no dough conditioners or preservatives. Spouted grain varieties enhance flavor and nutrition.

Focaccia (fa-KAH-chee-a)

An Italian flatbread similar to a thick pizza crust, focaccia is baked in sheet pans from a moist dough that creates a shiny, moist interior crumb. Before the proofing stage, the dough is lightly poked to dimple the surface with indentations and then brushed with olive oil and herbs, or with other toppings such as olives, mushrooms, or sun-dried tomatoes. Cheeses and salt may also be used before baking.

Fougasse (foo-GOSS)

A traditional, leavened flatbread from Provence, fougasse is shaped to resemble a ladder or tree, either baked plan or topped with fresh herbs, nuts, or cheese. Its interior crumb is moist, dense, and chewy but, because of its shape, which provides a higher percentage of exterior, fougasse is most known as a crust lover's delight. No need for a knife to cut fougasse. Its shape also makes it very easy to tear apart.

Grissini (gruh-SEE-nee)

Grissini are thin, crisp breadsticks thought to have been created in the seventeenth century in Turin. *Stirato* (straight) grissini are crisp and delicate in flavor. In contrast, rubata (hand rolled) grissini are thicker, less crunchy, more *breadlike* in flavor, and made with less yeast. Look for grissini made with basic ingredients such as flour, water, salt, yeast, and olive oil.

Kaiser Roll (KI-zur)

Also known as "Vienna roll" or hard roll, a Kaiser roll is a large round roll with a thin, hard crust and a soft, light interior. It is served at breakfast or used for sandwiches. It is also distinguished by the star pattern on the top.

Lavosh, also Lahvosh (LAH-vohsh)

Also known as Armenian cracker bread, lavosh is a traditional thin, large, round, pliable bread. It is often used for creating aram sandwiches, first softening the cracker bread by sprinkling it with water and letting it set for 5 minutes. Then it is spread with a filling and tightly rolled in plastic wrap to create the shape and help keep the bread pliable. As lavosh naturally dries out and becomes brittle quickly, aram sandwiches should be served and eaten soon after they are removed from the plastic wrap. When soft, lavosh can also be torn into smaller pieces to scoop dips or other foods or, when hard and dried, used as you would any cracker.

Naan (nahn)

A round, flat, soft bread native to India, naan is made from wheat and leavened with natural airborne yeasts or from commercial baking yeast. Some recipes also use yogurt or milk to increase the volume and produce a soft texture. After the dough is allowed to rise for a few hours, it is baked briefly on the sides of a hot vertical clay oven called a tandoor in which temperatures exceed 700°F. As a result, the bread will slightly expand and become brown and blistered. Naan is served hot, sometimes brushed with ghee or butter, as an accompaniment to meals, and to scoop up and roll around other foods.

Pagnotta (pahg-NAHT-ah)

Originally hailing from central Italy, pagnotta is a round, rustic Italian bread crusty on the outside with an open crumb on the inside. A simple loaf, it is great as an accompaniment to any meal.

Pain au Levain (PAN ah la-VAIN)

More a class of breads than a specific kind, pain au levain refers to bread that is naturally leavened with sourdough. It is often baked in a boule (round) or bâtard shape. Known for its thick crust, large open holes in the interior crumb, and hearty, mildly sour flavor, pain au levain will last up to a week.

Pain de Campagne (PAN deh cahm-PAHYN)

A country-style French bread, pain de campagne can be found in many shapes; most typically it is shaped into a large, round loaf. While its crust is chewy, thick, and dark in color, the interior crumb is airy and light. The flavor is full-bodied but slightly acidic from the sourdough starter or yeasted sponge that provides the base for lengthy leavening. As a rustic version of pain au levain, pain de campagne is often made with part whole wheat flour and sometimes rye flour.

Pain Paysan (PAN PI-zan)

Also known as peasant bread, pain paysan is a dark, rustic French bread made from a blend of wheat and rye. It is great for savory sandwiches or breakfast toast.

Panettone (pah-neht-TOH-nay)

Traditionally served at Christmas and at special celebrations, panettone is a sweet, cylindrical Italian bread made with candied citrus peel and raisins. Originating in Milan, Italy, and now symbolic of the city, panettone has a very light, airy texture and golden color, thanks to the addition of eggs and butter. It is at its lightest and best when made with the time-honored, although more time-consuming, method of using either Italian biga pre-ferment or natural wild yeast sourdough as leavening. Panettone is traditionally served at breakfast or brunch, cut into vertical slices.

Panini (pah-NEE-nee)

Translated from Italian, the word *panino* means "roll" or "a sandwich." When referred to as the Italian grilled sandwich by the same name, panini are made by splitting the roll in half lengthwise, filling it with cheeses, vegetables, meats, olives, etc., and grilling it, weighted down in a skillet or in a panini press. The high temperature of a panini press makes the crust crisp and golden brown.

Pita Bread (PEE-tah)

Also known as pocket bread, pita is a yeast-leavened, round, flatbread. Thought to have originated in Greece, it is considered a traditional bread served in Middle Eastern and Mediterranean cuisine. Whole wheat pita is significantly more flavorful and better complements the usual pita stuffings than white flour versions do. When pita is cut in half vertically, a handy pocket is revealed, ready to be stuffed with fillings such as hummus, baba ghanouj, tabouli, falafel, or any other sandwich filling or salad. The pocket is formed from the rapid conversion of water into steam, which makes the flat pita rounds puff up, a result of baking the bread at 500°F. Although the pita deflates after coming out of the oven, the upper and lower layers remain separated.

Pretzels

There are many colorful stories about how and where pretzels originated and the reasons for its characteristic twisted shape, often with a knot in the middle. The hard, crispy version, along with the name *pretzel*, is thought to be an Americanized adaptation. Like good bread, high-quality pretzels are made with simple ingredients: whole wheat or unbleached wheat flour, water, yeast or sourdough culture, and salt. Pretzels' brown glazed appearance and unique flavor can be attributed to the use of sodium hydroxide (caustic soda) as a processing aid. Pretzels get either a short bake for a soft pretzel or a long, slow bake to yield a dry, crisp product.

Pugliese (POOL-yee-ay-say)

This bread is named after the area in which it originated—Italy's Puglia region, located in the "heel" of the Italian boot shape of the country. Using bread dough with a high water content, as developed for ciabatta, Pugliese has a moist interior crumb along with the characteristic holes, although smaller. Authentic Pugliese bread is made either partially or entirely from finely milled golden durum flour (similar but finer than semolina flour), which accounts for its golden color, delicious nutty flavor, and delicate crust. Its overall shape is typically round. Eat with olive oil, top with spreads, or serve it to accompany any meal.

Schiacciata (sky-ach-CHA-ta)

Also known as Tuscan flatbread, schiacciata (which means "flattened" in Italian) is a thin round or rectangular bread that is typically baked with olive oil along with other simple toppings. Considered the typical focaccia of the Tuscan region, it has the customary dimpled surface and, like focaccia served anywhere, is used as a snack or part of a meal. The texture can be crackerlike to somewhat soft. Sweet schiacciata is made from the addition of sugar to the schiacciata dough.

Semolina Bread

Made with finely ground semolina flour, typically used for making pasta, and from refined hard durum wheat, semolina bread retains the grain's pale yellow color and captures its sweet and nutty flavor. Semolina breads will vary in the percentage of semolina flour within the recipe—the more semolina, the more flavorful the bread, but also more tricky for the baker to achieve. Exhibiting a delicate crust, semolina bread's crumb is uniquely fine and tender. Many semolina breads also have their crust coated with sesame seeds to enhance the grain's exceptional nutty flavor. Use for great sandwiches and toast or as an accompaniment to a meal.

Beyond Wheat

Breads can be further distinguished from one another by the special flavor and textural characteristics found in specific types of bread, the primary kind of flour used to make the bread, its shape, and where it originates.

Bread is most commonly baked using wheat-based flour, a factor of its high gluten content that, in comparison with other kinds of flour, can most easily produce bread that rises well, along with the specific variety of crumb, from soft to chewy, that is intended.

However, exceptional bread made with flour beyond common varieties of wheat provides an array of textures, flavor, and color.

■ GLUTEN-FREE BREADS

Gluten-free breads are made with one or a combination of flours from gluten-free grains, including brown rice flour, white rice flour, cornmeal, potato starch, sorghum flour, quinoa flour, garbanzo flour, fava bean flour, millet flour, amaranth flour, and tapioca flour.

Gums such as xanthan gum and guar gum are added to create the elasticity needed within bread dough. Emulsifiers are added to stabilize the gas bubbles in order to help make bread from nongluten flour look similar to typical bread. Some gluten-free breads are also made with nonfat dry milk and eggs to increase the protein content of the bread to counter heavy, gritty, or crumbly textures that could otherwise result from using nongluten flour, creating a more light and tender crumb that sticks together. Often gluten-free breads are baked with a fair amount of sweetener as a way to provide more flavor to either enhance an otherwise bland taste or to mask bitterness from

specific gluten-free flours that may be used. Toasting significantly improves the flavor and freshens up the texture of any gluten-free bread.

(For more information on gluten-free baking, see the Flour chapter.)

Injera Bread (in-JER-ah)

Injera is a traditional Ethiopian flatbread with a unique feature—it is used both as an eating utensil to scoop up thick meat or vegetable stews as well as a lining for the tray on which the stews are served. This spongy, slightly sour-tasting flatbread is made from teff flour, a grain commonly grown in Ethiopia, although wheat flour has become a more common addition in restaurants and households outside the country. The leavening agent comes from the wild yeast that lives on the grain itself. After the teff is ground into flour and made into a batter, it is allowed to ferment for a couple days, which accounts for its tangy flavor, to allow the yeast to become active. The batter is then cooked on a large flat skillet like a crepe, where it becomes light and airy as it rises slightly.

Kamut Bread (kuh-MOOT)

The name Kamut is a registered trademark used for products made a with variety of durum wheat said to have originated in Egypt. To protect the quality and integrity of the grain, bread labeled as Kamut bread must contain 100% Kamut brand flour or grain. If at least 50% but less than 100% Kamut brand grain is used, it can be called bread with Kamut grain. Breads made with Kamut brand grain will have a rich, buttery, sweet flavor and an amber color. Because the gluten in Kamut is weaker than that found in modern-day wheat, brands of Kamut breads can vary in lightness of the crumb depending on the skillfulness and expertise of the particular bakery. Just switch to another brand if you end up with one that is dense and heavy.

Pumpernickel Bread

Thinly sliced whole grain pumpernickel bread exported from Germany in shelf-stable packaging is a must-try. Its unique packaging keeps the bread fresh, without preservatives, for at least six months unopened, making it a great choice for traveling or for an emergency snack stash at work. Once opened, any remaining bread should be wrapped, refrigerated, and used within four days. Dense, richly flavored, and moist, all varieties are based on whole grain rye and slowly baked in steam-heated ovens before being vacuum-packed. These hearty, deceptively filling breads are perfect, toasted or untoasted, topped with cheese, butter, meats, nut butters, sandwich spreads, or sweet toppings. They are very high in fiber, too.

Rice Bread

Since rice flour has no gluten, it is a common base for gluten-free breads. Its typical gritty texture is modified by the addition of gums and starches, other gluten-free flours that have complementary characteristics, and sometimes milk or eggs to create a softer crumb. However, not all rice bread is gluten free; some are wheat-based, with cooked brown rice added for moisture, depth of flavor, and softer texture.

Rye Bread

Much of the rye bread sold in bakeries and grocery stores is considered light rye sandwich-style bread, a mild tasting, yeast-leavened loaf made primarily from wheat flour to take advantage of wheat's gluten to help make the bread rise higher. Rye flour, then, is used primarily for flavor, with varying proportions depending on the desired result. New York–style rye bread, also known as Jewish rye bread, is made by combining rye and wheat flours and is leavened with a sour rye starter and baking yeast. The dough ferments slowly to develop a full, slightly tangy flavor; it is baked to have a chewy caraway-seeded crust, and a soft interior texture. European-style 100% rye bread is made simply with organic rye flour, rye sourdough culture, water, and salt; using sourdough as the leavening agent is the key. The result is a very flavorful, slightly sour rye bread, not nearly as dense as a true, thinly sliced pumpernickel, which is perfect for sandwiches or at breakfast with either sweet or savory toppings. Although sometimes available fresh, it is also sold frozen or refrigerated.

Rye Crispbread

True to its name, rye crispbread is a brittle flatbread based on varieties originally created in Sweden more than a thousand years ago as a result of the quest for a type of bread that could be transported and stored for a long time. There are three basic types of rye crispbread, based on its method of production: a yeasted version, a sourdough rye crisp commonly produced in Finland and Germany, and a version made without yeast or sourdough using a process called the cold bread method, which relies on the incorporation of air into cooled dough. Crispbread made using simple recipes free of hydrogenated oils or added emulsifiers (such as monoglycerides and diglycerides) allow the delicious natural flavors of the grains to prevail; they also have a longer shelf life.

Spelt Bread

Spelt is derived from an ancient and distant cousin of modern wheat, making the texture and grain similar to that of wheat-based breads. Special strains of spelt that have been developed throughout the years for food consumption, including improved baking characteristics, although the grain has retained much of its original distinctive attributes, still making it unique from typical wheat flour in many ways. In terms of flavor, spelt is more nutty and sweet in comparison to wheat. The gluten in spelt is also different from that in wheat, specifically the gliadin protein component of the gluten. Not only does it mean that a few minor modifications in technique will be required when making bread, but it also means that the bread may be more digestible for those sensitive to gluten. For the best-tasting spelt bread with the lightest crumb, look for spelt bread that is naturally leavened with sourdough.

Sprouted Grain Breads

Sprouted grains are created from a variety of grains, and each is sprouted no longer than the length of the particular grain itself. During the sprouting process some of the grain's starch is broken down into the simple sugar maltose. Not only does this allow the bread to showcase the naturally sweet flavors of the grain, but it also provides great fuel for the leavening agents (sourdough or baking yeast) to help boost the bread to rise. Sprouting also allows for the absorption of minerals that would otherwise be trapped within the grain by breaking down phytic acid found in the bran layer of the grain. Although baking the bread destroys some of the phytic acid, as does fermentation during the bread making process (the longer the better), using sprouted grain greatly enhances the availability of the minerals. Overall, the sprouting process adds to the nutritional value and digestibility of the bread. Just how much depends on the percentage of sprouts used to make the breads.

How to Store Bread

For best flavor and texture, bread should be stored at room temperature or frozen.

Cold refrigerated air accelerates bread going stale. Storing bread in plastic bags inside the refrigerator or at room temperature is even worse. Moisture becomes trapped, encouraging mold growth and a soggy crust.

Instead, store bread in a bread box, paper sack, specially made perforated cellophane bread bag, or even a clean dishtowel. Each allows the bread to breathe, helping maintain good texture, crisp crust, and maximum flavor. Although the crust may become more chewy as the days progress, inside the bread will remain moist.

The only exceptions to this rule are quick breads such as tortillas, chapatis, and Essene bread. Unless refrigerated, they begin to mold within a day or two.

Because of their natural acidic character, sourdough breads last much longer at room temperature than yeasted breads, often tasting even better a couple days after the bread was baked.

Lean crusty breads such as French breads dry out within a day but, like all breads, can be revived by cutting into pieces and steaming in a vegetable steamer for 3 minutes. To reheat bread in the oven, sprinkle bread with water, wrap in foil, and bake 10 to 15 minutes at 350°F. Tortilla warmers give even better results.

If you can't finish the loaf within three days (five days for sourdough breads), slice the rest, double-wrap it in a plastic or foil, and pop it in the freezer. Freezing slows the staling process, trapping water inside the bread's cells. For best flavor, use within three months. Individual slices will thaw in about 10 minutes. Frozen bread can also be thawed in the oven in about 20 minutes at 350°F wrapped in foil. Toasting is obviously another way to revive bread that has been frozen.

Crispbreads such as crackers, pretzels, rice cakes, and tortilla chips should be stored tightly sealed in a dry environment. To rejuvenate their crispness, bake them in a 300°F oven for about 5 minutes. Cool before eating or repackaging.

Pasta and Noodles

With its rainbow of colors and variety of shapes and textures, pasta provides an option to fit any whim and enhance any meal, whether it's topped with a sauce, tossed into soup, or served on the side. Though there are a few exceptions, most varieties fit into two main categories—Italian-inspired pastas and Asian noodles—and many are available both fresh and dried. Within these broad groupings, they can be further distinguished by type of flour used, shape, and whether they have added ingredients for color and flavor. No matter which kind you choose, all pasta is quick and easy to cook, providing the perfect base for a meal in minutes.

A Healthy Choice

Cooked just to al dente, pasta is metabolized slowly, thanks to its unique combination of starches and proteins, and as a result, it helps maintain steady blood sugar levels. Among the foods rich in complex carbohydrates, it's one of the most easily digested, explaining why it's often a favorite food of athletes; it's one of the most nutritious ways to help restore depleted muscle glycogen.

Although most people assume pasta is only made from wheat, that's far from the case. Until recently, the predominant grain grown in a region often dictated what the local pasta was made from and how it was made. Over the millennia, pasta has been made from everything from rice to buckwheat, including many now-uncommon varieties of wheat. This was strikingly illustrated in 2005, when archaeologists found the oldest recognizable evidence of pasta to date, a four-thousand-year-old container of Chinese noodles made from millet. These days, the selection of pasta has expanded to include versions made from corn, quinoa, and even bean flour. Not only do these serve to accommodate wheat-free and gluten-free diets, they also provide even more variety in flavor, texture, and nutrition for anyone who loves pasta. And for visual interest, various coloring agents

The Shape of Things

Ever wonder why the shapes of pasta are so varied? Aesthetics has something to do with it, but the primary reason is that the different shapes have different properties in terms of retaining heat, absorbing liquids, and holding sauces.

Shape	Example	How to Use
Strands: long cylinders with or without a hollow center	angel hair (capelli d'angelo), bucatini, capellini, cellophane noodles, soba, somen, spaghetti, vermicelli	Italian varieties: Best with finely grated cheese and smooth, not-too-chunky tomato-based sauces that are intended to coat or cling to the pasta. Also good for tossing with olive oil or butter and seasonings. Asian noodles: Use in soups, salads, and side dishes, or in stir-fries with a sauce, dressing, or light broth.
Ribbons: flat strips	fettuccine, kluski, lasagna, lasagnette, linguine, mafalda, pappardelle, rice sticks, tagliatelle, trenette, udon	Italian varieties: Best with pesto, creamy or béchamel sauces, or rich ragout-type sauces. Dried ribbon pasta can stand up to thicker, heavier sauces while fresh versions call for lighter toppings. Asian varieties: Use like Asian noodles.
Tubular: hollow shapes	cannelloni, elbow macaroni, maccheroni, manicotti, mostaccioli, penne, penne rigate, rigatoni, trenette, trenne, ziti	Best with chunky vegetable and meat sauces, or thick cheese sauces that will cling to the pasta and be trapped in the bends and crevices. Match smaller shapes with sauces with more finely chopped ingredients. Also a good choice for casseroles and pasta salads. Larger versions can be stuffed and baked.
Novelty shapes	conchiglie (shells), farfalle (bowties), fusilli, gnocchi, orechiette, radiatore, rotelle, rotini, ruote	Use like tubular pasta.
Tiny soup shapes	alfabeto, ditali, fregola, orzo, stelline (stars), wonton noodles	Use sparingly in soups and stews to thicken and contribute texture, using larger shapes in thick soups and smaller shapes in broth-based soups.
Stuffed fresh pasta	cappelletti, mezzaluna, ravioli, ravioloni, tortellini, tortelloni	Traditionally, the shape of a given stuffed pasta was based on the filling, but these days anything goes!

may be added, from pureed vegetables, herbs, and spices to squid ink, creating striking green, golden, red, and even black pastas.

For optimum nutrition, choose whole grain pasta or pasta made from a combination of sprouted whole grains and beans. Since whole grain pasta contains all the nutrients and fiber in the whole grain, it needs no enrichment, as most of the semolina pasta sold in the United States does. Remember, enrichment only replaces five of the nutrients depleted during refinement of the flour, even though levels of up to thirty nutrients are significantly diminished. When it comes to taste and texture, whole grain pasta is also the most flavorful and hearty, commanding more of an equal footing in the meal rather than the subtle presence of pasta made from refined grains.

The next best choice in terms of nutrition is pasta made from a blend of whole grain flour and refined flour (usually wheat). Although it has less fiber and fewer vitamins and minerals than 100% whole grain varieties, it offers a good compromise, having a lighter texture while still containing more of the flavor and nutrients of the whole grain. A blended flour base also allows pastas to be made using grains (such as quinoa) and beans (such as pinto beans and soybeans) that couldn't be made into pasta on their own.

All of that said, fresh or dried pasta made from refined flour still has its place in good, wholesome meals, and it can be an appropriate choice depending on the recipe. To help ensure you get enough of the fiber, vitamins, minerals, and phytonutrients whole grains provide, work toward having at least 50% of the pasta and grains you eat be in whole grain form.

Exploring Pasta and Noodles

Fresh Pasta and Noodles

Like dried pasta, fresh pasta comes in many shapes, but the most common are ribbon shapes rolled out by hand or in a pasta machine. Unique shapes formed by hand are also available, often as specialties of a given region or pasta producer. Stuffed pastas are made by cutting squares or other shapes from sheets of pasta and encasing a vegetable, cheese, or meat filling seasoned with a variety of herbs and spices. With its wide range of imaginative and inspired flavors, colors, and fillings, fresh, artisanal pasta can be savored with all the senses.

At its best, fresh pasta is tender, delicate, and flavorful, needing only a light sauce or broth as accompaniment. Most familiar are Italian-inspired fresh pastas made from wheat. Since fresh pasta made with 100% semolina as used in good-quality, store-bought fresh pasta would be too difficult to roll out by hand or in many home pasta machines, homemade versions usually use unbleached all-purpose flour and eggs, sometimes with semolina flour added to provide more strength to the dough. The use of eggs makes for dough that is softer, more elastic, and easier to handle. Some of fresh pasta's amber color and subtle flavor can be attributed to the eggs, which also provide extra nutrients.

A wide variety of freshly made Asian noodles are also available, including Chinese wheat noodles made with or without egg, Southeast Asian rice noodles, and Japanese buckwheat soba and wheat-based udon. Fresh Asian noodles made with wheat use soft wheat flour, so they cook up softer than fresh pasta made with any amount of sturdy semolina. Most soba is also made with some wheat flour to increase strength and elasticity, making it more resilient during cooking.

When handmade with attention to detail and cooked the day it is prepared, fresh pasta is well worth seeking out. Think of gnocchi that melts in your mouth, chilled soba served with the simplest of dipping sauces to further spotlight its exceptional flavor, and heavenly fettuccine so soft and flavorful it takes your breath away. Outside of making it fresh at home, to find such high-caliber fresh pasta you'll likely need to go to a specialty market that makes its own pasta daily or to a small restaurant devoted to the craft of producing fresh handmade pasta.

Because of its high moisture content, fresh pasta is very perishable. To sell it beyond its usual two-day shelf life, many manufacturers steam pasteurize the pasta and pack it on trays enveloped with plastic barrier films to minimize spoilage. Many manufacturers further treat their fresh pasta using a packaging process in which oxygen present within the package is displaced by a high concentration of carbon dioxide, which helps control growth of microorganisms. The use of specialized oxygen-scavenging packaging materials can further extend shelf life. Depending on the product and the specific technology used to treat and pack the pasta after manufacture, the shelf life of fresh pasta can be extended to as much as 120 days. Although pasta treated as such can be labeled as "all natural" and may contain no preservatives or additives, it stretches the definition of the term "fresh." Unfortunately, flavor and texture can be adversely affected in the process, too, making the final result thick, heavy, and rubbery—and an unpleasant eating experience—in which case dried pasta is a better option.

Alternatively, all types of fresh pasta can be purchased frozen, which turns out to be the best way to extend the shelf life of fresh pasta. Unlike pasteurization, the flash-freezing can preserve the flavor and texture of fresh pasta. Another advantage is that frozen pastas generally don't have added preservatives, such as sorbic acid and potassium sorbate, or stabilizers, which may be added to the fillings of refrigerated stuffed pastas.

How to Cook Fresh Pasta

Plan on cooking about 4 ounces of fresh pasta for a 1-cup cooked serving. Add the pasta to a generous amount of salted boiling water, and cook for the amount of time recommended on the package. In general, fresh unstuffed pasta cooks within 3 minutes, whereas it can take up to 5 minutes until the edges of stuffed pastas are al dente. Uncooked fresh pasta should be refrigerated and used within three days or by the date indicated on the package. Stored in an airtight container, leftover cooked fresh pasta can be stored in the refrigerator for up to three days or in the freezer for up to a month.

Fresh pasta that has been frozen should be cooked without thawing in order to retain its integrity and texture. This adds a couple of minutes to the cooking time than as required for fresh pasta.

Italian-Style Dried Pasta

The best wheat-based dried pastas are made from durum wheat. High in gluten, durum flour makes sturdy dough that enables pasta to both stretch and expand without disintegrating during cooking. (There are three varieties of durum flour: whole durum flour, refined durum flour, and semolina.) Pasta made with durum wheat is a light amber color, and its cooking water should look fairly clear, not starchy.

Manufacturing Durum Wheat Pasta

Using good-quality flour is not enough to make great pasta. It also takes a great deal of skill and the right type of equipment. Because durum flour is so difficult to knead into a smooth, elastic dough, most of the manufacturing processes are done by machine rather than by hand. The dough is generally rolled into sheets, which are then cut into strands or shaped mechanically (extruded) by being forced through dies, metal molds designed to produce various shapes, sizes, and patterns.

The speed at which the dough is squeezed through the die is very important. If processed too fast, as is often the case in factories geared toward efficiency rather than quality, the excess heat affects the wheat and has negative impacts on flavor, quality, and nutrient levels. Even the composition of the die makes a difference. The best shaped pastas are extruded through bronze dies that produce pasta with a rough, porous surface, which will better capture sauces. In contrast, pastas with a smooth, polished look are extruded through Teflon dies. Although Teflon is a longer lasting material and also allows dough to flow more easily through the die, Teflon's effect on pasta is similar to what it does to pans: sauces don't tend to stick.

Dried ribbon pastas, such as fettuccine, linguine, lasagna, and egg noodles, are more tender and flavorful if made from dough that is rolled and cut (laminated) rather than extruded. In the lamination process, once the dough is mixed and kneaded it goes through a series of rollers until it reaches the appropriate thickness. The long, continuous sheets are then cut as they pass through a series of knives. Although it is a more time-consuming and intricate process, the extra effort makes for firmer pasta with better texture and taste.

Drying time and temperature also affect flavor. Pasta dries from the inside out. If dried too fast, it will become brittle; if dried too slowly, it could sour. At home, drying is accomplished by hanging fresh pasta on special drying racks (sometimes even on the backs of kitchen chairs!) for several hours, until it's very dry. The goal is to lower the moisture content, which is initially about 60%, down to 12.5%, so that it can be stored for a long time under normal conditions. The best commercial dried pasta are dried at low temperatures with circulating air. Drying time may be as long as fifty hours, depending on the type of pasta.

Beyond Durum Wheat

These days, Italian-style pastas are made from a wide range of ingredients beyond durum wheat. There are gluten-free options based on rice, corn, or bean flour; pastas made from heritage forms of wheat, including Kamut, spelt, and farro; and selections made from a combination of sprouted grains and beans. And sometimes the flavor and nutrition of durum wheat pastas are enhanced by the addition of unconventional flours, such as quinoa flour and Jerusalem artichoke flour.

Pasta made from durum wheat is often considered to be superior because of its texture and ability to cook al dente, whereas many alternative pastas tend to be stickier or more fragile. However, pastas made from other types of flour have improved significantly over the years. Better manufacturing techniques and refinement of cooking methods allow some of these pastas to rival durum-based varieties. Without gluten to bind them, many gluten-free pastas are made by cooking the starch before it is extruded; this allows the starch structure to hold the pasta together.

Even if you aren't on a gluten-free or wheat-restricted diet, it's worthwhile to explore the new generation of alternative pastas. They provide interesting variety in terms of appearance, taste, and texture. Plus, eating a wider variety of grains and grain products provides more well-rounded nutrition.

■ BEAN PASTA

Bean pastas may seem like the most unconventional alternative pasta, but they've been made in Asia for centuries in the form of cellophane noodles. Nutritionally, the Italian-style bean pastas have a lot going for them. The beneficial fiber, protein, iron, magnesium, zinc, and folate in beans creates a product with a better nutritional profile than that of other pastas. Some are made entirely from bean flour, whereas others use a blend of bean flour with other flours.

■ CORN PASTA

Corn pasta is available in several forms and shapes, including spaghetti, rotini, and elbows. Made from a blend of refined corn flours, it has a rich natural corn flavor that is nicely complemented by cheese and black, pinto, or kidney beans. In addition to plain corn pasta, look for colorful corn pasta made with dried vegetable powders. Corn pasta contains about half the amount of protein and less vitamins and minerals than pasta made from durum wheat. Since corn pasta doesn't have the benefit of gluten to help it keep its shape, it is particularly important to avoid overcooking.

■ JERUSALEM ARTICHOKE PASTA

Jerusalem artichoke pasta is made from a blend of durum wheat flour and flour made from dried Jerusalem artichokes. This root vegetable in the sunflower family looks like a knobby potato and is more typically cooked as a vegetable. In pasta, it contributes a somewhat nutty and sweet flavor, a lighter texture, and a lower level of carbohydrates. Up to 80% of the carbohydrate in Jerusalem artichokes is in the form of inulin, which isn't broken down in the digestive system by the enzymes that normally help digest starch. To the extent that it is digested, bacteria in the colon do the job. As a result, it functions more like fiber and has a stabilizing effect on blood sugar.

■ KAMUT PASTA

Kamut pasta is an exceptionally good whole grain pasta with a golden color and a rich, buttery flavor. Made from Kamut, a trademarked Egyptian variety of durum wheat, it has strong gluten, making it a perfect grain for pasta. There's a variety of Kamut pasta suitable for any recipe, from salads to soups to entrées. Kamut pasta also freezes well, retaining its cooked texture. Nutritionally, it is higher in protein, minerals, and essential fatty acids than are typical wheat-based pastas. And although Kamut is a variety of wheat, it has a different type of glu-

ten than modern hybridized versions, so some people who are sensitive or allergic to wheat may find they can eat Kamut pasta. Still, anyone who is severely allergic to wheat should consult with a medical professional before experimenting with Kamut pasta.

■ QUINOA PASTA

Quinoa pasta is always made by combining quinoa flour with another type of grain flour, such as corn, Kamut, or wheat. Along with adding a unique nutty flavor and lighter texture, quinoa flour also makes the pasta higher in protein and minerals.

■ RICE PASTA

Rice pasta, once heavy-textured and starchy, has improved a lot over the years and now looks and cooks up like traditional wheat-based pastas. Not to be confused with Asian rice noodles, these pastas are gluten-free versions of fettuccine, penne, elbow macaroni, and other Italian-style pastas. One reason they're better these days is because they incorporate parboiled white rice flour, which lends the pasta a drier, less sticky texture. It's made from brown rice that is soaked in warm water, steamed, and dried before it is milled into white rice and then ground into flour, a process that retains more nutrients. Brown rice pasta is also available. It is light brown and has a subtle nutty flavor.

■ RYE PASTA

Rye pasta made entirely from rye flour is dark brown and has a deep, rich flavor reminiscent of pumpernickel bread. It is particularly good with mild-flavored ingredients or as a side dish alongside salmon or cooked beans, especially white beans or garbanzo beans. It's a nutritional dynamo, especially because it's an excellent source of soluble fiber, which provides a sensation of fullness sooner, stabilizes blood sugar levels, and helps decrease absorption of cholesterol. If made from whole grain rye flour, it also contains lignans, which can help reduce the risk of cancer.

■ SPELT PASTA

Spelt pasta, made from a distant relative of modern-day wheat, has a somewhat sweeter, nuttier flavor that is equally wonderful whether it's served with a sauce, in a dish, or on its own. It's available in both whole grain and refined forms, and either can be used in any recipe that calls for wheat pasta. It is higher in protein than traditional pasta and very easy to digest. And because its protein profile is different than that of modern varieties of wheat, many people who are sensitive or allergic to wheat find they can tolerate spelt fairly well. Still, anyone who is severely allergic to wheat should consult with a medical professional before experimenting with spelt pasta.

■ SPROUTED GRAIN PASTA

Sprouted grain pasta is usually made from a combination of grains and beans that are sprouted then dried and ground into flour. It is higher in protein than most pastas, and the sprouting process makes the minerals more easily absorbed. These pastas are also high in fiber, making them very filling. The conversion of some of the grains' starch into maltose during the sprouting process also gives the pasta a sweeter taste and a darker color. To avoid stickiness, sprouted grain pasta must be rinsed before serving. Because their flavors are stronger than those of most pastas, sprouted grain pastas are best used in conjunction with mild-flavored ingredients and dishes.

Dried Asian Noodles

Although rice has long been synonymous with Asian cuisine, noodles have been an equally key component. Used in soups, salads, stir-fries, and braised dishes, noodles have been highly esteemed over the centuries, and these days they're also prized as a convenient and healthy fast food and snack. Asian noodles look somewhat like Italian strand and ribbon pastas, and in most cases the two could be used interchangeably. However, there are some important distinctions between the two, mostly due to the types of flour used to make Asian noodles.

In contrast to the firm Italian pastas made from durum wheat flour, most wheat-based Asian noodles are softer and more porous because they're made with soft wheat, or with hard wheat that contains less gluten. Other Asian noodles are made with rice flour, buckwheat flour, or a variety of vegetable starches, lending them remarkable flavors and textures. As none of these contains gluten, making noodles from them requires different techniques, and many of them are cooked differently, too. For example, many varieties of Asian noodles require presoaking before cooking. Others, including soba, somen, and udon, must be rinsed with cold water after cooking to remove excess starch.

Like Italian-style pastas, Asian noodles come in a wide variety of colors. They run the gamut from translucent to white, green, or brown. Because they're made from a wider variety of grains, they vary in flavor, too. Many have a rich, unique flavor, while others are neutral, allowing them to absorb the flavor of the foods they're cooked with. All of this variety makes exploring the world of Asian noodles an especially fun experience.

■ CHINESE EGG NOODLES

Made from refined hard wheat flour, eggs, and water, the golden yellow strands of Chinese egg noodles come in various round thicknesses or flat widths. Soft, silky fresh Chinese egg noodles are shaped into nests and sold refrigerated; dried, they're packaged in tight, rectangular bundles. While some of their yellow color can be attributed to the egg yolks, most of it is from the action of *kansui*, an alkaline solution made from potassium carbonate or sodium carbonate, on the natural pigments in wheat. *Kansui* also helps improve the elasticity of the noodles and contributes to their characteristic flavor. If the noodles are a very bright yellow, it's likely that artificial color was used.

Use Chinese egg noodles in soups, or serve them with a sauce; cold cooked egg noodles are especially good with a soy-sesame dressing. Depending on size, cooking time is 1 to 3 minutes for fresh noodles and 3 to 6 minutes for dried. Fresh Chinese egg noodles can be added directly to soups, whereas dried noodles should be precooked (actually slightly undercooked).

■ CHINESE WHEAT NOODLES

These are round or flat, cream to yellowish beige strands of various thicknesses and widths. Fresh Chinese wheat noodles are shaped into nests and sold refrigerated; dried, they're packed in tight, rectangular bundles. Made from hard wheat, water, *kansui*, and salt, they can be used in soups and stir-fries or served with a sauce. Depending on size, cooking time is 2 to 4 minutes for fresh noodles and 4 to 7 minutes for dried. After cooking, rinse the noodles in cold water and drain before using in a recipe. Fresh noodles can be added directly to soups, whereas dried noodles should be precooked (slightly undercooked).

■ CELLOPHANE NOODLES

Also known as bean thread noodles and glass noodles, cellophane noodles are very thin, translucent noodles made from mung bean starch and water. Before packaging, they are boiled, then dried; then they're soaked in water, shaped into bundles, and dried again. They have a slippery, springy, chewy texture and are virtually tasteless until they absorb flavors from other foods. Nutritionally, they are a good source of iron, and because they are primarily pure starch, they're easy to digest. Cellophane noodles are popular in many Southeast Asian countries and are especially prized as a key ingredient for refreshing summer salads. They shouldn't actually be cooked; rather, soak them in hot but not boiling water just until softened, about 5 to 15 minutes. Loosen and separate the noodles, then rinse and drain them before adding them to a dish. They may benefit from cooking a few minutes in a dish, but they'll become gelatinous if cooked too long. They are quite long and have a tendency to clump together, so you may wish to cut them into more manageable lengths with clean kitchen scissors. Since cellophane noodles can expand up to three times in volume, start with a small amount the first time you use them.

■ HARUSAME

These translucent 5- to 7-inch-long Japanese noodles look like cellophane noodles, but they may be made from rice starch, potato starch, or soybean starch. Like cellophane noodles, they are not boiled but rather are soaked in hot water just until softened, about 5 to 15 minutes. Loosen and separate the noodles, then drain and rinse them before adding to stir-fries, soups, and other dishes.

■ HIYAMUGI

These Japanese noodles made from wheat flour, salt, and water are somewhat wider than somen but thinner than udon. Like somen, they are traditionally served only in the warmer months in chilled noodle dishes with a dipping sauce. A whole wheat version is also available, sometimes referred to as whole wheat somen. Cook in boiling water for 4 to 6 minutes, just until tender, then rinse in cold water to stop the cooking and remove excess starch.

■ KUZUKIRI

These light colored, nearly transparent Japanese noodles are made from kudzu starch, and sometimes with added potato starch. Extracted from the fibrous root of a viny plant native to Asia, kudzu has long been valued for its thickening properties and, in Japanese folk medicine, as an easily digested, restorative carbohydrate. To make ku-zukiri, the starch is dried, then ground and mixed with water to make a batter, which is cooked briefly until it solidifies. After cooling, it is cut into strips and dried. It is cooked like regular pasta and used in salads, sukiyaki, or sweet-and-sour soup, or simply in a light broth.

■ RAMEN NOODLES

These familiar long, thin, extruded noodles are made from wheat flour, water, salt, sometimes eggs, and *kansui*, an alkaline solution made from potassium carbonate or sodium carbonate. *Kansui* is essential in making ramen noodles, giving them their springy texture and characteristic flavor, and also lending them their yellow color as a result of its action on pigments in the wheat flour.

In the United States and many other countries, ramen is synonymous with instant ramen, a cheap and easy noodle soup flavored with a seasoning packet. But in Japan, where some restaurants specialize in this traditional dish, it can be elevated to an art form. The noodles are served in a meticulously prepared broth and topped with everything from scallions, bean sprouts, and bamboo shoots to sea vegetables, wood ear mushrooms, and meat. Instant ramen, created in 1958 by the Japanese company Nissin Foods as way to make ramen available anytime and anywhere, is also extremely popular in Japan but is seen as distinctly different than its namesake dish.

Japanese standards for instant ramen noodles stipulate they are to be made with wheat flour, water, salt, and *kansui* to give the noodles their characteristic flavor, texture, and color. After the raw noodles are steamed and pressed into a mold, they are either dried in a hot air drying machine or deep-fried in palm oil, lard, or sesame oil for a couple of minutes to reduce their moisture content. Not surprisingly, there are noticeable differences in flavor and texture between deep-fried and air-dried ramen, with the air-dried noodles having a more delicate texture, fresher taste, and better retention of nutrients.

The flavor packet in packages of instant ramen provides a quick gauge of quality. If it contains monosodium glutamate (MSG), artificial flavors, sugars, artificial colors, preservatives, or flavor enhancers such as disodium inosinate and disodium guanylate, look for another brand. Although high-quality ramen costs more, you'll get a seasoning packet that contains natural ingredients such as shoyu powder from naturally aged soy sauce, freeze-dried miso, and preservative-free dried seaweeds, vegetables, and spices. You may even get ramen noodles made with some whole wheat flour—although perhaps not traditional, they are more nutritious.

■ RICE NOODLES (FRESH)

These fresh white noodles are made from a mixture of rice flour and water that is formed into a sheet and precooked by steaming, then cut into various widths (or sold as folded sheets), and coated with oil to prevent sticking. Since they are already cooked, all the cooking they require is a brief soak in hot or boiling water to soften them up and to rinse off the oil. Fresh rice noodles have a very limited shelf life and harden quickly, so ideally they should be used the day of purchase.

■ RICE PAPER WRAPPERS

These circular or triangular sheets used to make spring rolls are made with the same ingredients as fresh rice noodles and dried rice sticks, but they are much thinner and they're dried on bamboo mats. To use them as wrappers for spring rolls, either soften them in water for 30 to 60 seconds or brush them with water. Don't use hot water and don't soak them too long, or they'll start to fall apart. Like rice sticks, they are steamed before being dried, so they're ready to eat as soon as they're soaked and softened.

■ RICE STICKS

These brittle, opaque, white dried noodles made from rice are available in thin, medium, and wide widths. Popular throughout Southeast Asia, they are known by a plethora of names, including maifun, bifun, sen yai, and banh pho. To make them, rice is soaked in water, ground into a paste, made into dough, and then extruded in various widths. The noodles are precooked with steam, then cooled and maintained in this state for many hours to help stabilize their structure before they are dried with hot air.

Prepare Asian rice noodles by soaking them in hot water for 3 to 15 minutes, depending on the width of the noodles and how they will be further cooked or served. Drain the noodles after soaking, and rinse them in cold water to remove excess starch.

If you plan to use the noodles in soup, soak them in hot water for just 3 to 5 minutes, then add them to the soup for the last 2 to 3 of minutes of cooking. Presoaking time for stir-fries is, likewise, about 3 to 5 minutes before adding to the stir-fry for the last 3 to 5 minutes of cooking. For salads or serving the noodles with sauce, soak the noodles in hot water for 8 to 15 minutes, until tender.

Alternatively, the noodles can be soaked in cold water for an hour or until tender. This takes longer, but it helps prevent the noodles from sticking together during cooking and also gives more wiggle room in finishing the dish, as the noodles don't have to be used immediately.

■ SOBA

In Japanese, *soba* means "buckwheat," and these thin, square-cut brownish gray noodles are indeed made from buckwheat flour. Although all are based on buckwheat, the many types of soba vary in taste, texture, and color depending on the percentage of buckwheat flour used and whether any vegetables or other ingredients are included. The best soba is rolled (laminated) into sheets that are cut into long strands, slowly air-dried, and then hand cut,

similar to the traditional Japanese method of making soba by hand.

Soba is traditionally served hot during colder months, in a broth or stir-fry, and served cold in summer, in salads, in cold broths, or with a dipping sauce. It also makes excellent noodle sushi. And, it is great as a side dish with other meals beyond Asian cuisine, especially when served with smoked salmon, tofu, or tempeh, and vegetables such as peas, steamed potatoes, and sautéed onions and red bell peppers. For best results, avoid stir-frying 100% soba, ito soba, mugwort soba, and green tea soba.

Soba made from 100% buckwheat flour has a delicious flavor that's hearty and rich. As it contains no gluten, it is more delicate, so it's important not to overcook it, and to rinse it in cold water to stop the cooking process once it reaches the al dente stage. For this reason, most soba is made with at least 20% wheat flour to provide more strength and resilience. The more wheat used, the lighter the color of the soba and the milder its flavor. Soba made with added wheat also typically contains salt. Most varieties of soba are fairly thin, about like linguine. All vegetable soba noodles are based on soba made from a blend of buckwheat and wheat flours. Contemporary versions of soba sometimes use Kamut or spelt flour in place of the wheat flour, providing new options in flavor and nutrition. People who are sensitive or allergic to wheat may be able to eat these varieties. But as always, if you are allergic to wheat or gluten, consult with a medical professional before experimenting.

Ito soba is very thin, about the width of angel hair pasta, whereas most soba is about as thick as linguine. Ito soba is made from a blend of buckwheat and wheat and has a very light texture.

Yomogi soba (mugwort soba) is deep green, a color it derives from dried mugwort leaves. This mineral-rich plant lends the soba added nutritional value and a delicious, slightly bitter flavor slightly reminiscent of spinach.

Cha soba (green tea soba) is made with green tea powder, which contributes a lovely green color and a delicate, aromatic flavor. It is typically served cold with a simple dipping sauce on the side rather than in broth.

Jinenjo soba (wild yam soba) is light brown from the addition of dried Japanese wild mountain yam, a root vegetable that naturally contains diastase and amylase, two enzymes that help facilitate the digestion of starches. Wild yam soba has a particularly delicious nutty flavor and smooth, slightly slick texture. The wild yam also provides good binding qualities, making it sturdier than other sobas.

Lotus root soba, a light-colored soba similar to wild yam soba, contains dried, ground lotus root. It has a delicious nutty flavor and aroma similar to that of freshly cooked lotus root and a smooth texture.

Korean-style buckwheat noodles, known as *naengmyon*, contain some potato starch in addition to buckwheat flour, which makes them slightly chewier than Japanese-style soba. *Naengmyon* is typically served cold but can also be used in soups.

Cooking time is 1 to 4 minutes for fresh soba or 5 to 7 minutes for dried. Cook just until al dente, drain, and then immediately rinse with cold water to stop the cooking process. Alternatively, use the cold water shock method, in which the soba is added to boiling water, then 1 cup of cold water is added after it returns to a boil. Another cup of cold water is added two or three more times, until the soba is at the al dente stage. After cooking, drain and rinse with cold water.

■ SOMEN

These very thin, delicate, white, round noodles made from wheat flour, water, and salt are often found packaged in small bundles secured by a band. Light and refreshing, they are traditionally served cold during the warmer months, often in salads, and sometimes directly on ice with a light dipping sauce on the side. Somen was originally made by hand stretching, folding, and restretching the dough into one long strip, a process that took considerable time and skill, making somen an expensive food eaten primarily by the wealthy. Hand-stretched somen is still made by artisans, including two- and three-year-old varieties that are valued for their smooth texture and enhanced flavor. Needless to say, these varieties are significantly more expensive. Cook somen in boiling water for about 2 minutes, just until tender. Drain, rinse in cold water, and drain again before serving.

■ TANGMYON

Also known as dangmyun, tangmyon is a Korean version of cellophane noodles made with sweet potato starch. They are prepared as cellophane noodles are: soaked in hot water for 10 to 15 minutes. They're typically added to stir-fries and soups.

■ UDON

These thick and delicious noodles made from wheat flour or whole wheat flour, salt, and water are nearly as wide as linguine. Soft and slippery, udon is typically served in a hot or chilled broth or with a dipping sauce, but it is equally good in salads or topped with a simple sauce. Fresh udon is generally thick and flat, while the dried version is somewhat thinner and may be either round or flat. The best-tasting, best-textured udon is made using the roll and cut method, in which the kneaded dough is repeatedly rolled to yield thin, large sheets that are cut into shape, slowly dried, and then cut into the final length. Udon is also available made from a blend of unbleached white and whole wheat flour or from other types of flour. Genmai udon contains some brown rice flour, which contributes a nutty flavor. It's also available made from spelt and Kamut, and some people who are sensitive to conventional wheat find they can eat these forms of udon.

Cooking time is 2 to 4 minutes for fresh udon and 5 to 7 minutes for dried. After cooking, drain the udon and rinse with cold water to stop the cooking and remove excess starch. An alternative method for cooking dried udon is the cold water shock method, in which the udon is added to boiling water, then 1 cup of cold water is added after it returns to a boil. Another cup of cold water is added two or three more times, until the udon is al dente. After cooking, drain, rinse with cold water, and drain again.

Beans, Peas, and Lentils

∽

When I was growing up in Iowa during the 1950s and 1960s, beans were a common side dish and ingredient in my family's everyday menus. There was my mother's delicious chili, made with kidney beans and ground beef, savory baked beans served at summer picnics, reconstituted bean with bacon soup served with sandwiches at lunch, and hamburgers accompanied by pork and beans—a standard Saturday night dinner. As a time-saver, all were prepared using canned beans and soups. In fact, it wasn't until I was twenty-one years old that I first learned how to cook beans from scratch—both from sheer curiosity and, truth be told, to impress my husband in our early courting days.

Beans can be the spotlight of a meal or part of the supporting cast in salads, soups, spreads, snacks, casseroles, dips, and wraps. They can also play an important role in vegetarian versions of pâté, burgers, and meat loaf. Tofu and tempeh, made from soybeans, expand the horizons even more, with their ability to act as substitutes in a wide variety of traditional egg- and meat-based recipes.

Virtually every culture and cuisine incorporates dried beans, peas, and lentils in one way or another, often combined with regional grains, pastas, and vegetables in unique combinations. Falafel and hummus, both based on garbanzo beans, hail from the Middle East, while tempeh with peanut sauce is native to Indonesia. Soy-based miso soup is traditional in Japan, just as tofu pad thai is long established in Thailand. Italian pasta e fagioli and cannellini-based minestrone are both time-honored recipes, as is red kidney bean curry from India. This is just a minor sampling of the many ways beans have long been incorporated into menus worldwide.

Nutrition

Besides being flavorful and adaptable, beans are a storehouse of nutrition. In particular, they are the most important plant-based source of protein. However, with the exception of soybeans, the protein in beans is incomplete, with most of them containing insufficient amounts of the amino acid methionine. However, when grains, seeds, or dairy products are eaten on the same day that beans are consumed, they can supply the needed methionine, making it entirely feasible to obtain sufficient, good-quality protein from a plant-based diet.

Research has revealed many valuable nutritional contributions from beans, including their extensive array of nutrients. They are a good source of B vitamins, like folic acid, and are rich in many minerals, including magnesium, potassium, iron, calcium, phosphorus, and zinc. Some of these nutrients may help reduce the risk of cardiovascular disease. Beans are also one of the best food sources of soluble fiber, also known as viscous fiber. Soluble fiber has been shown to lower cholesterol and help decrease the risk of type 2 diabetes, as it helps normalize blood glucose and insulin responses. Collectively, all of the nutrients and fiber in beans have been found to work together to help reduce the risk of heart disease and certain cancers.

Resistant starch, also categorized as a type of dietary fiber, is present in beans at significantly higher percentages than found in many other foods, even grains. The type of starch within plant cell walls, resistant starch is so named because it is resistant to human digestive enzymes until it settles in the colon. Since its fermentation in the large intestine helps promote the growth and activity of beneficial bacteria, resistant starch is considered a "prebiotic." Health benefits include improved bowel function, balanced blood glucose and insulin responses, increased satiety, and increased absorption of micronutrients.

All beans are also a good natural source of phytonutrients. Anthocyanins, the compounds responsible for the beautiful red, purple, and black seed coats of beans, act as powerful antioxidants and are thought to fight cancer and heart disease. In fact, according to a 2004 U.S. Department of Agriculture study of antioxidants from food sources, dried red beans were the food highest in antioxidants based on total antioxidant capacity per serving size, edging out even the highly touted wild blueberries. Red kidney beans and pinto beans followed, placing in the number three and four positions, with black beans achieving eighteenth place in the top twenty foods highest in antioxidants per serving.

Digestion

Bean are very easy to digest as long as they are first presoaked for several hours and then cooked long enough to break down their complex sugars and starches, the compounds that cause flatulence. Because the complex sugars, called oligosaccharides, aren't easily digested, they generally remain intact until they reach the large intestine. Bacterial enzymes then go to work to break them down, creating by-products such as methane, nitrogen, oxygen, hydrogen, and carbon dioxide gases in the process—in other words, the intestinal gas often associated with beans. Even so, it is important to note that oligosaccharides also have their good side, in particular, helping support bacteria in the colon.

SEVEN WAYS TO AID DIGESTION OF BEANS

Fortunately, there are many ways to reduce and even eliminate any potential problems from the oligosaccharides in the beans.

1. Soak dried beans and discard the soaking water prior to cooking

Not only does soaking serve to rehydrate beans, making them easier and quicker to cook, but it's also a sure-fire way to get rid of a significant portion of the hard-to-digest oligosaccharides. When

The Three Sisters

In Native American lore, the Three Sisters is the concept used to portray the inseparable and mutually supportive nature of corn, beans, and squash in agriculture, in nutrition, and in spirit. In practice, the seeds of these three vegetables were planted together in little mounds rather than separately in rows. As a result, the corn stalks provided support for the beans and shade for the squash. The beans provided nitrogen-fixing bacteria to naturally fertilize the corn, and their winding vines helped stabilize the stalks. The squash served to shade the soil around the plants to retain moisture, and its prickly leaves discouraged wildlife on the prowl for a tasty meal.

This symbiosis also expresses itself in the complementary nutritional nature of three plants. Although corn was a primary staple in Native American diets, beans were the essential component filling in the gaps in protein, while squash provided additional nutrients in both its flesh and its seeds. Three Sisters gardens are still planted today, a tangible demonstration of the interconnectedness of nature at its best. And, when it comes to eating, the delicious combination of beans, corn, and squash further confirms the harmony of these three plants together, not only in spirit, but in their complementary flavors and textures, as well.

you discard the soaking water and rinse the beans before adding fresh cooking water, the oligosaccharides go down the drain. Although most beans should go through this process prior to cooking, lentils and split peas don't require presoaking.

There are two primary ways to soak beans: the traditional cold-soak method and the hot-soak method. In the cold-soak method, the beans are placed in a pot and covered with room temperature water to a level a couple of inches above the beans, to allow for hydration and expansion. The pot is then covered and set aside for 8 to 12 hours. After soaking, the beans are drained and rinsed and fresh water is added to the pot before cooking.

The hot-soak method is quicker, and it's also said to be the more effective way to break down the oligosaccharides, as the initial application of heat helps jump-start the process. In this technique, the beans are placed in a pot, again with enough water to cover them by a couple of inches, and brought to a boil for 3 minutes. They are then removed from the heat and soaked for 1 to 4 hours. Soaking the beans in hotter water speeds their absorption of water and also more effectively leaches out the water-soluble oligosaccharides. The drawback is that it also leaches out many of the water-soluble nutrients and some of the flavor and color components. However, if the cold-soak method doesn't remove enough of the oligosaccharides for you, using the hot-soak method and sacrificing some nutrients and flavor may be a good compromise. The hot-soak method is also handy when needed to prepare beans more quickly.

2. Cook the beans until tender

It's essential to ensure the beans are thoroughly cooked. The combination of presoaking and thorough cooking will ensure maximum breakdown of the oligosaccharides and other resistant starches. The simple way to test for doneness is with a fork. If the beans can be easily mashed, they're ready to eat. If there is some resistance, they need further cooking. Rest assured, properly cooked beans will still be able to retain their texture and shape.

3. Choose beans that are easier to digest

Navy beans, lima beans, and whole dried soybeans are notorious for containing higher levels of hard-to-digest oligosaccharides. In contrast, anasazi beans, azuki beans, black-eyed peas, lentils, and mung beans have the least amounts of these complex sugars. Even so, centuries ago, traditional cultures found ways to prepare soybeans to make them easier to digest and more nutritious. In the process of making tofu and soymilk, the oligosaccharides are removed, and the fermentation of tempeh, miso, tamari, and shoyu also eliminates or breaks down most of the oligosaccharides.

Sprouting beans before cooking them also makes them more digestible. Beans are actually seeds, and their oligosaccharides are a form of stored fuel to provide energy when the seed germinates. The sprouting process uses up virtually all of the oligosaccharides in the beans. To ensure food safety and optimum digestibility, it's best to lightly steam, stir-fry, or sauté sprouted beans rather than eat them raw. Never eat sprouted kidney beans and sprouted lima beans raw, as they contain toxic enzymes that must be inactivated by cooking at high heat for at least 10 minutes.

4. Eat smaller quantities of beans until your body adjusts

Many people who eat beans regularly find their digestive system gradually adapts, making for easier eating. Start off by eating only ¼ cup to ½ cup at a time a couple of times per week, gradually increasing the amount and frequency.

5. Avoid eating beans cooked with sweeteners

Some people who would otherwise have little difficulty digesting most beans have trouble with beans cooked with sweeteners, presumably because it adds more carbohydrate fuel for bacteria in the large intestine. Experiment to see whether this is the case for you. If the after-effects of baked beans made with a sweetener make life a bit uncomfortable, opt for plain beans. Or, if you prefer your beans sweetened, cook them with naturally sweet root vegetables such as carrots.

6. Cook beans with epazote, bay leaf, or cumin

Certain herbs have carminative (gas-reducing) properties in addition to their delicious flavor. While bay leaf and cumin are often used as carminatives when cooking beans, epazote is one of the most effective herbs for this purpose. A pungent plant native to Mexico and South America, it is also grown in the southern United States. A sprig or two of fresh epazote or a couple of teaspoons of dry epazote can be very helpful; add it to the pot of beans during the last 15 minutes of cooking to avoid a bitter flavor.

7. Use a commercial enzyme product containing alpha-galactosidase

If all else fails, you can take supplemental alpha-galactosidase in liquid or tablet form. This enzyme developed from a food-grade mold breaks down the oligosaccharides into smaller, more digestible sugars before they reach the colon. It helps improve digestion of beans by supplying an enzyme not normally found in the human body. Take the tablets (swallow or chew them, or crumble them on the food) or sprinkle the liquid form directly on the food with the first bite, using the amount indicated on the product label. While cooking beans with the alpha-galactosidase may sound like a good idea, it isn't. High heat will render the enzyme ineffective.

How to Buy and Store Beans

Not only are beans nutritious, but they are also inexpensive and readily available. Fresh shell beans, such as black-eyed peas, cranberry beans, fava beans, garbanzos, and tongues of fire beans, can often be found in produce departments or farmers' markets. Prepare and serve them as a tender vegetable. Unlike their dried bean counterparts, they cook quickly in boiling water, taking between 15 and 30 minutes, depending on the bean and its size, and don't require presoaking. Approximately 2½ pounds of fresh beans in their pods will yield about 3 cups of shelled beans. Although they're best used within a few days of harvest, they can be stored in a plastic bag in the refrigerator for up to a week.

Dried beans are available throughout the year. Virtually every grocery store sells a variety of packaged dry beans, and many sell them in bulk. You'll likely find packages of mixed beans specially formulated for soups and stews, too. Each year the catalog of beans continues to expand with new hybrid varieties developed for their appearance, flavor, and sometimes ease of growing. Specialty grocers and online merchants are a good source for the more unique beans, including heirloom varieties. Some of these previously popular varieties had lost favor due to low yields or simply because newly developed varieties came on the market, but they are now being rescued from obscurity, and even possibly extinction, as people have developed a new appreciation of their remarkable flavors, beauty, and nutrients.

Select dried beans with smooth surfaces and bright colors. While dried beans can, in theory, be stored for years, about a year after production they lose moisture and then require longer cooking. Beans that are stored too long at warm temperatures and high humidity will never get tender. To make sure you are buying "fresh" dry beans, look for an expiration date on the package and use them within the suggested time frame. If the package has no expiration date or if you're buying in bulk, stick to buying only common varieties of beans, as they have faster turnover, and select those that aren't wrinkled or dull in color. After purchase, store beans in an airtight container in a cool, dry place away from sunlight. Rather than topping off

a small amount of beans left in a container, use up the old beans first, implementing a "first in, first out" inventory control.

Canned precooked beans are also an excellent choice. While it's hard to beat the flavor of freshly cooked beans, canned beans are a lifesaver when you need to prepare a meal quickly. A bit of seasoning is all you need to perk them up. Before you buy, look at both the nutrition information panel and the ingredient label to ensure the brand you choose contains only beans, water, and low amounts of sodium or no added salt. Avoid brands that contain high-fructose corn syrup or other forms of sugar. Ingredients such as disodium EDTA (for color retention) or calcium chloride (a firming agent) are also unnecessary. Drain and rinse canned beans before adding them to a recipe. This will lower the sodium level by one-third, help to reduce any amount of oligosaccharides in the beans, and also freshen the flavor. For best flavor, canned beans should be used by the freshness date on the container or within a year of purchase. As a rule of thumb, a 15-ounce can is equivalent to approximately 1¾ cups of cooked beans.

Cooked beans, including canned beans, will keep for five days in the refrigerator and up to six months in the freezer. Planning ahead, cooking a quantity of beans at a time, and keeping a few varieties of canned beans around for quick meals can all make it easier to incorporate these delicious and nutritious foods into your diet.

How to Prepare Beans

Regardless of whether you use either the cold-soak or the hot-soak method, first sort through the beans to remove any defective beans, small pebbles, and other debris. Wash the beans several times under cold water, discarding any that float to the surface. For best flavor and nutrition, cook the beans with just enough fresh water, always making sure the beans are covered with water throughout the cooking process. Avoid using too much water. Not only will this dilute the flavor of the beans, but also any liquid you drain away after cooking will represent a loss of valuable nutrients.

SEASONING BEANS

Chopped onion, garlic, herbs, and spices may be cooked along with dried beans for added flavor. Adding the sea vegetable kombu will help tenderize the beans and enhance their flavor by virtue of its naturally occurring glutamic acid. It also helps replace minerals that are lost down the drain when the bean soaking water is discarded. Use about a 2-inch strip of kombu per pot of beans, rinsing it first to remove excess sodium.

On the other hand, don't add salt, sugars, tomatoes, wine, lemon juice, or vinegar until the end of cooking. Salting the beans before they are done will slow the rate at which beans absorb water, prolonging the time until they become tender. Sugar added before cooking reinforces the cell walls and slows down the process of softening the starch within the cells. Acidic ingredients added early make the cell walls more stable but won't allow the starches swell and soften. So while sugar or acidic ingredients like tomatoes, lemon juice, and vinegar added at the end of cooking can help retain the texture of beans, they'll prevent the beans from becoming tender if added during cooking.

Some cooks and books have suggested adding baking soda to beans while they're cooking. Unless your water is exceedingly hard and baking soda's alkalinity would allow the beans to cook more quickly, it's best to forgo it. Excess alkalinity can break down the cell walls of the beans. Not only will you be left with a mushy texture, but valuable protein and vitamins will also leach into the cooking water. Baking soda can also deplete thiamin (vitamin B_1). If you decide you still need or want to use baking soda in your beans, keep it to 1/8 teaspoon per cup of dry beans.

COOKING METHODS
Boil and simmer

In a large covered pot, combine the beans with fresh water, using 4 cups of water for each cup of beans. Bring the beans to a boil, then lower the heat to a simmer to help prevent the skins of the beans from bursting during cooking. Toward the end of the cooking time, it's okay if there isn't much water above the beans, but check periodically to make sure there's enough water to keep the bottom from scorching. The beans will be done when they are tender.

Pressure-cooking

With a pressure cooker, you can prepare beans in less than one-third the time it would take with the boil and simmer method. Since the temperature inside a pressure cooker is around 250°F, beans cook much faster, saving a lot of preparation time and eliminating the need to be at home and babysit the beans for a couple of hours while they cook. Because less water escapes as steam, you'll only need to add water to a depth of about 1 inch above the surface of the beans before securing the lid. Vegetables such as onions, carrots, and celery may be combined with the beans before cooking, if desired. Since some beans tend to foam and clog the pressure release vent, keep the total amount of beans and water to no more than two-thirds of the pressure cooker's capacity. To prevent the beans from splitting and losing their shape, after bringing the cooker to pressure, turn down the heat and keep the pressure at a low, even level. After the cooking is complete, let the pressure come down naturally. Pressure-cooking lentils and some beans are sometimes not recommended because of the tendency of their skins to loosen or for foam to develop during the cooking process, each of which can clog the pressure vent. The cooking guidelines for each variety listed below will indicate when that is the case.

Baking

Before baking beans, first boil them for 15 to 20 minutes in 4½ cups of water for each cup of beans. Then transfer the beans and their cooking water to a covered baking dish and bake at 350°F for about 3½ hours.

Slow-cooking

While slow cookers are good for making soups or stews with beans, manufacturers of these appliances recommend using precooked or canned beans in slow cooker recipes rather than starting with dry beans. The suggestion is based both on recipe testing conducted by the manufacturers and on concerns about whether the cooking temperature of slow cookers is high enough to safely cook beans from scratch. This is of special importance when cooking kidney beans, which need to be boiled or cooked at boiling temperatures for at least 10 minutes to inactivate toxins they naturally contain that could otherwise cause symptoms similar to food poisoning.

If you still want to use a slow cooker to cook dry beans, manufacturers recommend that you first boil the beans for at least 10 minutes before placing them in the slow cooker. Add water to cover the surface of the beans by about 1 inch, and then cook on the high setting, which is approximately 212°F, until tender, approximately 5 to 8 hours.

Finding Time for Cooking Beans

Cooking time is determined by several factors: the variety of bean, the simmering temperature, the soaking time, the size and age of the beans, and the altitude. Use the cooking times listed for each of the beans below as a general guide; actual cooking time will vary depending on the beans and the situation. Also adjust the time depending on the intended use. Beans destined to be used whole in salads are usually cooked less than those destined for soups. Even so, they should also be cooked until tender and easily mashed with a fork.

No matter how little preparation time you have to spare before mealtime, there's bound to be a bean or bean-based product you can use. Canned beans and seasoned baked tofu are ready to use as is. In 30 minutes you can cook a pot of red lentils or black beluga lentils, and prepare tofu and tempeh in a variety of ways. Got 40 to 60 minutes? Reach for French green lentils, brown lentils, or Spanish pardina lentils. For beans other than lentils, a pressure cooker will significantly decrease the cooking time, making them quick and easy to prepare even on busy days.

Exploring Beans, Peas, and Lentils

The range of colors and flavors within the wide array of beans is remarkable. You owe it to yourself to try each of them at least once. Within the vast family of beans there are eight major categories: dried peas, fava beans, garbanzo beans, soybeans, lentils, beans originating in Asia (which includes mung beans, black-eyed peas, cowpeas, and pigeon peas), and "common beans," originating in Central America, the category with the most extensive and seemingly diverse varieties, ranging from azuki beans to lima beans and pinto beans to black beans and even navy beans. (The eighth category within the legume family, peanuts, will be explored in the Nuts and Seeds chapter in keeping with its common usage.)

Anasazi Beans

Boil and simmer for 1 to 1½ hours. Pressure-cook for 18 minutes.

This heirloom variety has been cultivated in the American Southwest since about 130 CE. After the cliff-dwelling Anasazi abandoned their homes in the Four Corners region around 1200 CE, the beans were left to survive in the wild. Officially rediscovered in the Anasazi ruins by archeologists in the 1950s, cultivation of the bean had actually continued throughout the centuries in family gardens. Commercial production was rekindled by agronomist Bruce Riddell and entrepreneur Ernie Waller, who shared a common interest in this native bean. In 1983 they named it anasazi from the then-current name for the people now known as the Ancestral Puebloans.

Anasazi beans are as striking in appearance as they are delicious. While similar in both size and shape to pinto beans, they are dappled burgundy and white, markings that fade with cooking to a light pink. They are also sweeter and more flavorful

than pinto beans and hold their shape better once cooked. Much of the anasazi bean's popularity can be attributed to its ease of digestion. Many people report it is less problematic in terms of intestinal gas, and this is well grounded in reality. The levels of hard-to-digest oligosaccharides is 25% less than in many other beans. Anasazi beans can be used in any recipe that calls for pinto beans.

Appaloosa Beans

Boil and simmer for 1½ hours. Pressure-cook for 18 minutes.

This heirloom bean has a long, thin shape and is mottled dark purple and ivory white on the diagonal. Not surprisingly, the bean is named after the Appaloosa horse, whose markings are quite similar. During cooking their color fades to a pinkish burgundy. The remarkable flavor of appaloosa beans is mild and earthy, like an especially flavorful black bean. Use them in any soup, chili, dip, or refried bean recipe that calls for black beans, pintos, or kidney beans.

Azuki Beans

Boil and simmer for 1 to 1½ hours. Pressure-cook for 15 minutes.

Also known as aduki or adzuki beans, these are small, round, reddish brown beans marked with a distinctive thin white line down the side. Traditionally used in both Japanese and Chinese cuisines for festive meals, they are slightly sweet and nutty in flavor. Although azuki beans have often been used as an ingredient in desserts and confections, they are equally, if not more, delicious when prepared in a savory manner. Serve them with rice or barley or, for an exceptional dish, add cubes of winter squash during the last half hour of cooking and season with tamari. Stretch tradition and try azuki beans in Southwestern cuisine, too. Their color contrasts beautifully with yellow corn tortillas. Azuki beans are also easy to sprout.

Black Beans

Boil and simmer for 1½ hours. Pressure-cook for 15 to 18 minutes.

Also known as black turtle beans, these are small, oval shaped, and, of course, black in color. Particularly high in magnesium, black beans are also low in fat and particularly high in fiber. Their rich, earthy flavor is a perfect foil to the spicy seasonings used in South American, Caribbean, and Mexican dishes. Black beans are often accompanied by rice and tomatoes, cooked into a delicious soup, or served in or with enchiladas, burritos, chapatis, side dishes, dips, and salads. It's especially important to sort through black beans, as they are prone to having a few small black pebbles in them, masquerading as beans.

Black Calypso Beans

Boil and simmer for 1½ to 2 hours. Pressure-cook for 18 minutes.

Also known as yin yang beans, these are a black and white heirloom variety that bear an amazing resemblance to the Chinese yin yang symbol—complete with the contrasting polka dot. Somewhat sweet in flavor, Black Calypso beans are good additions to salads, soups, casseroles, stews, and baked dishes.

Black-Eyed peas

Boil and simmer dried black-eyed peas for 1 to 1¼ hours. Pressure-cook for 16 to 18 minutes.

Identified by a black "eye" amidst a creamy-white background, this oval-shaped bean has become synonymous with the southern United States,

where it's traditionally cooked with rice and greens or served with cornbread. It is also a requisite food in southern New Year's celebrations, when eating it is said to ensure good luck in the coming year. The most commonly grown variety of cowpeas and a relative of the mung bean, black-eyed peas have a mild, vegetable-like flavor somewhat reminiscent of peas. Despite the similarity of taste and the word *pea* in their name, black-eyed peas are, botanically, a bean. They are especially good when combined with sautéed onions, celery, and red bell peppers and served as a side dish alongside rice or spinach pasta.

To prepare shelled fresh black-eyed peas, cover them with water in a pot, bring to a boil, then lower the heat and simmer until tender, adding salt only after they're cooked.

Bolita Beans

Boil and simmer for 1½ hours. Pressure-cook for 18 minutes.

This heirloom bean, introduced to the New World by early Spanish settlers, was grown throughout the Southwest by Native Americans. These pinkish beige beans can be used in any recipe that calls for pinto beans, where they will improve the dish because of their deeper flavor.

Cannellini Beans

Boil and simmer for 1½ hours. Pressure-cook for 15 to 18 minutes.

Also known as Italian white kidney beans, cannellini beans are an heirloom variety that came to the United States in the early 1800s. They are best known as an essential ingredient in minestrone, pasta e fagioli, and traditional Tuscan tuna and white bean salads. Because of their smooth texture and nutty flavor, cannellini beans are delicious in any soup, especially tomato-based soups, or served simply with fresh tomatoes or finely sliced sun-dried tomatoes, fresh basil, and a splash of olive oil.

Christmas Lima Beans

Boil and simmer for 1½ hours. Pressure-cook for 18 minutes.

Also known as chestnut lima beans, these heirloom lima beans are as beautiful as they are delicious. Hailing from the 1840s, Christmas limas have mottled maroon and creamy white markings that become even darker and richer looking when cooked—not often the case with colorful beans. Their flavor is remarkably like roasted chestnuts, and their texture is similar to baked potato. Although their name implies holiday fare, use Christmas limas any time of year as a main dish, in casseroles, and in salads.

Cranberry Beans

Boil and simmer dried cranberry beans for 1 to 1¼ hours. Pressure-cook for 18 minutes.

Also known as borlotti beans and Roman beans, cranberry beans are an heirloom variety traditionally used in New England for succotash, as well as in Italian and Portuguese dishes. While they very closely resemble pinto beans in size and shape, cranberry beans are more pinkish tan in color and streaked with cranberry red markings that fade when they're cooked. The American red cranberry bean from Maine, which actually looks like a ripe cranberry when fresh, was a popular dried bean among the local Abenaki Indians and early settlers of the area. Cranberry beans have a sweet, mild, somewhat nutty flavor, with a firm texture that survives prolonged cooking. A classic in pasta e fagioli soup and stews, they are equally good in any pasta dish seasoned with moderate amounts of aromatic herbs or in any recipe that calls for pinto or kidney beans.

To prepare shelled fresh cranberry beans, cover them with water in a pot, bring to a boil, then lower the heat and simmer until tender, about 15 to 20 minutes.

Fava Beans

Boil and simmer for 1½ to 2 hours for whole dried fava beans, or 30 to 45 minutes for peeled and split fava beans. Pressure-cooking isn't recommended.

Fava beans are oval shaped, about 1½ inches long, and light brown. When cooked, they have a pulpy texture and nutty, earthy flavor. The many names for fava beans—broad beans, Windsor beans, horse beans, field beans, tickbeans, and more—reflect their widespread use and long history. They are one of the most ancient plants in cultivation and are thought to have been used for food in the Mediterranean region as early as 6000 BCE. First a staple in Europe, western Asia, and northern Africa, they were grown in China by about 3000 BCE. They had the distinction of being the only bean grown in Europe for centuries, until other varieties from the Americas were discovered. Although it's perfectly safe for most people to eat fava beans, some people of African, Mediterranean, and Southeast Asian descent have a rare, inherited disease, called favism, in which eating fresh fava beans can cause severe anemia. Favism can be diagnosed using a blood test.

Unless harvested when very young, fava beans have a thick seed coat that must be removed before cooking. To prepare fresh fava beans, first shell them by pulling the stem at the top to unzip the string on either side of the pod. Add the beans to boiling water, allow the water to come to a boil again, and cook for 1 to 2 minutes. Transfer the beans to ice water to cool briefly, then drain. Slit the skin on each bean and peel it off before using the beans in recipes. They can be served simply with olive oil and salt, added to risotto, or used in combination with other vegetables.

To peel dried fava beans, soak them in water for about 8 hours or overnight. Bring them to a boil for 5 minutes and then drain. Let them cool slightly and then slit the skin on each bean and slip off the tough, outer skin. Then combine the fava beans with fresh water and continue cooking them until tender. Use them in soups and salads or puree them to make a spread for crostini or crusty bread, or to make falafel. Peeled dried fava beans are also available, obviously requiring much less advance preparation time, and also about half the cooking time. However, they don't hold their shape very well, so they're best pureed or used in soup.

Flageolets

Boil and cook for 2 hours. Pressure-cook for 15 minutes.

Although these heirloom beans originated in the United States, they are more poplar, and more frequently cultivated, in France and Italy. In French country cuisine, flageolets are often served as a side dish with meat, especially lamb and poultry. Looking much like very pale green, miniature kidney beans, flageolets are indeed immature kidney beans. Their light flavor and delicate, creamy texture is enhanced by aromatic vegetables and herbs, such as onion, celery, carrots, garlic, bay leaf, and thyme. For an Italian variation, try mixing pesto into flageolets cooked until just tender.

French Navy Beans

Boil and simmer for 1 hour. Pressure-cook for 15 minutes.

These small heirloom navy beans are white in color with just a hint of green and have a slightly baconlike flavor. Like regular navy beans, they are perfect for soups and salads.

Garbanzo Beans

Boil and simmer for 3 hours for whole dried garbanzos, or 45 to 60 minutes for chana dal. Pressure-cook whole dried garbanzos for 25 to 30 minutes (not recommended for chana dal.)

Upon close scrutiny and with a good imagination, garbanzo beans resemble the head and beak of a chicken, perhaps accounting for their other common name: chickpeas. If you think that's stretching it, consider that ancient Romans thought the garbanzo bean looked like a ram's head with curling horns. In fact, its species name, *arietinum*, means "ramlike." Whatever you think this roundish bean does or doesn't look like, you'll appreciate its sweet, mild flavor and the fact that garbanzos keep their unique shape when cooked.

In addition to being a good source of protein and calcium, garbanzos are particularly high in iron. And even though garbanzos are somewhat higher in fat than other beans (except soybeans), they still contain only about 12% calories from fat, and it's primarily unsaturated. Garbanzos are widely used in traditional Middle Eastern, Mediterranean, and East Indian cuisines, where they're served several ways, including marinated and served alone or in a salad, mashed and combined with tahini to make hummus, cooked with vegetables and pasta in minestrone, or as the basis for falafel.

A smaller, charcoal black variety, called black Kabuli chickpea, hails from Central Asia. Their flavor is similar to that of regular garbanzo beans and the two can be used interchangeably. Chana dal refers to dried baby garbanzos that are split and polished (meaning their seed coat has been removed). A sweeter-tasting version of garbanzos, they look more like yellow split peas than garbanzo beans. Although they are split, they should still be presoaked, just as you would whole garbanzo beans. Chana dal is best in soups, pilafs, and salads. While garbanzo beans are typically purchased dried, fresh garbanzo beans, with one or two beans in a pod, are also available. In contrast to the light yellowish brown color of common dried garbanzo beans, when fresh and shelled they are bright green.

To prepare fresh garbanzo beans, steam or cook in boiling water for about 2 minutes, until tender.

Gigande Beans

Boil and simmer for 2 to 3 hours. Pressure-cooking isn't recommended.

Also known as hija beans, gigande beans are a large, cream-colored, slightly flattened type of lima bean. Their dry texture and slightly sweet, savory flavor is excellent cooked in soups, pan-fried in olive oil to create a crisp coating and creamy-textured interior, or topped with olive oil and served with fresh herbs in salads or appetizers. Unless cooking gigande beans for a soup, pressure-cooking is not recommended, as they can break fairly easily.

Great Northern Beans

Boil and simmer for 1½ hours. Pressure-cook for 18 minutes.

These white, oval-shaped, medium-sized beans look like a larger version of navy beans. Generally cooked in soups or baked bean casseroles, their mild flavor gives you the option to go assertive or mild when seasoning. When substituted for garbanzos, great northern beans make for a delicious twist on a traditional hummus recipe.

Jacob's Cattle Beans

Boil and simmer for 1 to 1½ hours. Pressure-cook for 15 minutes.

Also known as trout beans, these heirloom beans were formerly quite popular in New England and Germany. These long, slim, kidney-shaped beans are speckled maroon and white. Although these colors fade somewhat after cooking, they still remain apparent. Their earthy, slightly sweet flavor and mealy texture make them a terrific addition to soups, stews, and casseroles, as well as the basis for a simple salad when combined with fresh herbs and a splash of olive oil.

Kidney Beans

Boil and simmer for 1½ hours. Pressure-cook for 18 minutes.

These reddish brown beans are shaped like you-know-what. There are two main varieties of kidney beans. Dark red kidney beans have an earthy flavor and, because of their thicker skin, retain their shape better when cooked, especially in recipes that require a longer cooking time. In contrast, light red kidney beans are softer and have a more full-bodied taste. They can be used interchangeably in chili, soups, salads, and rice dishes. Cannellini beans, which are often referred to as white kidney beans, are indeed a white variety of kidney beans.

It is especially important to thoroughly cook kidney beans, boiling them for at least 10 minutes to inactivate a natural toxin that can cause symptoms similar to food poisoning if they're undercooked. In contrast, cannellini beans only have one-third the amount of this toxin as red kidney beans. Most instances of illness from kidney beans have occurred because people ate raw or undercooked kidney bean sprouts or cooked dried kidney beans on the low setting in a slow cooker.

Lentils

Lentils are the world's oldest cultivated legume, domesticated around 7000 BCE. The bean's name originates from the fact that the small, round, flat shape that distinguishes all varieties of lentils looks very much like a lens. Colors range from slate green, brown, and black to reddish orange, coral, and gold, with all varieties having unique, delicious flavors and textures but a similar nutritional profile. In general, the brown and green varieties retain their shape well, whereas the hulled and split red and yellow lentils disintegrate and therefore are best for soups or in applications where they'll be pureed. One of the easiest beans to digest, lentils also rate as a favorite because of their short preparation time and versatility. Unlike other beans, no presoaking is required. Pressure-cooking lentils is not recommended, as the foam that they create during the cooking process can clog pressure vents. Nor is it generally necessary, as most varieties cook quite quickly using the boil and soak method.

Brown lentils (regular lentils, brewer lentils)

Use 2½ to 3 cups water per 1 cup lentils. Boil and simmer for 45 to 60 minutes. Pressure-cooking isn't recommended.

Distinguished from other lentils by their khaki color and larger size, these are the most common variety of lentil. They're commonly used to make hearty soups, side dishes, and vegetarian meat loaf and burgers. Brown lentils and rice have similar cooking times, so they've long been cooked together, often with celery seed or other seasonings. Mild and somewhat earthy, brown lentils hold their shape well after cooking but are easily mashed or pureed.

Spanish pardina lentils (Spanish brown lentils, pardina lentils, continental lentils)

Use 2½ cups water to 1 cup lentils. Boil and simmer for 45 to 60 minutes. Pressure-cooking isn't recommended.

These are small (about one-third the size of green lentils) and nutty tasting, and range in color from a rich medium brown to brownish gray. Although now much of the production of Spanish pardina lentils occurs in the United States, they remain popular in Spain, as well as in Italy and

North Africa. Use them in any recipe that calls for brown or green lentils. Because pardina lentils hold their shape well, they are also excellent in longer-cooking soups and stews.

French green lentils (Puy lentils, Le Puy lentils, Du Puy lentils)

Use 2½ cups water to 1 cup lentils. Boil and simmer for 40 to 45 minutes. Pressure-cooking isn't recommended.

These lentils are slate green in color with bluish black undertones and about one-third the size of green lentils. Although they originated in the volcanic soils of the Le Puy region in central France nearly two thousand years ago, French green lentils are now also grown in Italy and North America. Still, lentils from the Le Puy area offer exceptional quality, flavor, and nutritional content. Look for the AOC (Appellation d'origine contrôlée) label to ensure authenticity. Known for their distinctive rich, peppery flavor, French green lentils can be used as a side dish, in salads, as a focal point in a meal, or even as a foundation when serving meat, fish, or game. Like other green and brown lentils, French green lentils hold their shape well. They are rich in antioxidant phytochemicals similar to those in blueberries and black grapes and are also high in minerals, particularly iron and magnesium.

Green lentils (also include the Laird and Eston varieties)

Use 2½ cups water to 1 cup lentils. Boil and simmer for 40 to 45 minutes. Pressure-cooking isn't recommended.

Commonly grown in Canada, the Laird variety is a large lentil with a robust, earthy flavor. The small Eston variety, also grown in Canada, is a small, khaki green lentil with a distinctive earthy, nutty flavor. Both varieties hold their shape well when cooked.

Black beluga lentils

Use 2¼ cups water to 1 cup lentils. Boil and simmer for 25 to 30 minutes. Pressure-cooking isn't recommended.

These are tiny black lentils that look remarkably like shiny, glistening caviar when cooked. Their rich, earthy flavor and soft texture is perfect in salads and soups or featured with pasta, rice, or sautéed vegetables. Not only does their deep black color present a striking contrast when cooked with a variety of colorful green and red vegetables, but it also indicates they are high in the antioxidant anthocyanin.

Split red lentils

Use 1¾ to 2 cups water to 1 cup lentils. Boil and simmer for 10 to 15 minutes. Pressure-cooking isn't recommended.

The beautiful coral color turns golden when they're cooked. Unlike their green and brown cousins, red lentils are hulled and split. As a result, they cook very quickly. They also lose their shape during cooking, a plus when making soups, stews, vegetarian pâtés, or spreads, or simply cooking them together with white basmati rice. With their mild, earthy flavor, red lentils work well with a gamut of seasonings and cuisines, from Indian spices to fragrant Italian herbs. When rinsing red lentils prior to cooking, they will appear soapy and tend to clump together—a result of the release of starch. Red lentils foam heavily during cooking, so keep the lid of the pot slightly ajar.

Petite crimson lentils

Use 1¾ to 2 cups water to 1 cup lentils. Boil and simmer for 10 to 15 minutes. Pressure-cooking isn't recommended.

The reddish orange color of these tiny lentils turns golden once they're cooked. Like split red lentils, they have their outer seed coat removed, so they cook just as quickly. As they lose their shape in cooking, they are good for thickening soup and cooking with white rice. They may be used in any recipe that calls for split red lentils. Their mild, celery-like flavor works well with a variety of seasonings and cuisines.

Petite golden lentils

Use 1¾ to 2 cups water to 1 cup lentils. Boil and simmer for 10 to 15 minutes. Pressure-cooking isn't recommended.

A small variety that is rounder in shape than other lentils, they hold their shape fairly well when cooked. Because they cook as quickly as petite crimson lentils, the two can be used interchangeably.

Lima Beans (Baby)

Boil and simmer dried baby lima beans for 1 hour. Pressure-cooking isn't recommended.

You may have assumed that baby lima beans are simply a smaller version of lima beans or lima beans harvested earlier. However, the two are entirely different species, with baby lima beans originating in Central America. Also known as sieva beans, baby limas are flat, thin-skinned, and small (just about ½ inch long), so they cook fairly quickly. Creamy-white with a hint of green, they have a sweet, rich flavor and creamy texture. Baby lima beans work well as a featured dish seasoned with herbs, as an accompaniment to a meal, and as an addition to pasta or a pilaf.

Shelled fresh baby lima beans are green, with a sweet flavor and creamy texture when cooked. Fresh lima beans should never be eaten raw because they contain a toxin that's released when the bean's seed coat is ruptured. Cooking, however, deactivates this compound, making them safe to eat.

To prepare shelled fresh baby lima beans, cover

them with water in a pot, bring to a boil, then lower the heat and simmer until tender, about 15 minutes.

Lima Beans (Large)

Boil and simmer for 1½ hours. Pressure-cooking isn't recommended.

Also known as butter beans and fordhooks, these flat, creamy-white, disk-shaped large beans (about 1 inch long) originated in South America. Their neutral yet buttery flavor and starchy texture, similar to that of Christmas lima beans, make them particularly good for soups, stews, and casseroles. Soaking will help loosen the skin of some of the beans before cooking. More skins will loosen during cooking. As these skins could clog the vent in a pressure cooker, it's best not to pressure-cook them.

Lupini Beans

Boil and simmer for 1 hour and use a 5-day brine soak process. Or boil and simmer for 3 hours followed by draining the cooked beans along with multiple rinsings to remove bitter flavor. Pressure-cooking isn't recommended.

These large, round, white, high-protein beans, also known as white lupins and tremoços, are most commonly prepared as a traditional Mediterranean snack food. This bean native to Italy requires a long soak in brine to get rid of its bitter alkaloids. Even the improved sweet lupin strain, developed to reduce the bitter flavor, still requires a long preparation time. To prepare them traditionally, soak the beans overnight. Drain, rinse, and then add fresh water, bring to a boil, reduce the heat and simmer for 1 hour. Drain and rinse again, then cover with salted water, using about 1 tablespoon of salt per quart of water. Refrigerate the beans in the brine overnight to leech out the bitter alkaloids. The next morning, drain yet again, then repeat the brining process every day for four more days to further

remove any bitter flavor. After the fifth brining, drain the beans one last time, then serve chilled as a snack or as an ingredient in salads, with or without the skins, marinated with olive oil and herbs if desired. Alternatively, you can use the boil and simmer method to cook them for about 3 hours or until tender. Even so, the cooked beans must be thoroughly drained and rinsed many times to ensure no bitter alkaloids remain.

Madeira Beans

Boil and simmer for 1 to 1¼ hours. Pressure-cook for 18 minutes.

A relative of the cranberry bean, this heirloom variety is distinguished by its large size and mottled brown color. Often used in traditional Portuguese and Italian dishes and in soup, Madeira beans have a floury texture and chestnutlike flavor.

Marrow Beans

Boil and simmer for 1½ to 2 hours. Pressure-cook for 25 minutes.

Similar to navy beans, this heirloom variety was popular during the 1850s for baked bean casseroles. More round and plump than navy beans, marrow beans have a creamier texture and are much more flavorful, tasting, oddly enough, similar to smoked bacon. Cook marrow beans in soups, stews, or baked bean casseroles or cook, puree, and serve as a side dish.

Mung Beans

Boil and simmer for 1 hour. Pressure-cook for 15 minutes.

These small, round, olive-green beans are most familiar in their sprouted form, often used as an ingredient in Chinese stir-fries and egg rolls. When the whole beans are cooked, they have a soft texture and somewhat sweet flavor. They have many merits, as they are easily digested, cook quickly, and need not be soaked in advance. An important component in Indian curries and dals, they are also very good cooked with brown rice and in soups, stews, and pilafs.

Navy Beans

Boil and simmer for 1½ to 2 hours. Pressure-cook for 18 minutes.

These small, white, oval-shaped, mild-flavored beans are considered a staple for soups, stews, and baked bean dishes. Likewise, they are also good for purees and sandwich spreads. As their name implies, sailors have long been more than familiar with the many ways navy beans can be served. They were a key component of U.S. Navy rations during the nineteenth century. Pea beans are a smaller version of navy beans, although often the two names are used interchangeably.

Peas

Boil and simmer for 1 to 1½ hours for whole peas and 1 to 1¼ hours for split peas. Pressure-cooking isn't recommended.

Peas have a long legacy in the human diet, going back to around 6000 BCE. Dried peas aren't a dried version of the peas we generally consume as a fresh vegetable; rather, they are a different variety with a higher starch content. Both green and yellow dried peas are available, often split. Although they are cooked similarly and are comparable nutritionally, green peas have an overall earthier flavor, while yellow peas taste milder and sweeter. Whole peas can be used in casseroles or as a side dish, or be pureed and made into spreads, dips, and croquettes. They should be soaked before cooking. Split peas have their skins removed by a machine, then are sent to another machine to be split in half. Although they don't require presoaking, if you soak them for at

least 30 minutes they'll keep their shape after cooking. Still, the creaminess achieved from unsoaked peas is the texture that most people expect and find most appealing.

Pigeon Peas

Boil and simmer for 1 hour. Pressure-cook for 16 minutes.

Most commonly used in Caribbean and African cuisines, pigeon peas are small, oval, brownish beans with a nutty, somewhat strong earthy flavor and mealy texture. Because they cook fairly quickly, pigeon peas are commonly cooked together with rice, or cooked ahead and served with seasoned rice, usually with hot, assertive seasonings.

Pink Beans

Boil and simmer for 1¼ to 1½ hours. Pressure-cook for 18 minutes.

These small, oval, pale pink beans are used extensively in Caribbean cooking, where they're served with rice. They're also commonly used in Southwestern cuisine. Their flavor is rich and meaty. Although they can be used interchangeably with pinto beans, pink beans have a firmer texture when cooked.

Pinto Beans

Boil and simmer for 1½ hours. Pressure-cook for 18 minutes.

In Spanish, the word *pinto* means "painted," an apt description for these oblong beans with a mottled salmon pink and brown pattern. Typically the bean of choice in Southwestern cuisine, their mealy texture makes particularly good refried beans. A natural served with rice, pinto beans are also great in dips, soups, chili, and stews.

Rattlesnake Beans

Boil and simmer for 1½ hours. Pressure-cook for 16 to 18 minutes.

The name of this hybrid variety of the pinto bean is derived from the fact that its growing pods twist like snakes. Although they're darker than pinto beans, the mottled patterns on rattlesnake beans are similar to those of pintos and their flavor, too, is similar, although richer. They can be used in any recipe that calls for pinto beans. They're especially good in Southwestern dishes and soups.

Red Beans

Boil and simmer for 1½ hours. Pressure-cook for 18 minutes.

These small, pea-shaped, dark red beans are used extensively in Creole and Mexican cuisines. Their flavor is reminiscent of kidney beans, although milder and slightly sweeter, and they hold their shape when cooked. While red beans and rice is their most well-known use, they also work well in soups, salads, and any recipe that calls for kidney beans.

Rice Beans

Boil and simmer for 1 hour. Pressure-cooking isn't recommended.

This is an heirloom bean hailing back to the 1860s in Germany. As the name implies, the white version looks like a plump version of cooked rice. They come in many colors, including green and various shades of brown. Delicate and slightly sweet in flavor, rice beans are a delicious addition to soups, casseroles, salads, and vegetable dishes. Because they are so small, they cook quickly, too, and presoaking is optional.

Scarlet Runner Beans

Boil and simmer for 1½ hours. Pressure-cook for 18 minutes.

This heirloom variety can be traced back to the 1750s in Great Britain, where the plant was used as an ornamental. Fairly large in size and sweet in flavor, scarlet runner beans have a deep magenta and black color and are shaped similarly to kidney beans. Use them in soups and stews, and in any recipe that calls for pinto beans or pink beans.

Soldier Beans

Boil and simmer for 1½ hours. Pressure-cook for 18 minutes.

Also known as European soldier beans, this heirloom bean was originally used in early New England for baked beans. They are long and white, with red markings along one side that look curiously like the silhouette of a toy soldier. Soldier beans have a mild flavor and firm texture that works well in soups, stews, and salads.

Soybeans

Soybeans originated in China around three thousand years ago and since then have won notoriety throughout the world for their versatility and nutrient value. They are most commonly eaten in the form of tempeh and tofu (see page 136). When it comes to nutrition, soybeans are the only bean containing all nine of the essential amino acids in the proper proportion to be recognized as a complete protein. Although they contain more fat than any other bean, the fat is primarily unsaturated, making them compare more favorably to many other high-protein foods that are high in saturated fat, including meat and eggs.

In 1999, the U.S Food and Drug Administration allowed a heart-healthy claim on food products that contain at least 6.25 grams of soy protein per serving, stating that soy could help lower a person's risk of heart disease if eaten as part of a diet low in saturated fat and cholesterol. Since that time, however, studies have not been able to support these assertions. Nevertheless, reducing the amount of saturated fats in your diet by replacing proteins such as meat, poultry, and eggs with soy, or alternating between these two types of protein, remains a very good idea.

In terms of phytonutrients, soy contains the highest amount of isoflavones, naturally occurring compounds in plants that can exert weak estrogen-like effects on the body. Classified as phytoestrogens, isoflavones can bind to estrogen receptors in various tissues, including those related to reproduction. The amount of isoflavones in soy foods depends on the level of processing and whether or not the isoflavones or soy protein is intentionally concentrated.

Although it was once theorized that the lower incidence of breast cancer in Japan was linked to higher consumption of soybeans, it is now thought that, with the exception of women who had a soy-rich diet during adolescence, higher intakes of soy do not necessarily correlate with a lower risk of breast cancer. Studies have also shown inconsistent results in regard to soy's ability to reduce the incidence of prostate cancer, improve bone density, or relieve symptoms of menopause.

Still, it is important to note that most of these studies used highly processed, fractionated forms of soy, such as isolated soy protein or soy isoflavones, not whole soybeans. Soy protein isolate is highly processed, created by extracting the protein components from soybeans to create various products that imitate meat or provide a concentrated source of vegetable protein. In addition, the isoflavones used in the studies were concentrated to levels significantly higher than those occur naturally, despite the fact that the long-term safety of high supplemental doses of isolated isoflavones is unknown.

Still, while soy is not the panacea it was formerly thought to be, it remains a very versatile, nutritious food when eaten in moderation and in whole or minimally processed forms that retain all of its vitamins, minerals, polyunsaturated fats, phytonutrients, protein, fiber, and other constituents in naturally occurring amounts. Accordingly, it is best to get both soy isoflavones and soy protein from cooked whole soybeans and minimally processed soy foods such as tofu, tempeh, miso, roasted soybeans, and soymilk, all of which are considered safe and potentially beneficial. However, those with a family or personal history of estrogen-sensitive cancer should talk with their doctor about whether it's okay to eat soy foods.

Fresh, immature, green soybeans, also known as edamame, are cooked by steaming or boiling them in their pods for 3 to 5 minutes. Drain and cool, then split open the pods, remove the beans, and eat them as an appetizer with or without added salt, or add them to soups.

Cooking whole soybeans is just as easy as cooking any other dry bean—it just takes longer. Soybeans must always be soaked and then cooked thoroughly to deactivate protease inhibitors that would otherwise block the body's enzymes from doing their job of digesting protein. Pressure-cooking and boiling and simmering are the preferred methods for cooking whole soybeans. If a slow cooker is used, the soybeans must first be boiled on the stove for 10 minutes to ensure that the protease inhibitor is deactivated. Because they contain less starch, they will remain more firm in texture and retain their shape rather than becoming creamy, even though they must be cooked longer than other beans. There are two types of dried soybeans: yellow and black. They may be used interchangeably and are suitable for use in salads, soups, and stews or can be served with pasta or grains, especially rice.

Yellow or beige soybeans are the basic variety of soybeans used for cooking and processing. As they have a bland but beany flavor and are less digestible than other cooked whole beans, yellow soybeans are most commonly eaten in the form of tofu and tempeh. Still, they can be jazzed up with a variety of seasonings or served in a flavorful sauce or stew.

Black soybeans, when cooked in their whole form, they are much more flavorful than yellow soybeans, with a flavor somewhat reminiscent of regular black beans. They are also used as the basis of salty, spicy Chinese fermented black beans, which are added to dishes before steaming or stir-frying. They're also featured in Chinese black bean sauce, a strong, salty sauce used in many Chinese dishes. For a delicious twist on hummus, substitute black soybeans for garbanzo beans.

Boil and simmer either yellow or black soybeans for 3 hours. Pressure-cook for 40 minutes.

Spanish Tolosana Beans

Boil and simmer for 1½ hours. Pressure-cook for 18 minutes.

Also known as prince beans, Spanish tolosana beans are an heirloom variety introduced in the late 1920s that are popular in Spanish cuisine. They are shaped like kidney beans, although smaller in size, and have a mottled cinnamon and burgundy color that fades slightly when cooked. Serve them in salads or as an accompaniment to seafood. Their creamy texture makes them a great bean to use in soups.

Steuben Yellow-Eye Beans

Boil and simmer for 1¼ to 1½ hours. Pressure-cook for 18 minutes.

This heirloom variety with many names, including molasses face, Maine yellow-eye, and butter-scotch calypso, dates from the 1860s in Maine and Vermont. Steuben yellow-eye beans are medium-size, white-colored beans with distinctive mark-ings similar to those of black-eyed peas; however, the "eye" is yellow and turns a light brown when cooked. Steuben yellow-eye beans are the variety most commonly used when making baked beans because of their mild flavor and firm texture. They are also very good in salads and soups.

Swedish Brown Beans

Boil and simmer for 1½ hours. Pressure-cook for 18 minutes.

These heirloom beans were introduced about one hundred years ago by Scandinavian immigrants. Small, and oval-shaped, they retain their honey-brown color when cooked. Considered another bean of choice for old-fashioned baked beans, Swedish brown beans have a rich, nutty, slightly sweet flavor and tender texture that makes them good not only for baked beans but also for soups and stews and as an accompaniment to any grain or pasta.

Tongues of Fire

Boil and simmer dried tongues of fire for 1½ hours. Pressure-cook for 18 minutes.

This Italian heirloom variety, known as *borlotto lingua di fuoco* in its native tongue, is a version of the cranberry bean distinguished by its mottled beige and brown markings. Their delicious, full-bodied flavor and mild texture makes them a nice addition to Italian pasta dishes and soups. They are also very good for baked beans and in salads.

To prepare shelled fresh tongues of fire beans, cover them with water in a pot, bring to a boil, then lower the heat and simmer until tender, about 15 to 20 minutes.

White Emergo Beans

Boil and simmer for 1½ hours. Pressure-cook for 18 minutes.

This white bean with a half-moon shape is an heirloom variety that's slightly larger than lima beans. Their sweet flavor and creamy texture make them a good choice for use in soups and salads, or in any recipe that calls for gigande or cannellini beans.

Tempeh and Tofu: Soybeans at Their Best

Two of the tastiest and most digestible ways to enjoy soybeans are tempeh and tofu. Quick to cook, both readily absorb seasonings, making them very versatile. Their textures also make them good substitutes for meat in sauces, sandwiches, stir-fries, and casseroles.

Tempeh

Tempeh is a traditional Indonesian soy food with a tender, chewy texture and a mild flavor reminiscent of mushrooms. Tempeh is made by culturing cooked, cracked soybeans with the fungus *Rhizopus oligosporus*, in a process similar to making blue cheese. After an incubation period of eighteen to twenty-four hours, the soybeans are bound into a cakelike form created by the mycelia of the fungus, a network of white cottony filaments. Grains such as rice, quinoa, and amaranth, as well as sesame seeds and peanuts, are often combined with the soybeans before inoculation for increased flavor.

Tempeh contains all the nutrients and phytonutrients of whole soybeans, including the beneficial fiber. Its protein is particularly high in quality and quantity, providing 18 grams of protein per 4-ounce serving. The fermentation process involved in its production makes it more digestible, a benefit common to all fermented foods, as their proteins, fats, and carbohydrates are broken down into simpler compounds during the fermentation process. Fermentation also neutralizes phytic acid, a compound found in many plant foods that binds with minerals and impedes their absorption. Therefore

the fermentation of tempeh makes it easier for the body to absorb the many minerals present in soybeans, including zinc, iron, and calcium.

Although there are many claims to the contrary, tempeh processed in the United States and Europe is not a vegetarian source of B$_{12}$, as tempeh produced traditionally in Indonesia is. However, the source of B$_{12}$ in Indonesian tempeh is neither the soybeans nor the *Rhizopus oligosporus*, but one of two bacteria, either *Citrobacter freundii* or *Klebsiella pneumoniae*, which develop as a result of "accidental" inoculation that can occur when sanitary conditions are less than optimal. As most Western tempeh producers use a pure *Rhizopus oligosporus* culture in tightly regulated environments, the presence of these bacteria, and the B$_{12}$ they produce, would be unlikely.

Tempeh can be found either in the refrigerated or frozen food department. Its texture, flavor, and overall quality vary widely depending on the specific methods and equipment used, the quality of the ingredients, and the manufacturer's skill, so it's a good idea to experiment with different brands. While the flavor of tempeh is milder when its surface color appears completely white, tempeh with small black spots, which can occur during the process of fermentation, is still safe to eat. Keep tempeh refrigerated, cooking it prior to the use-by date indicated on the product's label. Once cooked, it should be consumed within 5 to 6 days. Alternatively, uncooked tempeh can be frozen in its original packaging in the freezer for up to six months. Throw it away if it begins to smell like ammonia or grows patches of rainbow colors.

Preparation of tempeh is very simple. It's best to season it prior to cooking and cook it for at least 30 minutes. An easy and delicious way to prepare tempeh is to season it lightly with tamari and herbs or spices, add a little water, then bake it at 350°F for 30 to 35 minutes. Alternatively, it can be marinated for an hour prior to baking for deeper flavor. Use the baked tempeh as a filling for sandwiches or wraps, or serve it with pasta, rice, or a whole grain. Tempeh can be cooked in many other ways, as well, both on its own and with other ingredients: stir-fried, grilled, pan-fried, broiled, braised in a small amount of water or broth, or added to stews and soups. When crumbled, it has a meatlike texture that goes well in spaghetti sauces and on pizza instead of sausage.

Tofu

First produced in China about two thousand years ago and introduced to Japan a thousand years later, tofu remains an integral component of Asian cuisine while becoming a major source of protein worldwide. In 1770, Benjamin Franklin sent a friend soybean seeds from England, along with a note about the fascinating idea that soybeans were being used to produce cheese in China. But it wasn't until two hundred years later, in an era of increasing exploration of the diversity of global ideas and cultures, that tofu went from relative obscurity in Western nations to become a food emblematic of the times.

William Shurtleff and Akiko Aoyagi's comprehensive *The Book of Tofu*, first published in 1975, introduced its readers not only to the countless ways to prepare tofu but also to the idea of right livelihood through the production of tofu. Consequently, scores of local tofu shops sprang up, both large and small, many of which continue to thrive to this day.

Nutritionally, tofu is an excellent source of high-quality protein: 7 grams based on the Nutrition Facts reference serving size of 3.2 ounces of firm tofu. And, with the exception of fiber, which is removed as part of the tofu-making process, it contains all the nutrients, including isoflavones, found in whole soybeans. It is also very easy to digest, thanks to the fact that the oligosaccharides, the complex carbohydrates that make soybeans (and all beans) difficult to digest, are removed during the manufacturing process. Protease inhibitors found in raw soybeans that can impede the digestion of its protein are also mostly destroyed during the cooking process that occurs when making tofu. In fact, low concentrations of protease inhibitors are now considered to help reduce the risk of cancer in humans.

Although the flavor of plain, unseasoned tofu is mild, having little taste on its own, it is this very quality that makes tofu so versatile. Depending upon how it is seasoned, what it is cooked with, and how it is cooked, every tofu dish you prepare can be unique.

As with tempeh, one of the easiest ways to cook tofu is to bake it. Slice or cube it, sprinkle with tamari and any combination of herbs and spices, place it in an oiled pan, and bake at 350°F for 25 to 30 minutes. If you wish, marinate it for up to 30 minutes prior to baking to infuse more flavor into the tofu. When added to stews, soups, chili, and vegetable medleys, tofu will contribute its soft texture to the dish while absorbing the flavors in which it is immersed. It is delicious stir-fried with a lot of vegetables, and its soft texture makes it excellent for blending with other ingredients to make dips and sandwich spreads.

Tofu can also be substituted for dairy and eggs in recipes. It can be transformed to emulate the flavor and texture of dairy products such as cream cheese, sour cream, cottage cheese, and whipped cream, and it does a good job of replacing ricotta in pasta dishes. When crumbled and sautéed with onions, scrambled tofu makes a worthy stand-in for scrambled eggs, especially when a pinch of turmeric is added to give the dish its characteristic yellow hue.

There are four main types of tofu, differentiated by their density and texture: soft, firm, extra-firm, and silken. The first three, soft, firm, and extra-firm, are made somewhat like soft cheese is. The process starts by soaking soybeans overnight, then grinding them with water and cooking to make a soymilk slurry. After straining it to remove the fiber, a coagulant is added to curdle the soymilk. The curds are then separated from the "whey" and placed into containers or forms where they are pressed to expel more moisture, the extent depending on the density desired. The finished tofu is then either vacuum-packed or packaged in water-filled plastic tubs.

As tofu is a very perishable product, most packaged tofu is pasteurized during the manufacturing process to prevent spoilage from potentially harmful microorganisms while it remains in the unopened package. Avoid any packages that appear bloated and never use tofu that has a sour odor or a slimy texture upon opening. All of these indicate spoiled tofu caused by some glitch in the packaging process.

When using unpasteurized tofu in dips and other recipes that won't undergo any cooking, boil it in water for at least 5 minutes, then allow it to cool before proceeding with the recipe. For extra assurance, even pasteurized tofu should be briefly boiled before it's used in uncooked recipes. Any unused raw tofu can be kept in the refrigerator for up to six days as long as it's stored in water that is drained and replenished daily. Cooked tofu should be stored in the refrigerator and used within six days.

Although all types of regular tofu are made in the same basic way, there are distinct differences in flavor and quality among the various brands. The most important determinant of quality is the skill of the producer, but variations can also be attributed to the quality of the soybeans, the source of water, the kinds of coagulants used, and the type of equipment used—whether the tofu is mass produced by a largely mechanized method or is made in smaller batches requiring hands-on attention.

The type or blend of coagulant used determines the final density, texture, and flavor of the tofu. Magnesium chloride, which can be obtained from seawater or created synthetically, creates a firmer, denser tofu with a subtle natural sweetness. Cal-

cium sulfate yields a soft, smooth consistency and a mild flavor, as well as additional calcium content. Glucono-delta-lactone (GDL), an acidifying agent derived from corn, is more typically used to make silken tofu. It provides a very soft, smooth consistency and a bland flavor.

Silken tofu, popular in traditional Japanese cuisine, is much lighter, more delicate, and sweeter tasting than regular tofu, resembling a custard or thick cream. Modern manufacturing of silken tofu depends on a thicker, richer soymilk that is neither strained nor pressed. After mixing the pasteurized soymilk with coagulating agents, glucono-delta-lactone and calcium chloride, it is poured directly into individual cartons that are then sealed in an aseptic, sterile atmosphere. Immersion in hot water activates the coagulant to form the tofu inside the carton. Since the curds and whey are not separated in the process as with regular tofu, silken tofu has a higher water content, which accounts for its softer, smoother consistency. Firm and extra-firm versions of silken tofu are made by adding soy protein isolates during manufacture. An advantage of aseptic-packed silken tofu is that it's shelf stable under cool, dry conditions and need not be refrigerated until after it's opened. It must, however, be used by the date stated on the package.

Which type of tofu to choose depends on its intended use. Silken tofu has a creamy custardlike texture and therefore works well in dips, sauces, soups, smoothies, and salad dressings. Soft tofu can be used in similar ways, and because of its similarity to ricotta cheese, it can also be used as a nondairy substitute for ricotta and cottage cheese in recipes. Because firm tofu holds its shape better, it's a good variety to use in tofu salads and scrambled tofu and as the basis for nondairy cheesecakes. Extra-firm is best when using tofu in cubed or sliced form, whether baked, sautéed, stir-fried, or fried.

However, there are ways to make soft tofu harder and, conversely, hard tofu softer. Soft tofu can be made firmer by pressing some of the liquid out of the tofu. Place the tofu in a cloth or between paper towels on a hard surface, then put a plate or cutting board on top and place something heavy on top, such as a thick book or a skillet. Allow it to set for 30 minutes to expel the liquid. Conversely, if a recipe calls for soft tofu and you have hard tofu on hand, simply soak the tofu in water or, if the tofu is used in mashed form, mash it with a bit of extra liquid.

Another way to change the texture of tofu and increase its ability to absorb flavors is to freeze it. When thawed and cooked, it has a chewy, meaty quality. Once it's crumbled, it's a perfect substitute for ground beef in casseroles, pizza, stews, or spaghetti sauce. Sliced or cubed frozen tofu is delicious baked, sautéed, or stir-fried and finished with a sauce or seasoned with a splash of tamari and any variety of herbs and spices. To freeze tofu, simply place it in the freezer for a minimum of thirty-six hours but no longer than four months. Vacuum-packed tofu can be frozen as is. Water-packed tofu should be drained and then frozen in a container or plastic bag. Silken tofu should be removed from its aseptic packaging and sliced before freezing. The tofu will turn yellow while in a frozen state but return to its original color once thawed. Thaw frozen tofu in the refrigerator. Placing it in a pan of water while in the refrigerator will accelerate defrosting. Once it's thawed, squeeze out the excess liquid before cooking.

Freeze-dried tofu is an ancient version on the frozen tofu theme. In its packaged form it looks unusual, perhaps even inedible, resembling a pack of small, pale beige sponges, but when reconstituted, it has a finer, firmer-grained texture and is more absorbent than regular tofu. When available, it can be found in the Asian food section of natural foods stores or specialty grocers.

The traditional manufacture of freeze-dried tofu is just as intriguing as its appearance. In the mountains of Japan, the tofu is suspended on wooden racks, where it is allowed to freeze at night and thaw during the day, allowing for evaporation of its moisture. After about twenty days, the tofu is extremely dry, light in weight, and finely textured. Some freeze-dried tofu is now made in factories over a yearlong process, using tofu made with calcium chloride as the coagulant, for a softer version, instead of the more traditional tofu coagulated with nigari. Ammonia gas is used to set the color.

Freeze-dried tofu needs no refrigeration, but to ensure best flavor use it by the freshness date on the package. (Freeze-dried tofu past its prime will turn a yellowish brown color.) Once the package is open, the tofu should be stored in an airtight plastic bag or container and used within four months. To reconstitute, soak the cakes in hot water on each side for 5 minutes. Press between towels or the palms of your hands to squeeze out excess liquid. Then cover the tofu with hot water again, soak for an additional 5 minutes, and squeeze out the liquid. Repeat this process a few times, until the soaking water remains clear rather than becoming milky white. Cook reconstituted freeze-dried tofu for at least 20 minutes in soups or stews, with vegetables, or alone with your choice of seasonings. When shredded, it can be used as a meat substitute in spaghetti sauce, chili, and casseroles. It can also be marinated for 30 minutes before cooking. Since freeze-dried tofu is such a concentrated food, one cake is usually enough per person.

Nuts and Seeds

At my house, nuts or seeds are a fundamental food we couldn't do without.
Breads, appetizers, snacks, soups, salads, veggies, pasta, entrées, and desserts, you
name it—all are often enhanced with nuts and seeds in one way or another. Breakfast
might be almond butter on muffins or oatmeal and raisins sprinkled with roasted pecans. At lunch, combining tahini with pureed beans of any type makes for a quick and
easy sandwich spread, or the crunchy texture of roasted sunflower seeds might make
a welcome appearance in whole wheat wraps. Savory lentils and Kamut pasta topped
with roasted walnuts is a standard dinner at least once a week, and anything served
with rice and roasted almonds is an instant success.

Each type of nut or seed provides a unique taste, texture, and aroma that is both
satisfying on its own and a wonderful complement to other elements in a dish or meal,
adding depth, interest, and visual appeal. When you add in the variety of flavors,
textures, and functional properties provided by basic preparation techniques, such as
toasting, grinding into nut and seed butters, and making creamy nut and seed milks,
the possibilities these nutritious foods offer are endless. Cooking with their oils provides
yet another way to experience and benefit from nuts and seeds, but we'll explore that
in the next chapter.

A Compact Source of Nutrients

Botanically speaking, only a few of the foods we think of as nuts fit the technical definition of nuts: a dry indehiscent one-seeded fruit with a woody pericarp. Chestnuts,
hazelnuts, and acorns are all true nuts. Other culinary nuts fall into the less-than-
familiar category of drupes—a type of fruit with fleshy tissues surrounding a pit that
holds a seed inside. While we usually eat drupes in the form of fruit (apricots, cherries,
peaches, plums, and other stone fruits, as well as mangos and avocados), almonds and

Grams of Protein per Ounce

Almonds	6 grams
Brazil nuts	4.1 grams
Cashews	5.2 grams
Chestnuts	0.9 grams
Coconut (dried)	2 grams
Flaxseeds	5 grams
Hazelnuts	4.2 grams
Macadamia nuts	2.2 grams
Peanuts	7 grams
Pecans	2.6 grams
Pine nuts	4 grams
Pistachios	5.8 grams
Pumpkin seeds	7 grams
Sesame seeds (with hulls)	5 grams
Sesame seeds (without hulls)	5.8 grams
Sunflower seeds	6.5 grams
Walnuts, black	6.8 grams
Walnuts, English	4.3 grams

pistachios are a couple of drupes we think of as nuts. Other culinary nuts fall into other obscure botanical categories, like capsules and kernels, and as most of us know, the ubiquitous peanut is actually a legume and grows underground. Some of the "nuts" we eat are botanically defined as seeds, such as cashews and pine nuts. Of course, most of the foods we think of as seeds are indeed seeds, including sunflower seeds, sesame seeds, pumpkin seeds, and flaxseeds.

Regardless of how they are categorized botanically, all nuts are indeed seeds in the sense that they are reproductive structures and can sprout and grow into a new plant. As such, they are packed with nutrients to support the new plant until it begins producing nutrients on its own. The same is true of grains and beans, also foods with an excellent nutritional profile. So what is it that makes nuts and seeds so special? Their high protein content is one thing that sets them apart from most plant foods, but even more important is the healthful oils they contain.

A Good Source of Protein

It's not just by chance that nuts are sometimes referred to as nutmeats. While a few varieties provide only low to moderate amounts of protein, others contain significant amounts, most notably almonds, black walnuts, pistachios, and peanuts, supplying as much protein in a single ounce as 1 egg, ½ cup of cooked dried beans, or 1 ounce of meat, poultry, or fish. Most varieties of seeds provide a similar amount of protein, with pumpkin seeds, hulled sesame seeds, and sunflower seeds being exceptionally good sources. Whether as a primary source of protein or just an adjunct, nuts and seeds are a good source of protein that is low in saturated fat and free of cholesterol.

Healthy Fats, Phytosterols, and Antioxidants

The predominance of beneficial fats in nuts and seeds is another nutritional bonus. With few exceptions, their fats are monounsaturated and polyunsaturated, both of which are much more healthful than the saturated fat that predominates in most animal foods. Monounsaturated fat, often dubbed the heart-healthy fat, can reduce levels of LDL cholesterol (bad cholesterol) while sparing HDL cholesterol (good cholesterol). The polyunsaturated fats found in nuts and seeds provide essential fatty acids (EFAs): linoleic acid (an omega-6 fatty acid) and alpha-linolenic acid (an omega-3 fatty acid). Collectively, EFAs help maintain the structure of healthy cell membranes, particularly in nerve tissue and the retina, and promote healthy skin. EFAs also help regulate many vital systems within the body, including the inflammation response, immune function, blood pressure, and blood clotting. Because they're a good source of these healthful fats, regular consumption of nuts and seeds can help reduce the risk of cancer, diabetes, other chronic diseases, and even macular degeneration, an age-related eye disease that limits vision. It can also help reduce blood cholesterol levels and decrease incidence of cardiovascular disease.

Nuts and seeds provide an extra heart-healthy boost due to their high phytosterol content. These naturally occurring components of plant cell membranes have a chemical structure similar to that of cholesterol but act differently in the body. They block the absorption of dietary cholesterol that's circulating in the blood and reduce the liver's reabsorption of cholesterol that your body naturally produces.

Nuts and seeds are also a good source of certain vitamins and minerals, including calcium, vitamin E, iron, and zinc. As if all this weren't enough, they're also a good source of antioxidants, compounds that work within the body to help prevent and moderate damage from oxidative stress—whether from external sources, such as pollutants, toxins, and rancid fats, or from internal sources, such as the normal oxidation processes involved in metabolism and the production of energy. Although fruits and vegetables are the foods most commonly associated with high levels of antioxidants, nuts and seeds, particularly pecans, walnuts, hazelnuts, and pistachios, are also an exceptional source, often in the form of compounds that provide their color and astringent flavors.

What about weight gain from eating nuts and seeds? Because they're high in fat, they are indeed more calorie dense. However, as long as they're eaten in moderation and included as a substitute, rather than an addition, in place of other snacks or foods high in saturated fat, weight gain shouldn't be an issue. In fact, including more healthy fats in the diet can actually help with weight loss, providing not only the nutrients the body needs to function properly but increased satisfaction, as well.

BUYING AND STORING

As you can see, nuts and seeds are extremely healthful—if they're fresh and properly stored. However, once they become rancid, they pose significant health hazards, including weakening the immune system and promoting aging. Even worse, they are carcinogenic. Because many nuts are somewhat expensive, it can be difficult to discard them. Let this be your motivation to purchase only nuts in good, fresh condition. Buy them in smaller quantities, and store them properly. Consuming nuts that are even only slightly rancid is simply not worth the health risk.

The best way to purchase whole nuts and seeds is in the shell. If fresh and in good condition when purchased, they can be kept at room temperature for up to three months. They will last for up to six months if refrigerated or one year if frozen. Look for unshelled nuts that are heavy for their size and free of cracks or holes.

Shelled nuts are, however, more convenient, and some nuts, like cashews, macadamia nuts, and black walnuts, are only available shelled. For optimum freshness, flavor, texture, and nutrition, the best way to buy nuts and seeds is in bags or containers that have been vacuum-packed or nitrogen-flushed, or packed in oxygen-barrier plastic or foil packaging. This especially pertains to varieties that contain a high proportion of polyunsaturated fats, which are more susceptible to rancidity. Otherwise, look for whole and shelled nuts and seeds that are fresh and stored in cool and clean conditions away from direct light. In general, nuts and seeds should look firm and have uniform color inside and out. Avoid any nuts and seeds that are shriveled, moldy, or discolored.

Shelf life for shelled nuts can range from one month to one year, depending on the particular nut or seed and how well it has been stored from harvest to sale. After you purchase nuts and seeds, store them in glass jars or tightly sealed containers at temperatures below 50°F and away from light and moisture. It's best to refrigerate them if you have the space available to do this. Freezing will extend freshness, stretching shelf life from six months to one year. Chopped, sliced, or ground nuts are extremely susceptible to rancidity, so it's best to buy whole nuts and process them at home just prior to use.

Both raw and roasted nuts are available. Raw nuts have a milder, sweeter taste, while roasted nuts have a deeper color, intensified flavor, and crisper, crunchier texture. Roasted nuts are also less likely to sink to the bottom when baking them in muffins, quick breads, and cakes. However, because the fat within the nuts is exposed to oxygen during the roasting process, roasted nuts have a shorter shelf life than raw nuts do and require special attention for storage.

When buying roasted nuts, dry-roasted varieties are your best bet, since the oil used to roast them adds an extra element of risk, especially if the oil is less fresh or of poor quality. Not only can this make the nuts more susceptible to rancidity and subsequent oxidation, but it can also affect their flavor. In fact, unless you're confident the nuts are freshly roasted, just buy raw nuts and roast them at home, storing any extra in the refrigerator in a glass jar or tightly sealed container for up to four weeks; frozen, they'll keep for nine to twelve months. The process is very easy, and as a side benefit, the alluring aroma of roasting nuts will waft and linger throughout the house.

ROASTING AND BLANCHING AT HOME

Nuts and seeds can be toasted in a skillet on top of the stove or in the oven. To pan-roast, preheat a skillet over low heat and add a thin layer of nuts or seeds. Stir constantly, checking for doneness after 5 minutes and every few minutes thereafter to prevent burning. Don't even think of walking away, even if "just for a minute," as they can burn very quickly. Even though skillet-toasting may seem quicker, it's difficult to toast the nuts and seeds as evenly in a skillet as in the oven, where the heat is evenly distributed.

To oven-roast, preheat the oven to 275°F to 300°F, spread the nuts or seeds on a baking sheet, and bake for anywhere from 5 to 10 minutes, depending on the nut or seed, stirring occasionally. Using these lower temperatures will ensure more even roasting throughout the nut and actually increase shelf life. As with pan-roasting, check nuts frequently; it's all too easy to burn them. Since they will continue to roast while cooling, remove them from the heat just before you think they're done. The nuts will become crisper as they cool.

For a special treat, toward the end of roasting, sprinkle nuts with shoyu, stir to coat, and then place them back in the oven to dry for about 2 minutes. Alternatively, nuts can be immersed in shoyu prior to roasting, using about 2 tablespoons per cup of nuts, and then roast the nuts at 300°F for 10 to 15 minutes. Tamari-roasted nuts are terrific as a snack, especially when combined with raisins or sprinkled on foods as a condiment.

Blanched almonds or hazelnuts are also best prepared at home. Like roasting, blanching accelerates the oxidative process, even more so since the process removes the skin, which is a natural barrier to oxygen. You might also consider whether blanched nuts are truly necessary in a given application. Since the skin contains tannins and other phenolic compounds that are excellent antioxidants, removing the skin not only reduces fiber but also significantly lowers the phytonutrient value of the nut.

If you still choose to blanch nuts, the method for almonds is different than that for peanuts, hazelnuts, and pistachios. To blanch almonds, simply pour boiling water over the nuts, allow them to set for 3 minutes, and drain. Then put the almonds in cold water for 1 minute. Gently rub the almonds between your thumb and fingers to slip off their skins. If desired, the blanched almonds can be dried by lightly roasting them in 300°F oven for just a few minutes.

To blanch peanuts, hazelnuts, or pistachios, first roast them, then immediately wrap them in a clean terrycloth or coarsely textured towel to steam for about 5 minutes. Briskly rub them in the towel for 1 to 3 minutes, or until the skins are removed to the degree desired.

Nut and Seed Butters

Nut butter (referred to as nut paste in Europe if made without sugar) is another way to enjoy the flavors and nutrition of nuts. In general, 2 tablespoons of nut butter is the equivalent of 1 ounce of nuts. Typically used as spreads for bread and crackers, nut butters can also be used as the basis for sauces, gravies, dips, and cookies. Nearly any raw or roasted nut can be processed into nut butter, but the most commonly sold varieties are almond butter, cashew butter, hazelnut butter, sesame butter or tahini, and, of course, peanut butter. Nut butters are also sold freshly ground by a machine in the store. If made from very fresh nuts or seeds and ground at low temperatures, these usually provide the best flavor. All prepacked, freshly ground nut butters should be stored and sold refrigerated and labeled with a "best sold by" date.

Thanks to the force of gravity, the oils and solids of natural nut and seed butters tend to separate. However, once the oils are stirred in, they will remain suspended in the solids if the nut butter is refrigerated. Another trick is to store unopened jars of nut butter upside down at room temperature to help distribute the oils. You'll still have some stirring to do, but it will be much easier. Avoid nut butters that contain hydrogenated fat to prevent separation. Although palm oil can be used as a natural, nonhydrogenated stabilizer, not only is it unnecessary, but it also adds additional fat.

MAKING NUT AND SEED BUTTERS AT HOME

You can also make your own nut and seed butters at home. First roast the nuts, then process them in a blender or food processor until creamy. To facilitate the grinding and yield a better consistency, add 1 teaspoon to 1 tablespoon of oil per 2 cups of nuts or peanuts. Some juicers have attachments specifically for making nut butters.

Nut and Seed Milks

Nut and seed milks can be used like dairy milk: as a hot or cold beverage, poured over hot and cold cereals, as the basis for making yogurt or ice cream, as an ingredient when baking, and for all cooking applications, including sauces, gravies, puddings, and custards. However, they should never be used for infant formula, as their nutritional profile doesn't fulfill their dietary needs, even if enriched with calcium and other vitamins.

Nut and seed milks are hardly a recent phenomenon. Almond milk and walnut milk were common ingredients in European medieval cooking among both peasants and the aristocracy. Not only were they safer alternatives to dairy milk, which spoiled quickly in the days before refrigeration and pasteurization, but they also made the official list of foods approved by the Catholic Church for use during Lent and on other days when animal foods were not allowed. Even now, *latte di mandorle*, made from a sweetened almond paste (*crema di mandorle*), remains a traditional thirst-quenching summer drink in Italy and Sicily and an important ingredient in their delicious desserts and sweets.

On the other side of the ocean, Native Americans made pecan milk and sweet hickory milk for use as a beverage and as an ingredient in corn cakes and hominy. In the western part of what is now the United States, milk made from piñon nuts was left outside to freeze and made into a version of ice cream.

MAKING NUT AND SEED MILKS AT HOME

The basic process for making nut and seed milks hasn't changed much over the centuries: Grind any nut or seed and blend it with water, mixing in about one-fourth of the total amount of water before gradually adding the rest. One part nuts or seeds to four parts water is the proportion most commonly used when making nut milk. Less water makes it richer and creamier, which is handy for thickening soups or as a substitute for half-and-half. More water makes it thinner, with a consistency similar to that of skim milk. If you wish, you can pour the milk through a fine-mesh strainer or cheesecloth to filter out the gritty fiber. Nut and seed milks taste even better if you allow them to set for a couple hours for the flavors to meld before filtering and drinking.

The creamy texture of blanched almonds and cashews makes them the best candidates for nut milks, but any nut or seed or combination of them can be used. Blanching almonds and hazelnuts first to remove their skins isn't necessary, but it does make for a whiter color and smoother consistency. Nut and seed milks can be customized with other ingredients as desired. For a sweeter-tasting milk, blend in pitted dates, a banana, or any liquid sweetener, such as honey, maple syrup, agave nectar, or brown rice syrup. Fruit juice can be used for a portion of the liquid, too, and will also boost sweetness.

Homemade nut milk generally won't keep for more than three days in the refrigerator. Commercially prepared versions sold in aseptic packaging may last for seven to ten days, since they are sterilized to destroy microorganisms that could affect safety and shelf life of the product. Stabilizers such as guar gum, xanthan gum, carrageenan, carob bean gum, and soy lecithin are also typically added to help keep the fat and liquid components within the milk in suspension. Ground flaxseeds or lecithin granules can be added to homemade nut and seed milks as stabilizers, but giving the milk a vigorous shake before using it will usually do the trick.

Coconut milk is made in a different manner.

The fresh coconut water in the center of a young coconut has a slight almond flavor and is very nutritious, being especially high in potassium and other minerals. But it is the white pulp, or meat, of a mature coconut that is used to make coconut milk. Starting with a fresh coconut, remove the pulp from the shell, cut it into small pieces, then add boiling water to cover and let steep for about 10 minutes. Allow the mixture to cool briefly before transferring to a blender. Because hot liquids have a tendency to spew when blended, leave the lid slightly ajar and cover with a towel before blending. Process until the coconut is finely grated, about a minute or so. Then, using a strainer lined with a double layer of cheesecloth, strain the coconut milk into a bowl and squeeze the pulp to extract as much liquid as possible. You can add more hot water to the remaining pulp and strain and squeeze it again for a lighter coconut milk. For an extra-light coconut milk, do a third extraction.

Although the results aren't quite as tasty, dried unsweetened coconut can also be used if fresh coconut is unavailable. Combine 2 cups of coconut with 2¾ cups of water in a pan, bring to a boil, then lower the heat, cover, and simmer for 10 minutes. Transfer to a blender (observing the same cautions noted above) and process for about 1 minute. Strain the mixture as described above.

If allowed to set, coconut milk (including canned coconut milk) will separate just as raw whole milk does, with the higher fat "cream" rising to the top and the thinner "skim" layer on the bottom. Just shake the milk vigorously and the layers will combine once again. Use coconut milk as a beverage, on cereals, and in curries, desserts, soups, and sauces. Unless a recipe specifies otherwise, cook coconut milk and coconut cream over low heat, stirring constantly to avoid curdling and separation of the natural oils from the milk. Coconut milk is very perishable, lasting only about two days when refrigerated, so use it quickly.

Exploring Nuts and Seeds

Almonds

Predominantly monounsaturated fat
1 ounce = 22 to 24 almonds

Almonds are related to peaches, nectarines, and other members of the rose family. Originally native to the Mediterranean region, almonds are now grown throughout the world, with the United States (California), Spain, Syria, Iran, and Italy being the five countries with the greatest production. Sweet almonds are the edible variety, whereas bitter almonds are used as an ingredient in cosmetics and to make almond extract.

Both the standard nutrients and phytochemicals in almonds contribute to their cholesterol-reducing effects when eaten on a regular basis. They are high in heart-healthy monounsaturated fat, and their skins are not only a good source of fiber (3.3 grams per ounce), but they are also a good source of antioxidants. The skin contains most of the almond's flavonoids, including proanthocyanins, which are responsible for the slightly astringent flavor and brown color of the skin. Almonds also contain more calcium than any other nut, supplying 70 milligrams (mg) per ounce, and are one of the best nut sources of protein (6 grams per ounce) and vitamin E (7.3 mg of alpha-tocopherol per ounce). Beta-sitosterol is the primary phytosterol found in almonds, providing additional help with lowering cholesterol.

Varieties

There are hundreds of varieties of almond, each with its own unique combination of flavor intensity, shape, color, and texture, making some more appropriate than others for specific purposes. However, only a few are widely available. Here are some of the most common varieties:

- California almonds have a medium-thick shell and slightly wrinkled, medium-brown kernels. They're a good all-purpose nut and also good for blanching.
- Marcona almonds, from Spain, are a heart-shaped variety generally sold blanched, fried in oil, and salted. They have light brown, flat, smooth kernels and a very rich and somewhat sweet flavor. Fried Marcona almonds are good as a snack; raw, they're best for baking.
- Mission almonds have a thick, hearty shell; wrinkled, brownish red kernel; plump, rounded shape; and strong almond flavor. They're exceptionally good for roasting.
- Nonpareil almonds have a thin outer shell and smooth, flat, light brown kernels. They can be used for any purpose but are best for blanching.

Storage and Use

About 1 pound of almonds in the shell will yield 1¼ cups of shelled almonds. Store shelled almonds in the refrigerator for up to nine months and in the freezer for up to one year. Thanks to their edible but tough brown skins, which are retained after shelling, almonds resist rancidity better than any other nut.

Almonds can be ground into coarse flour for use as a thickener or to replace some, and sometimes all, of the flour in recipes for quick breads, pancakes, muffins, cookies, and cakes. Ready-made almond flour is typically ground from blanched almonds, which makes it somewhat ivory in color. But for ultimate freshness, make it at home by grinding raw almonds, blanched if you like, in an electric seed grinder, coffee grinder, blender, or food processor. Don't use warm almonds for this purpose and grind them using short pulses; otherwise, you're likely to end up with almond butter—also delicious, but not good for use as flour. For starters, experiment with replacing one-third of the wheat flour called for in a recipe with almond flour to see how it turns out, then increase or decrease the amount in subsequent trials until you're happy with the results. Because almond flour is heavier than wheat flour, slightly increase the amount of leavening agents. Expect the texture of the final product to be more fragile. Line the baking pan with oil and parchment paper so the baked goods can be removed more easily.

Almond butter can be used instead of butter or cream cheese as a delicious spread on muffins, toast, and bagels, or use it like peanut butter in sandwiches, cookies, sauces, and spreads. Whether made from raw or roasted almonds, its flavor is exceptional, with raw almond butter being more mellow. Like peanut butter, almond butter comes in smooth and crunchy versions. It has about the same amount of protein as peanut butter, but it's lower in saturated fat and higher in monounsaturated fat, giving it a preferable fatty acid profile.

Almond paste, a dense mixture of finely ground blanched almonds, sugar, corn syrup, water, and sometimes almond extract, is used as an ingredient in cookies, cakes, candies, and pastries, sometimes as a filling and sometimes standing in for flour. It's sold in tubes or cans that, once opened, should be stored in the refrigerator. Made with essentially the same ingredients, marzipan contains a higher percentage of sugar to create a more pliable consistency, making it easier to sculpt into decorative shapes to roll out for use as a covering on cakes.

Brazil Nuts

About equal monounsaturated and polyunsaturated
*   fat*
1 ounce = 6 to 8 Brazil nuts (but limit to no more
*   than 2 per day)*
Brazil nuts are the large seeds of trees that grow in the Amazon and reach heights of over 130 feet. They are grown primarily in Brazil, Peru, Bolivia, Columbia, Venezuela, and Guiana. The tree's fruit looks like a coconut with a woody shell, but inside are the long, wedge-shaped Brazil nuts with their own hard shells, found in clusters of twelve to twenty-four.

Remarkably, Brazil nuts contain 543 micrograms (mcg) of selenium per ounce. This trace mineral is known for its excellent antioxidant properties and ability to support the immune system, but a little goes a long way. Too much selenium over long periods of time can manifest in symptoms of selenium toxicity, most notably hair and nail brittleness and loss, as well as skin rashes, gastrointestinal disturbances, and fatigue. Since 400 mcg of selenium is the upper daily intake limit recommended for adults, consumption of Brazil nuts should be limited to no more than two per day.

Storage and Use

Brazil nuts are primarily sold shelled, as cracking the shell is a more challenging venture than with other nuts. Store shelled Brazil nuts in the refrigerator for up to six months or in the freezer for up to nine months.

Brazil nuts make a delicious snack, especially when eaten with fresh or dried fruit, such as apples, pears, raisins, dates, and figs. Their flavor and texture have a tropical flair, somewhat reminiscent of coconut and macadamia nuts, and they contribute a creamy texture to smoothies. Try a few chopped Brazil nuts in cookies, cakes, salads, and even poultry stuffing for extra texture and flavor.

Brazil nuts can be ground into a smooth, very creamy butter, although it's seldom sold commercially. It can be used like any other nut butter but, since it's exceptionally rich, it is best to use it more sparingly. In comparison to peanut butter, it is lower in protein and higher in fat, including saturated fat.

Cashews

Predominantly monounsaturated fat
1 ounce = 16 to 18 whole cashews

Cashews, which are in the same plant family as mangos and pistachios, grow near the equator on bushy medium-size trees. India, Mozambique, and Brazil are the principal producers. The grayish brown, kidney-shaped shell surrounding the cashew nut (the plant's true fruit) hangs from the lower end of the cashew apple, a pear-shaped, yellow or red fruit (technically a pseudofruit). After the cashew apple drops to the ground, the cashew nut is separated from the fruit. Cashew apples, which spoil very quickly, are eaten fresh locally or processed into juices, syrups, preserves, and alcoholic beverages.

Within the shell, the cashew is at one end and at the other end is a honeycomb of cells that contain a toxic fluid that can blister the mouth. Surrounding the nut itself is another thin brown shell. Because of the danger from the toxic oil that lies between the outer shell and the inner shell, cashews are sold only in their shelled form and are extracted using methods that ensure their safety.

Cashews contain more iron (1.9 mg) than other tree nuts. They are also a good source of beta-sitosterol, which helps reduce serum cholesterol. Since they contain more carbohydrates than most nuts, mostly in the form of starch, they're also lower in fat.

Storage and Use

Store cashews in the refrigerator for up to six months or in the freezer for up to nine months.

Their high starch content makes cashews a very effective thickener when ground and added to soups, smoothies, curries, and stews. They also yield creamy cashew milk and sauces. Their higher level of carbohydrates also means that raw cashews have a sweet flavor, one that develops more depth and complexity when they're roasted. If left whole, cashews are a wonderful addition to stir-fries and East Indian dishes. Since they become unpleasantly soggy when cooked too long, they should be added at the end of cooking to maintain crispness.

Most manufacturers add a small amount of oil when making cashew butter to compensate for the nut's higher starch content and drier consistency, creating a smoother texture. When buying cashew butter, check the label to ensure that only high-oleic oil is used; this will ensure optimum quality and greater resistance to rancidity. Cashew butter is a treat as a spread, in soups as a nondairy substitute for cream, and in dips, salad dressings, and sauces. Although it has a similar amount of saturated fat as peanut butter and less protein, it is higher in monounsaturated fat.

Chestnuts

About equal monounsaturated and polyunsaturated fat
1 ounce = 3 roasted and peeled chestnuts

Chestnuts have been used as food throughout the world for a very long time—in Asia for nearly six thousand years, in Europe for about three thousand years, in the United States certainly long before the pioneers settled the country, and in Australia since the 1850s. Though chestnut trees once grew prolifically from Maine to Georgia, a devastating blight introduced in 1904 from imported Chinese chestnut trees nearly wiped out native North American chestnut trees by 1950. Although a few surviving natives have been found and different hybrids have been developed in attempts to reinvigorate chestnut cultivation in the United States, most chestnuts purchased in the United States are imported. Worldwide, China reigns as the largest producer, with Korea as the second-largest producer. In Europe, Italy grows and exports the most chestnuts, followed by France and Spain.

Chestnuts are unique among nuts. They have a high water content, are very low in fat, and contain almost 50% carbohydrates, making them seem more like a starchy vegetable than a nut—which is exactly how they have been used and valued for thousands of years. They are also good sources of potassium and even a small amount of vitamin C. Although chestnuts are also low in protein, it is of high quality.

Varieties

The size and flavor of chestnuts vary widely among species. Though there are many wild varieties used locally, the primary types found commercially are as follows:

- American chestnuts (*Castanea dentate*) are small, with excellent, concentrated flavor. They have softer shells than other chestnuts and no astringent pellicle (a brown membrane that clings to other varieties of chestnuts).
- Chinese chestnuts (*Castanea mollissima*) are medium-size and have good flavor.
- European chestnuts (*Castanea sativa*) range in size from small to large and have good flavor. Smaller varieties are also fairly flat sided. The more commonly available variety is larger and more rounded, making it the better choice for roasting.
- Japanese chestnuts (*Castanea crenata*), confusingly, are sometimes called Chinese chestnuts, even though they are a different species. They have fair flavor and come in varied sizes.

Storage and Use

Boiled and mashed like potatoes, made into flour for bread or noodles, roasted for a snack, or even eaten raw, chestnuts have been for thousands of years a staple in the diet wherever chestnut trees have grown. They remain a highly valued snack and ingredient in contemporary times, to add flavor and texture to soups, stuffings, pastas, stir-fries, and desserts. Chestnut flour, ground from dried chestnuts, can be added to other flour when making pasta, bread, and other baked goods.

About 1 pound of chestnuts in the shell will yield 2½ cups of shelled chestnuts. Fresh chestnuts in the shell contain up to 50% water, making them prone to mold and thus highly perishable, so only purchase fresh chestnuts if they're sold refrigerated. Chestnuts should have smooth, shiny brown shells free of pinholes, mold, and splits. The best ones will feel heavy for their size. Store fresh chestnuts in a plastic bag in the refrigerator for up to three weeks or freeze them for up to nine months. Cooked chestnuts will keep for a similar period of time; store them in an airtight container.

Fresh chestnuts can be roasted, steamed, or boiled to remove the outer shell that envelops their richly flavored meat. It is actually very simple to do and, especially during holidays, creates a festive atmosphere. Before roasting or cooking chestnuts, the outer shell must be slit to keep it from exploding as the moisture within turns to steam. To make the cut, either lay the chestnut on its flat side and cut a slit halfway around the outer shell or make two slits in the form of a cross on the flatter side of the chestnut. The slits will also facilitate peeling off both the outer shell and the pellicle (the brown inner membrane). Next, cook the chestnuts using any of the following methods, but be aware that boiled chestnuts are the easiest to peel.

- Roasting over an open fire: Use a grill basket or fireplace popcorn popper. Put the chestnuts (already slit) in the basket, one layer deep, and hold them several inches over the fire, shaking frequently. To prevent charring, don't hold them too close to the fire. When they're done, their skins will be blackened. Immediately wrap roasted chestnuts within a cloth or dish towel and squeeze them until they crackle. Set them aside, still wrapped in the cloth, in a warm place for 5 minutes, then peel off the shell and pellicle while they're still warm. Once they cool, the task becomes difficult and frustrating.

- Oven-roasting: Place cut chestnuts on a cookie sheet and roast at 400°F to 425°F for 15 to 20 minutes, until the edges of the slit curl back and the chestnut meat becomes soft. Peel while still warm as instructed above.
- Stovetop toasting: This is best done with a chestnut roasting pan, which looks like a skillet with holes in the bottom. Put the slit chestnuts in the pan one layer deep and sprinkle water over them. Place the pan over medium heat, using a heat diffuser or metal trivet on an electric stove to create some space between the pan and the element and help prevent burning. Shake the pan back and forth frequently. The chestnuts are done when their skins have blackened, usually about 5 to 10 minutes. Peel while still warm as instructed above.
- Boiling: Add pierced chestnuts to a pan of boiling water, and cook at medium heat for about 15 minutes, until they can be easily pierced with a knife. Drain and allow them to partially cool, just enough until they can be handled, removing the chestnut meat from the shell with a fork. Overcooked chestnuts will have a mealy, crumbly texture.
- Steaming: To steam chestnuts, you must first cut them in half lengthwise rather than slitting them. Place a steamer basket in a pot, add water to about 1 inch below the basket, and bring to a boil. Put the chestnuts in the steamer basket and steam for 8 to 10 minutes, until the meat separates from the shell and the desired level of softness is reached.

Fresh chestnuts are fun and festive, but they're only available a few months per year. As an alternative, roasted and peeled chestnuts are available in vacuum-packed cans and bags. Once opened, they should be stored like freshly cooked chestnuts. Dried chestnuts are also available, and because they're shelf stable, they're very convenient. Store them as you would dried beans, in airtight containers for up to a year. As the natural drying process converts some of the starch within fresh chestnuts into sugar, dried chestnuts are sweeter in flavor when reconstituted. They also double in size after they are reconstituted, so use half the volume of dried chestnuts as the total amount you want when cooked. To use them in recipes in place of shelled fresh chestnuts, first soak them in cold water for six to eight hours. Or, use the quicker hot soak method by covering them with boiling water and allowing them to soak for an hour. The chestnuts can then be added directly to a recipe that will be simmered for at least an hour. Alternatively, precook the soaked chestnuts if the they will be added to recipes that require less cooking time, adding extra water, if needed, to cover the surface of the chestnuts by about 1 inch. Bring them to a boil, reduce the heat, and simmer them for an hour or until tender. For a richly flavored rice dish, cook dried chestnuts with rice in a pressure cooker.

Coconut

Predominantly saturated fat
1 ounce = ⅓ cup dried shredded coconut

The coconut palm has been highly valued since ancient times as a source of water, nutrients, fiber, and fuel. Although fresh coconut meat is often classified as a fruit, in its dried form it is treated more like a nut. Chewy and subtly sweet, coconut meat is the endosperm—nutrients designed to support the palm tree embryo as it sprouts through one of the eyes in the hard, hairy husk. Coconut palms grow in hot, rainy tropical regions, with the Philippines, Indonesia, India, Brazil, and Sri Lanka being the top five producers. Dried shredded or flaked coconut is made from coconuts that have been split open to remove the internal liquid. The endosperm is dried in the sun or in kilns until it has a 2.5% moisture content, at which point it's known as copra.

Dried coconut is high in fiber (4.6 grams per ounce). Unlike other nuts and seeds, it is primarily composed of saturated fat. However, unlike the saturated fats in meat and dairy products, which are comprised primarily of long-chain fatty acids, the saturated fat in coconut is made up of short- and medium-chain fatty acids, primarily of lauric acid followed by myristic, caprylic, and palmitic acid, which have been found to not increase cholesterol levels. These medium-chain triglycerides, also known as MCTs, are not stored as fat but rather are metabolized quickly. Caprylic acid and lauric acid are also known for their antiviral and antimicrobial properties.

Storage and Use

One medium fresh coconut will yield 3 to 4 cups of freshly grated coconut. Use a vegetable peeler to make coconut flakes. Store fresh coconut in a tightly sealed container for up to four days in the refrigerator or up to four months in the freezer. Dried coconut also keeps best when refrigerated, tightly sealed, and used within six months. Purchase only unsweetened coconut rather than the presweetened varieties. Not only is it more nutritious, but it also has better flavor. And because the amount of sweetener added varies, you can most effectively control the sweetness of foods cooked with coconut if you use the unsweetened form. Like other nuts, coconut's flavor is enhanced when it is roasted. Preheat the oven to 275°F to 300°F, spread fresh or dried unsweetened coconut on a baking sheet, and bake for about 5 to 10 minutes, until the coconut becomes golden in color.

While coconut milk made from fresh or dried coconut is a familiar ingredient in sweet and savory Asian, Indian, Hawaiian, Latin, and Caribbean cuisines (see Making Nut and Seed Milk at Home, page 145), flaked and grated coconut can also be used like nuts, added to cookies, muffins, granola, puddings, cobblers, and cakes. Or it can be simply sprinkled on fresh fruit or cereal, or used as a flavorful garnish on vegetables, main dishes, and desserts.

Flaxseeds

Predominantly polyunsaturated fat, primarily omega-3 fatty acids
1 ounce = 2¾ tablespoons of whole flaxseeds
1 tablespoon whole flaxseeds = about 1½ tablespoons ground flaxseeds

Flaxseeds are tiny, oval, reddish brown or golden seeds from the blue-flowered flax plant, now grown primarily in Canada, China, the United States, and India. Flax fiber has been used for food, clothing, and even building materials throughout the world for more than seven thousand years. When it comes to food, flaxseeds have long been prized for their flavor, fiber, and nutrient value. Flaxseeds were a valued remedy in ancient Egyptian and Greek medicine, and around 700 CE, Charlemagne thought flaxseeds so essential for health that he enacted laws requiring their regular consumption.

Half of the total fat in flaxseed (and 80% of its polyunsaturated fat) is from alpha-linolenic acid, making it the richest plant source of omega-3 fatty acids. Each tablespoon of ground flaxseeds supplies 1.8 grams of omega-3 fatty acids. Omega-3 fatty acids are deficient in most modern diets, and they're also consumed out of proportion to omega-6 fatty acids. Because flaxseed contains three times more omega-3 fatty acids than omega-6, adding flaxseeds to your diet can help correct the typical imbalance and provide significant health benefits, including reducing inflammation and lowering the risk of heart disease and cancer. And although polyunsaturated fats are normally very sensitive to heat (this is discussed in the next chapter), when flaxseeds are included in baked goods or otherwise cooked, their omega-3 fatty acids have shown to be very heat stable.

Flaxseed is also very high in fiber, providing 2.2 grams of fiber per tablespoon of ground flaxseeds. Mucilage gum is the main type of soluble fiber found in its seed coat, and when moistened, it both expands and becomes thick and sticky, making it effective in helping prevent constipation. Soluble fiber also helps maintain blood glucose levels and lower cholesterol levels.

Flax is also an excellent source of lignans, a type of fiber found within its cell walls that is acclaimed as a phytoestrogen, and also for its antioxidant capabilities. Its primary lignan, secoisolariciresinol diglycoside (SDG), is broken down by bacteria in the digestive tract and converted into the hormonelike substances enterodiol and enterolactone. (These are referred to as mammalian lignans because they are produced in the mammalian colon and not by plants.) Depending on the amount of stronger estrogens, like estradiol, available in the body, these can either act as weak estrogens and help balance hormone levels or function as estrogen antagonists, possibly helping protect against hormone-sensitive cancers, such as some forms of breast cancer. Flax contains many antioxidants beyond its lignans: flavonoids, carotenoids, lutein, zeaxanthin, and gamma-tocopherol (a form of vitamin E). All of them, as well as the metabolites enterodiol and enterolactone, help protect the body from oxidative damage and thus help guard against chronic diseases.

Although flax oil is a more concentrated source of omega-3 fatty acids than whole and ground flaxseeds, it lacks the fiber and, consequently, the potential benefits of the lignans. Some flax oil manufacturers add purified lignans back into their oils, but a better solution may be to use both flax oil and flaxseeds to get the best of both worlds.

Varieties

There are two types of flaxseed available: brown and golden. Both provide similar nutritional benefits. The main differences between the two are color, flavor, and price. Brown flaxseeds are reddish brown and have a nutty flavor. They are best for use in hearty-flavored foods or those that would be complemented by a stronger flavor. They're typically less expensive. Golden flaxseeds are light yellow and have a milder flavor. They are best for use in lighter-flavored foods. They're typically more expensive because they aren't as widely available.

Storage and Use

Whole flaxseeds can be stored in a glass jar or other airtight packaging in a cool, dry place for up to a year after harvest. However, since few labels indicate a use-by date or you may have purchased flaxseeds from a bulk bin, using whole flaxseed within six months after purchase is probably a good idea. When indoor temperatures are warm, store whole flaxseeds in a tightly sealed container in the refrigerator.

Flaxseeds have many uses in the kitchen. They are often used in their whole form to provide extra crunch, color, a lot of fiber, and a pleasant nutty flavor, perhaps as a topping applied before baking, or as an ingredient in cereals, crackers, breads, muffins, and other baked goods. But because their tough, protective seed coat is so hard, it isn't broken down by either chewing or digestion, so they must be ground if their omega-3 fatty acids and other nutrients are to be assimilated. Simply sprinkle ground flaxseeds over cereals, soups, salads, or vegetables, or mix it into juices or smoothies.

Because flaxseeds are high in fiber and swell and increase in bulk when moistened, start out with just a couple of teaspoons, and be sure to consume them with plenty of liquid. These same mucilage properties of flaxseeds allow them to be used in place of eggs to help increase volume of baked goods. For the equivalent of 1 egg, combine 1 tablespoon of ground flaxseeds with 3 tablespoons of water. Set the mixture aside for a few minutes to allow it to gel, and then add it to your recipe as you would an egg.

Ground flaxseed can be substituted for one-fourth to one-third of the flour in muffins or quick breads; however, too much flaxseed will weigh down the batter, limiting the amount it can rise. Flaxseeds can also be used to replace some of the fat within a recipe, substituting three parts of ground flaxseed for the amount of fat being replaced. Just as extra liquid is needed when sprinkling ground flaxseeds over food, add 1 tablespoon of extra liquid for every 3 tablespoons of ground flaxseed used in a recipe. Baked goods made with ground flaxseed tend to brown quickly, so you may need to reduce the baking time slightly or lower the oven temperature by 25°F. Unlike most other seeds, flaxseeds don't make a good seed butter, as they are too gritty when ground.

Hazelnuts

Predominantly monounsaturated fat
1 ounce = 18 to 20 hazelnuts

Hazelnuts, which have been consumed for nearly five thousand years, are prized for their mild, rich, slightly sweet flavor and crisp texture, which is enhanced when they're roasted. They range in color from reddish brown to dark brown on the exterior and cream to tan-colored in the interior. Today, the principal countries producing hazelnuts are Turkey, Spain, Italy, and the United States (Oregon).

The names *hazelnut* and *filbert* are often used interchangeably, and different authorities make different distinctions between the two (wild versus cultivated varieties, or American versus European varieties, for example). Given that both are delicious, don't worry too much about the nomenclature, which is apt to be misapplied anyway. Several explanations have been given for the origin of the name filbert. Some say it arose because the day that harvesting of the nuts usually began was on the feast day of St. Philbert, a French monk who lived in the seventh century. Others believe it to be derived from the German word *vollbart*, which means

"full beard," referring to the appearance of the shell that covers the entire nut. Practically speaking, large, round hazelnuts are the kind usually sold for snacking, roasting, and general cooking. The European variety, more often called filberts, are smaller in size and easier to blanch; they're preferred by many European bakers and confectioners, who often grind them to use as flour.

In addition to their heart-healthy monounsaturated fat, hazelnuts are an excellent source of phytochemicals, ranking third among all the nuts in total antioxidant capacity. Proanthocyanidins, a type of flavonoid found in hazelnuts, are present in particularly high amounts. These compounds, which are responsible for the astringent flavor of hazelnuts' skins, can neutralize both water-soluble and fat-soluble toxins in the body. Hazelnuts are also a good source of phytosterols, which help reduce cholesterol and boost the immune system, as well as vitamin E in the form of alpha-tocopherol.

Storage and Use

About 1 pound of hazelnuts in the shell will yield 1½ cups of whole nuts. Hazelnuts in the shell can be kept at room temperature in dry conditions for two to three months or kept in the refrigerator or freezer for up to one year. Store shelled hazelnuts in the refrigerator for up to six months or in the freezer for up to one year.

Simply appreciated when eaten out of hand, especially when roasted, whole hazelnuts are also exceptional in salads, providing a nice contrast in shape, texture, and flavor. As with almonds, many cooks like to blanch hazelnuts to get rid of the fibrous, somewhat astringent brown skin that surrounds the meat. However, removing the skins also strips away the protective action of their phytochemicals. Use whole hazelnuts, including the skin, for optimum nutrition and complexity of flavor, and blanch them only when truly necessary. Chopped or sliced, they make a nice addition to baked goods. Both blanched and whole hazelnuts can be ground into flour and substituted for one-fourth to one-third of the flour called for in a recipe. Hazelnut flour is particularly good in muffins, breads, and biscuits.

Hazelnut butter or paste is another way to enjoy hazelnuts while taking advantage of their many nutritional benefits. It is usually ground from roasted hazelnuts and has a very rich flavor and a smooth, silky texture. Use it like peanut butter, add it to cookie recipes, or spread it on bread and baked goods in place of butter. Thinned with fruit juice, it makes a terrific sauce for sliced bananas, apples, and pears. In comparison to peanut butter, hazelnut butter is lower in protein and higher in overall fat; however, it has a higher percentage of monounsaturated fat and is lower in saturated and polyunsaturated fats. Since it contains more natural oil than peanut butter, it will also have a thinner consistency.

Macadamia Nuts

Predominantly monounsaturated fat
1 ounce = 10 to 12 macadamia nuts

Macadamia nuts are produced by evergreen trees indigenous to Australia. Named after John Macadam, the Scottish scientist who first cultivated the tree in the mid-1800s, the macadamia tree was originally grown only for ornamental purposes. Fortunately, somewhere along the line someone realized that beyond the tree's natural beauty, its nuts are delicious. They are mildly sweet and buttery with a smooth, creamy texture. About the size and shape of a marble, they are light beige in color. Introduced to Hawaii in 1882, the macadamia tree is now the most important tree crop grown there, making Hawaii one of the top producers, along with Australia and New Zealand.

Since the shells of macadamia nuts are very hard to crack, requiring special equipment to do the job, they are sold shelled. Once the husk and shell are removed, the actual kernel ends up being only

15% of the whole macadamia nut, explaining why macadamia nuts are one of the more expensive nuts.

Macadamia nuts are a good source of phytosterols, especially beta-sitosterol, which can help lower cholesterol. They also have the highest percentage of calories from fat of all nuts, although most of it is monounsaturated. Their percentage of polyunsaturated fat is low, and they don't contain an inordinate amount of saturated fat.

Storage and Use

Store macadamia nuts in the refrigerator for up to six months or in the freezer for up to nine months.

Because macadamia nuts can stand up to higher heat, they are a good, flavorful addition to stir-fries and sautés. Like hazelnuts, they are a complementary addition to salads because of their unique shape and taste. And, of course, they are often added to baked goods and are delicious eaten as a snack. Macadamia butter is very rich. Because it is very high in fat in comparison to other nut butters, it should be used in moderation, but you can use it as you would any other nut butter. It's a wonderful nondairy alternative to cream in soups.

Peanuts

Predominantly monounsaturated fat
1 ounce = 28 peanuts

First cultivated thousands of years ago in South America, peanuts have since become an important component of traditional cuisines worldwide. The three top producers worldwide are China, India, and the United States. Although peanuts are actually members of the legume family, they are higher in fat and lower in carbohydrates than other legumes, so they're commonly used like other nuts and included in many of the same reference charts. They mature underground (explaining their other common moniker—groundnuts), yielding two or three peanuts within each brown shell.

In addition to their high protein content (7.3 grams per ounce), niacin, and heart-healthy monounsaturated fat, peanuts are an excellent source of phytochemicals. The phytosterols in peanuts can help reduce cholesterol levels in the blood. They are also very high in antioxidants, including proanthocyanidins, resveratrol, and p-coumaric acid. Although resveratrol is most often associated with grapes and wine, 1 ounce of peanuts contains the same amount as 2 pounds of grapes or about ½ ounce of wine. Resveratrol has been associated with reduced risk of atherosclerosis and increased blood flow to the brain, which can help reduce the risk of stroke. And because it's been shown to help stop the growth of damaged cells within the body, it also reduces risk of cancer. P-coumaric acid is known for its strong antioxidant properties. Roasting peanuts actually increases their p-coumaric acid content by as much as 22%.

Peanuts are often added to many kinds of foods to boost nutrient values. Nonetheless, nutritious as they are, peanuts are one of the most common allergy-causing foods, causing severe reactions in highly sensitive individuals.

Varieties

There are four primary varieties of peanuts, each with a different size, shape, flavor, and intended use:

- Runner, a higher-yield variety with uniform intermediate kernel size and good flavor when roasted, is used for peanut butter and salted peanut products.
- Virginia, a variety with large oval kernels and good peanuty flavor, is used for candies, salted peanut products, and nut mixes, and is sold both raw and roasted in the shell.
- Spanish, a small, mild-tasting variety with round kernels with reddish brown skin, is used for peanut candies, nut mixes, snacks, and peanut butter.

- Valencia, a medium to small, sweet, richly flavored variety with oval kernels with bright red skin, is a good roasting peanut, in or out of the shell. They are used for boiled peanuts and peanut butter, and are sold both raw and roasted in the shell.

Storage and Use

About 1½ pounds of peanuts in the shell will yield 1 pound or 3½ cups of shelled peanuts. Although peanuts are susceptible to contamination by aflatoxins, carcinogenic substances produced by certain strains of a mold, better storage and handling methods, along with testing, have lowered rates of contamination in recent years. Since the fungus grows in humid, hot conditions, especially between 86°F and 96°F, and because peanuts tend to go rancid quickly, it's especially important to store peanuts in cool, dry conditions. Store peanuts in the shell in a cool, dry place for up to two months or in the refrigerator for up to nine months. Shelled peanuts should be refrigerated and used within three months or frozen for up to six months. For best flavor, freshness, and nutrition, avoid buying and storing chopped peanuts. Instead, chop them by hand or in a food processor immediately before use.

As a garnish for soups, salads, noodles and rice dishes, chopped and whole peanuts provide a complementary flavor and a crunchy textural contrast. Add them to stir-fries, too. Blend ground peanuts into sauces and spreads to provide extra nutrition, flavor, and bulk. They are also often used as the basis for Asian sauces and dressings. And, freely substitute peanuts for other nuts when making cookies and muffins. In addition to being convenient and having great flavor, peanut butter is a good source of protein and monounsaturated fats, although somewhat higher in polyunsaturated fats than many other nut butters. The antioxidant capacity of peanut butter is, likewise, increased by 22%, which occurs when whole peanuts are roasted, as they are when making any commercial peanut butter.

Peanut butter is made by grinding roasted peanuts until smooth and creamy, and peanut granules are added for chunky versions. The differences among the various brands of peanut butter begin after this point.

The standards for peanut butter in the United States require that it consist of at least 90% peanuts from either blanched peanuts, with or without the highly nutritious germ, or unblanched peanuts, including the skins and germ. Up to 10% seasonings and stabilizing agents may be added, such as salt and sweeteners, along with emulsifiers and stabilizers to help keep the peanut oil from separating and rising to the top. Since 1996, adding vitamins has also been permitted. Artificial sweeteners, artificial flavors, chemical preservatives, lard and other animal fats, and coloring additives are not allowed.

Commonly used sweeteners include sugar, evaporated cane juice, honey, dextrose, corn syrup, and high-fructose corn syrup, often in combination with one another. Molasses is sometimes added, but more to complement flavor than as a sweetener. Emulsifiers, typically mono- and diglycerides derived from vegetable oil, interact with the proteins in peanut butter to help keep them suspended within the oil base. Stabilizing ingredients help prevent oil separation and make the peanut butter more stable in terms of oxidation so it doesn't need refrigeration. Stabilizers include a blend of vegetable oils, both fully and partially hydrogenated vegetable oils, with rapeseed, cottonseed, and soybean oil most often used.

Be aware that the trans fat listing on the nutrition panel may not tell the full story. Even though the ingredient label may list hydrogenated fats, labeling regulations allow a zero claim to be used if the amount of trans fat per serving is less than 0.5 gram. Unlike the process of partial hydrogenated fats, full hydrogenation, which transforms an oil into a hard fat, doesn't create trans fats. When fully hydrogenated fats are combined with partially hydrogenated fats, they're easier to work with, and also keep the overall amount of trans fat low enough to be under the radar of labeling requirements. A better type of stabilizer is palm oil. A natural alternative to hydrogenated vegetable shortening that's free of trans-fatty acids, it functions similarly, including helping protect against oxidation.

Brands made with fresh, high-quality peanuts need no additives, including flavor enhancement from sweeteners. Although oil separation occurs soon after production, an initial stirring followed by refrigeration will keep the oil from separating again without additional emulsifiers or stabilizers.

Peanut butters made from unblanched peanuts that include the skin and the germ of the peanut offer more full-bodied flavor, aroma, and nutrients. Like wheat germ, the germ of the peanut is the part that would develop into an embryo if the whole raw peanut were planted. As such, the germ is richer in vitamins and minerals than the bulk of the peanut, which, like the endosperm in wheat, is composed primarily of protein and starch to nourish the embryo as it sprouts and begins to grow. While some manufacturers claim the skins can make the peanut butter taste bitter, in reality the blanching process is largely used as a roundabout way to lengthen shelf life. During the process of removing the reddish skins loosened by blanching, mechanical rollers also remove the nutrient-dense germ, which is processed into peanut oil. Since the germ contains many natural oils, peanut butter from peanuts without the germ can be stored unrefrigerated longer than varieties made with unblanched peanuts.

The leftover peanut skins are typically sold for animal feed, which is good for the animals but unfortunate for human consumers of peanut butter, who would be better served if the peanuts weren't blanched, getting the benefit of all the nutrients within the skins. Eight different flavonoids have been found in peanut skins, including proanthocyanidins. Blanching has been found to significantly lower their levels, reducing their ability to provide antioxidant protection within the body. Resveratrol, a beneficial phytochemical associated with reduced risk of chronic diseases such as heart disease and cancer, is completely removed in the process, along with other important polyphenols.

The answer is simple: Go for the flavor and nutrition of peanut butter made with unblanched peanuts, since it retains the healthful skin and germ. There is also no need for additives; 100% peanuts is the best bet.

Pecans

Predominantly monounsaturated fat
1 ounce = 18 to 20 pecan halves

Pecans are one of the few tree nuts indigenous to North America. Their use as a staple food by Native Americans can be traced back eight thousand years in what is now southern Texas and northern Mexico. Actually a species of hickory family, they are also in the same plant family as walnuts. The name pecan is derived from an Algonquin word that roughly translates to "nut so hard as to require a stone to crack"—an apt description of what faces anyone who has ever shelled a tough native pecan. The United States remains the top producer of pecans, followed far behind by Mexico. Texas leads the nation in native wild-harvested pecans, while Georgia produces the most pecans from hybrid trees selected for particular attributes, including larger nut size.

Pecans are truly an antioxidant powerhouse, ranking as the nut highest in total antioxidant capacity, including both fat-soluble and water-soluble antioxidants and a wide range of flavonoids. Among the nuts, they have the most proanthocyanidins and also the highest level of gamma-tocopherol, a form of vitamin E (6.9 mg per ounce). All of their antioxidants work both singly and in concert to neutralize free radicals—those highly unstable molecules that can potentially injure cells and set up the body for disease. As a result, pecans can help reduce the risk of cardiovascular disease, cancer, and blood clots. They also provide a moderate amount of phytosterols, which help reduce serum cholesterol.

Storage and Use

About 2 pounds of pecans in the shell will yield 1 pound or 4 cups of shelled pecans. Pecans in the shell can be stored at a moderately cool room temperature (70°F) for up to four months or refrigerated for nine months. For longer storage, freeze them in sealed plastic bags for up to nineteen months. Shelled pecans should be crisp, golden brown, and relatively plump. Since they can easily go rancid, purchase them whole instead of in pieces or ground. Because of their soft texture, they can easily be processed at home using a blender or food processor. Store shelled pecans in an airtight container in the refrigerator for up to six months or in the freezer for up to one year.

Pecans are a great snack and also have myriad uses in both sweet and savory foods. They can be used interchangeably with walnuts in any recipe. Try them in baked goods, salads, cereals, and casseroles or as a garnish on vegetables, fruits, desserts, or anything you can imagine. Ground pecans make an interesting coating for fish or chicken.

Although not as common as other nut butters, pecan butter is occasionally available, usually ground from raw pecans, sometimes with cashews added for a creamier texture. Much lower in protein and overall fat than peanut butter, it has a higher percentage of monounsaturated fat.

Pine Nuts

Predominantly polyunsaturated fat (pignoli); about equal monounsaturated and polyunsaturated fat (piñon nuts)
1 ounce = about 3½ tablespoons of pine nuts

Mention pine trees and most people will conjure up images of fragrant evergreen forests, holidays, or perhaps simply cabins or cabinets made from their wood. But for thousands of years, the seeds from their cones, two on each scale, have provided food for humans and animals alike. Pine trees grow throughout most of the northern hemisphere, and some varieties have seeds large enough to be worth the effort to extract them, first from the pinecone itself, and then from the shell that surrounds each seed. Spain, Italy, China, Portugal, and Turkey are the principal producers.

Piñon is both Spanish for "pine nut" and the name of a type of pine tree, and technically speaking, *piñon nuts* should be used to refer to the rich, sweetly flavored, small, dark seeds from various small species of pines that grow in western North America, including the piñon. These are most often gathered and sold locally, making them difficult to obtain elsewhere. They help lend a distinct regional flair to Southwestern cuisine. Chinese pine nuts are from completely different species of pine trees grown in Asia, primarily the Korean pine. This strongly flavored, somewhat stocky, triangular, ivory-colored pine nut is available in Asian markets. Pignoli (pignolia is the singular form) is the more appropriate name for the seeds of the stone pine, which grows in southern Europe. This European variety of pine nut is the kind most frequently sold in retail markets. They are delicate, oblong, and creamy white, with a sweet, buttery flavor.

European pignoli are quite high in total phytosterol content, while piñon nuts contain much lower amounts. As their fat is primarily polyunsaturated, pignoli are very susceptible to rancidity, requiring constant refrigeration after shelling to keep them stable. Piñon nuts are somewhat lower in fat, with almost equal percentages of monounsaturated and polyunsaturated fats. As piñon nuts are often kept in their shells until they're consumed, they tend to have a better shelf life but should still be stored carefully.

Storage and Use

Because pignoli are so vulnerable to oxidation, it can be hard to find them in really good, fresh condition. Look for plump, creamy white nuts that are sold refrigerated or in vacuum-packed bags. Store them in the refrigerator for up to one month or in the freezer for up to six months.

Use pine nuts raw, or roast them for crisper texture and enhanced flavor. They are a favorite for use in pesto and dolmas. Penne pasta with broccoli and pine nuts is a classic. Toss in a few pine nuts when cooking any kinds of greens. And be sure to add them to couscous and rice pilafs for subtle crunch and extra seasoning.

Pistachios

Predominantly monounsaturated fat
1 ounce = a scant ¼ cup of shelled pistachios

The delicious pistachio nut is unique in many ways. Not only does it come with a precracked shell, but also the color of the kernel is green, thanks to the presence of chlorophyll. Pistachios, which originated in the Middle East and have been used for food for more than ten thousand years, are now primarily cultivated in Iran, the United States (California), Turkey, Syria, China, and Greece. The pistachio is a small tree that thrives in hot, dry, desertlike conditions. Its fruits, which grow in clusters, consist of a thin hull that tightly surrounds an inner shell and the kernel. When the fruit ripens and the internal kernel matures, the hull begins to loosen its grip on the inner shell and changes to a rosy pale yellow color. In the meantime, the internal kernel (the pistachio nut) expands, ultimately cracking the inner shell as it fills it to capacity.

Traditionally, the ripe fruits were knocked to the ground and dried with the rosy-colored hulls still attached, which meant that some of the inner shells, which are naturally grayish beige, became stained from the pigments in the hull. Early importers decided to stain all the shells red to disguise the staining, as well as to make pistachios more noticeable amidst the other nuts in the marketplace. These days, pistachios are typically hulled before they are dried, which eliminates any staining issues, and most consumers view dyed shells as unnatural.

Pistachios have the distinction of being slightly lower in fat than most of the other nuts and seeds, and a majority of their fat is monounsaturated. They also have an outstanding range of phytochemicals. They are highest in phytosterols of any nut, ranking alongside sesame seeds and sunflower seeds as one of the top three in the nuts and seeds category. Because of their phytosterols, pistachios can help control blood cholesterol levels. They are ranked fourth among all nuts in total antioxidant levels, containing proanthocyanidins, lending them their slightly astringent flavor, and also making them helpful for reducing risk of cardiovascular disease and cancer.

Likewise, they contain a significant amount of carotenes, especially lutein, an antioxidant associated with eye health. They also contain high levels of the antioxidant gamma-tocopherol, a form of vitamin E that helps prevent oxidation of fats both in foods and in the body. To top it off, pistachios are high in protein, earning them a high rating as a snack.

Although pistachios are available shelled, most are sold in their shell, either raw or roasted. Discard any shells that are not split open, as they usually contain immature kernels. Slightly split shells are usually fine, but they just require a bit of extra effort to wedge them open. Cooking raw pistachios at low temperatures or roasting them can help retain the green color of the pistachio kernel. Pistachios are also available salted in the shell. These are made by first dipping them into a salt solution before they are dried or roasted.

Storage and Use

About 1 pound of pistachios in the shell will yield 2 cups of shelled pistachios, or in terms of cup measurements, 1 cup of pistachios in the shell yields ½ cup shelled. Store pistachios in an airtight container in the refrigerator for up to six months or in the freezer for up to one year.

Although typically eaten as snacks out of hand, pistachios also make a great addition to salads, vegetables, pasta dishes, muffins, quick breads, and desserts—including, of course, ice cream. Another option is pistachio butter, which is green like the nut and mildly sweet. It is best served as a rich dip for fruit or vegetable slices, making for a nice snack or a simple, satisfying dessert. Try a dab stuffed into a halved, pitted medjool date. In comparison to peanut butter, pistachio butter is somewhat lower in protein but similar in terms of its fat profile.

Pumpkin Seeds

Predominantly polyunsaturated fat
1 ounce = about 3½ tablespoons of pumpkin seeds

Pumpkins are native to North America, where they have been used for food for thousands of years, primarily in areas that correspond to current-day central and northern Mexico and the southwestern United States. All parts of this squash were used for food, including the seeds. Today, the pumpkin seeds sold commercially come from special varieties of pumpkin that yield long, flat, dark green seeds that are typically hull-less, rather than from jack-o'-lantern pumpkins or sugar (pie) pumpkins, which have small pale seeds encased in pale fibrous hulls. Pumpkin seeds, also known as pepitas, have a subtle sweet flavor and a chewy texture.

Pumpkin seeds are especially celebrated for their impressive nutritional portfolio. High in protein (7 grams per ounce), pumpkin seeds are also a very good source of zinc (2 grams per ounce) and iron (4 grams per ounce). Their green color comes from chlorophyll, and their carotenes, lutein and beta-carotene, provide important antioxidants. They're high in gamma-tocopherol (5.4 grams per ounce), a form of vitamin E that prevents oxidation of fats, and lignans, a type of fiber in its cell walls, adds extra antioxidant depth. Pumpkin seeds are also an excellent source of phytosterols, which can help lower cholesterol levels, ranking them fourth among all the nuts and seeds in phytosterol content. The virtues of pumpkin seeds have been known for quite some time, as they've long been used medicinally for bladder conditions and as a remedy for parasitic worms. More recently, they've seen use as an alternative treatment for benign prostatic hyperplasia.

Storage and Use

Because they are high in polyunsaturated fat, pumpkin seeds need special attention to keep them from going rancid. Their freshness window is a couple months at best when they aren't refrigerated, so it can be hard to find them in top condition unless they are sold in vacuum-packed containers. Look for seeds that have a deep green color and are full, not shriveled. Store them in an airtight container in the refrigerator for up to six months or in the freezer for up to one year.

Pumpkin seeds are commonly used as a snack and in Mexican and Southwestern cooking. However, they're very versatile and can be used in many other ways. Roasted, they're a nice addition to vegetables, any cooked grain, muffins, and cookies. Garnish soup or any kind of entrée, especially enchiladas, with pumpkin seeds just before serving. Ground roasted pumpkin seeds can imbue sauces with a deep, rich flavor while also serving as a thickener.

Greenish and richly flavored, pumpkin seed butter can be used as a spread, in salad dressings and sauces, and in baking. Although it has about the same overall fat content as peanut butter, pumpkin seed butter has a higher percentage of polyunsaturated fat and is lower in monounsaturated fat, so it should be kept under constant refrigeration and be used quickly.

To roast seeds removed from a fresh pumpkin, first wash them to remove any lingering stringy membranes and blot them dry. Roast in a 325°F oven for about 15 minutes. Although much smaller and more fibrous than commercially available pumpkin seeds, they are tasty and nutritious. Shelling them is a lot of work; fortunately you can eat them whole—shells and all.

Sesame Seeds

About equal monounsaturated and polyunsaturated fat

1 ounce = about 3 tablespoons of sesame seeds with hulls or 3½ tablespoons hulled

Sesame seeds are yet another ancient crop, with cultivation most likely originating in Africa. They have been used for both food and medicinal purposes for several thousand years. Today, about two-thirds of the world's sesame seeds, grown primarily in India, China, Mexico, and Sudan, are processed into oil, with the rest being used predominantly as a topping, seasoning, or condiment. A sesame plant stands about 2 to 4 feet high and produces flowers that mature into seedpods; the hulls of the seeds within range in color from light tan to red, brown, or black. Inside each hull is a tiny, oval-shaped, creamy-colored seed. The seeds may be gathered by hand, collecting the seeds that emerge from the pod after it bursts; however, hybrid varieties created to prevent the usual scattering of the seed have been developed to allow harvesting by machine.

Despite their small size, sesame seeds pack in an impressive amount of nutrients and flavor. Grinding the seeds will ensure that more of their nutrients will be absorbed. Sesame seeds are a good source of protein and iron, but calcium is another issue. Although nutritional charts for whole sesame seeds show them to be very high in calcium, how much of it is really absorbed remains a question because their hulls contain oxalic acid, which can bind with the calcium and prevent its absorption.

Whole sesame seeds with the hull intact are an

excellent source of fiber. Like flaxseeds, sesame seeds are an excellent source of the beneficial class of fiber called lignans, containing their own unique lignan, which is called sesamin. In a metabolic process similar to the conversion of flax lignans, sesamin functions as a precursor of the hormonelike substances enterodiol and enterolactone. These compounds are thought to help protect against hormone-sensitive cancers, such as certain forms of breast cancer, or to exert weak estrogenic effects that can help balance hormone levels in the body. The lignans in sesame seeds also have potent antioxidant effects.

Sesame seeds are especially noteworthy for containing more phytosterols than any other nut or seed. This phytochemical has been shown to enhance the immune response and also help reduce cholesterol levels and decrease risk of cardiovascular disease and certain cancers. Unfortunately, removing the hull removes some of their other beneficial phytochemicals, including phytic acid, which is being studied as an agent that may prevent cancer. Hulled sesame seeds are also much lower in iron, calcium, and copper. But in the end, hulling is a mixed bag. Although the nutrients in the hull are lost, it makes the nutrients within more accessible.

Varieties

Sesame seeds are sold both whole and hulled, or decorticated. Whole sesame seeds, which are light brown in color, are used extensively in the baking industry since they tend to stick well to crackers and bread while also providing a pleasant crunch. Black sesame seeds are an unhulled variety that has a strong, earthy flavor. They are typically consumed raw as they can become bitter when toasted. They are often used in Asian cooking as an ingredient or a condiment both for flavor and to create a striking color accent on vegetables, rice and noodle dishes, and fish. They are particularly beautiful on salmon.

Hulled ivory-colored sesame seeds have had their hulls removed to make them easier to digest or for a milder flavor. When buying hulled sesame seeds, look for the phrase "mechanically hulled" to ensure the hulls were not removed using caustic soda or other chemical solvents. Hulled sesame seeds are often used in Asian cooking as a seasoning, both sprinkled on and incorporated into the dish. Hull-less varieties are also used in candies and sprinkled on conventional hamburger buns.

Storage and Use

Store both whole and hulled sesame seeds in moisture-proof containers in the refrigerator for up to six months or in the freezer for up to one year. Because the fiber-rich hull provides a protective covering for the creamy white seed inside, whole sesame seeds last longer when not refrigerated, remaining relatively fresh for about two months, assuming they were purchased in top condition. Hulled sesame seeds are more prone to rancidity and therefore have a much shorter shelf life.

Toasting gives sesame seeds a more full-bodied nutty flavor and an attractive deep golden color. To toast them, place them in a dry skillet over medium-low heat for just a few minutes, until golden brown. Stir constantly to prevent burning, and don't even think of turning your back, even for just a moment—that's exactly when they'll burn.

Sesame seeds are also the main ingredient in gomasio, also known as sesame salt, a delicious, flavorful condiment made by roasting and grinding sesame seeds with salt. Proportions usually range from eight to fifteen parts sesame seeds to one part salt. Use it as a lower-sodium alternative to salt, and as an additional source of protein and other nutrients on grains, noodles, vegetables, beans, tofu, or fish.

As peanuts are to peanut butter, sesame seeds are to sesame butter and tahini. These delicious, creamy spreads, often used in Middle Eastern, African, and Asian cooking, are made by grinding sesame seeds, either raw or roasted. They provide an easy, convenient, and delicious way to get maximum nutrient value out of sesame seeds. In comparison to peanut butter, sesame butter and tahini are lower in protein but higher in iron, magnesium, and zinc. They have similar amounts of total fat, but the sesame-based products are lower in monounsaturated fat and higher in polyunsaturated fat.

Sesame butter, made from ground whole sesame seeds, is darker in color and stronger in flavor and has a thicker consistency. It is used primarily as a spread for breads and such or as an ingredient in sauces rather than as an ingredient in classic dip recipes like hummus. Because it's ground from whole sesame seeds, it is also more nutritious, containing all the phytochemicals, vitamins, and minerals found in the whole seed. Black sesame butter, sometimes incorrectly called tahini, is a variety of sesame butter made from ground whole black sesame seeds. It has a rich, complex, naturally smoky flavor.

In contrast, tahini is made from ground, hulled sesame seeds, which gives it a thinner consistency than that of sesame butter. Both raw and roasted versions of tahini are available, and each has distinctive flavor qualities. Raw tahini is nutty and subtly sweet, while tahini made from roasted sesame seeds has a deeper, richer flavor. Which to choose is simply a personal decision.

All forms of sesame butter and tahini are versatile and can be used at any meal. The possibilities are endless. At breakfast, spread some on toast instead of butter, add a spoonful to a smoothie, or thin it with a bit of juice to make a sauce for fruit salads. At lunch or dinner, tahini can be both a binder and a flavor component in sandwich spreads, fillings, or dips. Or use it to make salad dressings or creamy nondairy soups. A simple nondairy milk substitute can be made by blending 1 tablespoon of tahini with 1 cup of water and a dab of sweetener. Use it as you would milk, whether as a beverage or in cooking and baking.

Sunflower Seeds

Predominantly polyunsaturated fat
1 ounce = about 3 tablespoons of shelled sunflower
  seeds

Sunflower seeds have their roots in what is now the southwestern region of the United States, where they are thought to have been cultivated by Native Americans by 3000 BCE. They were domesticated in Mexico about 3,500 years ago and are now used extensively throughout the world. Their popularity got a big boost in the eighteenth century when the Russian Orthodox Church declared them to be an acceptable food during Lent. By crossbreeding them for higher oil yield and larger seeds, Russia set the stage for commercial production, and Russia remains the world's largest producer, followed by the European Union, Eastern Europe, Argentina, China, India, the United States, and Turkey.

Sunflower seeds are particularly high in vitamin E (9.8 mg per ounce)—the highest of any nut or seed—making them an excellent source of antioxidants. They're also especially rich in phytochemicals. They rank third-highest in phytosterols, which can help reduce cholesterol and the risk of certain types of cancer. They also provide a good amount of fiber (3 grams per ounce), including lignans, the type of fiber that can help lower cholesterol and protect against heart disease and some cancers. Phenolic acids, like chlorogenic acid, provide extra antioxidant protection. Sunflower seeds have a high protein content, too, providing 6.6 grams per ounce, near the amount found in pumpkin seeds and peanuts.

Varieties

There are two basic types of sunflower seeds: Oilseeds are small, oil-rich, black seeds used to make sunflower oil and meal; they're also the sunflower seed of choice for birdseed. Non-oilseeds are larger, black-and-white striped-seeds used for snacking and general food use; they're available both in-shell and shelled. This type of seed has been developed so that its fibrous hull is only loosely attached to the kernel, making it easily shelled by hand or even with one's teeth, spitting out the shell.

Storage and Use

About 1 pound of in-shell sunflower seeds will yield a bit over ½ pound (8.5 ounces) of shelled sunflower seeds, or approximately 1¾ cups. For best nutrition, choose unsalted sunflower seeds, either raw or dry-roasted. In-shell sunflower seeds should be clean and unbroken and have a firm texture. Refrigerate or freeze in-shell sunflower seeds for up to one year, keeping out only the amount that will likely be consumed within a week. Shelled sunflower seeds should be uniform in color with no broken or discolored seeds, indications that the seeds may be rancid. If purchased in top condition, shelled sunflower seeds can last for up to six months in the refrigerator or nine months in the freezer, tightly wrapped.

Besides being a nutritious snack, sunflower seeds are a good addition to baked goods and a crunchy substitute for bacon bits and croutons on cooked vegetables and salads. Roast them for best flavor. Raw in-shell sunflower seeds can be sprouted. Crisp in texture and slightly bitter, sunflower seed sprouts are a great addition to salads and sandwiches.

Sunflower butter is sometimes available. It provides about the same amount of protein as peanut butter, as well as all the valuable phytochemicals and nutrients in sunflower seeds. However, it is very prone to rancidity due to its high percentage of polyunsaturated fat, so it's hard to find it in good shape. Once opened, its shelf life is very limited, even if it's refrigerated.

Walnuts

Predominantly polyunsaturated fat, including omega-3 fatty acids
1 ounce = 14 English walnut halves or about 3½ tablespoons of black walnuts

Walnuts have been used for food since at least 7000 BCE, also serving medicinal purposes throughout the millennia. There are a variety of native species found throughout the world, including in southeastern Europe, ancient Persia (now Iran and Afghanistan), Asia Minor (Turkey), the Himalayas, and the Americas. Today, the top five producers are China, the United States (California), Iran, Turkey, and Ukraine.

There are more than a dozen species of walnut trees with edible nuts, but English walnuts (*Juglans regia*) and black walnuts (*Juglans nigra*) stand out as the two varieties most widely known and used. English walnuts, also called Persian walnuts, are much more commercially significant than black walnuts. Though the species originated elsewhere, "English" became associated with its name because this type of walnut was widely transported by English merchant sailors during medieval times. Black walnuts, native to North America, are more distinctly flavored and stronger in taste than English walnuts. Because their hull is very thick and hard to crack, requiring the nuts to be shelled between heavy rollers or wheels, black walnuts are usually sold in pieces rather than as halves.

Walnuts are most widely known for their alpha-linolenic acid content, making them one of the few plant foods and the only nut that contains appreciable amounts of this omega-3 fatty acid—2.6 grams per ounce (0.56 grams per ounce for black walnuts). When in proper balance with linoleic acid (an omega-6 fatty), omega-3 fatty acids serve to increase immunity and reduce inflammation, risk of cardiovascular disease, and total and LDL (bad) cholesterol.

Walnuts also rank as the second-highest nut, after pecans, in total antioxidant capacity, a measurement of both the fat-soluble and the water-soluble antioxidant components. A number of phytochemicals contribute to this impressive antioxidant activity. Walnuts contain high amounts of gamma-tocopherol, the form of vitamin E that reduces oxidation of fats (6 mg per ounce in English walnuts; 8 mg per ounce in black walnuts). Walnuts are also a good source of melatonin. Although this hormone is more commonly known for its role in maintaining regular sleep patterns, it also serves as an antioxidant, protecting cells from oxidative damage and inhibiting certain types of cancer. The walnut's pellicle, the thin brown skin surrounding the meat of the nut, contains most of the phenolic substances found in walnuts. The function of the pellicle is to protect the kernel from oxidation and fungal attack, but it is also responsible for the nut's mild astringent flavor and the source of much of its antioxidant activity. For example, the pellicle includes ellagic acid, flavonoids, and proanthocyanidins—all of which help protect against cardiovascular disease and cancer.

Phytosterols, which help reduce cholesterol and enhance overall immunity, are also present in walnuts. Though the amount in English walnuts is low in comparison to most nuts and seeds, black walnuts are a richer source. Black walnuts are also higher in protein (7 grams per ounce) than English walnuts (4 grams per ounce).

Storage and Use

About 1 pound of English walnuts in the shell will yield 2 cups of shelled nuts. For best flavor and texture, avoid walnuts that rattle within their shell. Store walnuts in the shell at room temperature for two to three months, or for longer storage, keep them in the refrigerator or freezer for up to one year. Once shelled, walnuts tend to go rancid quickly. When possible, ask for a sample before purchasing. The more surface area exposed on a nut, the more opportunity for oxidation to occur, so when buying shelled walnuts, choose English walnut halves instead of walnut pieces; they can be easily chopped or crushed at home. (Black walnuts are only available in pieces since they are so hard to extract from the shell.) Store shelled walnuts in the refrigerator for up to three months or in the freezer for up to a year.

Use walnuts to top cereals, grains, vegetables, and salads, or as an ingredient in breads, stuffings, entrées, and cookies and other desserts. Walnut butter is sometimes available, usually made from English walnuts. Lower in protein than peanut butter, it is also very rich and vulnerable to oxidation, and thus requires constant refrigeration.

Culinary Oils

Just as juice is extracted from whole fruits and vegetables, culinary oils are extracted from nuts, seeds, and oil-rich plants. As a concentrated fat, culinary oils lack the fiber and phytonutrients found in the nuts, seeds, and other plant parts from which they're derived. They're also employed in ways quite different from how their whole plant counterparts are used. They act as a lubricant to prevent sticking and are also used as a medium to transfer heat to foods during the cooking process, allowing higher temperatures than are possible with water, with it's boiling point of 212°F. Within recipes, oil acts as a tenderizing agent in baked goods, as an emulsifier, and as an aerating agent, holding and setting air bubbles to aid the leavening process.

Olive oil is considered to be one of the first cooking oils, coming into used soon after olive trees were initially cultivated, around 5000 BCE. Although almond, walnut, and flaxseed oils were also produced thousands of years ago, they were most often used for lighting, heating, and medicinal purposes.

Choosing the Best Oils for Health

Fat is comprised of varying proportions of all three types of fatty acid: saturated fat, monounsaturated fat, and polyunsaturated fat, which includes essential fatty acids. The predominant type of fat in a particular oil is something you can actually easily discern with a glance. Saturated fats, like lard or butter, are solid when cold and fairly solid at room temperature. Monounsaturated fats, like olive oil, are thicker when cold but liquid at room temperature. Polyunsaturated fats, like safflower oil, are liquid whether cold or at room temperature.

While appreciation of the importance of oils and fats in the diet has waxed and waned throughout the years, these days it's better understood that getting the right kind of fat in one's diet is important for optimum health and well-being. In addition to eating

Culinary Oils High In . . .

Monounsaturated Fats
Almond oil
Apricot kernel oil
Argan oil (also 37% polyunsaturated fat)
Avocado oil
Canola oil (also 11% omega-3 fatty acids)
Hazelnut oil
Olive oil
Peanut oil
Safflower oil (high-oleic)
Sesame oil (also 50% polyunsaturated fat)
Sunflower oil (high-oleic)

Polyunsaturated Fats
Corn oil
Cottonseed oil
Flaxseed oil (57% omega-3 fatty acids)
Grapeseed oil
Pumpkin seed oil (15% omega-3 fatty acids)
Safflower oil
Sesame oil (also 50% monounsaturated fat)
Soy oil (8% omega-3 fatty acids)
Sunflower oil
Walnut oil (10% omega-3 fatty acids)

Saturated fats
Coconut oil
Palm oil (also 40% monounsaturated fat)

heart-healthy monounsaturated fats, it's critical to achieve a proper balance between omega-3 and omega-6 fatty acids, as this can also help reduce inflammations, as well as the risk of heart disease and certain types of cancer.

In the Paleolithic hunter-gatherer diet on which humans evolved, omega-3 fatty acids were abundant in the diet from eating both wild edible plants and the game animals that also ate these plants, providing about equal amounts of omega-3 and omega-6 fatty acids. For coastal peoples, seafood was an excellent source of omega-3 fatty acids. In contrast, modern-day diets are too high in polyunsaturated vegetable oils that are rich in omega-6 fatty acids, including corn, cottonseed, safflower, sunflower, and peanut oils and products made from them, including hydrogenated fats.

Such an imbalance has been linked to heart attacks, stroke, thrombosis, arrhythmia, cancer, arthritis, asthma, and even menstrual cramps and headaches. Ironically, drugs such as aspirin, acetaminophen, and ibuprofen and other NSAIDs

(nonsteroidal anti-inflammatory drugs, used to deal with pain, swelling, and inflammation) often work by blocking the effects of excessive omega-6 fatty acids in the diet. Rather than resorting to drugs, a more healthy way to correct the imbalance would be to use less omega-6-rich oils, replacing them with oils high in omega-3 fatty acids, such as flaxseed oil, along with oils high in monounsaturated fats, such as olive oil and canola oil.

How Oils Are Produced

Although the idea of extracting oil from corn or soybeans in the same manner as from olives would have been considered quite far-fetched even a thousand years ago, modern innovations have made the seemingly impossible commonplace. In many ways, we have gained valuable knowledge about how to produce, choose, handle, and store oils more appropriately. On the other hand, not all of the novel products that have been created have turned out to be beneficial for health, particularly hydrogenated fats—proving yet again that sometimes it is better to leave well enough alone, and that the most healthful foods are those closest to their natural, whole form.

PRESSING

There are two basic steps involved in extracting oil: pressing and refining. Oil can be pressed in a variety of ways, with some methods being more suitable than others depending on what the oil is extracted from and how it will be used. Although refining (discussed below) is optional, whether it's done and what methods are used also depend on the specific oil, as well as its intended use and market.

Stone pressing is the traditional method of extracting oil from olives and some seeds, and it's still sometimes used to produce olive oil. Stone pressing generates little heat and protects the olives' natural antioxidants, which help preserve the integrity of the oil.

Hydraulic pressing works by squeezing the oil out of the source material by means of a weight applied from above. This method allows for an extraction level of about 50% to 70% of the oil. This is the method typically used to produce extra-virgin olive oil, and it's also often used with walnuts and soft-fleshed fruits, such as avocados. After World War II, the oil industry shifted from using mostly hydraulic pressing, even for cottonseed oil, to the more economical methods of mechanical pressing and solvent extraction.

Mechanical pressing, also known as expeller pressing, removes oil by using continuously driven screws to crush the source material into a pulp from which the oil is expressed. Although there is no external heat applied during expeller pressing, friction created in the process can generate temperatures between 120°F and 190°F, depending on the hardness of the nut or seed.

Cold pressing is a non-chemical, mechanical process that extracts oil from the source material at temperatures below 122°F. Products labeled "cold-pressed" can be created using any of the methods described above—stone pressing, hydraulic pressing, or mechanical pressing—as long as the temperature remains below 122°F. Cold-pressed oils may also be filtered naturally to remove any impurities. Extra-virgin and virgin olive oils are the most readily available cold-pressed oils. This process is also used for specialty oils that are used primarily for their nutritional benefits, such as flax-seed oil, borage oil, and wheat germ oil.

Solvent extraction was invented in Germany in 1870 as a way to maximize the efficient removal of oil from the source material, since the pulp left over from mechanical pressing can have a residual oil content of up to 7%. During solvent extraction, ground or flaked seeds are steamed and then pressed to remove oil. The seed pulp, which still contains some oil, is then combined with a solvent mixture featuring hexane, a highly flammable, colorless, volatile solvent that further removes as much of the residual oil as possible.

The U.S. Environmental Protection Agency considers hexane a toxic air pollutant that can cause permanent nerve damage with long-term exposure, yet they still allow its use in solvent extraction, since they expect that much of the hexane will be removed from the final oil, recycled, and reused. To remove the solvent from the oil, the mixture is exposed to steam. The solvent is then condensed from the steam and recovered so it can be reused. The oil is then refined, removing any lingering solvents in the process. As it is recognized that solvent losses can occur at several points in the oil production process, facilities that use hexane to extract oil from seeds are subject to regulations to ensure only minimal emissions of hexane and smog-forming volatile organic compounds.

Oils made using natural, non-chemical extraction methods are readily available. Because it's always good to limit toxic chemicals, both in the environment and in the body, whenever possible, it makes sense to choose oils processed without

Culinary Oil Selection Guide

Uses	Oil Type	Smoke Point
High heat: suitable for all purposes, especially frying, stir-frying, high temperature baking, and other high-heat applications	Avocado (refined)	510°F
	Almond (refined)	495°F
	Apricot kernel (refined)	495°F
	Canola (super high-heat), refined	460°F
	Safflower (very high-oleic), refined	460°F
	Sunflower (high-oleic), refined	460°F
	Corn (refined)	450°F
	Palm fruit (refined)	450°F
	Peanut (refined)	450°F
	Soy oil (refined)	450°F
	Safflower (high-oleic, refined)	445°F
	Sesame (refined)	445°F
	Hazelnut (refined)	430°F
Medium-high heat: sautéing and baking	Canola (refined)	425°F
	Grapeseed (refined)	425°F
	Walnut (refined)	400°F
	Safflower (high-oleic, unrefined)	390°F
	Coconut (refined)	365°F
	Soy (semi-refined)	360°F
Low to medium heat: sautéing and baking at lower, more moderate heat	Peanut (unrefined)	350°F
	Sesame (unrefined)	350°F
	Toasted sesame (unrefined)	350°F
	Olive (unrefined)	325°F
	Corn (unrefined)	320°F
	Soy (unrefined)	320°F
	Coconut (unrefined)	280°F
No heat	Argan (unrefined)	225°F
	Almond (unrefined)	225°F
	Avocado (unrefined)	225°F
	Flaxseed (unrefined)	225°F
	Hazelnut (unrefined)	225°F
	Pumpkin (unrefined)	225°F
	Safflower (unrefined)	225°F
	Sunflower (unrefined)	225°F
	Walnut (unrefined)	225°F

Adapted from Spectrum Organic Products, Inc. "Kitchen Guide."

hexane. Extra-virgin and virgin olive oils aren't processed with hexane and are always easy to come by. To find other oils processed without chemical solvents, look for the phrase "mechanically pressed" or "expeller-pressed." Because it takes more raw material to produce an equivalent amount of mechanically pressed oil, they are typically more expensive than those produced with solvents, but think of it as an investment in your health—and the health of the planet.

REFINING

Once extracted, oils may remain unrefined or be lightly filtered, or they may be refined and further processed. Refining is generally done to remove components within the oil to make it more neutral in flavor, less cloudy, or less prone to oxidation. Unfortunately, many nutrients are removed during refining, including a fair amount of phytosterols and vitamin E. However, the essential fatty acids do remain.

The full refining process involves many steps. First, oils such as soybean oil and sunflower seed oil, which contain high amounts of naturally occurring lecithin and other phospholipids, are degummed. The phospholipids are removed using water and citric acid or phosphoric acid, resulting in oil that's less thick and less susceptible to darkening at high temperatures. In the refining stage (not to be confused with the general term for the entire process), the oil is combined with an alkali, such as caustic soda, to reduce the presence of unbound fatty acids and peroxides, which can accelerate the oxidation of the oil.

During bleaching, the oil is mixed with fuller's earth, a type of absorbent clay, to remove plant pigments. The bleached oil is then filtered to remove the clay. Further clarification is accomplished through deodorizing. In this process, steam is blown through the oil at temperatures up to 470°F to remove flavors and remaining odors. Oils that naturally contain high amounts of waxes, stearines,

sterols, or other solids are winterized to reduce cloudiness. This involves subjecting the oil to temperatures around 45°F, causing the waxes or stearines to solidify so they can be separated from the liquid oil by filtering.

While unrefined oils are highly valued for their full-bodied flavor, enticing aroma, deep color, and richer nutrient content, refined oils can actually be the better choice for cooking at medium to high temperatures. Many of the nutrients and phytonutrients in unrefined oils make the oil more vulnerable to oxidation, especially at higher temperatures. Long-term use of oxidized fats can increase risk of arterial damage, cancer, inflammation, and premature aging of cells and tissues. In contrast, refined oil has fewer unstable components, making it more suitable for high-temperature cooking. Refined oils also work better in recipes where the flavor of the oil is not desired in the final outcome.

Smoke Point

Different types of oil have different smoke points, the maximum temperature the oil can be heated to before it starts to smoke and discolor, indications that the oil is being damaged by heat. When oil begins to smoke, it releases carcinogens into the air and creates free radicals within the oil. These highly reactive molecules can cause cellular damage and breakdown and lead to disease. Even from a purely culinary standpoint, heating oil beyond its smoke point is a problem, as it will give rise to an off taste in the dish and an acrid smell in the kitchen.

The fatty acid profile of an oil determines the temperature at which dangerous compounds are formed and its stability in terms of its resistance to oxidation. Oils higher in saturated fats are the most stable, followed by monounsaturated fats, and polyunsaturated fats are the most vulnerable.

There are some basic rules of thumb you can use to decide whether to use unrefined or refined oil in various cooking applications. Use unrefined oils when preparing dishes that need only low to moderate heat (temperatures below 320°F), such as steaming, light sautéing, and drizzling over cooked vegetables or grains. They're also suitable for salad dressings and most sauces, and can be used in baking when the oven temperature doesn't exceed 350°F, as the internal temperatures of cookies, cakes, and breads will remain below 320°F.

On the other hand, it is best to use refined oils when oiling baking pans, since they can heat up to higher temperatures than are advisable for unrefined oils. For cooking at medium to high heat (350°F to 425°F), such as stir-frying, sautéing with high heat, popping popcorn, grilling, and high-temperature baking, use only refined oils. Even so, different types of refined oils have different smoke points. For example, refined avocado oil, which is high in monounsaturated fat, can withstand temperatures up to 510°F, while refined walnut oil should only be used up to 400°F.

Cold-pressed nutrient-focused oils such as flax-seed, borage, and wheat germ oil are very sensitive to heat and should never be used in cooking. Instead, use them as a butter substitute on bread, in smoothies and uncooked sauces and salad dressings, or as a condiment on raw or cooked vegetables, soups, and entrées.

Storage of Culinary Oils

Constant refrigeration is the best way to store oils to maintain optimum flavor and nutrition for longer periods of time. When refrigerated, unrefined oils may keep for up to fourteen months, while refined oils may keep for up to twenty months. Oils high in saturated fat, such as coconut oil and palm oil, are an exception. Because their fatty acid profile makes them so stable, they can be stored at room temperature for up to two years. Monounsaturated oils that are used frequently can be kept unrefrigerated for up to two months if they're not stored at temperatures above 77°F. At warmer temperatures,

these oils should be refrigerated. Because oils high in polyunsaturated fats are less stable and more vulnerable to oxidation, they should always be stored in the refrigerator. For the same reason, it's best to buy smaller amounts of polyunsaturated oils so you'll use them up more quickly. Cold-pressed nutrient oils are even more prone to oxidation, so they must be refrigerated at all times and be used even more quickly than other polyunsaturated oils. To ensure freshness, use within eight weeks of opening and no later than the date indicated on the container.

The manner in which oils are bottled is also important. For maximum flavor and nutrition, look for oils labeled that they have been flushed with an inert gas, such as argon or nitrogen gas, before being sealed. This ensures that oxidation won't begin before you even open the bottle. Most unrefined cooking oils are sold in clear glass or plastic bottles. Ideally, they would be packaged in opaque, nonreactive, inert containers to protect them from light, which can also cause oxidative damage. Fortunately, avoiding damage caused by exposure to light is easy: Buy oils in darker containers or store them in a dark pantry or, even better, in the refrigerator.

While many oils have healthful properties when they're fresh and stored properly, rancid oils can present a significant health risk. Knowing that rancid oils are carcinogenic should be enough to keep you from using them, but be aware that they can also weaken immunity and promote aging. Once an oil has been burned or has become rancid, discard it. No matter how much you paid for it, it's simply not worth using.

The Lowdown on Hydrogenated Fats

Margarine was first developed in 1869 by a French pharmacist in response to the opportunity to win a substantial prize offered by Napoleon III to the first person to produce a synthetic, edible fat. At the time, a serious disease affecting cattle made butter both scarce and expensive. The pharmacist's first prototype was a mixture of beef fat, milk, chopped sheep's stomachs, and cow's udders. He named it after a fatty acid, margaric acid (a name derived from the Greek word for "pearl"), that he mistakenly believed to occur in the animal fat he used. Nonetheless, calling the synthetic fat margarine did make some sense as, not only did the substance he created form pearly drops, but it was also hard, white, and glossy.

A more palatable option, using vegetable oils instead of animal parts, became possible with hydrogenation. This process, first developed in Germany in 1903, artificially alters liquid polyunsaturated vegetable oils into more solid, stable fats, such as margarine and shortening. Hydrogenated fats became popular with food manufacturers because they are cheaper than butter, emulate the consistency and mouth-feel of saturated fats like butter and lard, and are resistant to oxidation, thus allowing extended shelf life.

During the process of hydrogenation, polyunsaturated vegetable oils are mixed with hydrogen gas under pressure at high heat. A metal catalyst like nickel, zinc, or copper is added to react with the hydrogen gas in order to break some of the polyunsaturated fats' carbon double-bonds, forcing them to bond with the hydrogen. Since total hydrogenation would produce a very dense and brittle fat, oils are usually partially hydrogenated to various degrees of saturation depending on the intended use of the finished product. This is the point where trans-fatty acids are created. The double bonds where hydrogen hasn't been added are broken and reformed into a new shape in which one of the existing hydrogen molecules at a double-bond is flipped and rotated, creating a molecular structure that seldom occurs in natural fats. The molecule becomes more straight and rigid, lending the hydrogenated oil a higher melting point and giving it a plastic quality.

The bad news is that as the body tries to incorporate these unnatural trans-fatty acids into its cell membranes, deformed cellular structures may result. Trans fats have been linked to a long list of health problems, including obesity, infertility, increased risk of cancer and heart disease, and accelerated aging and degenerative changes in tissues. The more trans fats consumed, the higher the risks. Trans fats also inhibit action of the enzymes that transform alpha-linolenic acid into longer-chain omega-3 fatty acids (EPA and DHA), compounds that have many important functions within the body.

As a final clincher in regard to the dangers of hydrogenated fats, according to the U.S. National Academy of Sciences, as recommended in their 2002 "Letter Report on Dietary Reference Intakes for Trans-Fatty Acids," the tolerable upper intake level should be considered *zero*—a decision based on the undeniable relationship between trans-fatty acid intake and increased risk of coronary heart disease. In other words, avoiding hydrogenated fat is best for optimum health.

Mandatory labeling of trans fat content in foods is required in many countries. Confusingly, sometimes labels on meat and dairy products indicate the presence of trans fats even though they don't contain hydrogenated fats. It is true that low levels of naturally occurring trans-fatty acids may be present in these foods. However, the trans fats found in meat and dairy products are the result of a natural process in which microbes in the stomach of ruminant animals transform unsaturated fatty acids into trans fats. Their chemical structure is different from that of man-made trans fats, with the trans fat bonds occurring at different locations, and as a result, the body metabolizes them differently. In particular, hydrogenated oils contain a higher percentage of a type of trans-fatty acid (trans-9) that has been shown to have significant negative effects on heart health. It's unfortunate that the same term is used for both man-made and naturally occurring trans fats.

Natural trans-fat-free, plant-based substitutes for hydrogenated fats, based on palm and coconut oils, are now available. Ironically, these very ingredients were widely used in food processing rather than hydrogenated fats until the mid-1980s, when consumer groups in the United States pressed for their replacement because of worries about saturated fats, leading to a widespread switch to hydrogenated fats. Since then, palm and coconut oils have been exonerated and are now recognized for their unique saturated fatty acid profile that allows them to function as trans fats do, but without the disastrous health effects.

Exploring Culinary Oils

Almond Oil

Predominantly monounsaturated fat
Unrefined or refined

While almond oil maybe more familiar as the base of massage oil and as an ingredient in other personal care products, it is a delicious oil in its own right and one that is now recognized for its nutritional benefits, as well. Made from almonds that are ground and then roasted to help release their oil, almond oil is a mildly sweet and delicate cooking oil with a flavor reminiscent of roasted almonds.

Studies on almond oil, which is high in monounsaturated fat, have shown it can significantly reduce triglycerides and total and LDL cholesterol, as well as increase HDL cholesterol when used on a regular basis. Beta-sitosterol, the primary phytosterol found in almonds, plays a role in reducing cholesterol and also enhances immune function.

Both unrefined and refined almond oil are available, each suitable for specific uses. Unrefined almond oil is only lightly filtered, making it more flavorful and deeply colored than refined almond oil. However, it is more sensitive to heat and should, therefore, only be used in no-heat or low-heat cooking applications. Try it as a delicious flavoring oil drizzled over finished dishes, as a base for salad dressings and low-heat sauces, or for almond-inspired sautés cooked at low temperatures.

Refined almond oil, with its smoke point of 495°F, is an all-purpose oil that can be used for all types of cooking, from salad dressings to stir-fries, and for coating baking pans or cookie sheets. It also works well in recipes where only a very subtle almond flavor is desired.

Apricot Kernel Oil

Predominantly monounsaturated fat
Refined

Apricot kernel oil is pressed from the kernels found within apricot pits, which, botanically, are very similar to almonds. It has a mild, slightly sweet flavor. Apricot kernel oil is widely used in cosmetics, lotions, and massage oils.

Like other monounsaturated oils, apricot kernel oil is considered a heart-healthy oil that can help promote good cardiovascular function and healthy cell membranes. Apricot kernel oil is always sold in refined form. It has a smoke point of 495°F, making it a good all-purpose oil for all types of cooking. It's especially nice in salad dressings.

Argan Oil

Slightly higher in monounsaturated fat (44%) than
*   polyunsaturated fat (37%)*
Unrefined

Extracted from the nut of the argan tree, argan oil is a deep golden color and has a flavor similar to pumpkin seeds. The argan tree, which can live to be 200 years old, grows only in a small area in southwestern Morocco. The hard-shelled nut, still typically cracked by hand, is found inside the tree's small green fruit. Each nut can contain up to three kernels from which the oil is extracted. Argan oil has been used for many centuries as a flavoring ingredient in Moroccan cuisine. Due to its high omega-6 content, it is also used in traditional medicine—externally as a massage oil and internally as a good source of beneficial essential fatty acids.

Argan oil is light, similar in viscosity to sesame oil. Mix it with honey and serve with bread for a traditional Moroccan breakfast, or drizzle it over tagines—Moroccan stews made from meat or poultry simmered with vegetables, olives, and spices and served over couscous. It also makes a delicious salad dressing when mixed with lemon juice or vinegar. Or use it as a condiment to enhance the flavor of soups, vegetables, grains, pasta, grilled meat or fish, or beans, especially lentils.

Avocado Oil

Predominantly monounsaturated fat
Unrefined or refined

Avocado oil is pressed from the oil-rich pulp of the avocado fruit and may have some of the flavor and color of avocados depending on the degree of refinement the oil has undergone. Because it's rich in monounsaturated fats, regular use of avocado oil can help reduce the bad LDL cholesterol while raising levels of good HDL cholesterol. It is high in beta-sitosterol, which inhibits absorption of cholesterol from the intestines. Studies have also shown that avocado oil can significantly increase absorption of two important antioxidants, beta-carotene and lutein, when it's added to salads.

Avocado oil is available both unrefined and refined. Unrefined avocado oil has a delicious, buttery, nutty flavor that's exceptional in salad dressings, sauces, and light sautés or simply drizzled over crusty bread, steamed vegetables, or pasta dishes. As processing essentially involves only pressing the oil from the pulp, unrefined avocado oil retains the beautiful green color of the original

fruit. For best flavor and nutrition, use it only in no-heat or low-heat cooking applications.

In contrast, refined avocado oil has a very light color and is almost flavorless. It is distinguished from all other plant-derived culinary oils as having the highest smoke point—510°F. In addition to being the best oil to use for high-heat cooking, such as stir-frying, grilling, broiling, and frying, it also works well in salad dressings and low- to medium-heat applications when a mild flavor desired.

Canola Oil

Predominantly monounsaturated fat, including 11%
  omega-3 fatty acids
Refined

If you want to keep things simple and keep only one kind of oil in your refrigerator, this is the one to choose. Canola oil is an excellent, all-purpose oil made from a fairly recently developed variety of mustard rape, a plant related to kale, cabbage, brussels sprouts, and other members of the *Brassica* genus. Although oil from conventional rapeseed plants has been a traditional cooking oil in China, Japan, and India for more than three thousand years, in the 1970s questions were raised about its safety because it contains fairly high levels of erucic acid, which had detrimental health effects on rats in a single animal study. As a result, several hybrids with lower levels of erucic acid were developed, even though subsequent studies have failed to show detrimental effects from erucic acid in humans.

Nonetheless, this relatively new variety of oil, sometimes referred to as LEAR oil (low erucic acid rapeseed oil) turned out to be worth the effort. Canola oil (a name that abbreviates the unwieldy descriptor Canadian oilseed, low-acid) is a nutritional powerhouse. High in heart-healthy monounsaturated fat, as olive oil is, and lower in saturated fat than any other oil, canola oil is also a good source of hard-to-find omega-3 fatty acids, with 1.2 grams of alpha-linolenic acid in each tablespoon. It also is a good source of phytosterols, which have been shown to lower blood cholesterol levels and protect against certain types of cancer.

Canola oil is always refined, making it heat stable at fairly high temperatures. Accordingly, it is suitable for all types of cooking, from salad dressings to sautéing and baking up to 425°F with regular canola oil and up to 460°F with super high-heat canola oil, which has been bred to have a higher percentage of monounsaturated fats. Its neutral flavor and aroma are mild enough to allow the flavors of the foods it's cooked with to be the focus.

Although canola oil was developed before genetic engineering was used as a tool in plant breeding, genetically engineered versions of low-erucic-acid rapeseed have since been created. To ensure you aren't getting oil from genetically modified plants, use only certified organic canola oil.

Coconut Oil

Predominantly saturated fat
Unrefined or refined

Coconut oil is made from the fruits of coconut palm trees, which grow in hot, rainy tropical climates. It is thought to be one of the earliest plant oils used by humans, especially in tropical regions. More recently, coconut oil has gone through a cycle of appreciation and then vilification because of its high percentage of saturated fats. Now we're back to appreciation, as we've grown to better understand both the role of fats in health and the unique properties of the fats found in coconuts oil.

Not all types of saturated fat behave the same in the body. Studies have confirmed that moderate consumption of coconut oil doesn't have the same harmful effects on the heart that occur with most foods high in saturated fats. This is due to the specific types of saturated fatty acid found in coconut oil, including lauric, myristic, palmitic, and caprylic acids. Lauric acid, the most prevalent of the four, increases good HDL cholesterol and

helps reduce the ratio of total cholesterol to HDL, which is really the most important measure as far as cardiovascular health is concerned. Both myristic and palmitic acids have an overall neutral effect on total cholesterol. Lauric acid and caprylic acid also have antiviral and antimicrobial properties, so they provide valuable immune support.

The lauric, caprylic, and capric acids in coconut oil fall into a special class of fatty acids known as medium-chain triglycerides (MCTs). In contrast to the long-chain triglycerides that usually predominate in saturated fats, MCTs are metabolized immediately by the liver rather than needing pancreatic enzymes or bile salts for digestion and absorption. This means they digest quickly and are used for energy and biochemical processes rather than being deposited in the body as fat. MCTs from coconut oil have long been prescribed by doctors in nutritional formulas for patients who are critically ill or have problems with absorption.

One of the benefits of saturated fats is that, unlike polyunsaturated fats, they are very stable, resisting oxidation and thus rancidity. This lends products made with coconut oil a longer shelf life and explains why it is widely used in food manufacturing, in nondairy creamers, and for frying products like potato chips and popcorn, for example. It is also appreciated for its subtle, slightly sweet and nutty flavor, making it a key ingredient in popcorn and many other products.

The coconut flavor is much more pronounced in unrefined coconut oil. Because all of the flavor components and the full spectrum of phytonutrients remain intact in unrefined coconut oil, it also has a lower smoke point (280°F), making it more appropriate for medium-heat cooking, including light sautéing in dishes where its coconut flavor will enhance the recipe. In comparison, refined coconut oil has fewer nutrients, but its smoke point of 365°F makes it the better option for cooking and baking at medium-high heat.

Different brands of coconut oil vary widely in

quality. Coconut oil can be processed in many ways, some retaining nutrients and the natural coconut flavor better than others. Typical commercial production of coconut oil starts with copra, coconut meat that has been scraped out of ripe coconuts and dried for a couple of days in the sun or in a kiln, often by individual farmers in communities where coconut palms are grown. Because the copra is usually processed into coconut oil at facilities far from where it was dried, it can start to deteriorate along the way, especially because of the high humidity and unsanitary conditions that often prevail. To make it safe for human use, the coconut oil expressed from the copra undergoes a thorough refining process, often at high temperatures and using solvents.

In contrast, expeller-pressed coconut oil is processed without solvents. It can be either lightly filtered and left unrefined or further refined, filtered, and distilled, giving it a higher heat tolerance but also removing some of the flavors and aroma of fresh coconut.

Virgin coconut oil is unrefined and may be processed in a couple of different ways. It can be expressed from quickly dried coconut meat within an hour of cracking open the coconut, using minimal heat and filtration, directly at the site where coconut palms are grown. Or it can be expressed from wet coconut meat by first making coconut milk and then separating the oil out of the coconut milk in any of a number of ways: by boiling, fermentation or refrigeration, or by using enzymes or a centrifuge. For example, in the fermentation method, the coconut milk is fermented for twenty-four to thirty-six hours, during which time the oil separates out. Then, depending on the manufacturer, the oil may be heated at low temperatures for a short time to remove moisture that could eventually cause the oil to deteriorate. Finally, it is filtered. The best virgin coconut oils will have a wonderful taste and aroma of coconuts.

Free of trans fats and cholesterol, coconut oil is an excellent alternative to hydrogenated fats and butter for frying, sautéing, or baking cookies, piecrusts, and cakes. When stored below 78°F, coconut oil has a thick consistency like shortening and is sometimes referred to as coconut butter. At warmer temperatures, it melts into a liquid oil. If your coconut oil is in a more solid form and a recipe calls for coconut oil in its liquid state, just put the container in hot water until it liquefies. Likewise, you may want to refrigerate liquid coconut oil until it solidifies if you're using it in a recipe that calls for fat in a solid form, such as shortening.

Corn Oil

Predominantly polyunsaturated fat
Unrefined or refined

An old American standby, corn oil was first produced in the late 1800s, several years after the development of processes for hydrolyzing cornstarch, in which the starch is separated from the oil-rich germ. Because it's inexpensive, corn oil is used extensively in making margarine and vegetable shortening, as well as for cooking and salad dressings.

Like other oils high in polyunsaturated fats, corn oil is a good source of omega-6 fatty acids. However, the average person in the United States eating a highly processed diet already consumes an adequate amount of this fatty acid, especially given the prevalence of corn oil in conventional food processing. In fact, the overuse of corn oil is one of the main contributors to the excess of omega-6 fatty acids in proportion to omega-3 fatty acids in the average diet. On the other hand, corn oil does contain a high amount of phytosterols, which help reduce cholesterol levels, and has one of the highest amounts of vitamin E of any culinary oil. How much of the phytosterols and vitamin E is removed during refining depends on the manufacturer and the processing method used. Unrefined corn oil will, of course, retain the most.

Corn oil has a smoke point of 320°F if unrefined and 450°F if refined. Because of its tendency to foam and smoke at high heat, neither form of corn oil should be used for deep-frying. It's usually refined, in which case it has an almost nonexistent flavor and a light golden color. When unrefined, it has a buttery corn flavor and a deep yellow color that make it a good choice for baking, sautéing, and cooking pancakes. When using unrefined corn oil, don't exceed medium-hot temperature cooking and keep oven temperatures at or below 350°F. As the majority of corn is genetically engineered, use certified organic corn oil to ensure that it isn't derived from genetically modified corn.

Flaxseed Oil

Predominantly polyunsaturated fat, including 57% omega-3 fatty acids
Unrefined

Flaxseed oil, a golden-colored oil with a nutty, buttery flavor, is pressed from the tiny, oval seeds of the blue-flowered flax plant. As its polyunsaturated fat is comprised of an amazing 57% alpha-linolenic acid, flaxseed oil is prized as the best plant-based, and therefore vegetarian, source of omega-3 fatty acids. Designated an essential fatty acid because it must be obtained in the diet, alpha-linolenic acid helps support heart health, reduce inflammation, and improve cellular integrity, which helps reduce the risk of some forms of cancer. The human body can convert about 10% of the alpha-linolenic acid (ALA) in flaxseed oil into the more biologically potent longer-chain forms of omega-3 fatty acids, EPA (eicosapentaenoic acid) and DHA (docosahexaenoic acid). The estimated adequate intake of alpha-linolenic acid (ALA) is a minimum of 1.6 grams per day for men and 1.1 grams per day for women. Just 1 teaspoon of flaxseed oil provides 2.8 grams of ALA.

Lignans, a beneficial form of fiber found in the thin outer membrane of whole flaxseeds, are removed as a result of expressing the oil from the seeds. However, they are sometimes added back into flaxseed oil as an enrichment. The primary lignan found in flaxseed, secoisolariciresinol diglycoside (SDG), is known for its antioxidant properties and balancing effect on hormones. Flaxseed oil enriched with lignans provides enhanced nutrition, richer texture, and nuttier flavor. As the lignans will sink to the bottom of the bottle, the oil must be shaken vigorously before use.

Flaxseed oil should only be used in no-heat recipes or added to foods at temperatures lower than 225°F, such as salad dressings, sandwich spreads, and dips. It makes a delicious and healthy replacement for butter or any oil on baked potatoes, steamed vegetables, rice, pasta, and cooked grains, and even drizzled on bread. Or you can add a spoonful to smoothies, shakes, or yogurt. Because flaxseed oil is so high in polyunsaturated fats, it is quite sensitive to light, heat, and oxygen, explaining why it's packaged in dark bottles. It should be refrigerated at all times, including in grocery stores.

Grapeseed Oil

Predominantly polyunsaturated fat
Refined

Grapeseed oil, a traditional oil produced in many countries where wine grapes are grown, is pressed from the tiny seeds of grapes. Not surprisingly, it is a popular component in French and Italian cooking. Because of its nongreasy nature, it is also popular as a base for massage oils. Because the seeds are so small and hard and contain only 10% oil, most grapeseed oil is extracted with solvents and refined. However, varieties that use alcohol, rather than hexane, as a solvent are available and would be the better choice.

Very high in polyunsaturated fat, grapeseed oil is a good source of linoleic acid (the omega-6 essential fatty acid). However, the ratio of omega-6 to omega-3 fatty acids in the typical U.S. diet is already higher than optimal, so this isn't necessarily beneficial. Still, grapeseed oil is also a good source of polyphenols and phytosterols, which help reduce cholesterol levels.

Unlike other oils high in polyunsaturated fats, grapeseed oil has a relatively high smoke point (425°F), due to its low levels of impurities, which are naturally present in most oils. Another benefit of its relative purity is that salad dressings and marinades made with grapeseed oil don't cloud when refrigerated. Chefs often prefer it for its neutral flavor and light consistency, and also because it's suitable for a wider range of temperatures and cooking applications than olive oil is. Grapeseed oil is a good choice when making sauces, sautéing, baking, and frying at medium-high heat. Because of its mild flavor, it's a good choice when making infused oils, and it's also commonly used with other oils to tone down strong flavors.

Hazelnut Oil

Predominantly monounsaturated fat
Unrefined

Hazelnut oil is a distinctively delicious oil made by hydraulically pressing hazelnuts that have been ground and then roasted. The monounsaturated fats in hazelnut oil can help reduce total cholesterol. And like hazelnuts themselves, hazelnut oil is also a good source of phytosterols, phytonutrients that help reduce cholesterol while boosting the immune system.

To best appreciate it's flavor, drizzle hazelnut oil on salads, bitter greens, steamed vegetables, cooked grains, or pasta as a flavoring accent, or use it in marinades, vinaigrettes, and sauces. Although hazelnut oil can also be used in baking, its flavor can dissipate when subjected to heat.

Olive Oil

Predominantly monounsaturated fat
Unrefined or refined

A hallmark of the Mediterranean diet, olive oil is a ubiquitous ingredient and flavoring agent that weaves together all of the key foods in this healthful cuisine. All good-quality olive oil is pressed from coarsely crushed olives, most often in a hydraulic press, sometimes in a stone press, and occasionally by letting gravity take its course, allowing the oil to drip out of the crushed olives and through a fine screen. The many types of olive oil vary in flavor, color, and aroma depending on the variety of olives used, the soil and climate in which they were grown, when and how they were harvested, and the skill of the processor.

The most flavorful and nutritious olive oils come from handpicked semi-ripe olives and have a fruitier, more robust taste accented by a spicy, peppery flavor. This latter characteristic signifies the higher level of antioxidant phytochemicals present in olives before they ripen. Early-harvest olive oils contain at least thirty antioxidant phytochemicals, which provide not just health benefits, but also flavors, colors, and aromas.

Some of these compounds are visually apparent, such as the chlorophyll and carotenoid pigments that give the oil its greenish gold color. Olive oil is very high in monounsaturated fat, a feature that became the focus of many scientific studies when it was discovered that people eating traditional cuisines that include liberal amounts of olive oil had the lowest incidence of heart attacks. Olive oil raises levels of good cholesterol (HDL) and lowers bad cholesterol (LDL), creating a more healthful ratio of the two. Further, it can significantly reduce the absorption of cholesterol.

Studies have also shown that when tomatoes are cooked with olive oil, absorption of their lycopene skyrockets—something that doesn't occur to the same dramatic extent when other oils are used. Lycopene is a powerful phytochemical that may reduce the risk of certain cancers and macular degeneration. All of these nutritional benefits come together to explain why the Mediterranean diet is not only delicious but also extraordinarily healthful. It also underscores how things that may seem very simple and basic can be profoundly beneficial—perhaps because of, rather than in spite of, their simplicity.

Oils from olives harvested later in the season also have considerable merit. While somewhat lower in antioxidants, they have the same healthful fat profile, high in monounsaturated fats. Olive oil from riper olives is also delicious, albeit different in flavor, having a nuttier, milder, less spicy flavor. And they are also less expensive, as the olives yield more oil than those that are less ripe.

The particular variety of olive, coupled with the soil quality and climate where they are grown, also has a significant effect on flavor and color. For example, olive oil from Italy can range from Tuscany's hearty, peppery oil to Liguria's flowery oil to Umbria's nutty and buttery oil to Puglia's fruity and herbaceous oil. And that's just olive oil from Italy. Spanish olive oil is generally fruity and nutty, with just a hint of almond. Greek olive oil is often described as strong, buttery, and aromatic. Many French olive oils are mild and sweet. Olive oil from California can be reminiscent of peppery Tuscan oil, or it may be mild, light, and fruity. Let your taste buds, and the intended use, be your guide. The optimum way to experience olive oil is to try a new variety each time you buy it. As with choosing wine, with more experience you'll discover which varieties you most enjoy.

Each of the official categories for olive oil—extra-virgin, virgin, light, and so on—is recognized globally, based on guidelines that were updated in 2003. A primary distinguishing point between the categories is the concentration of residual oleic acid present in the oil, also known as the percentage of free fatty acids or free acidity, and the number of positive and negative sensory attributes found in the oil.

Free acidity has nothing to do with an acid or sour flavor. Fatty acids are often attached to other molecules, such as triglycerides (three fatty acids bound together) or phospholipids (in which fatty acids are bound to phosphoric acid and other compounds). When they exist just on their own, rather than as components of larger molecules, they're known as free fatty acids. In terms of olive oil, the amount of free fatty acids gives a rough indication of the quality of the olives used to make the oil and how carefully the olives were handled, from picking through pressing. The lower the free acidity percentage, the better overall quality of the olive oil. Fatty acids can be freed up when the harvested olives or their oil is exposed to light, heat, and air before being bottled. Accordingly, the more quickly olives are pressed before they start to deteriorate, the better the flavor and the lower the free acidity. In addition, the riper the olives are, the higher the free acidity level.

The sensory evaluation of olive oil considers both positive and negative attributes in terms of taste, aroma, look, and feel. Traits perceived as negative include musty, winey or vinegary, rancid, greasy, earthy (unwashed olive flavor), and burnt. Attributes considered positive include fruity, bitter, and pungent. Either unripe or mature olives can be high in fruitiness, generally indicating that fresh, sound olives were used, and that they were processed carefully. Both bitter and pungent are characteristics that can only be achieved with unripe olives, which have more polyphenols than ripe olives do. Both of these traits are readily perceived—bitterness as flavor experienced on the back of the tongue and pungency as a biting sensation perceived in the throat.

The overall category of virgin olive oil indicates oil obtained exclusively by mechanical or other physical means (stone pressing or, more commonly, hydraulic pressing). Treatments such as washing, decanting, centrifuging, and filtration are allowed, but solvents are not. Olive oil processed with solvents is classified as olive-pumice oil, and can never be marketed as olive oil.

Extra-virgin, representing the best in flavor and aroma, must contain no more than 0.8% free acidity, and the best versions are as low as 0.1%. Extra-virgin olive oil must also have no negative attributes and at least one positive attribute. Its flavor should taste like the specific variety of olives from which it was made. Virgin olive oil is slightly lower in quality than extra-virgin olive oil. It has good flavor, but its free acidity may be as high as 2.0%, and it can have up to 2.5 sensory defects.

Both extra-virgin and virgin olive oils have medium heat smoke points (325°F), making them appropriate for cooking at low to medium heat, such as in sauces, savory breads, and sautéing at moderate heat. They are especially good in marinades and salad dressings and drizzled on bread, pasta, pizza, and vegetables.

For cooking at medium-high to high heat, choose products labeled "olive oil" or "light olive oil." Products labeled simply as "olive oil" comprise the majority of olive oil sold to consumers worldwide. A blend of unrefined virgin olive oil and refined olive oil, it has a free acidity of not more than 1%. Any olive oil with free acidity higher than 3.3% or with more than six defects—indications that the oil was processed improperly or made from bad olives—is a good candidate for refining. Free fatty acid levels are lowered by treatment with sodium hydroxide, and compounds causing objectionable flavors, colors, and aromas (including many antioxidants) are removed, but without using solvents. The refined olive oil is always blended with an unrefined virgin olive oil to ensure the final oil has some flavor. Because refining removes polyphenols responsible for the oil's full flavor, color, and aroma, refined olive oil has a higher smoke point. As a result, when it's mixed with virgin olive oil, the resulting blend has a higher smoke point—around 425°F to 450°F.

Light olive oil is a subcategory of "olive oil." Rather than referring to low calorie content, the term *light* here refers to less flavor, aroma, and color, all of which are filtered out during process-ing. Although it has little flavor, it may be able to take slightly more heat than those labeled "olive oil"—sometimes up to 465°F, depending on the brand.

Like all unrefined oils, extra-virgin and virgin olive oils should be stored in a cool, dark place. Better-quality oils are usually sold in tinted bottles to help protect them from light. Although olive oil can be stored at cool room temperatures, no higher than 77°F, for up to ten weeks, for optimum shelf life, keep it refrigerated. Although it will cloud and slightly solidify in the refrigerator, it quickly returns to a liquid state at room temperature.

Palm Fruit Oil

*Predominantly saturated fat (50%), along with a
high amount of monounsaturated fat (40%)*
Unrefined or refined

Palm fruit oil is pressed from the oily pulp of the plum-size fruit from a variety of palm tree that grows in Southeast Asia, western Africa, and Central and South America. Oil is also made from the nut-like kernel within the fruit, usually referred to as palm kernel oil. The name palm fruit oil is used to help distinguish the two, but many ingredient labels simply list "palm oil." A common cooking oil used since around 3000 BCE in western Africa, its strong, unique flavor and natural reddish orange color lend a distinctive flair to traditional dishes of the region.

Once scorned as no different than other saturated fats, palm fruit oil has since returned to popularity as a trans-fat-free alternative to hydrogenated fats, often used in cookies, crackers, pastries, and piecrusts. Unlike the saturated fats in meat and dairy products, palmitic acid, the main kind of saturated fat in palm oil, has been shown to have a neutral effect on cholesterol. Its high monounsaturated fat content is another plus, helping make palm fruit oil a positive alternative that doesn't promote heart disease. The phytosterols in palm oil also help keep cholesterol levels in check.

The crude red oil expressed from mature, ripe

palm fruit is extraordinarily rich in various carotenoids, primarily beta- and alpha-carotene, two powerful antioxidants that help boost the immune system and protect against certain forms of cancer. Carotenes may also prevent diseases of the eye, such as cataracts and age-related macular degeneration, which are thought to be caused by damage to the lens and retina by free radicals. Carotenoids are fat-soluble and thus best absorbed with fat, so palm fruit oil is a perfect medium for their absorption. Palm fruit oil is also naturally resistant to oxidation and rancidity, protected by both the chemical structure of its saturated fats and its naturally high levels of vitamin E—another antioxidant.

The best source of all these antioxidants is unrefined red palm oil. The traditional processing method starts with steaming the fruit to soften the pulp. The fruit is then pounded to separate it from the kernel and help facilitate separating out the oil, which is skimmed off the top. Excess water is removed by gently heating the oil. The oil is then allowed to settle, any impurities that sink to the bottom are removed, and then it is filtered. Red palm oil retains 80% of the carotenoids naturally found in crude palm oil, which accounts for its characteristic color.

Being such a stable fat, palm oil serves to naturally extend the shelf life of manufactured foods. Its stability also allows it to be stored at room temperature for months and makes it suitable for higher temperature cooking. The smoke point for unrefined palm oil can vary widely depending on how it was processed, including how much of the palm particulates are retained in the oil. In many African cultures, it is customary to burn red palm oil before cooking, essentially burning off some of the sediment not previously filtered out of the oil. However, burning any type of oil can cause it to become unhealthful, so a good rule of thumb is to keep engaged during the cooking process and

remove the pan from the heat if wisps of smoke begin to appear—a point generally somewhere below 450°F. Red palm oil imparts a uniquely nutty flavor that can be used to accent stews, sauces, and other recipes. As it is thicker and heavier than other common cooking oils and more strongly flavored, be sparing if using it for sautéing.

Since the traditional process extracts only about 50% of the oil from the pulp, modern methods are often used. Generally, palm fruit oil is made by pressing the pulp in a hydraulic or expeller press and then refining it to remove the oil's bright color and strong flavor components, yielding a light yellow, more bland-flavored oil. The refinement process is also a handy way to use lesser quality fruit. Although the palm fruit oil's healthy monounsaturated and palmitic fatty acids are retained in the process, a significant amount of the natural antioxidants are lost. Refined palm fruit oil has a higher smoke point than that of unrefined red palm oil. To make a creamy product resembling hydrogenated shortening, refined palm oil is whipped and often blended with other kinds of oils. Shortenings made with palm oil can be used in any recipe calling for vegetable shortening.

Although palm kernel oil comes from the same tree, the two oils are completely different from one another and used for different purposes. Palm kernel oil has a very different fatty acid profile, consisting primarily of saturated fat (82%), with small amounts of monounsaturated and polyunsaturated fats (14% and 2%, respectively). Palm kernel oil is not generally available for home use. Instead, it is primarily used in commercial food production to make products such as margarine and coatings on candies and frozen confections. Fractionated palm kernel oil, not surprisingly, is created through a process known as fractionation. First, the oil is melted and then slowly cooled. As the oil cools, a solid layer of fat rises to the surface, but rather than discarding the fat, as you would when making gravy at home, manufacturers collect the various layers that rise throughout the process and combine certain ones to yield a manipulated fat with a higher melting point for specific applications, such as making candy.

Peanut Oil

Predominantly monounsaturated fat
Unrefined and refined

Peanuts, a legume higher in fat than other beans, contain almost 50% oil, primarily in the form of monounsaturated fats, making it both heart-healthy and resistant to oxidation. Its saturated fat content is fairly high for a nontropical oil but consists primarily of palmitic acid, which is neutral in terms of raising cholesterol levels, and it also helps increase peanut oil's stability. Research into creating a peanut oil with even longer shelf life has resulted in the development of peanuts with a significantly altered fatty acid profile. Referred to as high-oleic peanuts, they yield an oil that has levels of monounsaturated fats equal to or higher than those of olive oil, and lower levels polyunsaturated and saturated fats than are typically found in peanuts.

Like the whole peanuts from which it's derived, peanut oil is very high in antioxidants and phytosterols. Heating the peanuts before processing also significantly boosts the amount of the antioxidant p-coumaric acid.

To make peanut oil, peanuts are crushed, heated, and pressed, generally in an expeller press with or without hexane. Unrefined peanut oil has an exceptional roasted peanut flavor and aroma and contains most of the nutrients found in peanuts. It has a fairly dark color and a medium-high smoke point of 350°F, somewhat high in comparison to other unrefined oils. Refined peanut oil is blander, paler, and, like other refined oils, lower in antioxidants and phytosterols. Refining does, however, push its smoke point up to 450°F, making it a better choice for stir-frying and high-heat cooking.

Although peanuts are native to South America, peanut oil is most often used in Asian stir-fries, sauces, marinades, and salads. Peanut oil is also a good choice when baking. Either unrefined or refined peanut oil would be appropriate; use unrefined when a stronger peanut flavor is desired.

Note: Those who are allergic to peanuts shouldn't use unrefined peanut oil, as it contains small amounts of peanut protein—the part that causes the allergic reaction. They may be able to tolerate refined peanut oil, since the refining processing removes most of the protein, to the point that none would be detectable by standard laboratory methods. But with so many other choices available, it may not be worth the risk.

Pumpkin Seed Oil

Predominantly polyunsaturated fat, including 15%
omega-3 fatty acids
Unrefined

Pumpkin seed oil has a dark, opaque green color and the rich flavor of roasted pumpkin seeds. Like pumpkin seeds, it is very high in antioxidants, including vitamin E, carotenes, and chlorophyll, as well as phytosterols, which can help reduce cholesterol levels.

Though it is sometimes refined for use in cosmetics, for culinary purposes it's usually unrefined. And since it is very high in polyunsaturated fats, its smoke point is quite low. It is best used as a flavoring accent on salads, soups, hot crusty bread, and steamed vegetables or fish. For salad dressings or general cooking purposes, mix a small amount of pumpkin seed oil into a larger amount of another oil, preferably one high in monounsaturated fats. Not only will the combination moderate the robust flavor characteristic of pumpkin seed oil, but it will also increase its smoke point. Store pumpkin seed oil in the refrigerator, and for optimum flavor and nutrition, use it quickly.

Safflower Oil

■ REGULAR SAFFLOWER OIL

Predominantly polyunsaturated fat
Unrefined or refined

■ HIGH-OLEIC OR VERY HIGH-OLEIC SAFFLOWER OIL

Predominantly monounsaturated fat
Refined

Safflower oil is expressed from the seeds of a thistlelike plant whose flowers have long been used as a dye and as a coloring agent in food in place of the more rare and costly saffron. This is why the plant is sometimes referred to as saffron thistle or bastard saffron. Because regular safflower oil has the highest polyunsaturated fat content of any culinary oil, it was particularly popular in the 1970s, when then-current nutritional theory praised the virtues of polyunsaturated fats. Since then, however, newer information about fats indicates that polyunsaturated fats should be used in moderation because they are very vulnerable to oxidation.

Unrefined safflower oil, which has a unique nutty flavor and golden color, is best used unheated as a condiment on cold dishes and to make salad dressings. When cooking with it, don't exceed 225°F. It can also be blended with other oils that have a higher smoke point and used for cooking at medium heat. The smoke point of refined safflower oil, which has a very light color and flavor, is 320°F, making it appropriate for medium-heat cooking.

For cooking at medium-high to high heat, which includes sautéing, pan-frying, searing, stir-frying, grilling, broiling, and baking, choose high-oleic or very high-oleic safflower oil. Both are made from new varieties of safflower developed through traditional plant breeding techniques, not genetic engineering, to significantly modify the fatty acid profile from predominantly polyunsaturated fats to monounsaturated fats. The term *high-oleic* simply refers to its high percentage of monounsaturated fats in the form of oleic acid. Not only do the high-oleic forms of safflower oil have a heart-healthy advantage over regular safflower oil, but they are also much more stable against oxidation and have a smoke point of 390°F. Very high-oleic safflower oil has an even higher percentage of monounsaturated fat, giving it a higher smoke point of 460°F.

Sesame Oil

About equal monounsaturated and polyunsaturated fat
Unrefined or refined

Sesame oil has been enjoyed for thousands of years for many reasons. Its rich, nutty flavor has long been used to enhance cooking, but sesame oil has also been used in Ayurvedic medicine, where it's revered for its beneficial essential fatty acids.

Sesame seeds contain more phytosterols (which help lower cholesterol) than any other nut or seed, and their oil has a very high amount, especially when it undergoes minimal processing and isn't refined. Unlike other culinary oils, sesame oil's fatty acid profile consists of almost equal amounts of monounsaturated and polyunsaturated fats. Although such a high proportion of polyunsaturated fats would generally result in increased vulnerability to oxidation, sesame oil contains unique lignans, sesamin and sesamol, which act as potent antioxidants. They help protect the oil from rancidity and also allow it to be used at medium-high temperatures even in its unrefined form. The smoke point of unrefined sesame oil is 350°F, and that of refined sesame oil is 445°F.

As usual, the flavor and color of unrefined sesame oil is much richer. Its nutty flavor makes it a natural for sautés, sauces, salad dressings, and marinades, and it's also excellent simply drizzled over any cold or hot vegetable, pasta, or grain dish. Use refined sesame oil when stir-frying, for higher-heat sautés, or for general cooking purposes. It's a good choice for mixing with other oils to increase their smoke point.

Extracting the oil from toasted sesame seeds creates a very rich flavor and aroma, making toasted sesame especially good as a flavoring agent. It is often used in Asian cuisine, drizzled over soups, noodles, stir-fries, and vegetables. When using it as a cooking oil, rather than a condiment, don't exceed 350°F.

Soy Oil

Predominantly polyunsaturated fat, including 8% omega-3 fatty acids
Unrefined and refined

For a long time, soy oil was considered to be inedible due to its tendency to have off flavors, so it was used primarily in the manufacture of industrial products. But by the early 1940s, new processing and refinement methods, including hydrogenation, were developed to remove or neutralize the various components responsible for its unpalatable flavor. Shortly thereafter, soy oil became the leading cooking oil in the United States and one of the oils most often used in vegetable shortening, margarine, and salad dressings. In fact, it became so common in the United States that it was often referred to generically as "vegetable oil." Even now, most vegetable oil is predominantly soy oil.

Because soy oil is so high in polyunsaturated fat, including an appreciable amount of the esteemed alpha-linolenic acid (an omega-3 fatty acid), it is more vulnerable to oxidation. Hydrogenation can help stabilize the oil, but given all of the health risks associated with consumption of hydrogenated fats, this ends up doing more harm than good. Over the years, techniques have been developed to modify the fatty acid composition of soy oil. While helpful for increasing shelf life and preventing rancidity, it sacrifices much of the alpha-linolenic acid, which oxidizes at a much quicker rate than does linoleic acid, the other main form of polyunsaturated fatty acids.

Soy oil is also known for being high in vitamin E. About 30% of its vitamin content is lost during refining; however, it is collected and is often used in dietary supplements.

Unrefined soy oil has a deep amber color and a very distinctive flavor, making it one that should be used sparingly, as it can easily overpower other ingredients within a dish or meal. It is best reserved for low- to medium-heat cooking no higher than 320°F. With its light flavor and smoke point of 450°F, refined soy oil can be used for almost any application. Semirefined soy oil, mechanically expressed without harsh chemical solvents, is also available, with a smoke point of 360°F. Check product labeling to know whether you are buying unrefined, semirefined, or fully refined soy oil. Since the majority of soybeans grown in the United States are genetically engineered, use certified organic soy oil to ensure it isn't derived from genetically modified soybeans.

Sunflower Oil

■ REGULAR SUNFLOWER OIL
Predominantly polyunsaturated fat
Unrefined or refined

■ HIGH-OLEIC OR VERY HIGH-OLEIC SUNFLOWER OIL
Predominantly monounsaturated fat
Refined

Although sunflowers have grown wild for millions of years and their seeds have been used for food for thousands of years, a method of extracting sunflower oil from the seeds wasn't developed until the early 1700s. Newer strains of sunflower, developed to contain up to twice the amount of oil in the seeds as traditional varieties, make the process even easier.

Sunflower oil is a very good source of vitamin E, having the highest alpha-tocopherol level of any of the primary culinary oils. It also contains a moderate amount of phytosterols, which help cholesterol levels. While its specific fatty acid pro-file can vary depending on the strain of sunflower and the climate in which it was grown, sunflower oil is usually very high in polyunsaturated fats, making it more vulnerable to oxidation. Accordingly, unrefined sunflower oil, with its light yellow color and mild sunflower seed flavor, is best used for no-heat applications, such as salad dressings.

Refined sunflower oil can be made from traditional varieties of sunflower seeds, which are rich in linoleic acid (an omega-6 fatty acid), but most sunflower oil now available is made from new varieties of sunflowers developed to have high levels of oleic acid (a monounsaturated fat). First developed in Russia in the mid-1970s, these varieties were created using crossbreeding rather than biotechnology. In 1995, the oil industry made a wholesale switch to high-oleic seeds because their oil is more stable. Because it has a smoke point of 460°F and is more resistant to oxidation, high-oleic sunflower oil is a good choice for cooking at medium-high to high heat, including sautéing, pan-frying, searing, stir-frying, grilling, broiling, and baking.

Walnut Oil

Predominantly polyunsaturated fat, including 10% omega-3 fatty acids
Unrefined or refined

Walnut oil is extracted from English walnuts that are first ground and then roasted before being pressed. It is one of the rare plant sources for omega-3 fatty acids, with 1 tablespoon of walnut oil providing 1.4 grams of alpha-linolenic acid, which is a precursor for eicosapentaenoic acid (EPA) and docosahexaenoic acid (DHA), the more biologically active omega-3 fatty acids. Like walnuts themselves, walnut oil is high in antioxidants. It has especially high amounts of gamma-tocopherol, a form of vitamin E that helps guard against the oxidation of fats, both in foods and in the body.

Unrefined walnut oil has a more vibrant color than does refined, and a rich, nutty flavor, but because it's more vulnerable to oxidation and has a fairly low smoke point (305°F), it isn't suitable for general cooking. Use it in salad dressings and sauces, or drizzle it over pasta, cooked grains, and steamed vegetables as a flavoring agent. Refined walnut oil has a higher smoke point (400°F), so it's suitable for baking, where it makes for especially delicious cakes and cookies, and is good for greasing baking pans. Or try brushing it on fish or chicken before baking or grilling.

Meat, Poultry, and Eggs

It wasn't until April 1981, seven months after Whole Foods Market initially opened, that the company even started to sell fresh meat and poultry. I became the company's first meat department clerk upon volunteering to work with the newly hired butcher. My husband and I had sold locally raised, organic meat in our own small natural foods store in Wisconsin, and the idea of having that quality of meat, raised with care and concern, available as the only option at a larger grocery store was very exciting to me. That same enthusiasm and support for compassionate raising of farm animals remains with me today.

The Mutualistic Approach

The term *mutualistic* best describes how we should view our connection with farm animals. At its core, this is a specific type of symbiotic relationship in which two very different species reciprocally benefit from their interaction and affiliation with one another. In this case, the mutualistic, or symbiotic, relationship is between humans and animals raised specifically for their meat or eggs (or dairy products, covered in the next chapter). The farmer's or rancher's commitment is to provide the animals as good a quality of life as possible for the duration of their lives. In turn, consumers who buy meat and eggs raised in this way increase the demand and, therefore, the likelihood that animals will be raised in a more compassionate manner. With their undeniably better flavor, "the way meat and eggs used to taste," and enhanced nutrition as extra incentives, it's a win-win situation for animals and humans alike.

That such care should be provided as a basic right to all creatures is based on the belief that animals are sentient beings, aware of themselves, their surroundings, and what is happening to them. They can also experience sensations such as pain, hunger, cold, warmth, and fear; learn from their experiences; and respond to new and challenging situations. More specifically, quality of life for livestock entails allowing them to express their natural behaviors. This is facilitated by providing appropriate, comfortable living conditions geared specifically to the species and plenty of feed and water appropriate to their natural needs and desires. Good physical care should be provided, including preventative care as well as swift treatment when animals are injured, sick, or in pain. Ensuring quality of life also involves minimizing fear and distress by ensuring proper handling while on the farm and during transport and slaughter.

Nutrition

Meat and poultry are undeniably excellent sources of protein. They are also good sources of B vitamins, zinc, and, in particular, iron. Although iron can be obtained from leafy green vegetables and dried beans, peas, and lentils, the form of iron in meat is more easily absorbed by the body.

On the other hand, the saturated fat content of meat, especially when consumed in excess, has cast a shadow on the nutritional benefits of meat. In response to consumer fears about fat and its relationship to heart disease, cancer, and a variety of largely preventable diseases, many meat producers have bred their animals to be leaner. Unfortunately, this can take a toll on the health and behavior of the animals. For example, pigs bred for less fat have exhibited aggressive behavior toward each other, including tail biting, something that conventional producers have "solved" by cutting off their tails. This is clearly a step in the wrong direction. Rather than using such drastic approaches, the real solution lies in raising animals on pasture, allowing them the opportunity to forage and to express their natural behaviors.

EFFECTS OF MEAT PRODUCTION METHODS ON NUTRITION

Animal husbandry, the practice of raising animals, began around ten thousand years ago. Before that time, the typical Paleolithic hunter-gatherer diet consisted of plants and wild animals that also ate plants. Because the food supply for wild animals varied seasonally, the amount of fat in animals' bodies fluctuated accordingly. This meant that the fat content of the meat consumed by our early ancestors was, by and large, primarily polyunsaturated and monounsaturated due to the higher dependence on and availability of plants in the animals' diets, with a far lower percentage of saturated fat than is typically found in meat today as a result of animals often being confined to feedlots for much of their lives and fed high-calorie grains rather than pasture and plant-based forage.

Until very recently, most animal husbandry practices were relatively simple and natural. Animals were raised, fed, and bred in ways that didn't differ all that much from how they lived in the wild. Until the end of World War II, most animals were raised on diversified crop-livestock operations where farmers provided pasture, forage, and feed for their animals. In turn, the animals provided manure for fertilizer and meat, milk, or eggs for consumption. Climate permitting, animals were allowed to graze year-round on open pastures, eating perennial and annual grasses, broad-leaved plants, legumes, and a wide variety of seasonal plants, all of which were rich in nutrients and fiber. Outside the growing season, animals received supplemental forage from dry hay or from crops that had undergone fermentation as a result of their storage, known as silage, haylage, or baleage. This natural fermentation process converts them into sweet-smelling, succulent, nutritious animal feed that is easy to digest.

Meat from animals that spend their lives grazing on grasses has a more favorable ratio of omega-3 to omega-6 fatty acids. As too high a proportion of omega-6 fatty acids in the diet can increase the potential for heart attacks, strokes, thrombosis, arrhythmia, cancer, and arthritis and other inflammatory diseases, the more favorable ratio of omega-3 fatty acids in grass-fed meat helps reduce these risks. This is also true of chickens and other poultry. Eggs from hens that forage extensively outside on natural grasses and insects naturally contain more omega-3 fatty acids than those from hens confined to crowded wire cages or even uncaged chickens kept in poultry houses. Some brands of eggs are marketed as high in or enhanced with omega-3 fatty acids because the chickens' feed has been supplemented with flaxseed. Although flaxseed is good for the hens and makes their eggs more nutritious, it would be even better if the hens also had the opportunity to forage outside, where they could obtain omega-3 fatty acids naturally.

Meat from grass-fed ruminant animals, including cattle, sheep, bison, goats, deer, and elk, is also higher in conjugated fatty acids (CLAs), due to the high proportion of linoleic acid found in pasture grasses. CLA is the collective term for a variety of very specific forms of linoleic acid, and although they are trans fats, they occur naturally and appear to have certain health benefits, including helping to reduce or inhibit the effects of cancer-causing substances. The health benefits of CLAs are similar to those of omega-3 fatty acids, but CLAs appear to be more potent.

Unfortunately, producers began to turn away from natural, grass-fed raising practices when experiments during the latter part of the nineteenth century demonstrated that feeding grain to livestock in concentrated animal feeding operations produced more flavorful, tender meat marbled with fat. During the second half of the twentieth century, grain-fed rather than grass-fed meat became the norm rather than the exception, in part because feeding with grain results in lower production costs and greater efficiency. The result is that the majority of cattle and sheep spend most of their lifetime in barren feedlots eating specialized, high-energy feed rations consisting of a variety of grains mixed in with hay, soybean or cottonseed meal, and minerals, along with other supplemental forms of feed, including by-products from regional food processing.

These industrial methods of livestock production have transformed rural landscapes, degrading land and water quality and significantly altering the nutritional composition of animal foods. Not only does the high grain content in animal feed cause the unfavorable ratio of omega-6 fatty acids, but it also boosts weight gain, and as such has the potential to make foods from these animals higher in saturated fat.

Cows Mad about Animal By-Products in Feed

Getting away from natural forage can have other, even more devastating results. For many years, animal by-products from ruminant animals were commonly added to feed. Outbreaks of bovine spongiform encephalopathy (BSE), a fatal degenerative neurological disease of cattle also known as mad cow disease, provided a painful but much needed wake-up call, making the meat industry rethink the practice of adding animal by-products to animal feed. Other related diseases within the general category called transmissible spongiform encephalopathies (TSEs) can, likewise, affect sheep, deer, and elk. Because by-products from infected animals are considered the main way BSE is transmitted, the use of meat and bonemeal from ruminant animals is now prohibited in feed for ruminant animals in the United States, Canada, and many countries throughout the world.

Even so, blood, blood products, and protein from pigs, horses, poultry, and fish are still allowed in feed manufactured for ruminants. Fortunately, some meat producers, who are dedicated to natural production and want to provide only the best feed for their animals, use none of these animal by-products, with the possible exception of milk and milk-derived ingredients.

Drugs in Meat Production

The nutritional qualities of meat, poultry, and eggs are also affected by the overall living conditions in which an animal is raised. Any kind of stress, whether from inappropriate breeding, crowded and unsuitable living conditions, or denial of normal social interactions, can impair an animal's immune system and increase susceptibility to a variety of diseases. Tethering calves and sows, raising veal calves in crates on solely a liquid milk-replacement diet, overcrowding chickens in cages, and force-feeding geese and ducks for foie gras production are especially reprehensible examples of raising animals with solely the end product in mind and no regard for the animals' welfare. Drugs administered to try to keep these and other farm animals alive and sellable have created their own problems, too.

ANTIBIOTICS

In the United States, livestock producers are generally unrestricted in their use of antibiotics. As a result, only a very small percentage of antibiotics administered to animals are actually used to treat active infections. The vast majority are used in subtherapeutic doses as a preventive measure, to compensate for the increased probability of disease because of overcrowding and other intensive production techniques. Supplemental antibiotics can also cause animals to gain 10% to 20% more weight more quickly than normal, so they're also used to improve feed efficiency.

While this subtherapeutic use of antibiotics may help increase profitability, it also has hidden costs. It's been linked to the growing emergence of antibiotic-resistant strains of bacteria, a problem that's impairing our ability to effectively treat serious and life-threatening bacterial infections in humans. When bacteria are exposed to antibiotics, hardier strains resistant to the effects of the antibiotic survive exposure and multiply. In addition to passing on the genes responsible for their resistance as they multiply, even more disconcerting is that they can transfer their DNA to other, unrelated bacteria, making them resistant, as well. Because any drug given to an animal can ultimately end up in the environment, foods derived from the animal, and even farmworkers, are potential vectors for the spread of antibiotic-resistant bacteria. As a result, it's increasingly difficult to find antibiotics that remain effective against the growing array of superbugs, which can withstand not just specific antibiotics but also several classes of antibiotics.

A few food supermarkets, specialty retailers, and restaurants in the United States refuse to purchase meat from animals treated with antibiotics, thus creating an incentive for producers to prevent disease by managing the animals' environment to reinforce health and well-being. Likewise, many nonorganic meat producers voluntarily avoid using antibiotics, claiming no need for them due to extra efforts to provide better care and conditions for their animals.

Organic regulations in the United States specifically ban the use of antibiotics in meat sold as organic. However, organic standards also require that any ill or injured animal be treated in any manner needed to help the animal heal quickly. Even so, meat from animals that don't respond to alternative treatment and subsequently receive antibiotics cannot be labeled as organic.

In most countries in the European Union, all meat producers, including those who produce organic meat, are allowed to use antibiotics when necessary to treat disease. They are, however, specifically prohibited from using antibiotics as a growth promoter or for any other nontherapeutic use. In contrast to the United States, where those who raise livestock have free access to antibiotics, in Europe only veterinarians are allowed to dispense antibiotics, thus helping to reduce gratuitous use of these drugs. In short, there is no place for antibiotics in meat production, especially when it comes to unnecessary nontherapeutic use of antibiotics.

SUPPLEMENTAL HORMONES IN MEAT

Hormones are not allowed in raising poultry and pigs in the United States and Canada, but beef producers are allowed to inject hormones in their cattle as a way to stimulate weight gain and produce leaner meat. This also saves them money, since animals treated with growth hormones get to market quicker, which translates into reduced feed costs. Accordingly, many producers view hormones as a key tool that enables them to make a profit while selling beef at a cheap price. Five hormones can be used in the United States and Canada to make cattle grow faster, larger, and leaner. Regulations require that the hormone be administered via a time-release pellet implanted behind the animal's ear in muscle tissue that won't be eaten.

Most of the concerns about injected growth hormones is due to their potential links to increased cancer risk. A particular type of synthetic estrogen, diethylstilbestrol (DES), was used in livestock as a growth promoter for more than twenty years before it was banned by the U.S. Food and Drug Administration. DES was banned because it was found to cause cervical cancer in women whose mothers had taken the drug years earlier, prescribed by their doctors to help deal with certain complications of pregnancy. Hormones are powerful chemicals that exert their effects throughout the body in both subtle and obvious ways. Their actions are complexly interrelated and finely tuned. Although DES was banned and a different form of estrogen is now used to treat livestock, the problems associated with DES serve as a powerful reminder of the potentially harmful effects of tinkering with hormones in general—a risky practice that's especially hard to justify when hormones are used solely for economic benefits.

Because of these concerns, the European Union banned hormone-treated beef in 1989, cutting off beef exports from the United States and bringing the safety of supplemental hormones directly into the limelight. As it stands, in the United States we're currently caught in a limbo between dueling scientific studies looking into whether the overall costs of supplemental hormones in terms of human and animal health are truly worth a lower price for beef. But when it gets right down to it, meat from animals treated with hormones may not even be as tasty. And in fact, many producers don't use them because they believe meat from animals given hormones is generally tougher and less flavorful than meat from animals who live a natural life cycle. Supplemental hormones certainly aren't needed to support the health and welfare of an animal. So no matter how you look at it, eating meat from animals who don't receive supplemental hormones is definitely the way to go.

Meat from Cloned or Genetically Engineered Animals

Starting in December 2006, meat derived from cloned cattle, pigs, or goats, or from their offspring, has been allowed to be sold in the United States. The usual reproduction techniques used for livestock, including natural breeding and artificial insemination, produce animals that are genetically different from their parents. It's quite the opposite with cloning, which creates offspring that are genetically identical to a single animal. As such, the traits deemed desirable in the donor, such as disease resistance or specific meat qualities, are expressed in what amounts to animal carbon copies.

Cloning works by replacing all the genetic material in an egg with a mature cell containing the complete genetic code from the donor. The embryo that results from this process is then implanted into a surrogate mother, who carries the pregnancy to full term and gives birth to the cloned animal. However, cloning heightens the risk of adverse effects on the animal, including deformities and premature death. Like many other modern methods of raising livestock, cloning is focused more on potential economic benefits than on animal welfare. Beyond that, it is a wholly artificial act, corresponding to nothing found in nature.

Genetic engineering is different from cloning. Because cloning is the transfer of a complete set of genetic material to a host cell to create genetic duplicates of the original animal, it involves no changes to the DNA. In contrast, genetic engineering is the deliberate modification of genetic material. In order to promote the expression of one or more desirable traits, the sequence of genes may be modified, or extra genes may be inserted or deleted—including genes from other species. As an example, genetic engineering could be used to develop an animal with a specific fatty acid profile, to create an animal with parts in specific sizes that are seen as more desirable, or to create a drug, using the animal as the medium for its production.

As with cloning, an animal's health and well-being is far down the list of concerns when it comes to genetic engineering. Unfortunately, genetic engineering is, indeed, being explored as a potential tool in breeding programs for food-producing animals. Given our limited understanding of all of the implications and potential long-term outcomes of this powerful technology, it must be viewed as an unnecessary, unnatural, and unethical way to produce and treat animals.

Animal Welfare Labeling

Trying to make informed decisions when buying meat, especially if you're trying to buy only from producers who raise their animals compassionately, can be frustrating. "Free-range" and "free-roaming" certainly seem to imply that the animals have access to the outdoor world. But does access mean more than a small pen crowded with other animals? Neither term tells us how long they are allowed to stay outside and what their outdoor environment is like. When it comes to raw meat, the term *natural* is fairly meaningless, since its definition, "minimally processed with no added color-

ings or artificial ingredients," is more applicable to processed meat.

To help guide you through this confusing maze, look for labels that clearly state how the animal was raised, including living conditions, feed, and permissible and prohibited production and handling techniques. Standards for labels with animal welfare claims should be designed to minimize the suffering of animals and encourage systems of production that promote mental and physical health. Ideally, animals should be raised in an environment that allows them to express their natural behaviors.

In addition to stating that the animal was raised without antibiotics, supplemental growth hormones, and animal by-products in it's feed, the label should indicate whether the animal was raised on well-managed pasture or in a natural outdoor habitat for all, some, or none of the animal's life. When animals are housed, labeling should indicate indoor conditions, where conditions would ideally include dry, clean bedding and litter several inches in depth; good indoor air-quality control; and plenty of room for the animals to move, express natural behaviors, and rest. Requirements that workers are well trained in respectful handling of animals, including no kicking, dragging, or other mistreatment, should also be high on the list of expectations for an animal welfare label. Transportation of the animals to slaughter should be in a vehicle that is in good condition with good ventilation, and the actual slaughter should be done quickly, effectively, and humanely by highly trained workers who respect animals. The more detailed the labeling criteria the better, as this will help you identify producers who are trying to provide the best possible conditions to support the physical, emotional, and behavioral needs of the animals they raise.

Organic meat and eggs are produced by feeding the animals a diet of organically raised foods that aren't genetically engineered. Organic regulations prohibit the use of hormones and antibiotics (as mentioned above, antibiotics may be used in certain circumstances, but then the meat can't be labeled in the United States as organic). They also require that livestock be given some access to pasture or an outdoor environment. The best organic meat and egg producers go beyond the minimum regulations, using pasture and foraging areas as the foundation of their production systems rather than as an adjunct. Basic principals related to humane treatment of animals and environmental sustainability are addressed in organic regulations worldwide, to varying degrees.

Exploring Meat, Poultry, and Eggs

Cured meats, including ham, bacon, sausage, hot dogs, and luncheon meat, are typically made with sodium nitrite, a synthetic quick-curing agent, in order to maintain the pink or red colors, enhance flavor, and help protect against bacterial growth. Concerns about the safety of nitrites were raised in the 1970s, when it was discovered that they can combine with amines (substances derived from protein) to form nitrosamine, a very potent carcinogenic compound, especially when cured meat is heated at high temperatures; frying bacon is particularly problematic. In addition to mandating the use of significantly less sodium nitrite when curing meat, governmental regulations also require the addition of a compound closely related to ascorbic acid (vitamin C), such as sodium ascorbate, which serves to effectively block the formation of nitrosamines.

Many no-nitrite varieties are also available, labeled as "uncured meat." These are smoked or made with salt or ingredients like celery juice, which contain trace amounts of sodium nitrate. While they taste fairly similar to meat cured with sodium nitrite, they don't appear as richly colored, instead depending on natural coloring agents such as beet juice. Preserved by freezing, they are sold either from the frozen meat department, or they may be thawed and sold within a specified time frame.

Dry-aged beef has been stored for ten to twenty-eight days at temperatures between 34°F and 36°F and at 85% humidity, a process that allows the beef's natural enzymes to further tenderize the meat by breaking down the connective tissues in the muscle. At the same time, evaporation of moisture from the muscle concentrates the flavors of the meat. In contrast, most meat is wet-aged in vacuum-sealed bags for just a couple of days, resulting in less tenderization.

Grass-fed beef is a labeling term whose meaning may vary depending on the company that claims it. Ideally, it should designate that the meat is from cattle raised solely on pasture with grass and other forage rather than on grain, with no time spent being fattened up or finished in a feedlot. Grass-fed beef is delicious, with a stronger, more gamey flavor than grain-fed beef. It varies in consistency depending on the climate conditions, variety of grasses and other forage found in the pasture, and the skills of the producer. As it is lower in fat than meat from grain-fed animals, a couple of key cooking hints can help enhance its full flavor and texture. In general, it is important to add or conserve moisture. To help lock in natural juices, sear the meat before roasting, then cover with a lid or foil while cooking; alternatively, it can be cooked in a slow cooker. Other cooking methods can also help retain moisture. The meat can be braised, stewed, cooked in a sauce, marinated before cooking, or basted during cooking. Add oil to the pan before browning the meat. Adding sautéed onions and peppers or cooking them along with the meat will also help add moisture, along with extra flavor. Because grass-fed beef is low in fat, keep cooking temperatures low; high heat can

How Much Meat to Buy per Person

Cut	Description	Amount
Boneless cuts	ground meat, boned roasts and steaks, stew meat	¼ lb.
Meat with some bone	rib roasts, unboned steaks, chops	⅓ lb.
Bony cuts	ribs, shanks	¾–1 lb.

How Much Poultry to Buy per Person

CHICKEN

Cut	Amount
breast quarters	1
broiler/fryer,* bone-in	¾–1 lb
broiler/fryer,* bone-less	⅓–½ lb.
drumsticks	2
ground	¼ lb.
leg quarters	1
thighs	2
roaster	½ lb.
sausage	¼ lb.
wings	4

* A 3½ lb. whole broiler/fryer chicken with neck and giblets yields slightly over 3 cups of cooked, diced chicken meat without the skin.

TURKEY

Cut	Amount
boneless breast	⅓–½ lb.
boneless roast	⅓–½ lb.
fryer/roaster	¾–1 lb.
ground	¼ lb.
hen/tom	½–¾ lb.
sausage	¼ lb.
thigh (bone-in)	½–¾ lb.

DUCK/GOOSE

Cut	Amount
Whole bird	1 lb.

make for tough eating. It is at its best when cooked no longer than medium rare, or medium at most. After cooking, allow it to rest for a few minutes before serving, to distribute the natural juices.

Heritage meat is a term used to describe classic breeds of livestock that had commercial viability in the past. Unlike modern breeding programs that focus on operational efficiency or enhancement of isolated traits, heritage breeds better support the health and well-being of the animal, including preserving characteristics more in tune with the animal's natural behaviors. Meat from heritage breeds usually has better flavor, too, in part due to genetics, and also because they usually have a more varied diet and more opportunities to graze and roam. Their size, shape, and texture may be unique, as well, preserving the genetic diversity that was common in the past.

Veal production typically involves confining the male offspring of dairy cows in small, individual crates that severely restrict their movement and normal behaviors, as well as interaction with their

Grading Eggs

Eggs are graded for quality based on the interior characteristics of the egg and the condition and appearance of the shell. Grade AA eggs, with round yolks that stand tall and firm whites are best for poaching, frying, and boiling when the cooked appearance of the egg is important. Grade A eggs have similar characteristics, but the white is less firm. While they may not be as satisfactory for poaching, Grade A are still a very good choice for frying, boiling, and general cooking.

When stored properly under constant refrigeration, fresh eggs can generally be used for three to five weeks after purchase. Look for the use-by date stamped on the carton. To avoid any risk of salmonella, all eggs should be cooked thoroughly until their yolks are firm.

mothers or other calves. Although calves would normally begin to eat solid food a couple of weeks after birth, in order to maintain the tender white flesh and mild flavor characteristic of prime veal meat, their nourishment is restricted to a liquid milk replacement. Fortunately, some producers are concerned about animal welfare and have refused to treat calves in this appalling manner, raising them instead in a group setting with other calves and giving them free access to grain in addition to the milk replacement. Even better are operations that allow veal calves to be out in pasture with their mothers. The meat from these calves is rosy in color and more flavorful than pure white, bland-tasting veal from crated calves, an indication that the calf had the opportunity to graze on pasture and lead a healthier, more enriched life.

Game meat can come from many different animals, such as deer, bison, rabbit, pheasant, duck, geese, guinea fowl, quail, and squab. Although these and many other animals are hunted in the wild for personal consumption, game meats sold in supermarkets in the United States must be farm raised. Like beef, pigs, and poultry, game animals can be raised any number of ways, from outdoor habitats where they forage on natural grasses and plants to confinement in small areas where they are given grain-based feed. Wild game is generally less tender because the animals eat a natural diet and get a lot of exercise in their natural habitat. In the end, the flavor, texture, and nutritional value of game meat vary according to living conditions, feed, and other factors. Game animals aren't treated with hormones, but, depending on the producer, they may receive antibiotics. Game birds can generally be cooked like their poultry counterparts, and venison and bison can be cooked using techniques similar to those for preparing grass-fed beef.

Cage-free eggs are produced by hens that aren't confined to the cramped and crowded wire cages as typically used in conventional egg production. Instead, they are allowed to move freely within a chicken house or, better yet, allowed to scratch and peck within a natural outdoor habitat, where they can experience direct sunlight and explore all the wonders of a natural environment.

In the past, fertile eggs were popular because producing them requires the presence of a rooster, which implies that the eggs are from cage-free hens. They were also considered to have a better, richer flavor than nonfertile eggs, but this is probably because such hens usually received a better quality feed, whether foraged or commercial. There is little, if any, nutritional difference between a fertile egg and a nonfertile egg. Fortunately, as more producers are raising their chickens outside in response to consumer demand, fertile eggs no longer need to be the key to finding eggs from cage-free hens. Even so, eating fertile eggs is perfectly acceptable, and you need not worry that they will hatch into chicks on the way home from the store. The eggs are chilled to a cold temperature shortly after they are laid, which prevents them from developing into chicks.

Dairy Products

As a child, I knew it was a special meal when my mother bought Gouda cheese to accompany her apple pie. Other days it was a popular brand of pasteurized processed cheese, and even at that young age, I knew it didn't hold a candle to that smooth, nutty Gouda that seemed to make her wonderful pie taste even better.

These days, one of my favorite pastimes while grocery shopping is to peruse the specialty cheeses from around the world and pick one I've never tried before. I'm the same way with yogurt and other cultured milk products. And when I travel, I always seek out the ones produced locally.

Cow's Milk and Beyond

Distinctions in taste, consistency, and nutrition among the wide variety of dairy products comes down to the source—the milk from which they were produced and, of course, the animals that supply it. While cow's milk may be the most familiar, whether in the form of milk, cultured dairy products, or cheese, products that use milk from other animals, including goats, sheep, and water buffalo, are also available. In contrast to cow's milk, in which the fat naturally separates out when the unprocessed milk is allowed to set, milk from these other animals contain smaller fat globules, so the fat tends to remain in suspension.

The color of milk from goats, sheep, and water buffalo is consistently white, as they lack the yellowish carotene pigment that sometimes occurs in cow's milk. This is because these other animals convert nearly all of the carotene they derive from plants into vitamin A, leaving little to none of it available to affect the milk's color. Difference in flavor and consistency in these alternative milks, and products made from them, arise due to variations in amino acid profile and fatty acid composition. Digestibility may also be affected; some people find they can tolerate dairy products from one particular milk source more easily than others.

■ GOAT'S MILK

Goat's milk is a popular alternative for people sensitive to proteins in cow's milk. Unlike cow's milk, which has high levels of alpha-s-1-casein, the protein involved in curd formation and firmness, goat's milk is fairly low in this protein. Not only does this help explain why some people are less sensitive to goat's milk, but it also helps explain why goat cheese is more crumbly in nature.

Goat's milk is only slightly higher in fat than cow's milk, and its fat profile is unique. It contains about twice the concentration of medium-chain fatty acids (MCTs) as cow's milk. (As the Latin word for "goat" is *caper*, the names of three of these MCTs—caproic, caprylic, and capric acid—are quite fitting.) MCTs, also found in coconut, are metabolized immediately in the liver rather having to go through the usual digestive and absorption process involving pancreatic enzymes and bile salts in the gall bladder. Because MCT fatty acids are absorbed well and quickly, they are often used in the treatment of people with malabsorption issues. This unusual fat profile may be another reason why some people find goat's milk easier to digest than cow's milk. And, because MCT fatty acids provide readily accessible energy, they aren't stored in the body as fat.

Goat's milk has a lot more going for it. Two of its medium-chain fatty acids, lauric and caprylic acid, have antiviral and antimicrobial properties and thus provide valuable immune support. What's more, goat's milk is more than three times richer than cow's milk in lauric acid, which increases good HDL cholesterol and thus helps minimize the potentially harmful effects of saturated fats on heart health.

■ SHEEP'S MILK

Milk from sheep contains twice as much butterfat as cow's milk. About 25% of the fat in sheep's milk is made up of medium-chain fatty acids, providing the same benefits as goat's milk in terms of enhanced absorption and utilization. While it contains less caproic, caprylic, and capric acid than goat's milk, it is almost twice as high in two long-chain fatty acids—palmitic and stearic acid—both known to have an overall neutral effect on cholesterol. As such, they can help moderate the health risks otherwise associated with saturated fats.

Sheep's milk is very concentrated, containing a higher percentage of solids than cow's milk. This means it contains higher amounts of many nutrients as well, including protein, calcium, magnesium, iron, and zinc, along with several of the B vitamins. However, because it is so thick and rich, sheep's milk is most commonly consumed as cheese or yogurt rather than in its liquid form. Its thickness also means that a lower volume of milk is needed to make cheese and other dairy products.

■ WATER BUFFALO'S MILK

Long-lived animals with many important functions in southern and eastern Asia, water buffalo look very similar to cattle, other than their long, curved horns. They are highly valued for their work power and their milk, with the river buffalo variety, in particular, used for dairy production. Appreciation for water buffalo continues to grow, to the point that they are now being raised on five continents, including North America.

Like sheep's milk, the milk from water buffalos contains twice as much fat as cow's milk. Also like sheep's milk, milk from water buffalo has a higher percentage of total solids and less water, making it more concentrated than cow's milk, and richer in nutrients, including protein, calcium, and iron. One benefit is that there's no need for additional thickeners in yogurt made with milk from water buffalo, and as with sheep's milk, a lower volume of milk is needed to make cheese.

Lactose Intolerance

Lactose intolerance is a condition caused by a deficiency in lactase, an enzyme produced in the small intestine that's responsible for digesting lactose (the natural sugar found in milk) to yield glucose, the form of sugar the body requires for energy. Symptoms of lactose intolerance, which are usually experienced soon after consuming dairy products, include bloating, cramps, flatulence, and nausea. A deficiency in lactase is fairly common. Although 96% of people of northern European descent are able to digest milk, people with genetic roots in other parts of the world often have difficulties with milk. Sometime between weaning and young adulthood, about 70% of the world's population begins to lose the ability to produce lactase.

Milk from cows, goats, sheep, and water buffalo all have about the same amount of lactose. However, a lactase deficiency doesn't necessarily preclude a person from being able to drink milk or consume other dairy products. Depending on the person, sensitivity to milk may be dose-related, dependent on frequency of consumption and the amount of dairy products consumed at one time. Cultured dairy products can also help circumvent the problem, thanks to the predigesting of lactose that occurs in the process of their production. A wide range of cultured dairy products have arisen throughout the world, including cultured butter, buttermilk, sour cream, crème fraîche, kefir, quark, and yogurt. These cultured products provide viable dairy options for some people who are lactose intolerant. Another alternative is nondairy milks, made from soybeans, grains, and nuts.

Cultured Dairy Products

Not long after people first domesticated mammals such as cows, goats, sheep, water buffalo, and yaks, they began to develop techniques for making cultured dairy products and cheese. This was an effective method of preservation because, without any means of keeping milk cold, certain types of bacteria, both within the milk and in the environment, will eventually make milk spoil. Though it may seem counterintuitive, early cultures discovered that they could significantly extend the opportunity to consume milk by adding bacteria and molds and thus transforming it into cultured dairy products and cheese.

More recently, we've begun to understand the beneficial effects this processing has on the digestibility of the milk, and its positive impacts on overall health. As occurs in the process of making naturally leavened breads, cultured dairy products like yogurt or sour cream are created through a fermentation process initiated by lactic acid–producing bacteria that break down, or predigest, the lactose in milk. The extent to which the lactose is broken down, making the product more easily digestible, depends on the length of the fermentation process and the specific type of culture starter used. The end result is an enhancement of fresh milk: a more flavorful, slightly tart, health-promoting, digestible food.

Another key health benefit of cultured dairy products is their complement probiotics, also known as "friendly bacteria," which are introduced during the culturing process. Each of us has an internal ecosystem with many players, including both "friendly" and "unfriendly" bacteria. The friendly bacteria are essential to proper functioning of the immune and digestive systems and help ensure proper digestion and absorption of food and nutrients. But just as in the external environment, things can get out of balance. Unfriendly bacteria can become too numerous, and friendly bacteria can be destroyed by antibiotics.

Cultured dairy products can help remedy any imbalances, whether due to illness, poor food choices, or antibiotic use. All yogurt will at least be cultured with *Lactobacillus bulgaricus* and *Streptococcus thermophilus*. To ensure optimum probiotic activity, look for labels on cultured dairy products that indicate they contain live cultures. Although it's hard to comprehend the numbers, the live bacteria count in a good-quality yogurt can be in the billions per teaspoon. Additional types of lactic acid bacteria, such as *L. acidophilus*, *L. casei*, *L. rhamnosus*, or *Bifidobacterium bifidum*, may also be added to dairy products, both for the unique flavor each contributes to the overall taste profile, as well as for their beneficial health effects.

Cheese

The cheese-making process also results in lower lactose levels, with the lowest amounts found in cheeses aged for long periods of time. Cheese is made by first souring the milk with a starter bacterial culture, which converts some of the lactose in the milk into lactic acid, just as in cultured dairy products. A curdling agent is added, which coagulates the solids in milk. The curds are then consolidated and the liquid whey is extracted. The curds are pressed into a specific shape or form, and then the cheese is matured through a ripening or aging process until it reaches the state desired for consumption. Since a great deal of any remaining lactose will be hydrolyzed during this maturation process, the longer a cheese is aged, the less lactose it will contain.

RENNET AND VEGETABLE RENNET

Animal rennet is most traditionally used as a coagulating agent. Also called bovine chymosin, it is an enzyme extracted from the membrane lining the fourth stomach of a bovine calf. In a calf, rennet aids digestion of milk by causing the milk to curdle. Observant folks in ancient times, who noticed that the milk they stored in pouches made from animal stomachs curdled, eventually got the idea that they could extract whatever was responsible for this to make cheese. High-quality cheese with good flavor and a firmer, denser texture has long been associated with the use of animal rennet. However, due to the high price of animal rennet and consumer requests for cheeses without animal

rennet, both microbial enzymes and a genetically engineered version of rennet have increasingly been used as alternatives.

Microbial enzymes are made from a variety of microorganisms derived from a controlled fermentation process. There are debates about whether cheese made with microbial enzymes can match the flavor and aroma of a rennet-based cheese, but their biggest drawback is that they cannot be used to make Cheddar or other hard cheeses. Genetically engineered chymosin, also called recombinant rennet, is made through a cloning process in which the calf chymosin gene is transferred into a bacteria or molds, which then produces chymosin. Rennet produced in this way functions nearly identically to animal rennet. And unlike microbial enzymes, genetically engineered chymosin can be used to make Cheddar or other hard cheeses. A high percentage of cheeses, especially those made in the United States, Ireland, and Great Britain, are now made with genetically engineered chymosin.

It's very easy to figure out if packaged cheese has been made with animal rennet, as it will generally be stated on the ingredient label simply as "rennet." However, with the exception of Cheddar and other hard cheeses, in which only genetically engineered chymosin can be used as a nonanimal rennet alternative, differentiating between cheeses made from microbial enzymes and genetically engineered chymosin can be difficult. To further complicate the issue, there is no ironclad guarantee that the term "enzymes" means that animal rennet isn't used.

Although microbial enzymes may be listed on a label as "vegetable rennet," in reality authentic plant-based rennet is rare. Some traditional Portuguese and Spanish cheeses are the exception, made with a coagulant extracted from the flowers of the cardoon thistle. This is considered a hallmark of Portuguese cheeses such as Quiejo Azeitão, Queijo de Évora, and Queijo Serra da Estrela and Spanish cheeses such as Queso de la Serena and Torta del Casar. Since the curdling properties of thistle work only on goat's milk and sheep's milk, no cow's milk cheese is available coagulated with true plant-based rennet.

Salt, too, plays a major role in the processing of cheese. It helps draw out the whey to reduce moisture content, which slows the growth of microorganisms that promote spoilage and lactic acid bacteria. It also helps control the rate of ripening. The overall effect of adding salt is a cheese with better flavor, texture, and appearance. While some cheeses are specially made to be lower in sodium, the difference in flavor is quite marked. And because salt also functions as a natural preservative, low-sodium cheeses will be more susceptible to spoilage and have a shorter shelf life.

Pasteurization and Homogenization of Milk

While cultured dairy products and cheese provided a solution for how to safely preserve milk, opportunities to consume fresh fluid milk increased with the advent of improved ways to keep milk cold, along with pasteurization, a method that emerged in the latter part of the 1800s.

Pasteurization, a heating process that destroys bacteria that contribute to spoilage or are pathogenic, ensures the safety of milk within a specified time period. But in the early days of its use, particularly up to the 1930s, pasteurization wasn't unanimously popular, largely due to fears that pasteurization destroyed most of the nutritious and health-enhancing properties of raw milk. Instead, many encouraged dealing with contaminated milk and poor sanitation issues by focusing attention directly on dairies to ensure clean production facilities and equipment and improved storage practices.

Although a system of sanitation was indeed created by which clean milk could be produced on any farm, between 1910 and 1920, pasteurization was highly promoted in the United States and Canada. Soon after the U.S. Public Health Service developed the Standard Milk Ordinance in 1924, pasteurization became a routine practice throughout most of the country. Since it also extended the shelf life of milk to as much as twenty days, pasteurization was also valuable as a way to deal with the challenges of extra time and distance required for distribution within an ever-widening network. Several revisions have been made to the original ordinance, now known as the Grade "A" Pasteurized Milk Ordinance, which sets forth requirements for the processing, packaging, and sale of milk and milk products that dairy farms and plants must meet to use the Grade "A" label and ship milk between two or more states.

Regulations for pasteurization require that milk be heated to a minimum of 161°F for at least 15 seconds to kill yeasts, molds, pathogenic microorganisms, and most of the less harmful strains of bacteria. Also called the high-temperature, short-time method (HTST), basic pasteurization provides an extended shelf life of up to twenty days.

In contrast, ultra-pasteurization, also known as UP, uses a higher temperature and a shorter time frame. The milk is heated to a minimum of 280°F for at least 2 seconds, although usually for about 5 seconds. Even more bacteria and microorganisms are eliminated with the UP procedure, extending shelf life to sixty to ninety days. Some people buy ultra-pasteurized milk for its convenience factor, as it allows them to keep milk on hand for longer periods of time. Ultra-pasteurization also enables processors to sell more of the milk they process, along with providing them a lot of extra time to distribute "fresh" milk across the country and still have plenty of shelf life remaining.

Although pasteurization of milk has been generally accepted as a public health measure, the process is still not supported by everyone. In fact, regulations on the sale of raw, unpasteurized milk within state borders remains up to each state, which is why the sale of raw milk is allowed in a few states, through retail stores or directly from the farm.

Advocates of raw milk believe that unpasteurized milk tastes better, promotes better health, and protects the natural enzymes present in the milk. Because heating milk at any temperature causes some destruction of nutrients (including cooking with milk at home), both the HTST and UP methods cause slightly decreased levels of folic acid and vitamins B_1, B_6, B_{12}, and C. Ultra-pasteurization also causes greater degradation of some of the protein components in milk, although the nutritional value of caseins remains stable. This explains why similar protein levels are stated on milk nutrition labels regardless of the method of pasteurization. Heating milk to higher temperatures also inactivates some of its good bacteria and natural enzymes, and this can affect the flavor and aroma of cheese and yogurt made from pasteurized milk.

The counterargument is that any possibly negative effects of pasteurization are a small price to pay for the safety and sanitation measures they provide, especially for those with weakened immune systems, such as the elderly, children, and people with diseases or conditions that put them at heightened risk. Pasteurization is also viewed as a way to ensure that milk can be widely distributed. In addition, some scientists believe that the bovine enzymes destroyed by pasteurization aren't useful to humans for digesting and metabolizing food.

Although the debate about pasteurization of milk will likely continue for years to come, when it comes to cheese, starting with raw milk instead of pasteurized milk really does make a big difference in flavor, texture, and overall character of the cheese.

To ensure that any potential harmful bacteria are eliminated, U.S. regulations require that cheese made with raw milk, whether imported or domestically produced, must be aged for a minimum of sixty days prior to sale at temperatures not greater than 35°F. With these added precautions, such cheeses remain safe, not to mention exceptionally delicious, when made properly by skilled producers. Since some heat is needed in the process of making cheese, the main difference between raw and pasteurized cheese is the initial level and duration of heat the milk is subjected to. The natural aging process of cheese also ensures safety through: the protection of the rind, the natural acidity of the cheese, and the higher levels of good bacteria, which can control any dangerous bacteria.

Periodic evaluations of appearance, flavor, aroma, and texture are also stipulated by U.S. law during and at the end of the sixty-day period. Any cheese that is unsafe to eat, whether made from raw or pasteurized milk, won't look, taste, or smell good. Its texture and consistency would also be off the mark. Thus raw milk cheese is not only safe to eat, but also a better representation of the complexity of flavor and character possible for any given cheese.

Homogenization, another widely used method for processing cow's milk, involves distributing the fat particles evenly throughout the milk so the cream doesn't separate from the rest of the milk. Because the fat globules in milk from goats, sheep, and water buffalo are smaller and stay suspended, homogenization isn't necessary with these alternative milks. Homogenization is accomplished by spraying milk at high pressure through a small nozzle onto a hard surface to break the fat down into very small particles.

Many people prefer unhomogenized milk, finding it more flavorful, less sensitive to spoilage from light, and less likely to curdle when heated. Unhomogenized milk also affords the opportunity to enjoy the cream that floats to the top, which can be carefully skimmed off and used as a topping for fruit, desserts, and cereals, or it may be whipped. Whirled in a blender or food processor, the cream can be transformed into homemade butter. It can also be stirred in to disperse it throughout the milk.

Better Flavor and Nutrition from Better Animal Welfare

Just as with meat, poultry, and eggs, the relationship between humans and all milk-producing animals should be one of mutualistic synergism. When we provide the animals feed and living conditions that support their natural behaviors, they reciprocate with good-quality, flavorful milk. And as with animals raised for their meat, pasture is the basis of good flavor, superior nutrition, and animal welfare. As observed by dairy farmers and corroborated by studies examining the effects of pasture on animal health, the rates of lameness, mastitis (an udder disease), reproductive difficulties, and premature mortality are lower when animals have access to well-managed pasture. Behavior differences have also been observed, with cows on pasture exhibiting less restlessness.

Milk quality is improved, too, with lower total bacteria counts in milk from herds that graze in comparison to those that are confined. Plus, milk from animals raised on pasture has a preferable ratio of omega-3 to omega-6 fatty acids, which helps minimize the potential for heart problems and inflammatory diseases that can occur with excessive consumption of omega-6 fatty acids. Milk from grass-fed animals is also higher in conjugated fatty acids (CLAs), forms of linoleic acid found primarily in foods from ruminant animals. Pasture grasses are high in linoleic acid, providing source material for microbes within the animal's gut to transform into CLAs. As CLAs are known to help reduce or inhibit the effects of carcinogens, it's advantageous to obtain as much as we can from dairy products, providing extra incentive to make sure the animals we obtain milk from are pasture-raised. There is no doubt about it. Grazing animals on pasture can make a real difference in nutrition for both dairy animals and the humans who consume their milk.

It also makes sense to graze animals on pasture that hasn't been treated with synthetic pesticides, herbicides, and fertilizers that can be persistent in the environment, in the bodies of the animals, and in our own bodies. Choosing organic milk is the best way to ensure the animals are raised on high-quality pasture that's monitored and well maintained. Integrated pest management and biological pest control are also excellent measures, but few, if any, products labeled as such are as well-defined as organic in terms of what the label really means and who can use the label.

Plant variety and soil conditions in the pasture, along with the time of year the pasture is grazed, can affect both the nutrients the animal consumes as well as the flavor of the milk. Seasonal effects on the natural color of cow's milk is most apparent in cheese, due to the concentration of milk that occurs in production, though this doesn't apply to dairy products from goat, sheep, and water buffalo, whose milk is always pure white. In dairy products made from cow's milk, those created from summer milk will be darker, changing from an off-white to more yellow because of the increased smorgasbord of plants available, from which the cows naturally obtain more beta-carotene. Other differences in milk and dairy products can be attributed to the specific breed of animal, the particular time within the animal's lactating cycle (the milk is more concentrated and rich toward the end of the cycle), and the time of day the animal is milked (evening milk is higher in fat than is morning milk). In fact, Morbier, a rich and delicious two-layered, semisoft French cheese, showcases this difference in milk quality. The bottom layer is made from morning milk and the top layer from evening milk, with the two separated by a thin layer of ash.

Dairy Animal Health without Antibiotics or Growth Hormones

The benefits of pasture aren't just about advantages for humans. Well-managed pasture with a variety of grasses and plants provides superior nutrition for the animals, too, and gives them the freedom of movement and ability to exercise that are so important to their health and well-being. Too often, in the name of efficiency or as a result of competition to be the lowest priced brand, dairies confine their animals to indoor housing for much or most of the day, and there's a very real possibility that the animals are tethered. Such restriction, combined with inadequate bedding, can result in painful foot problems and lameness, and poor air quality can allow disease to spread. As a result, antibiotics are often used both therapeutically and as a preventive measure. Keeping animals on pasture remains the better solution.

Dealing with disease can involve drastic measures. Docking the tails of dairy cows and sheep, a practice prohibited in Denmark, Germany, Scotland, Sweden, the United Kingdom, and some Australian states, is done on some farms in New Zealand and is on the rise in the United States. One-third to two-thirds of the animal's tail may be removed, based on anecdotal accounts of enhanced udder cleanliness and decreased mastitis. However, studies have shown that tail docking not only subjects animals to acute and chronic pain, but it also inhibits their ability to use their tail to deal with flies, causes increased stress, and increases risk of infection (and subsequent antibiotic use). Fortunately, research has turned to working on improving basic conditions for the animals, along with improved genetics to breed sheep with shorter tails.

Antibiotics are also used to deal with metabolic disorders and infectious diseases, many of which can be attributed to the negative effects of focusing on breeding animals for high milk yields. But as is the case with using antibiotics in animals raised for their meat, using them in dairy animals contributes to the growing emergence of antibiotic-resistant bacteria, limiting the effectiveness of antibiotics when they are genuinely needed to treat serious and life-threatening bacterial infections in both humans and animals.

This drug-based approach to raising livestock is also evident in the treatment of dairy cows with genetically engineered bovine growth hormones, referred to as rBST (recombinant bovine somatotropin) or BST. Injected into the cows every fourteen days, rBST can increase milk production, on average, by about 10%. It's no bonus for the cow, however. Even the label for this synthetic hormone states that cows administered rBST may have reduced pregnancy rates, increased risk for mastitis, enlarged hocks, and disorders of the foot region. Dairy producers who use rBST provide excuses similar to those of beef cattle producers who use hormones, saying that the resulting increase in production can make the difference between profitability and loss.

Labeling isn't much help when trying to choose milk produced without rBST. Unfortunately, it is impossible to test whether rBST in milk or dairy products occurs naturally or is the result of injections with the genetically engineered form. Increased confusion can arise due to labeling requirements of the U.S. Food and Drug Administration (FDA), which state that rBST-free claims on a label must include the following accompanying statement: "No significant difference has been shown between milk derived from rBST-treated and non-rBST-treated cows." Although FDA consumer fact sheets do not deny that some differences exist, they agree with the developer of the drug that, for all practical purposes, there are none. Ironically, the FDA doesn't also insist on revealing the significant adverse effects rBST can have on the health of the animal.

The FDA further explains that their insistence on the "no significant difference" labeling is due to their support for the drug developer, who fears that without such labeling, producers who don't use rBST might have a marketing advantage with consumers (who could rightfully question why such a drug is needed in the first place). As a result, producers and consumers who prefer that dairy animals not be treated with rBST are at a disadvantage. Nonetheless, consumers are increasingly demanding milk produced without rBST. Until labeling regulations are reformed, buying organic dairy products is an easy way to avoid milk from cows treated with rBST, as organic standards prohibit use of the drug.

In every way imaginable, milk produced from animals raised on well-managed pasture, without antibiotics or growth hormones, is best for the health and well-being of the animals. It's also best for us, in terms of health, nutrition, and flavor, and we can feel better about eating a wide variety of delicious dairy products when we know the milk is produced by animals who are healthy and enjoy a good quality of life.

Exploring Cultured Dairy Products and Cheese

The vast variety of cultured dairy products and cheeses available from around the world is astounding, with offerings in every flavor, consistency, and style imaginable. An exploration of this wide array provides both a journey through history and an opportunity to experience flavors and sensations unique to other countries and regions without leaving the comfort of your home. The passion and ingenuity demonstrated by individual artisanal cheese makers is also inspiring. When you factor in the different types of milk and the diversity of cultures and molds used, the possibilities are endless. This delicious world is a lot of fun to explore.

Artisanal Cheeses

As is so often the case in our modern world, mechanized processing methods, complete with computers to monitor every step along the way, have been developed for making cheese. This allows manufacturers to produce larger quantities of cheese and use less skilled labor, as well as make cheeses that are consistent in flavor and texture from one batch to another. Many of these cheeses can be very good and satisfying.

Fortunately, however, the fine art of creating hand-crafted cheese still exists, preserving traditional methods that have been used for centuries. Demand for these cheeses is, in fact, increasing as appreciation for their unique and full flavors, as well as the people behind them, continues to grow. Although fairly new on the scene, U.S. artisanal cheeses have earned deep respect and appreciation, with many now included in lists of the world's great cheeses.

Designated as artisanal cheeses, they are, by definition, produced on a small scale, providing more opportunity to produce distinctive, seasonal cheeses that reflect the breed of animal from which the milk is obtained, the plants foraged upon, and the character, passion, and skill of the producer. Some of these artisans use milk from animals they raise on their own farms, creating cheeses referred to as farmstead or farmhouse cheese. Enhanced attention to detail also means more opportunity to age and ripen cheeses to their full potential, allowing for just the right humidity, temperature, and amount of time to develop the complexity of flavor and aroma to extraordinary levels.

Artisanal cheeses are produced on a small scale locally and regionally throughout the world. Differences in cheeses from different countries and regions, or attributable to climate, types of livestock adapted to the area, local plants, and time-honored techniques, can be quite significant. Special designations have been created to protect the labeling of such cheeses, such as the French

"Appellation d'origine contrôlée" (AOC), the Spanish "Denominación de origen" (DO), and the Italian "Denominazione de origine controllata" (DOC).

Any producer granted the right to use these name-controlled origin labels must follow very detailed production methods that help preserve cheese-making traditions and the physical characteristics and other attributes of different types of cheese. Species and breed of animal, amount of pasture, and time of year the cheese is produced can be among the many aspects specified for the production of a particular variety of cheese.

Given that the United States represents an amalgamation of cultures arising from global immigration into the country, it isn't surprising that U.S. cheese makers have a long history of creating a wide variety of cheeses based on methods passed down by previous generations. But now American artisanal cheese is coming into its own, with innovative twists on traditional cheeses reflecting America's melting pot culture and the country's wide variety of climates and communities.

Types of Cheese

With so many kinds of cheese to choose from, it can be helpful to arrange and explore them within smaller groupings. Cheese can be categorized in many ways, but one fairly universal method is to arrange them according to their appearance, texture, and general characteristics. Let's take a look at some of these categories and the cheeses found within them.

Fresh Cheeses

These cheeses, which are unripened and don't have a rind, are typically mild and have a milky flavor. Their moisture content is very high because the cheeses are only a few days to a few months old.

Chèvre
Cottage cheese

Cream cheese (natural and without gums is best)
Crème fraîche
Feta
Fromage blanc
Kefir cheese
Mascarpone
Mozzarella (plain and smoked)
Neufchâtel
Ricotta
Skyr
Yogurt cheese

Soft-Ripened or Bloomy-Rind Cheeses

These high-moisture cheeses are surface-ripened for up to twelve weeks after being exposed to specific strains of mold, which are resident in the ripening room or sprayed on. They are then grown under humid conditions, creating the characteristic soft, white, fuzzy, or bloomy rind. Their flavors are typically buttery and rich.

Brie
Brillat-Savarin
Camembert
Explorateur
Humboldt Fog
Mt. Tam
Pièrre Robert
Saint André

Soft Washed-Rind Cheeses

These high-moisture cheeses ripen for up to twelve weeks from the outside in, during which time the exterior of the cheese is rubbed or washed regularly with a solution of brine, wine, beer, cider, or marc (grape brandy). The rind-washing process encourages the growth of certain bacteria (*Brevibacterium linens*), which create a distinctive orange rind and further develop the strong, complex flavor for which these cheeses are renowned. The process also keeps the cheese smooth and soft, although denser than bloomy-rind cheeses.

    Chaumes
    Chimay
    Espoisses
    Limburger
    Livarot
    Mont St. Francis
    Morbier
    Munster (French)
    Reblochon
    Red Hawk
    Saint-Nectaire
    Taleggio

Blue-Veined Cheeses

These soft or semisoft cheeses are pierced and inoculated with a type of mold (from the genus *Penicillium*) during the ripening process. The bluish-green mold then grows throughout the cheese, creating the characteristic flavor of blue cheese through the action of enzymes that break down fats in the cheese.

    Bleu d'Auvergne
    Blue Castello
    Buttermilk Blue
    Danish Blue
    Fourme d'Ambert
    Gorgonzola
    Maytag Blue
    Roquefort
    Saga
    Shropshire Blue
    Stilton
    Valdeon

Semi-Soft Cheeses

These cheeses ripen from the inside out and are aged between three and twelve months. They are usually supple to the touch and mild in flavor.

    Asiago
    Bel Paese

    Colby
    Edam
    Fontina
    Gouda
    Havarti
    Kasseri
    Monterey Jack
    Muenster (American)
    Provolone (plain or smoked)
    Pyrenees
    Swiss (baby)

Semi-Firm Cheeses

These cheeses also ripen from the inside out, but they're generally aged longer—anywhere from three months to two years. These cheeses develop more complex flavors as they age, and many of them have nutty and fruity flavors.

    Cheddar
    Cheshire
    Comté
    Double Gloucester
    Emmental (French and Swiss)
    Gruyère
    Jarlsberg
    Manchego
    Pleasant Ridge Reserve

Firm and Aged Cheeses

These cheeses also ripen from the inside out, and most are aged more than six months, creating a dry, low-moisture cheese. These cheeses are typically more complex in flavor with sweet overtones.

    Aged Asiago
    Aged Gouda
    Aged Manchego
    Aged Provolone
    Grana Padano
    Parmesan
    Parmigiano-Reggiano
    Pecorino Romano
    Vella Dry Monterey Jack

How to Store Cheese

Similar to other fresh foods, like fruits and vegetables, all cheese continues to ripen after purchase. Proper moisture and temperature are key components to keep cheese at its best while in its prime.

Plastic shrink-wrapped or cheese sold vacuum-packed in heavy plastic should always be transferred to more suitable, fresh wrappings after purchase. Although cut-to-order cheese is optimum, such packaging can be appropriate in retail operations for added grab and go convenience when displaying pre-cut cheese. However, keeping cheese in shrink-wrapped packaging beyond the few days in which it should be sold can cut off air supply to the cheese, essentially suffocating it. Long storage of cheese in shrink-wrapping also invites the growth of not-so-friendly bacteria and molds, adversely affecting the overall quality of the cheese, as well as the potential for the migration of volatile compounds from the plastic into the cheese.

Although home refrigerators are set up for a drier, colder atmosphere than is best for storing most cheeses, put it where in the area that has the highest humidity such as a vegetable drawer or, if available, special deli drawer set at the warmest temperature possible.

The particular kind of container or wrapping used, chosen according to the specific category in which a cheese can be classified, can also help compensate for less than ideal conditions.

Fresh and soft cheese: Keep them in the plastic or glass containers in which they are purchased, using them before the product's "use by" date.

Soft-ripened bloomy-rind or washed-rind, high moisture cheeses: loosely wrap in waxed or parchment paper which can then be wrapped in light plastic wrap to retain moisture

Semi-soft cheeses: wrap in waxed or parchment paper which can then be put in a plastic bag, leaving it unsealed or loosely wrapped in plastic to help retain moisture

Semi-hard cheeses: wrap in waxed or parchment paper, folding to seal the edges. If it begins to dry out, loosely cover the paper-wrapped cheese in plastic.

Hard/grating cheeses: wrap in plastic or unwaxed parchment, leaving the rind exposed to allow it to breathe

Rewrap the cheese frequently, daily if possible and, at the least, each time some cheese is cut from the remaining piece. Most mold that develops on cheese can be cut away, adding an additional ½ inch or so as extra protection, leaving the cheese still safe to eat. Flavor, odor, and texture are good guides, too. If a piece of cheese looks suspicious or smells or tastes "off", it is best to throw away the whole thing.

Avoid the idea of freezing cheese. While some semi-hard and hard cheeses can be frozen their texture will be crumbly when thawed, making it only usable for cooking. The best idea is just to buy cheese frequently, buying only enough to allow you to enjoy it while its flavor and texture is at its prime.

Seafood

⁓๑

I was about fifteen years old when I finally understood why people liked shrimp. Up to that point, I had only experienced rubbery, frozen breaded shrimp that got most of their taste from the sea of ketchup I immersed them in on my plate. Several years later, while on a family excursion to Texas to visit my older sister, we found ourselves in a ramshackle hut in Galveston, a restaurant my brother-in-law swore had better shrimp than exterior appearances might indicate. The shrimp were freshly caught and simply boiled, and eating them was akin to a religious experience. The flavors were so extraordinary as to bear no relationship to the shrimp I had previously eaten.

Nutrition

Seafood consumption has soared recently. While its ease of preparation and versatility no doubt have played a large part in its widespread popularity, its nutritional attributes are equally appealing. A commonly heard phrase used long ago to summarize the benefits of fish—fish is brain-food—is actually remarkably true. It's recommended that healthy adults consume at least two 3-ounce servings of seafood per week, particularly those varieties high in two long-chain polyunsaturated omega-3 fatty acids: eicosapentaenoic acid (EPA) and docosahexaenoic acid (DHA). The human body can synthesize both EPA and DHA, in limited amounts, from alpha-linolenic acid, the plant-based omega-3 fatty acid found in flaxseeds, walnuts, and canola oil. However, the preformed, longer-chain EPA and DHA found in fish, which they derive from their diet of algae, plankton, and other fish, are a more reliable source and more easily used by our bodies.

EPA and DHA offer health benefits throughout life, starting even before we are born. In addition to helping reduce overall risk of cardiovascular disease in adults, the EPA and DHA in fish help facilitate the growth of brain and nerve cells in the developing fetus and nursing infant. DHA, in particular, is a component in phospholipids, components of all

209

Seafood High in EPA and DHA

Anchovy
Atlantic mackerel
Herring
Mussels
Pacific oysters
Sablefish
Salmon
Sardines
Trout

cell membranes, including brain cell membranes, where they help facilitate release of neurotransmitters and general cell-to-cell communication within the brain. These fatty acids in fish may also play a role in supporting mental health by helping to reduce depression and neuropsychiatric disorders.

Although virtually all seafood contains some EPA and DHA, some, especially oily cold-water fish, are much better sources of EPA and DHA. It all depends on the species and the diet of the fish. Farm-raised fish can have comparable amounts of these omega-3 fatty acids as their wild cousins, but whether this is the case depends on the amount and quality of fish meal, fish oils, or algae included in their diet.

The way fish is processed can also affect its nutritional profile, in terms of both essential fatty acid content and its ability to reduce risk of heart disease. In particular, frozen or fast-food-style fried fish made from white-meat fish and cooked in partially hydrogenated fat or reused cooking oil will not provide the heart-healthy benefits fish is touted for. It's not so much that most of the fish used in such prepared foods is typically low in omega-3 fatty acids. The problem is that the trans-fatty acids in hydrogenated fats are known to increase the risk of heart disease and cause degenerative changes in tissues, negating any positive effects

the fish would have provided. If the fish is cooked in canola or soy oil, both of which contain plant-based alpha-linolenic acid, any trans-fatty acids present due to hydrogenation would also inhibit the conversion of some of its essential fatty acids into EPA and DHA. Likewise, the free radicals that form in cooking oil that is used more than once pose significant health risk. If you choose to eat fish, make sure it's working to benefit your health: Consider not only the source of fish, but how it is prepared, as well.

Concerns about Contaminants

Reports about the effects of industrial pollution, runoff from agricultural chemicals, and accidental and illegal dumping of synthetic chemicals has created a conundrum for consumers about whether the benefits of fish outweigh the risks. These toxic substances can persist in the environment, entering the food chain at its most basic level: plants and other organisms that produce energy through photosynthesis. Through a process called bioaccumulation, toxins progressively accumulate in fatty tissues at each successive stage of the food chain, from small plant-eating fish to larger fish that eat them, and finally to humans who consume the various types of seafood.

MERCURY

Mercury provides a prime example of bioaccumulation. Though it often originates as an air pollutant from chlorine processing plants, coal-fired power plants, and the burning of medical waste, it can ultimately make its way into bodies of water. It's initially released in an inorganic form, but bacteria in the water convert it into a more readily absorbed and more toxic form: methylmercury. Longer-lived predatory fish, including shark, swordfish, tilefish (golden bass), king mackerel, and tuna (fresh or frozen), tend to accumulate higher concentrations of mercury from their consumption of organisms lower in the food chain.

Some varieties of fish obtained from recreational fishing in rivers, lakes, and streams may also be high in mercury, not to mention other contaminants. Each state's Department of Health or Department of Natural Resources should be able to provide information about fish in certain areas that have a high risk of contamination, along with specific food consumption advisories. Neither cooking nor trimming can reduce mercury levels in fish, as it is most concentrated in the muscle tissue rather than in fat or oils.

Human health risks depend not only on the methylmercury level in the fish but also on how much is eaten, the body weight of the consumer, and individual variation in the body's ability to handle mercury. Babies in the womb and young children are most vulnerable to mercury, as it can adversely affect the development of the cognitive, motor, and sensory centers within the brain. The more mercury that gets into a person's body, the longer the exposure time, and the younger the person, the more severe the effects are likely to be.

In addition to children, all women of childbearing age are advised to avoid eating fish containing more than 50 parts per million per serving. Therefore, because of the benefits of consuming seafood, especially those relatively high in EPA and DHA, it's recommended that both women and children eat a variety of fish and shellfish known to be lower in mercury. About a 3-ounce serving twice per week is suggested, although it's safe to consume up to 12 ounces of fish per week. Fortunately, there are many varieties of seafood known to have low mercury levels. In general, smaller fish have less mercury than larger fish, as the older and larger the fish, the greater the potential for them to accumulate high levels of mercury.

Guidelines on albacore tuna have been highlighted in particular. Unlike canned tuna labeled "chunk light" or "chunk," which tends to come from smaller species, deciding whether to eat albacore tuna (labeled "solid white" or "chunk white")

Fish with Lower Levels of Mercury*

Catfish (farm-raised)
Clams
Crab
Haddock
Hake
Herring
Oysters
Pollock (Alaskan)
Salmon
Sardines
Scallops
Shrimp
Tilapia
Trout (farm-raised)

*Based on "Levels of n-3 Fatty Acids and Contaminants in Commonly Consumed Fish, Shellfish, and Other Foods" (Mozaffarian and Rimm, "Fish Intake, Contaminants, and Human Health," *Journal of the American Medical Association*, vol. 296, no. 15, October 2006) and "Methylmercury Concentrations in Seafood" (Institute of Medicine, *Seafood Choices: Balancing Benefits and Risks* [Washington, DC: National Academies Press, 2007]).

can be difficult. It's a convenient source of EPA and DHA, but this long-lived, higher-fat species can accumulate higher levels of methylmercury. Total weekly consumption of albacore tuna shouldn't exceed 6 ounces per week. As such, it's best to use it only occasionally, rather than as a primary fish choice; in its place, eat a variety of different species of fish low in mercury to help minimize any risk of methylmercury accumulation.

Women not of childbearing age and men are recommended to eat high-mercury fish only occasionally, and instead focus more on low mercury options. They are also encouraged to eat at least two 3-ounce servings of fish weekly to reduce risk of cardiovascular disease and take advantage of the other health benefits of fish, including the positive neurological effects from fish higher in EPA and DHA. There is some speculation that the high natural selenium content of fish may help mitigate some of the negative effects from heavy metals such as mercury, but this hasn't been clearly established.

POLYCHLORINATED BIPHENYLS (PCBS) AND DIOXINS IN FISH

Polychlorinated biphenyls (PCBs) and dioxins are classified as persistent organic pollutants—compounds that are resistant to environmental degradation through chemical, biological, and other means. Because they persist in the environment for long periods of time, they often make their way into bodies of water, where they are absorbed and transported into fatty tissues in fish and marine mammals. Although they are distinctly different than mercury in chemical composition, they also bioaccumulate up the food chain, and some fish may contain all three contaminants.

PCBs are synthetic organochlorine compounds once used in electrical equipment such as transformers and condensers and as plasticizers in paints, plastics, and rubber products. Dioxins are organochlorine by-products of waste incineration, paper bleaching, and production of both pesticides and polyvinyl chloride plastics. Although PCBs were banned in 1977 and the use and incidental production of dioxins has been reduced since 1987, their persistence means they continue to exert their influence as low-level contaminants. High exposure to PCBs has been associated with damage to the immune, reproductive, and neurological systems. Both PCBs and dioxins have also been linked to cancer. Although news stories and exposés about PCBs and dioxins seem to focus primarily on seafood, in reality meat, dairy products, and vegetables are actually the major sources of exposure. Nonetheless, fish from some lakes

in the United States and certain areas of Europe can register quite high levels of PCBs and dioxins. Unlike mercury, exposure to PCBs and dioxins can be minimized by removing the skin and surface fat from fish before cooking.

All in all, if you use common sense and reliable information when choosing which fish to eat and consume moderate amounts, the positive health benefits of fish generally outweigh the risks, even for age groups and populations most at risk.

Sustainability: Wild or Farmed or Both?

Even if seafood is nutritious, a key question remains: Is there enough fish to go around? A recent comprehensive review of seafood sustainability suggested the possibility that all current commercial fisheries could collapse by the year 2048. This grim conclusion was based on analysis of available worldwide catch data for all fish and invertebrates from 1950 to 2003, along with historical data covering the last one thousand years related to significant species in twelve specific coastal regions. The greater the decline in diversity of species in an ecosystem, the faster fisheries were expected to collapse.

Drastic reductions in fish populations typically result from overfishing (catching fish faster than they can reproduce) or taking too much bycatch, meaning catching and discarding fish and other aquatic creatures other than the specific species sought. But the problem goes beyond excessive fishing. Dwindling seafood stocks can also be a consequence of building in and polluting coastal areas, estuaries, and reefs, which can destroy nursery habitats for young fish. This can set off a chain reaction, adversely affecting the productivity and stability of entire ecosystems and also resulting in reduced water quality and increased human health risks.

Still, all is not doom and gloom. The good news is that a return to abundance and biodiversity within the world's fisheries remains a very real possibility. Restoration can readily occur through pollution control, strict fishing quotas that are followed and respected, careful ecosystem management for healthy habitats, and at least temporary closures of protected areas to allow species to recover before they're fished to extinction. Many such turnarounds have, indeed, taken place as a result of putting intent into action.

Seafood sustainability is the term used to describe fishing practices that not only contribute to long-term viability of the species of fish, but are in balance with the marine environment and local ecology, as well. The Marine Stewardship Council (MSC), an independent, global, nonprofit organization, was created to help consumers identify fish from wild fisheries proven to be well managed by looking for the distinctive blue and white MSC label. The program also allows those who engage in sustainable fishing practices to get recognition for doing so, thus creating extra incentive for others to do the same. The Principles and Criteria for Sustainable Fishing that underlie the program are based on the Code of Conduct for Responsible Fisheries of the UN's Food and Agriculture Organization. Input from a multi-stakeholder group of scientists, fisheries experts, environmental organizations, and seafood-related businesses helps keep the organization and its programs current and relevant.

Assessments of fisheries are done by accredited certification agencies independent of the Marine Stewardship Council to ensure evaluations are unbiased and credible. Credibility of the label is further secured by a chain of custody system that guarantees MSC-labeled seafood can be traced from the label right back to the fishery itself to make certain only fish from certified fisheries is labeled as such.

The Marine Stewardship Council program has started putting sustainability of wild fisheries back on track, with fisheries showing continued improvements in management methods and in-creasingly more MSC-certified products available to consumers. Even so, given the ever-increasing world population and our growing appetite for seafood, both wild fishing and aquaculture will be required if we are to have enough seafood for future needs. Several seafood sustainability advocacy groups have also created consumer guides to choosing fish. Although they can be handy for helping reduce the confusion when buying fish, they are quite general in nature, lacking the MSC's specificity regarding the species of fish and the location where they're caught, both of which can make a great deal of difference.

THE BEST METHODS FOR CATCHING WILD FISH

The most environmentally responsible ways to catch wild fish include harpooning, hook and lining, traps and pots, and trolling, all terms that are increasingly being used to help consumers identify fishermen who are trying to make a difference. In general, these practices help reduce accidental bycatch by allowing the fisherman to focus on the species at hand and also make it easier to release any species inadvertently caught, hopefully with minimal injury. Different methods are used depending on the type of fish or seafood sought.

Harpooning can be used to catch large fish like bluefin tuna and swordfish, using a long aluminum or wooden harpoon, thrusting it directly into the animal, and then hauling it on board.

Hook and lining can be used on a wide range of fish, from those that swim near the surface to those deep below, such as tuna, mahi mahi, and cod. It may involve using a rod and fishing line with one too many hooks, or even just a line with hooks that is simply held in the hand. After the fish takes the bait, it is hauled into the boat.

Traps and pots can be used to catch bottom-dwelling species, such as sablefish, Pacific rockfish, lobsters, crabs, and shrimp. Wire or wooden cages with bait are submerged and later lifted into the boat to retrieve the catch. Escape hatches are included in many traps to allow unwanted species to escape, or they can be returned to the water once the trap is on board.

Trolling can be used for fish like salmon, mahi mahi, albacore tuna, and any other fish that follows moving bait. Using a hook and line approach, fishing lines are towed behind or alongside a boat and reeled in after the fish takes the bait, allowing for the release of unwanted catch.

AQUACULTURE

Aquaculture, the raising of fish in tanks on land or in cages in open water, is hardly a recent phenomenon. The Chinese have been raising fish since before 1000 BCE, both as a source of fresh food and for ornamental purposes, to beautify the gardens of the wealthy. Over the years, they also developed polyculture practices, where raising fish was integrated with plant and animal husbandry, with each system supporting the others and all flourishing from their interaction. Ideas about aquaculture spread to other Asian countries and eventually to Europe, where, in the Middle Ages, fish ponds became common as a means of providing fresh protein.

Toward the end of the nineteenth century, it became apparent that widespread environmental destruction and pollution as a result of the Industrial Revolution was decimating lakes, rivers, and streams. This instigated scientific research into ways to recover fish stocks, including the development of fish hatcheries to augment the populations of wild fish. In the latter part of the twentieth century, there was a resurgence of interest in these techniques, and aquaculture in general, as people began to realize that the oceans were being overfished. Innovative techniques and sophisticated equipment brought aquaculture to a new level, giving it the status of darling or damned, depending on one's perspective.

Although fish farming increased the supply of fish and allowed people to buy less expensive fish,

with experimentation came new problems that needed solving. Interbreeding of farmed stocks with wild fish threatened the viability of natural strains. Wastes generated by intensive production degraded habitat. Antibiotics and parasiticides began to be used to deal with the novel fish diseases that emerged due to poor nutrition or unhealthy living conditions, and some producers even used hormones to create all-female stock to achieve better flesh quality and more consistent size. The specter of genetically engineered fish, manipulated to alter size, performance, and other qualities, has loomed in the background for years, fueling debate not only about the welfare of the farmed fish, but also about the future effects on native stocks.

Fortunately, many aquaculture operations have addressed these problems with innovative solutions. As with the sustainability of wild fish populations, consumer demand for excellence and ingenuity from producers can help ensure long-term protection of the environment along with healthy, well-cared-for stocks. When purchasing aquaculture products, look for farmed fish from operations that use no antibiotics, supplemental hormones, or toxic chemicals. Pens should be positioned in areas with active water exchange and away from vulnerable marine species or habitats. Seafood should test low for environmental contaminants, and feed should be based on the natural requirements of the species being raised, sourced as much as possible from fish meal and fish oil derived from by-products of fish or shellfish processed for human consumption or, at the very least, from sustainably managed fisheries. Good water quality should be maintained within and outside the pens or tanks, for the benefit of both the fish and the environment. Systems should also be well designed to prevent any farmed fish from escaping.

Organic certification of farmed fish is an option that helps producers get recognition for their work and also makes it easier for consumers to choose. But be aware that organic standards vary depending on the country, with some regulations being stricter than others. When conducted in a conscientious manner, aquaculture can be one of the answers, rather than a problem, in the quest to protect our world fisheries, ocean habitats, and the earth itself, which depends on the health of the oceans.

Humane Treatment of Aquatic Animals

The idea that humane treatment of fish and crustaceans like lobsters and crabs is something to be seriously considered is a big surprise for most people. As they are not particularly cuddly creatures, it can be easy to forget that they, like other animals, have some degree of awareness, including feeling pain and having the ability to learn. But that is just what is being discovered. In addition to commonsense measures, like providing good water quality, appropriate stocking densities, and wholesome nutrition geared to the specific species, other factors can have a big impact on the welfare of aquatic species, including how they are handled, transported to processing facilities, and slaughtered.

Recent studies of fish have revealed complex behaviors we weren't previously aware of, including purposeful behavior adjusted to adapt to information previously learned. Responses beyond the purely reflexive have been exhibited by fish when confronted with an aversive situation. Chronic stress responses can be observed through disease and other physiological and behavioral indicators. This new understanding has led to reconsideration of slaughter methods, unique to each species, to explore how best to render fish and other aquatic animals unconscious until death in order to minimize their stress, pain, and suffering. Live fish at retail outlets need special attention, including clean conditions, along with water temperature and chemistry appropriate to the species, and time spent in the tank, outside their natural habitat, should be minimized.

The issues surrounding the sentience of aquatic animals is particularly apparent with lobsters. Solitary animals by nature, they are typically piled on top of one another in a crate on the boat. Sometimes they are sold locally, but more often than not they are kept in tidal ponds, where they are crowded with other lobsters for up to several months and often fed antibiotics to deal with disease issues created by water conditions that are less than ideal. They are then shipped to stores, again piled on top of one another in a box or crate, and displayed in a brightly lit tank at temperatures high enough that lobsters remain active for the entertainment of consumers. Although an active metabolism means they can become hungry, lobsters in tanks typically are not fed. Stress from hunger and being in a tank with no place to hide can often manifest in the chewing of another lobster's antenna. Once purchased, they must endure transport to the customer's home, where they are ultimately subjected to death by boiling water.

Killing lobsters soon after capture, as is done with most finfish, rather than keeping them alive in artificial conditions, is the better option. New high-pressure processing methods can be used to kill lobsters immediately within a chamber, and then the meat can be hand shucked or frozen in the shell. In addition to eliminating stress on the lobster, the high-pressure method has the added bonus of yielding better-tasting, higher-quality meat than lobster kept in artificial conditions for an extended period of time and finally killed live, in boiling water.

All things considered, it only makes sense to provide both wild and farmed aquatic animals humane treatment as much as possible. In addition to being the right thing to do, as with other animals raised humanely and with respect, and processed accordingly, fish and shellfish will be significantly better tasting as a result.

Exploring Seafood

Ironically, although seafood is one of the easiest proteins to cook, people often have more apprehension cooking it than they do meat or poultry, with many people more frequently ordering fish at a restaurant than preparing it at home. The crux of the problem is that while seafood is easy to cook, it is equally easy to overcook. Nevertheless, it's easy to learn how to cook fish well. It's all a matter of adapting cooking techniques to the type of fish or seafood at hand and keeping it simple. Accompanying sauces and side dishes should be complementary, subtly enhancing the flavor of the seafood rather than overpowering.

Fresh Seafood

Fresh fish is a good, delicious choice when purchased from merchants that have their supply of fresh fish flown in several times per week (the same is true of ordering fish in a restaurant). Whether wild-caught or farm-raised, visual cues of freshness for whole fish include shiny skin and eyes that are bright, glassy, and convex, not sunken. Fillets should be translucent and light in color, not yellowed or uncharacteristically dark, with firm flesh that is springy when pressed. What we think of as a fishy smell is largely the product of decomposition, and as such shouldn't be apparent in either the fish or in the market from which it is purchased.

Frozen Seafood

Frozen seafood can often be better than fresh, given the fact that by the time fresh fish gets to a market hundreds or thousands of miles away, it could be several days old. Fortunately, frozen food technology has advanced dramatically over the years, so we can now buy fish frozen either immediately, on the boat, or very soon after coming to shore. Both the flavor and the texture of such frozen fish can belie the idea that fish must be bought and cooked fresh to be at its best.

However, do avoid frozen fish treated with sodium tripolyphosphate (STP) and sulfites. STP is used to inhibit potential moisture loss in the freezing and thawing process, control enzymatic breakdown, and aid in the removal of shells from shrimp. While it's relatively harmless to health, STP retains water, so some of the cost per pound for a product may be for this elevated water content. STP can also adversely affect the overall flavor and texture of the fish.

Sulfites, which can cause severe allergic reactions in sensitive individuals, are a different issue. A collective term for sulfur dioxide, sodium sulfite, potassium or sodium bisulfite, and potassium or sodium metabisulfite, sulfites are often used to help prevent development of a black pigment on shrimp shells called melanosis or "black spot," or to bleach it out once it's occurred. This discoloration is the result of a natural chemical reaction that occurs in warm-water shrimp if they aren't properly rinsed and iced once their heads are removed. Melanosis itself is harmless, similar to the blackening of a banana peel as it ripens. However, its presence could indicate poor handling—that the shrimp were left out too long in warm temperatures after being caught. Ultimately, both sodium tripolyphosphate and sulfites are unnecessary additives, as evidenced by the many frozen seafood products processed without them, and they are usually indicative of a lower quality product.

Smoked Fish

Curing fish with smoke and salt is a centuries-old method of preserve fish for months on end. Because refrigeration is now so readily available, most smoked fish is cured using new methods

Buying by Flavor and Texture

The flavors of various types of seafood range from mild to moderate to robust, with something to appeal to virtually any taste buds out there. Varieties with robust flavor usually have a higher fat content. Textures vary as well, from very delicate to very firm. Here's a guide to flavors and textures to help you in shopping.

MILD FLAVOR

Delicate Texture
Flounder
Sole
Wahoo

Medium-Firm Texture
Catfish (farm-raised)
Cod
Crab
Grouper
Haddock
Hake
Hoki
Lingcod
Lobster
Orange roughy
Pacific snapper (red)
Pollock
Scallops
Shrimp and prawns
Tilapia
Walleyed pike
White sea bass

Firm Texture
Halibut
Monkfish

MODERATE FLAVOR

Delicate Texture
Sablefish (black cod)

Medium-Firm Texture
Golden trout
Patagonian toothfish
    (Chilean sea bass)
Rainbow trout
Rockfish (ocean perch)
Steelhead trout
Striped bass
Tuna (canned)

Firm Texture
Mahi mahi
Shark
Sturgeon

ROBUST FLAVOR

Delicate Texture
Herring
Mussels
Oysters
Sardines

Medium-Firm Texture
Arctic char
Bluefish
Mackerel
Salmon

Firm Texture
Clams
Swordfish
Tuna

How Much Fish to Buy per Person

Whole fish		¾ to 1 pound
Dressed fish	(gutted and scaled, with head, fins, and gills removed)	½ to ¾ pound
Fish steaks	(sliced crosswise, with a section of backbone and skin)	⅓ to ½ pound
Fish fillets	(boneless sides of fish)	¼ to ⅓ pound

that concentrate on the absorption of flavors from aromatic smoke. The process begins with coating the fish in salt or placing it in a brine to bring out flavor and inhibit the growth of harmful bacteria. For extra flavor, sugar and other seasonings may also be used. Then the fish is rinsed and dried in cool, circulating air until the surface becomes glossy; this creates a natural seal on the exterior. Cold or hot smoking is the next step, using smoke from a variety of hardwoods, each contributing its own unique flavor. Cold-smoked fish, known for its delicious flavor and moist, tender texture, is processed at temperatures between 60°F and 110°F for twenty-four hours or more. In contrast, hot-smoked fish is cured at a minimum internal temperature of 145°F, perhaps up to 200°F, for a much shorter period of time than cold-smoked fish. Because hot smoking essentially cooks the fish, moisture content is reduced, yielding a firmer, drier texture and a slightly less rich flavor.

Since fish smoked by either method isn't processed enough to fully preserved it, both types must be refrigerated and consumed within fourteen days after processing, or by the date indicated on the package. For longer storage, smoked fish may be frozen for up to two months. Smoked fish sent through mail-order specialty houses needs no refrigeration until its special packaging is opened. Although it may be hard to imagine how the fish inside could be safe to eat, they are processed similar to canned fish except in this case the "can" is a thin metallic pouch.

Cooking Methods

As a general estimate of cooking time, plan on about 10 minutes per inch of thickness when baking, poaching, grilling, sautéing, or broiling. Measure the fish at its thickest point and add or subtract 2 minutes for each ¼ inch above or below the nearest inch. The fish is done when it turns opaque and just begins to flake when pierced with a fork in its thickest part. Be careful not to overcook. Keep in mind that fish will continue to cook for a few minutes after it is removed from the heat, no matter what cooking method you use. While most fish can be prepared using almost any cooking method, there are a few key exceptions. Grilling is best for medium-firm to firm fish and shouldn't be used for delicate fish. Poaching is best for lean fish.

Baking: Preheat the oven to 425°F to 450°F. Place the fish in an oiled baking dish, skin side down if the skin is present. Brush with oil, then top with fresh or dried herbs and tamari or your favorite sauce, if desired. Gauge the baking time according to the thickness of the fish.

Poaching: In a pan large enough to hold the fish in a single layer, pour in enough vegetable or chicken stock, water, or a combination of dry white wine and water to cover the fish by 1 inch. Bring the liquid to a boil, then add the fish, lower the heat, cover, and cook, basing the cooking time on the thickness of the fish.

Steaming: Add about 1 inch of plain or seasoned water to the bottom of a pan in which a steamer can be placed. Bring to a boil, then add the fish, cover, and steam for 6 to 8 minutes per inch of thickness.

Broiling: Position an oven rack so the fish will be 3 to 4 inches from the heat and preheat the broiler. Brush both sides of the fish with oil, then lay the fish on a broiling pan. Gauge the broiling time on the thickness of the fish, and turn the fish over halfway through cooking.

Stir-frying: Cut steaks or fillets into thin strips or ½-inch cubes. Shrimp and scallops can stay whole. Preheat a wok over medium-high heat, then add 1 to 2 tablespoons of oil per pound of seafood. Add a small amount of seafood, stir-fry until fish is opaque and flaky or, if cooking shrimp or scallops, firm and opaque. Remove the first batch from the wok, then add another batch and stir-fry, continuing in this way until all the fish is cooked.

Sautéing: Preheat a frying pan over medium-high heat. Cook the fish for 2 to 3 minutes per ½-inch of thickness, and until lightly brown on one side, then turn the fish over and finish cooking on the second side for about the same amount of time, once again until lightly browned.

Grilling: If you want to grill fish that isn't big or firm enough to be made into steaks, use only fillets that have the skin attached to keep them from falling apart while grilling. Diagonal slashes cut ¼ inch deep into the fillets will help keep the fish from curling and shrinking. Small, whole, scaled and gutted thick-skinned fish can also be used. Fish that weigh no more than 3 pounds should be scored diagonally across the thickest part to permit uniform heat penetration. To avoid losing natural juices over their long grilling time, large whole fish shouldn't be scored.

Prepare a moderately hot grill—hot enough to sear the surface of the flesh but not so hot that the outside is charred before the fish is cooked all the way through. Place the fish on the grill perpendicular to the grill bars to minimize contact with the grill. Brush with melted butter, oil, or an oily sauce to prevent sticking to the grill. Baste frequently with a pastry brush while cooking to seal in the natural juices. Whole, scaled, and gutted fish weighing more than 3 pounds require a grill cover and slow cooking over a low fire. Test with a small bamboo or metal skewer in the thickest part of the fish. Any resistance of the flesh means it needs more cooking. Since fish continues to cook after it leaves the heat, remove it from the grill as soon as it just begins to flake.

Essential Seasonings

There are many seasonings I just couldn't do without. Salt, miso, tamari, umeboshi plums, and umeboshi vinegar are some of the essential seasonings I use to enhance flavors. And, although edible seaweeds might seem more like a vegetable than a seasoning, they play a valuable role in heightening the flavor of other foods with which they are cooked or served.

Ask people to describe the primary flavors in food, and they're likely to list four: sweet, salty, sour, and bitter. That a fifth flavor exists may be surprising, but that elusive savory sensation experienced when all the flavor and aroma components come together in a food now has a name: umami (oo-MOM-ee). In fact, umami has been around for a long time. It was first identified in 1908, when research was conducted on kombu, the seaweed that provides the flavor-enhancing properties of dashi, a fundamental broth in Japanese cuisine. The study determined that when the amino acid glutamic acid exists in an unbound form, not linked to other amino acids, it helps provide the subtle taste of umami and its ability to expand and round out flavors. Mushrooms, ripe tomatoes, Parmesan cheese, and cured ham all provide umami, as do sea vegetables, soy sauce, and miso. Use any of these ingredients when cooking and a kind of magic begins.

Long after discovery of the link between glutamic acid and umami, two other compounds, inosinate and guanylate, were also determined to provide the fifth taste. Most known for their work as building blocks for creating RNA and DNA within our cells, these compounds are found in bonito flakes and shiitake mushrooms, two ingredients that, like kombu, are also considered essential flavor enhancers within traditional Asian cooking. In effect, science is merely corroborating what intuition already determined centuries ago.

Synthetic monosodium glutamate (MSG), a salt form of glutamic acid, was developed once the amino acid was determined to be a source of umami, in an attempt to capture the taste and provide it cheaply with a shake of the wrist rather than through the natural foods that contain it. However, given the serious side effects MSG causes in sensitive individuals, trying to imitate nature turns out to be problematic, as is often the case. Synthetic forms of inosinate and guanylate are often used in combination with MSG to further enhance flavor. In addition to their questionable effects on health, these attempts to add the taste of umami artificially also deny us the opportunity to experience the extraordinary textures, colors, and other flavors in real foods—not to mention the nutrients.

Umami can also be accentuated through fermentation and curing of foods. During the process of fermentation, proteins are broken down into their constituent amino acids, providing the opportunity for glutamate to exert its flavor-enhancing properties. Umami is further heightened by the synergistic effect of combining foods known to be high in glutamate, inosinate, and guanylate, adding mushrooms to tomato sauce, for example, or serving ham with cheese.

Many different sauces, seasonings, and condiments from across the globe provide umami including, for example, ketchup, cocktail sauce, anchovy paste, and clam sauce. While each of these essential seasonings can be associated with a particular style of cooking, their use is truly universal and they can enhance flavor in any type of cuisine. Common to each of them is salt, the most essential seasoning of all.

Salt

As an indication of salt's significance to health and wealth throughout the ages, wars were fought over it, towns were founded around salt deposits, and civilizations lived or died by its availability.

Salt, which is a combination of sodium and chloride, was valuable in historic times because it allowed people to preserve food without freezing or refrigeration. As a result of its dehydrating ac-

tion, salt helps to inhibit growth of both mold and bacteria. Pickled vegetables and cured meat and fish are classic examples of the superior preserving abilities of salt. It also is a key element in making both cheese and bread, responsible for development of the rind and better consistency of texture in the former, and strengthening gluten and controlling the rate of fermentation in the latter.

In the human body, the sodium in salt is a key player in maintaining the pressure and volume of blood and the correct balance of water in and around cells and tissues. Transmission of nerve impulses and proper digestion also depend on having enough salt in the diet. But we really don't need much salt to remain healthy, just about 500 mg per day. This number is remarkably close to the estimated daily sodium intake of our hunter-gatherer ancestors: about 690 mg, with 148 mg of it from plant foods and the remaining 542 mg from wild game. Today, however, some people may consume up to ten times that amount per day. Fast foods and processed foods are the biggest culprits, responsible for as much as 75% of the sodium intake of people who eat a lot of these foods.

In terms of dietary sodium from sources other than fast foods and processed foods, only 60% comes from the salt or salty seasonings we intentionally add, while 40% occurs naturally in foods. It should come as no surprise, then, that the most effective way to moderate sodium intake is to minimize consumption of processed foods, opting instead for simply prepared foods, seasoned only as needed to accentuate the natural flavors within.

NUTRITIONAL DIFFERENCES AMONG SALTS

Although all salt is mostly sodium chloride, with amounts ranging from 97% to 99.5%, there are distinctive nutritional differences between refined salt and unrefined salt, as the latter retains the spectrum of macrominerals and trace minerals found in the particular area from which it originates. However, despite unique local and regional variations in the mineral profile of seawater, the relative concentration of minerals has actually remained the same for millions of years.

The correlation between the profile of salts and trace minerals found in the sea and those within our bodies was recognized as far back as 1684. At that time, the noted scientist Robert Boyle discovered that the profile of salts in whole blood, excluding organic matter, was virtually identical to that found in seawater. This was further corroborated in 1776, when Hilaire-Marin Rouelle isolated cubic crystals that were similar to sea salt from inorganic materials in blood serum.

While the amount of minerals beyond sodium chloride that one actually receives in the small volume of salt consumed on a daily basis is fairly minimal, our growing understanding of the power of phytonutrients, found in trace amounts in plant foods, has repeatedly challenged the concept that nutrients in seemingly insignificant quantities have little value. The whole is typically greater than the sum of its parts, even if we don't always know exactly what we would be missing if the whole were fragmented. So when it comes to choosing between salt that retains the natural spectrum of minerals and refined salt, opting for more natural forms seems a prudent way to go, not only for finishing salts but for salt used in general cooking, too. Even when looking at the issue on a purely practical basis, the extra minerals in sea salt have been found to be helpful in gluten development when making bread. And salt with a more diverse mineral profile tastes better, too.

One nutrient not to bank on in sea salt, however, is iodine. Even though most of the world's naturally occurring iodine comes from the oceans, it is present in seawater only in very small amounts that, even when concentrated, do not provide enough to ensure proper functioning of the thyroid gland and prevention of goiter. But rather than depending on commercial iodized salt, try to get enough

iodine by eating fish or sea vegetables, or get it through a dietary supplement. Dairy products can also be a source of iodine, as iodine solutions are commonly used to clean the milking equipment and cows' udders.

Iodized Salt

Potassium iodide is often added to commercial salt to ensure that people get enough iodine. This critically important nutrient can prevent the development of goiter, an early warning sign of iodine deficiency. However, on a basic level, iodine helps ensure proper functioning of the thyroid gland, which regulates a wide variety of processes within the body, including growth, development, metabolism, and reproductive function. Iodine deficiency is also recognized as the number one cause of preventable brain damage worldwide.

Supplemental iodine was first added to salt in 1924, particularly for the benefit of people living in mountainous or landlocked regions where iodine is especially deficient in the soil. It also helps fill in the gaps for those whose diets do not include regular consumption of seafood or sea vegetables, both of which provide concentrated natural sources of iodine.

A very small amount of dextrose (0.04%) is added to iodized salt to stabilize the potassium iodide and prevent it from breaking down and evaporating. Pickling salt specifically developed for pickling applications isn't fortified with iodine or anticaking agents because they could discolor the pickles. In addition, the anticaking agents aren't water-soluble, so they could settle on the bottom of the jar.

VARIETIES OF SALT

All salt originates somewhere along the line from the sea or saltwater lakes, whether dehydrated from a current source of water or extracted from salt deposits formed as ancient bodies of water dried up. Even so, where the salt originates and how it is produced can make a big difference in how it affects the experience and flavor of food, and also in terms of what minerals it can provide beyond plain sodium chloride.

Mined Salt

Also known as rock salt, salt obtained from inland salt mines is used in a wide variety ways: as an agent to de-ice roads in the winter, as a salt lick for livestock in the fields, as a freezing aid for making homemade ice cream, and, of course, as a seasoning agent. Through an extraction method called room-and-pillar mining, miners blast and drill to remove big chunks of salt, leaving large pillars of salt in place to hold up the roof of the mine. The extracted salt is brought up to the surface, crushed, and screened. Mined culinary salts may occur in a variety of colors, such as soft pink Himalayan Crystal Salt from Pakistan or pinkish gray Redmond RealSalt from Utah, each manifesting and retaining the range of natural minerals of a long-gone ocean, as well as the sediment that settled between the different crystallization layers. Subtle flavor differences will also be apparent.

Mined culinary salts, with their cubic crystal structure, are best used in cooking, although they could also be used as a finishing salt to provide a more flavorful and colorful alternative to common table salt. Typically, these mined culinary salts are available both finely ground or in larger chunks to be used in home salt grinders.

Common table salt is often produced from deep underground salt deposits using the solution mining method. This involves pumping water down into the salt deposit to create a brine solution, then pumping it back to the surface and on to a purification plant, where impurities are removed, along with the more bitter chloride and sulfate salts of magnesium and many trace minerals, leaving about 99.5% sodium chloride. Evaporation in huge vessels yields very fine, dense, cubic crystals of salt that look like grains of sugar. Anticaking agents are often added, such as calcium silicate and magnesium carbonate, both white odor-free and taste-free compounds that absorb moisture within the package.

Salt from Evaporated Salt Water

Salt that is made by evaporating salt water is often generically referred to as sea salt. Quality varies widely among these salts. Some brands of sea salt are hardly different from typical mined table salt, being harvested and dried on a large scale and refined to remove most minerals, ultimately yielding 99.5% pure sodium chloride. They may even be evaporated in such a way as to create the same small dense, cubic crystals found in common table salt, and anticaking agents and iodine are often added. While refined sea salt, like common mined table salt, is fine for general cooking, its flavor is too sharp to function as a finishing salt, which needs to be able to complement and complete a dish.

At the other end of the spectrum, unrefined salt from unpolluted areas is still traditionally produced in much the same manner as it was centuries ago. In this seasonal process, which takes advantage of spring tides at their saltiest, seawater is first trapped in inlets, estuaries, large shallow ponds, or clay-lined pools (commonly referred to as salt pans). The water is then almost completely evaporated in the open air under the sun or, in humid, colder areas, with a controlled external heat source.

Next, during the crystallization stage, the salts in the seawater are encouraged to precipitate using unique techniques that ultimately determine the size, shape, texture, and color of the finished salt. This process includes carefully skimming off the delicate crystals that form on the surface, along with raking the crystals that form at the bottom. Special care is taken to minimize stirring up any clay or sediment to keep the salt crystals as pure and flavorful as possible. Traditional long wooden rakes are still used by many artisan producers, as metal implements are considered to have the potential to adversely affect the final flavor.

The surface crystals that are formed and collected each day are considered the crème de la crème of sea salt. These are known as fleur de sel in France or flor de sal in Portugal. Both terms translate to "the flower of salt," which reflects both how the crystals blossom on the surface of the water and the aroma of violets that has traditionally been claimed to develop as the crystals dry in the sun, which accentuates its special character. Like the cream that rises to the top of unhomogenized whole milk, this type of salt, with its light, flaky texture and sweet, delicate flavor, is considered the perfect condiment to complement simple dishes and foods. In fact, it is best used only as a finishing salt, as its nuances of flavor and its texture would be lost during most cooking processes due to high temperatures and the duration of cooking. However, a light dusting of fleur de sel can accentuate the flavors of vegetables, meats, fish, beans, and baked potatoes once they're cooked. Surprisingly, even though various brands of French fleur de sel and Portuguese flor de sal are produced in essentially the same manner, they have subtle differences in flavor and aroma because they come from specific harvesting areas.

French sel gris (gray salt) and the comparable, although naturally whiter, traditional Portuguese sea salt are made from the second layer of salt that doesn't rise to the surface. Skimmed off after the fleur de sel is collected, sel gris is coarser and somewhat bolder in flavor. Both French and Portuguese gray salt are excellent for all types of cooking, including roasting, baking, grilling, and brining, and also provide a more flavorful, mineral-rich alternative to common table salt.

Maldon Sea Salt is hand harvested off of England's Essex coast, a centuries-old salt-producing region that has low rainfall, strong winds, lots of sunshine, and low-lying salt marshes, qualities that come together to naturally trap seawater and begin the process of evaporation. The concentrated brine is collected and evaporated in large stainless steel pans over controlled natural gas heat. As the brine concentrates, small crystals shaped like hollow pyramids form, accumulate, and are hand harvested daily using traditional long-handled rakes. The result is very soft, light, flaky crystals of salt that are exceptional as a finishing salt.

Natural sea salt from the west coast of Sicily is also a special find. Look for salts like Ittica d'Or, a sea salt from the medieval saltworks along the salt road between Trapani and Marsala that is now designated as a natural preserve to protect it from industrial pollution.

Flower of Bali is an unusual finishing salt obtained by gathering crystals from the top of seawater evaporating in hollowed-out trunks of palm trees.

Flavor-Enriched Sea Salt
Each sea salt has a unique flavor and color, reflecting the minerals found in the area where the salt originates and the skill of the salt worker, which can make a difference in how much of the clay bottom of the salt pan is scraped up in the raking process. Beyond these inherent differences, some salts are enriched with natural minerals. Comprising up to 2% to 3% of the final product, the minerals retained or added to sea salt can make the final product taste slightly sweet, bitter, or briny.

Red Alaea sea salt from Hawaii derives its color from the natural iron oxides found in red volcanic clay. The red salt originally formed naturally, when, as a result of heavy rains, red clay river sediments seeped into tide pools. When evaporated naturally, the salt from these pools was dyed red. Hawaiian red sea salt, traditionally used in blessing and healing rituals, was valued as a sacred representation of the meshing of earth and sea. Today it is also used in Hawaiian dishes, not only for its flavor, but also in honor of tradition. Another example of enriched sea salt is Cyprus black lava salt. This flaky salt from tidal pools formed by lava flows has activated charcoal added for its dramatic color and smoky flavor and aroma.

Sea salt can also be infused with a distinctive smoked flavor. A variety of shells or types of wood can be used to impart different aromas through a cold-smoking process. Examples include Danish Viking Smoked Salt which is smoked over juniper, cherry, elm, beech, and oak; Fumée de Sel, which uses Chardonnay oak chips from seasoned French wine barrels; and Salish Smoked Salt, made from Pacific Ocean sea salt smoked over red alder wood.

EFFECT OF CRYSTAL SIZE ON FLAVOR

Despite the many nuances in flavor depending on where and how salt is obtained and whether it's enhanced with minerals or other substances, the primary differences among salts in terms of flavor and its effect on food is largely determined by the specific processing techniques used to create the salt and the skill of the manufacturers. This is especially the case in terms of the size and structure of the salt crystal.

Small, dense, cubic crystals are produced in closed evaporation tanks in which crystallization occurs throughout the brine. In contrast, salt produced in open pools or containers with monitored, slow drying and hands-on processing creates broad, irregular plate-shaped or pyramid-shaped crystals. Not only do these provide the crunchy texture characteristic of fine finishing salts, but their very structure also enhances the tasting experience, producing a pleasant burst of flavor on the palate, very unlike the sharp taste that results from the small solid crystals of common table salt. And here, too, the irregular crystals of fine finishing salts are superior. The size and shape of the crystals helps the salt adhere to the surface of foods, allowing it to better perform as a condiment or topping.

Kosher salt, which can either be mined or made from seawater sources, provides yet another texture of salt. Its name derives from the fact that it is used to prepare meat according to Jewish dietary guidelines. Through the process of continually raking salt brine during evaporation, coarse, irregular crystals are created, which tend to cling to meat. This means the salt stays on the surface longer and does a better job of drawing blood and juices out of just-butchered meat, as kosher guidelines require. Beyond this traditional use, kosher salt works well in recipes that include enough water to allow it to dissolve and disperse. It can also be used as a crunchy, salty topping on meat, fish, pretzels, and breads.

Many chefs appreciate kosher salt for its flavor, which is less harsh. And due to its large crystal size, kosher salt is easier to pick up with the fingers when adding a pinch of salt to a recipe. Brands of kosher salt do, however, vary in the shape of crystal, depending on the manufacturer's processing methods. Some are cubic, with the large grains composed of many cubes stacked together. Other brands have crystals with a hollow, pyramidal shape, and as a result they dissolve twice as fast as table salt and granular kosher salt do. Because the pyramid-shaped crystals are less dense, it takes a larger amount to achieve the same saltiness. Most brands of kosher salt also are free of additives, including iodine. Still, some brands do include sodium ferrocyanide as an anticaking agent, which may leave a slight chemical aftertaste.

Gomasio (goh-MAH-see-oh), a traditional Japanese condiment used instead of raw table salt, is a blend of roasted sesame seeds ground with sea salt, generally using eight to fifteen parts sesame to one part sea salt. Especially good on whole grains, cooked vegetables, baked potatoes, cooked beans, and pasta, gomasio can be used to enhance the flavor of other foods while minimizing the amount of sodium consumed.

HOW TO MEASURE AND STORE SALT

The amount of salt called for in recipes is based on the assumption that the small crystals commonly found in table salt will be used. How much to use when substituting salt with larger crystals depends on the specific density of the salt in comparison to table salt. Finely ground salt can generally be substituted for common table salt on a one-to-one basis, whereas with flake salt you may need to use almost twice as much. You'll have to experiment to figure out how much to use of different varieties.

Finishing salts should be stored in a glass, ceramic, or wooden container with a loose-fitting lid, such as a cork stopper, which allows some air flow to the salt but still keeps it dry. If a utensil is used to measure the salt or sprinkle it over food, it should be nonmetal. Cooking salts can be stored in similar containers. To keep excess moisture from causing clumping in salt shakers, add a couple of grains of uncooked rice.

Miso

Sea salt is a significant ingredient in miso (MEE-so). Although this thick, versatile seasoning paste originated in China 2,500 years ago, it is most commonly associated with Japan, where it is one of the hallmarks of traditional Japanese cuisine. It is made from cooked soybeans mixed with water and koji, the name for cooked grain or soybeans inoculated with a mold that starts the fermentation process. Depending on the type of miso being produced, the aging process may range between two months and three years. Each variety of miso reflects the microorganisms native to the area in which it is made, with a unique flavor, and sometimes a unique appearance.

The fermentation process enhances the fifth flavor, umami, explaining why miso is widely recognized for its ability to enhance flavor in soups, with classic miso soup being the most familiar. It also sets the stage for exceptional sauces, stews, gravies, salad dressings, dips, spreads, and marinades, and can even serve as a stand-in for Parmesan cheese for a new spin on pesto.

HEALTHFUL PROPERTIES OF MISO

An additional bonus of miso is its healthful, probiotic properties, arising from the "friendly" lactobacillus bacteria that proliferate during the process of making miso. Probiotics can help support the body's own internal friendly bacteria, effectively providing a boost to the immune system, helping protect against disease, and aiding in digestion of food and absorption of nutrients. Since pasteurization is designed to kill microbes, unpasteurized miso has the best probiotic activity. This type of miso will always be sold refrigerated in glass jars or plastic containers. While pasteurized miso is fine in terms of flavor and easier to ship, the pasteurization process reduces the health benefits of miso, trading nutrition for convenience.

Studies have also shown that frequent consumption of miso soup is correlated with decreased risk of stomach cancer and breast cancer. Other studies indicate that miso consumption can reduce the effects of radiation exposure and increase survival, particularly dark miso that has been fermented for a long time.

HOW MISO IS MADE

The thick texture of miso and its inherent complexity of flavors result from a unique production process involving alternating cycles of fermentation and aging. The process begins by steaming grain, typically rice or barley, or cooked soybeans, and inoculating them with *Aspergillus oryzae*, the type of mold most widely used in Japan for initiating food-related fermentation processes.

After a two-day incubation period, the mixture, now called koji, is mixed in with cooked, mashed soybeans or garbanzo beans, sea salt, and water. During the subsequent aging process, the enzymes in the koji, along with natural microorganisms in the environment, break down the complex carbohydrates, fat, and protein in the beans and grains, with glutamic acid, which is responsible for umami, being produced as the proteins are broken down.

Because fermentation requires warm temperatures, this phase occurs during the warmer months. Cold temperatures during the winter aging phase slow enzyme activity and kill undesirable bacteria that could otherwise taint the flavor and character of the miso. Both cycles are essential to the process of making miso. One-year miso has been fermented at least one summer, while "two-year" miso has gone through two summer fermentation seasons and at least one full summer-winter cycle. Similarly, "three-year" miso has gone through at least three summer fermentation seasons and at least two full summer-winter cycles, which accounts for the deeper flavors and thicker texture of three-year miso.

VARIETIES OF MISO

Differences among the various types of miso are based on the specific type of koji used, proportions of each of the ingredients, and the total fermentation time. There are two fundamental categories of miso based on color and taste: light miso and dark miso.

Light Miso

Light miso includes all one-year misos, which are typically labeled generically as "mellow miso" or "sweet miso," or by the type of grain used in the koji, such as shiro (sweet rice miso). Misos in this category are less salty, lighter in color (white, yellow, or beige), and higher in carbohydrates than are dark misos. To achieve these characteristics, light miso is made with a high proportion of grain koji, along with a low percentage of salt (ranging from 4% to 6%) to speed up fermentation. Fewer soybeans are used than in dark miso since they have a high protein content and thus require a longer fermentation time to break down the protein.

Sweet miso varieties have even less salt and more koji than does mellow miso, producing a smooth, creamy texture and a flavor that's mild, slightly tart, somewhat sweet, and cooling. It's a good choice for use in soups, sauces, dips, spreads, and dressings in warmer seasons and climates. Using sweet miso can be as simple as mixing a small amount into mashed avocado and tofu for a fusion-style guacamole, or blending it with pureed cooked beans and fresh herbs for a quick spread. The creamy texture of light miso also makes it an effective substitute for dairy in soups, spreads, dressings, and even mashed potatoes, though you'd use only a moderate amount.

Try making a miso glaze by combining light miso with oil, honey, and vinegar, and brushing it on roasted vegetables or grilled fish, chicken, or tofu near the end of cooking. Miso marinades are yet another way to explore light miso, combining it into a pastelike mixture with ingredients such as mirin (sweet rice wine), lemon juice, or sake. It's an especially good way to prepare tofu or fish; not only does the marinade help accentuate flavors, but it also serves as a natural tenderizer. Marinate tofu for 2 to 24 hours in the refrigerator. Firm fish like salmon or sablefish can be marinated (in the refrigerator) for anywhere between 4 hours and 3 days.

Dark Miso

Dark miso includes two- and three-year misos made with rice (red, kome, genmai, or brown rice miso), barley (mugi miso), soybeans (hatcho miso), or buckwheat (soba miso), with colors ranging from russet red to deep brown. Proportions used to make dark miso are largely the opposite of those used in light miso, with a lower percentage of koji, more soybeans, and more salt (ranging from 10% to 12%). Fermented longer and richer in flavor, dark miso is more warming to the body and therefore more appropriate for colder seasons and climates. In addition to complementing hearty root vegetables, onions, winter squash, nuts, and nut butters, dark miso provides an excellent foundation for cooked beans, stews, tomato sauces, and soup of all varieties, not just miso soup. Miso tahini sauce is a classic and delicious all-purpose sauce. To make it, combine one part red miso with four parts tahini in a saucepan and thin with broth or water, adjusting the amount of water depending on whether you'd like to make a spread or a sauce. Stir constantly over low heat for 2 to 3 minutes before serving; don't allow the mixture to boil. It's even better topped with a bit of grated fresh ginger or freshly chopped parsley.

COOKING WITH MISO

Miso is high in sodium, so it can be used to replace salt. In general, 1 teaspoon of dark miso is approximately equivalent to 1½ to 2 teaspoons of light miso, which, in turn, is equivalent to about ⅛ teaspoon of salt. A good rule of thumb is to use no more than ½ to 1 teaspoon of dark miso or 1 to 2 teaspoons of light miso per serving. For extra depth of flavor and an interesting interplay of sweet and salty, miso can be used instead of salt when making desserts or be added to oatmeal and other hot cereals just before serving, substituting about 1 tablespoon of light miso or 2 teaspoons of dark miso for ¼ teaspoon of salt.

For best results, mix miso in a small amount of broth or water and stir it to form a paste before adding it to soups, sauces, or other dishes. Adding it just 3 to 4 minutes before serving will activate its beneficial bacteria and enzymes, but to avoid destroying those beneficial components, only add miso to foods when their temperature is far below a boil. In spreads, dips, and salad dressings, miso is primarily used for flavor, so the heat activation step isn't necessary; however, many of the other health benefits of miso will still be available.

To protect its taste, color, and texture, store miso in the refrigerator, preferably in a tightly sealed glass jar, although a plastic container with a snug lid will work well, too. When properly stored in the refrigerator, miso can last for many years, in part due to its high concentration of salt.

Tamari and Shoyu

Naturally brewed soy sauce, like miso, is another key condiment that provides the taste of umami. There are a couple of reasons for this. First, its ancient Chinese origins are linked directly with miso production. And because the modern manufacturing process still involves several months of fermentation, this allows microbial enzymes to free up amino acids from the proteins in soy, including glutamic acid, setting the stage for its ability to blend and intensify the flavors in food. While soy sauce is the generic term applied to all forms of this liquid condiment, the three main categories it encompasses—tamari, shoyu, and nonbrewed chemically hydrolyzed soy sauce—are actually very different from each other, not only in how they are produced but also in how they are used.

Originating as a by-product of soy-based miso production in China 2,500 years ago, tamari (which translates as "that which accumulates") was the rich liquid that naturally accumulated in the wooden miso kegs. Many years later, in the seventh century CE, Japan was introduced to miso and, consequently, tamari. Tamari soon became as appreciated and sought after as the miso itself. However, since it takes more than 2,000 pounds of miso to yield only about 5 gallons of tamari, enterprising producers eventually developed a way to make tamari directly from soybeans without going through all of the stages of miso manufacture. The solution was a higher ratio of brine to solids in the fermentation mash.

Japanese tamari-makers went a step further. In the seventeenth century, they began adding wheat to the fermentation mix to create a soy sauce with a naturally sweeter taste, a seasoning they called shoyu. Fermentation naturally transforms the sugars in the wheat starch into alcohol, creating the unique aromatic characteristics responsible for shoyu's flavor profile, which is so different than that of tamari.

HOW TAMARI AND SHOYU ARE MADE

Similar to the process for making miso, both tamari and shoyu are made by first combining cooked soybeans (and roasted wheat if making shoyu) with *Aspergillus oryzae*, the mold commonly used in Japan and China to start the fermentation process in food. After an incubation period of about three days, the mixture, known as koji, is transferred to fermentation tanks where it is combined with salt and water. The salt helps control the lactic acid and yeast activity during the fermentation process and also acts as a natural preservative. During the five- to six-month fermentation period, the soy proteins are broken down into individual amino acids, including the all-important glutamic acid, and many complex flavors and fragrances develop. Thanks to the conversion of wheat into sugars and alcohol, shoyu develops different flavors and fragrances. The koji and brine mixture (called *moromi*) ultimately transforms into a reddish brown, semi-liquid mash. Next, the *moromi* is pressed to yield liquid tamari or shoyu, which is strained, pasteurized, and, finally, bottled.

Pasteurization is done for a couple of reasons. In addition to improving the stability of the product by inactivating most of the enzymes and creating acids that inhibit the growth of microorganisms, the brief heat that occurs during pasteurization further develops compounds that contribute additional flavors and aromas. However, even though both tamari and shoyu are pasteurized, both should still be refrigerated after opening to protect their color and flavor.

Even though a small amount of ethanol develops naturally in the process of making shoyu, food-grade grain alcohol is added to virtually all brands of tamari and shoyu during the bottling process to provide extra protection against spoilage and help retain good flavor. Despite pasteurization and the addition of alcohol, some brands still include preservatives. This is an unnecessary additive, especially if these products are refrigerated after opening, so check ingredient labels before purchase and opt for preservative-free brands.

Unfortunately, unless specifically labeled as naturally brewed or traditionally brewed, much of the soy sauce commonly available in grocery stores and restaurants is nothing more than a chemically hydrolyzed liquid seasoning. Instead of using natural enzymes and several months of fermentation time to break down the soybean protein into its flavorful constituents, nonbrewed soy sauces do the job by boiling the soybeans in hydrochloric acid. This quick process takes only a couple of days, then the liquid is neutralized and filtered and caramel color, salt, and corn syrup are added to provide color and some flavor. Preservatives are added as the final step. Although expedient and inexpensive, this process yields a harsh, salty, one-dimensional flavor enhancer, and food seasoned with chemically hydrolyzed soy sauce will be dull, lacking vibrancy and flavor.

VARIETIES OF TAMARI AND SHOYU

Tamari and shoyu can range from thin to thick, from light to dark in color, and have complex flavors that range from mild to rich, and from salty to slightly sweet. Authentic tamari produced as a by-product of miso manufacture is occasionally available. Lighter in color, sweeter in flavor, and lower in salt content, it is ready to use as a seasoning, essentially as a kind of liquid miso. Typically left unpasteurized, miso tamari is generally sold in the refrigerated section. However, just like centuries ago, its availability remains limited, as removing too much tamari from the miso could adversely affect the flavor and character of the miso.

Japan actually recognizes five types of soy sauce. The first three—shiro, tamari, and koikuchi—differ from one another in color and flavor based on their specific ratio of wheat to soybeans. The other two kinds of Japanese soy sauce have stronger flavors. Saishikomi soy sauce is fermented twice and is dark, and usukuchi, which is made with added amasake, is salty and has a light color.

Chinese soy sauce is made primarily from soybeans, more in line with the original way tamari was made. Light Chinese soy sauce, made from the first pressing of the *moromi* mash, is a premium seasoning that is both saltier and lighter in color than the thicker, brownish black dark Chinese soy sauce, which is aged longer and has added molasses for a distinctive look.

However, the main difference comes down to tamari or shoyu. Choosing between tamari and shoyu is not an either-or decision. Instead, it is matter of being aware of which is best to use at various stages of cooking or as a condiment at the table.

Tamari is the kind of soy sauce to use when cooking food such as sauces, especially tomato-based sauces, soups, stews, stir-fries, and casseroles and other baked dishes. It's also best for roasting and grilling. Unlike shoyu, which contains more aromatic flavors that burn off under high temperatures, tamari has a deeper, stronger flavor that holds up better under higher heat and longer cooking. Tamari is also a better flavor enhancer. Because it is made only from high-protein soybeans, tamari contains over one-third more glutamic acid than shoyu does. Because it doesn't contain wheat, which causes alcohol to develop, the flavor of tamari is smoother, richer, and more complex. Its color is a deeper brown than that of shoyu, and its consistency is somewhat thicker.

Shoyu, on the other hand, is best at the table as a condiment or dipping sauce and in marinades and salad dressings. Its toasty, caramel-like, sweeter flavor is the result of the breakdown of wheat starch into different natural sugars. Like a fine wine, shoyu also provides a rich aroma and enticing, robust bouquet.

SODIUM IN TAMARI AND SHOYU

With just slightly less than 1,000 mg of sodium per tablespoon for both tamari and shoyu, it's best to use them with a light hand. Like miso, tamari and shoyu are meant to enhance, not overwhelm. Low-sodium versions of shoyu are also available, from which salt is removed after the fermentation process. This allows the complexity of flavor to develop as much as possible before the sodium is removed using an ion exchange process. In this method, the salt precipitates out onto two electrically charged plates from the shoyu between them. These low-sodium forms should be used just as you would use regular tamari and shoyu.

Umeboshi Plums

Umeboshi plums are made from sour, unripe fruits of the ume tree, which is native to China. Though they're called plums, they're actually more closely related to apricots. To make umeboshi plums, the fruits are pickled with sea salt for about a month and then removed from the brine to dry in the sun. In the meantime, dark red shiso leaves, also known as beefsteak leaves, are placed in the brine, both for their natural preservative qualities and for the benefit of their natural red dye. The dried fruits are returned to the now red brine to soak for several days, which changes their color from green to red. They are then removed from the brine once again and aged in barrels for around a year. They are sold in the whole pickled plum form as well as a convenient paste form, with the pits removed. The red brine drawn off of the pickled umeboshi plums and shiso leaves is sold as umeboshi vinegar, even though it isn't a true vinegar. With its unique, salty, tangy flavor, umeboshi vinegar is delicious in salad dressings, dips, and marinades, or used as a condiment and splashed on vegetables, beans, and grains.

The distinctive sour and salty flavor of umeboshi plums is most commonly associated with nori rolls and rice balls. However, dips, spreads, salad dressings, sauces, broths, cooked grains, and vegetable dishes are all enhanced by a dab of umeboshi. Try it spread lightly on cooked corn on the cob instead of butter. Because umeboshi plums are high in citric acid and a good source of potassium and iron, they've also served as an important traditional remedy, both as a digestive aid and for their natural antibacterial effects.

Sea Vegetables

A beautiful and extraordinary universe of plants lies just beneath the surface of the ocean, and people living in proximity to the coast have harvested and eaten many of these plants since ancient times. It's a shame they aren't better understood or more widely used in our modern Western world, as they're a valuable source of nutrients and can impart complex and unusual flavors to food. Although they are commonly called seaweeds, edible versions are often referred to as sea vegetables, a moniker that attempts to restore them to a position of esteem, and also differentiate them from annoying versions associated with entangling arms and feet while swimming.

Throughout the world, both traditional and modern recipes use sea vegetables as a delicious addition to soups, sauces, salads, side dishes, snacks, and garnishes. They are found in recipes from Japan, China, Ireland, Scotland, England, Wales, Russia, Canada, Iceland, Norway, Sweden, Africa, Australia, New Zealand, Hawaii, the Pacific Islands, and the northeastern and northwestern coastal areas of the United States. Because they are a source of umami, the fifth taste that helps pull together and expand the flavors in a dish synergistically, the continued widespread use of seaweeds is no wonder. While research on umami was originally conducted on kombu, other sea vegetables contain varying levels of glutamic acid, the amino acid responsible for their ability to enhance other flavors. And since they grow and reproduce within salty waters, minerals found in the sea, especially sodium, are also abundant in seaweeds, providing another aspect of seasoning that further explains their ability to accentuate flavors. Sea vegetables also play another, less apparent role in foods and cooking. Some, like Irish moss (carrageenan), contain gelatinous carbohydrates, making them a useful ingredient in food processing in the form of stabilizers, thickeners, emulsifiers, and suspending agents.

GETTING TO KNOW SEA VEGETABLES

Classified as marine algae, seaweeds are chlorophyll-containing plants without true stems, roots, or leaves that live in the sea or brackish water, often attached to rocks or other surfaces. Successful and resilient species, they've been around for more than two billion years. Most seaweeds are photosynthetic, relying on sunlight as an energy source from which to produce food. Although all have chlorophyll, many also contain other pigments in order to better absorb various wavelengths of light and capture more of the sun's energy. As a result, they occur in three main color groups—red, green, and brown—which is a handy way of classifying them.

Green seaweeds, such as sea lettuce, mainly contain chlorophyll, similar to their land-based brethren. Red seaweeds, which include dulse, laver, nori, agar, and Irish moss, primarily have red pigments, although they can look purple as well as a whole range of other related colors depending on the specific kinds of accessory carotene pigments present. Because this class of pigments can be water-soluble and heat sensitive, seaweed that looks red when uncooked may change to a dark green after cooking. Brown seaweeds, such as kelp, kombu, alaria, arame, wakame, sea palm, and hijiki, depend on brown pigments from other carotenoid pigments, fucoxanthin in particular. Although chlorophyll is also a component of brown seaweeds, its green color is masked by the brown.

NUTRITIONAL AND MEDICINAL ATTRIBUTES

Seaweeds have long been known for their nutritional attributes. Traditional Chinese medicinal texts as far back as 2700 BCE mention seaweed's medicinal qualities, including reference to its ability to reduce goiter. The Ebers papyrus, the ancient Egyptian dissertation on medical care thought to have been written in 1550 BCE, also specifically includes the therapeutic use of seaweeds, as do Ayurvedic medicinal texts from the fourth century CE.

Current scientific research has keyed in on the phytonutrients in seaweeds, including lignans that may help prevent certain forms of cancer, including breast cancer. Tumor reduction, inhibition of cancer cell proliferation, free radical scavenging, and significant antioxidant activity have also been exhibited by red and brown seaweeds. In addition, sulfated polysaccharides, a type of carbohydrate found in some of the brown seaweeds, are being explored as antiviral agents and for helping prevent blood clots. Studies exploring polysaccharides in bladderwrack and kelp have also shown them to be a highly effective agent for reducing the effects of radiation toxicity.

With their ocean origins, sea vegetables are a valuable source of a wide array of trace minerals and, depending on the variety, small amounts of calcium, magnesium, and potassium. Sodium and iodine are the most predominant, and it is iodine that's responsible for the long history of use of seaweeds to treat goiter, even though this element was not identified and isolated until fairly recently. Iodine was discovered by accident in 1811 and isolated as a specific component of seaweed when Bernard Courtois, a manufacturer of saltpeter (potassium nitrate), was in the process of making gunpowder for France. Rather than using wood ashes, as he usually did, to extract sodium carbonate, a necessary component when making saltpeter, he decided to use burned kelp instead.

When the characteristic violet-colored vapors we now know to be iodine rose from the mixture, he quit the saltpeter industry and spent several months investigating the chemical reactions and properties of the newly discovered element.

Most of the iodine used commercially is obtained as a by-product of various mining operations because this is an inexpensive source, but seaweeds are still noted as the most concentrated food source of the mineral, and they have the benefit of providing an array of nutrients beyond iodine itself. The amount of iodine in different types of sea vegetables varies, depending on the age and condition of the plant, season and geographic location of harvest, the part of the plant consumed, how it is prepared, and how the seaweed is stored.

While iodine is an extremely important nutrient, it is possible to get too much if excessive amounts of seaweed are consumed. This can have disruptive effects on the thyroid and cause a host of other problems. Recommended daily iodine intake for most healthy adults with normal thyroid function aged nineteen years and older is 150 mcg, and the upper limit for this group of people is 1,100 mcg. Recommended daily amounts and tolerable upper intake levels for children and adolescents are lower and vary depending on age group. Within these ranges, the amount that's safe to ingest depends on the individual. Some people are very sensitive iodine and need to keep their daily intake on the low side. On the other hand, in some cultures where sea vegetables are a consistent part of the everyday diet, people may have adapted, making them able to tolerate higher levels.

As a class, red varieties of sea vegetables are consistently much lower in iodine than are brown ones, with nori containing the least (around 16 mcg per gram), and kelp and kombu containing the most (averaging around 1,300 to 1,500 mcg per gram, although sometimes as much 2,500 mcg per gram). Even within the brown varieties there is a wide range of iodine content, with alaria as low as 110 mcg per gram, a marked contrast to the much higher levels found in kelp.

All in all, a little seaweed goes a long way, especially the brown varieties because of their higher iodine levels. Use common sense and moderation in deciding how much to eat and how frequently, and also be aware that how they are cooked and what is also included in the meal can affect the amount of iodine ingested. The iodine in sea vegetables is mostly water-soluble, which means that boiling them in water will result in much of the iodine being extracted into the cooking water. The roasting method appears to release the least amount of iodine, while steaming and frying may release moderate amounts.

Eating sea vegetables in a meal that also includes goitrogenic foods may also help to lessen the effects of their high iodine content. Goitrogenic foods are those that contain substances that interfere with the thyroid gland's uptake and utilization of iodine, which is necessary for thyroid hormone production. They include soybeans (and products made from them), millet, peanuts, and cruciferous vegetables, such as broccoli, cauliflower, bok choy, brussels sprouts, rutabaga, turnips, and cabbage. For most people with healthy thyroid function, the potential negative effect of these foods is of no concern unless excessive amounts are consumed. Although some of the goitrogenic compounds in these foods may also be deactivated when they're cooked, ultimately, eating goitrogenic foods with seaweeds not only provides a tasty combination but may help provide a healthy balance in terms of iodine, as well.

Sea vegetables can be quite high in sodium, not surprising given that they grow in seawater. Excess salt can be removed by rinsing them with water. When you use them in a dish, you can reduce the amount of other salty seasonings or forego them altogether.

Seaweed can also contain heavy metals, such as lead, arsenic, mercury, and cadmium, which are unhealthful to the human body at certain levels. Given that these heavy metals occur naturally worldwide because they may be leached from bedrock, sea vegetables may often contain at least trace amounts. But to minimize your exposure, it's important to buy sea vegetables only from areas unpolluted by industrial waste. Good sea vegetable companies are very particular about where and how their seaweed is harvested, dried, and stored and test it regularly for heavy metals, as well as herbicides, pesticides, and microbial contaminants. Always purchase sea vegetables from companies that have a commitment to providing a high-quality product.

HOW TO COOK AND STORE SEA VEGETABLES

Adding small amounts of sea vegetables to soups, stews, or beans is a good way to start experiencing their unique flavors, textures, and colors. The mild flavors of nori, dulse, sea palm, and arame make them good choices to start with. Seaweeds are especially good cooked with grains, beans, and most root vegetables.

Since seaweeds can expand in volume up to sevenfold when rehydrated, only a small amount of dried seaweed is usually required. Most should be quickly rinsed with water to remove any surface dust, sand, or excess naturally occurring sea salt. Depending on the variety, they should then be briefly soaked before cooking in any quickly prepared dish. No soaking is needed when they're simmered in soups and stews for a long period of time.

Dried sea vegetables will keep indefinitely if stored in a tightly sealed container in a cool, dark place, such as a cupboard or pantry away from the stove. Cooked sea vegetables will keep for four to five days refrigerated.

Exploring Sea Vegetables

Agar

Agar is made from several varieties of red algae processed into lightweight translucent bars that may be further processed into flakes or powder. The primary use of agar is as a gelling agent to make vegetarian gelatin-like desserts, vegetable aspics, puddings, and pie fillings.

Its name *agar* is derived from a Malaysian word that means "seaweed." Using a traditional process that dates back to the seventeenth century, the red seaweeds used to make agar are harvested in autumn and sun-dried. During the winter, they are transported to the mountains, cooked into a thick mixture, poured into trays, and cut into bars after the mixture has gelled. The bars are then put outside on suspended bamboo mats, where they undergo a repeated freeze-thaw process for ten days, freezing solid during the night and thawing during the day. As a result, water and other impurities are removed, leaving the bars of agar nearly white.

To make agar flakes and powder, the bars are simply crushed. Quicker to use, the flakes and powder are also less expensive and yield a harder gel than the more traditional agar bars. Check the ingredient label and avoid any agar in which sulfuric acid is used as a softening agent or inorganic bleaches or dyes are used to whiten and chemically deodorize the agar.

Cooking Guidelines

To gel 2 cups of liquid, use 3 to 4 tablespoons agar flakes, 2 teaspoons agar powder, or 1 agar bar. Agar flakes and powder do not have to be soaked prior to use. When using an agar bar as a thickening agent, first break it into pieces and soak them for 30 minutes, or until spongy. Squeeze out the excess water before using. Whatever form of agar you use, add the amount indicated above to 2 cups juice, broth, or water. Bring to a boil, lower the heat, and simmer for 10 minutes, stirring to thoroughly dissolve the agar. Transfer the liquid to a heatproof mold or glass baking dish and allow it to set. Agar will set at room temperature, but the gelling process is much quicker in the refrigerator, taking only about 45 to 60 minutes.

Alaria

Alaria is a North American variety of wakame that grows off the northeastern coastline. Golden brown when fresh, it is very dark green, really almost black, once dried. Alaria has a taste similar to, but more delicate and slightly wilder than, Asian types of wakame, to which it is related. Like wakame, alaria is delicious in salads, miso soups, and stews, as well as cooked with grains. It requires a longer cooking time than wakame.

Cooking Guidelines

In soup, use about a 5-inch-long strip of alaria per quart of liquid. To bring out its sweet, mild taste and soft, chewy texture, alaria should be simmered for at least 10 minutes or pressure-cooked for 5 to 6 minutes. In salads, use alaria that has already been cooked or soak it in water or diluted lemon juice for 12 hours. For a salty snack or condiment, roast alaria in a 300°F oven for 3 to 5 minutes or pan-fry it in a well-oiled skillet over medium-high heat until crisp.

Arame

Arame is a branched, feathery brown seaweed. Once the fronds are harvested, they're steamed and left to soak in the cooking water for up to 12 hours to make the arame more tender. The arame is then drained, shredded into long black strands, and sun-dried. Although it looks somewhat like hijiki, its flavor is milder and sweeter and its texture softer. Arame is especially good in vegetable sautés, salads, and casseroles.

Cooking Guidelines

Before using arame, rinse it and soak for about 15 minutes. Once soaked and cooked, arame doubles in volume. Always cook arame before adding it to salads or casseroles. As an excellent introduction, soak 2 cups arame, drain, and sauté it with onions and carrots over low heat for about 30 minutes, mixing in a couple of tablespoons of sesame tahini diluted with equal amounts of water or mirin (sweet rice wine) during the last 5 minutes of cooking. Serve as a vegetable side dish or use it as the filling for a savory vegetable strudel.

Dulse

Dulse is a reddish purple sea vegetable harvested from North Atlantic coastlines. Highly valued as a traditional staple in Ireland, Scotland, Wales, coastal Canada, and parts of the northeastern United States, it can be eaten raw as a tangy, salty, soft but chewy snack, or it may be cooked. Rinsing will make dulse tender, less salty, and milder in flavor. Because its red pigments are water-soluble, dulse will become dark green during cooking. It will become more tender as it cooks and may dissolve with longer cooking times.

Cooking Guidelines

To reduce its natural sodium content before adding it to sandwiches or salads, briefly rinse dulse or soak it for up to 5 minutes then squeeze out the salty water. When cooking, add dulse about 5 minutes before the dish is done. To dry-roast dulse, place it in a skillet over medium-high heat or in a 300°F oven until the leaves turn greenish and crisp but not black. For richer flavor, pan-fry in a well-oiled skillet.

Dulse is delicious in sandwiches (though it may seem odd, try it with peanut butter), playing a dual role as both vegetable and tangy seasoning. When dry-roasted and crumbled, dulse can be used as a salty, savory condiment to sprinkle over soups, salads, pasta, popcorn, and cooked grains. Pan-frying dulse in a well-oiled skillet gives it a delicious, baconlike flavor. Prepared in this way, it can be sprinkled on pizza, stirred into scrambled eggs or tofu, or used to make a vegetarian version of a bacon, lettuce, and tomato sandwich. When cooked in chowders, stews, and grains, especially oatmeal, dulse provides a pleasant seafoodlike flavor.

Hijiki

Traditionally, hijiki (sometimes called hiziki) was considered a good food for helping maintain better-looking hair and skin. In fact, its Japanese name is translated as "bearer of wealth and beauty." The plant is also said to resemble strands of hair, due to its many branches, and the best hijiki is harvested from the tiny, thick curls that grow on the smaller branches near the surface of the water. Somewhat resembling a chubby version of arame, hijiki has a more pronounced flavor and tougher texture. In order to soften it, hijiki is washed after harvest, sun-dried, steamed for 4 hours, and left to cool and dry again. It is then soaked in the juice of cooked arame to enhance its black color.

Unfortunately, many countries have advised consumers to avoid this delicious sea vegetable because it often contains inorganic arsenic at a level that may present health risks. Likewise, most of these countries have asked retail establishments and restaurants not to offer hijiki. Arsenic is a semi-metallic element that occurs in nature mainly in combination with other minerals. The inorganic form of arsenic, found in combination with one or more other elements such as oxygen, chlorine, and sulfur, can increase the risk of cancer if regularly consumed. Gastrointestinal problems, anemia, and liver damage are other possible effects.

Although the levels of inorganic arsenic found

in many samples of hijiki were found to be above the regulatory limits of 1 mg per kilogram, government health officials from the United Kingdom and Canada have claimed it is unlikely that past consumption of small amounts daily or occasional larger portions would have caused harm. Nonetheless, they advise against continued regular consumption of hijiki, as it could significantly increase dietary exposure to arsenic. Only consume hijiki if you're sure that its inorganic arsenic levels are significantly lower than the regulatory levels of 1 mg per kilogram.

Cooking Guidelines

Before cooking hijiki, rinse it thoroughly and soak it in water for about 15 minutes. Then discard the soaking water and simmer the hijiki for 30 to 40 minutes. If hijiki will be added to a recipe that requires further cooking, the initial simmering of hijiki can be reduced by about 10 minutes. Hijiki expands fourfold after soaking and cooking. Like arame, hijiki is delicious cooked with sweet vegetables, tahini sauces, tofu, and tempeh. It is also a good addition to casseroles, salads, noodle dishes, cooked rice, soups, and stews.

Irish Moss

Irish moss, a red variety of seaweed, is the primary source of carrageenan, a gelatinous polysaccharide used in commercial food production as a thickener or stabilizer. The term *carrageenan* is from the Irish word *carrigín*, which means "moss of the rock," and in Ireland, the gelling properties of this seaweed have been utilized since at least 1810. Not surprisingly, Irish moss grows in rocky areas along the Atlantic coast of Ireland, as well as other parts of Europe and North America. When fresh, it has a greenish yellow to dark purple color and a soft texture, albeit tough and flexible in nature. When sun-dried, it is yellow and translucent and has a hard, smooth, hornlike consistency.

Cooking Guidelines

Unlike most sea vegetables, Irish moss is often used in its fresh form, cooked just after harvest. When soaked in lemon juice or water and chilled for a couple of hours, it forms a gel similar to what's achieved with agar. The gel can be cut into cubes and used as a refreshing ingredient in salads. If cooked with sugar, it can be made into Irish moss jelly. Fresh Irish moss can also be cooked in water to use as a thick, hot soup stock or to use in its gelled form once cooled.

To reconstitute dried Irish moss, first rinse it in warm water, then soak it for 10 minutes, at which point it's ready to add to broth, juice, or milk as a thickening aid. Use about ½ ounce of dried Irish moss to thicken about 3 cups of liquid. Combine the soaked Irish moss and liquid, bring to a boil, then lower the heat and simmer for 15 to 20 minutes. Strain the liquid through a fine-mesh strainer to remove the carrageenan. At this point, other ingredients or flavorings can be added to the liquid. Pour the mixture into a dish or mold and refrigerate until set.

Kelp

Also called Atlantic kelp or Atlantic kombu, kelp is harvested from North Atlantic waters. Although its thinner fronds give it a somewhat different appearance than Japanese kombu, the two can be used interchangeably in most recipes. Like kombu, Atlantic kelp is naturally high in glutamic acid, so it functions as a natural tenderizer and flavor-enhancer. However, it is much more tender than Japanese kombu, and will actually dissolve if allowed to cook for more than 20 minutes.

Cooking Guidelines

When using Atlantic kelp as a flavoring agent for a broth or sauce or adding it to recipes, first rinse it quickly under cold running water to remove excess salt. For a light-flavored broth, add a small piece, about 5 inches in length, to water, place over medium heat, and remove the kelp just before the water comes to a boil. For a moderate amount of flavor, allow the kelp to simmer for 10 minutes before removing, and for even richer flavor, leave it for the full duration of cooking, letting it fully dissolve into the broth. To use Atlantic kelp while cooking beans, add a small piece, about 5 inches long, to the cooking water and leave it in the pot. In addition to enhancing flavor and tenderizing the beans, the kelp will also slightly thicken the broth.

Atlantic kelp is best simmered for 15 to 20 minutes or pressure-cook for 5 minutes. For use as a condiment, dry-roast kelp for 3 to 4 minutes in a 300°F oven or pan-fry it in a well-oiled skillet for 4 to 5 minutes, until crisp. Because it isn't rinsed prior to dry-roasting or pan-frying, it will be too salty to use as a snack. Any white powder on the dried kelp is merely natural salts and sugars that may have precipitated from the seaweed during storage. Expect Atlantic kelp to expand up to 40% when rehydrated or cooked in water.

Kombu

Kombu, one of the mainstays of Japanese cooking, is the key ingredient in dashi, the all-important broth used as a stock for soups and noodle dishes. Stiff, dark green, broad, and flat when dried, kombu is harvested from large, thick, leafy fronds that grow off the southeast coast of Hokkaido, Japan's northernmost island. After harvest, the fronds are washed, folded, and sun-dried before they are cut and packaged. What makes kombu so unique and invaluable is its naturally high levels of glutamic acid, which accounts for its ability to enhance the flavor of other foods. Unlike MSG, kombu is a safe and nutritious flavor enhancer.

Cooking Guidelines

When using kombu as a flavoring agent for a broth or sauce or before adding it to recipes that include a moderate to high amount of liquid, rinse it quickly under cold running water or wipe it with a clean, damp cloth to remove the excess salt. For a light-flavored broth, add a small piece of kombu, about 3 inches long, to water, place over medium heat, and remove the kombu just before the water comes to a boil. The longer the kombu remains in the cooking water, the stronger the broth will be.

When preparing kombu as a cooked side dish or condiment, presoak it in cold water for 3 to 5 minutes prior to cooking. If you soak it much longer, the kombu can become very slippery and hard to cut. When gauging how much to use, keep in mind that kombu doubles or triples in size after soaking or cooking. For use as a salty condiment or snack, dry-roast kombu in a 300°F oven for 3 to 4 minutes; grind it after roasting if you wish to use it as a condiment.

Like its cousin Atlantic kelp, Japanese kombu is an excellent addition to soup stocks, broths, and vegetable dishes. Beans are especially delicious when cooked with a small piece of kombu, about 2 or 3 inches long. It can also be used as a featured ingredient in side dishes, condiments, and candies.

Laver

Consider laver (LAY-ver) to be the wild North Atlantic version of nori. Both are derived from the same species of red seaweed. Purple to black in color, laver is a traditional food in Scotland, Wales, and Ireland, where it is harvested in the winter from rocks, piers, and other vertical surfaces. Unlike cultivated Japanese nori, laver is left whole and not processed into sheets.

Cooking Guidelines

Traditionally, laver is slowly simmered for many hours into a thick, gelatinous puree and then eaten as a side dish, often served with butter. It is also used as the basis for laverbread, a recipe with a four-to-one ratio of laver to finely cut whole oats. The mixture is then formed into patties and fried. To make a salty condiment with a nutty flavor, dry laver in a 300°F oven for 5 to 8 minutes until crisp, then crumble it over soup, salad, pasta, stir-fries, potatoes, or popcorn. Dried laver can also be eaten without further cooking, although it will be quite chewy in this state. To use it in salads, marinate it in salad dressing for at least 18 hours to tenderize it. The laver can then be left whole and added to the salad along with its marinade. Alternatively, you can discard the marinade and chop the laver before adding it.

Nori

Nori (NOR-ee), the familiar wrapping used when making sushi and nori maki, is the cultivated form of laver grown in coastal areas of Japan, Korea, and northern China on nets suspended at the surface of the ocean. After harvest, it is washed and then, either manually or by machine, shredded and pressed between woven reed mats, drying it into the distinctive paper-thin sheets. Good-quality sheets of nori have a dark, greenish black color with a somewhat iridescent sheen. Flavor and digestibility improve if the raw nori sheets are toasted. Large sheets of nori made specifically for preparing sushi have typically been toasted before packaging.

Cooking Guidelines

To toast nori, simply hold it a couple of inches above a flame stove burner. Within seconds, it will change from greenish black to a more vibrant green and become crisp. Use it to make rice balls or sushi, or crumble it or cut it into strips for use as a garnish for soups, salads, grain dishes, noodles, casseroles, and popcorn. A rich-tasting condiment for grains and beans can be made by cooking nori with a small amount of water and tamari until the water evaporates and the mixture becomes a thick paste.

Sea Beans

Sea beans are collected fresh during the summer in salt marshes and tidal waters along the Pacific and Atlantic coasts. Also known as glasswort and marsh samphire, sea beans have crisp "branches" and stems that look like very thin, miniature cacti. Typically cooked, pickled, or used raw as a garnish, they retain a briny flavor that brings the ocean to mind.

Cooking Guidelines

To cook sea beans, first wash them thoroughly, then boil in unsalted water for 5 to 15 minutes, until the thin branches can easily be removed from the stalks with your fingers. Drain and serve the succulent green stems warm with butter or vinegar. This method makes a wonderfully complementary side dish for seafood.

Sea Lettuce

One of the few sea vegetables in the green category, sea lettuce looks like its land-based namesake when fresh, consisting primarily of bright green, crumpled, extremely thin fronds. It grows along rocky or sandy coasts, often attaching itself to rocks and shells but sometimes floating freely.

Cooking Guidelines

When fresh, sea lettuce can be eaten raw in salads. For cooking, it's best to combine it with other ingredients to minimize its slightly bitter taste. Dried sea lettuce makes a nice addition to soups.

Sea Palm

A sea vegetable unique to the Pacific Northwest, sea palm has a delicious, subtly sweet flavor that makes it a favorite even among those who are otherwise reluctant to try edible seaweeds. While growing, sea palm looks remarkably like a miniature palm tree, complete with a hollow, trunklike structure flexible enough to withstand the waves and leaflike blades at the top.

Cooking Guidelines

Sea palm is generally available only in dried form. For use in salads, soak sea palm in water for 1 hour prior to use. Alternatively, simmer it in water for 5 minutes, then cool and add it to other salad ingredients (it complements avocado nicely). For soup, soak it first for 10 minutes before proceeding with the recipe. Sea palm is good in vegetable sautés, too. After a 10-minute presoak, cook the sea palm until tender, about 30 minutes, before adding it to the sauté.

Wakame

Wakame is a common ingredient in miso soup and a tasty addition to vegetable dishes and salads. This member of the brown seaweed category is harvested along the coasts of Korea, China, and Japan using long poles with blades to cut off the long dark green fronds, allowing them to float to the surface. The fresh wakame is then taken to shore, dried, trimmed, graded, and packaged. Like kombu and Atlantic kelp, wakame is high in glutamic acid, making it a good flavor enhancer and tenderizing agent. Instant wakame is made by a process of washing the wakame, simmering it very briefly in salt water for less than 1 minute, and then rinsing it several times to reduce the salt content. The tougher main rib and leaf tips are then trimmed away and the tender fronds are air-dried into the tight curls characteristic of instant wakame.

Cooking Guidelines

Wakame is one of the most tender sea vegetables, so only minimal soaking and cooking are needed for any recipe. Before using wakame uncooked or as an ingredient in cooked soups or foods, rinse it first to remove surface dirt. Presoak it for 3 to 5 minutes, and then squeeze out the excess water. Don't soak it longer, as it will become too slippery. After its tough ribs are trimmed away, wakame can be added to salads or cooked for at least 5 minutes in soups, stews, or with veggies. Two must-have classics are miso soup with wakame and cucumber-wakame salad. When using instant wakame in soups, broths, and stews, no presoaking is necessary; just add it to the cooking water. Presoak instant wakame for 2 to 3 minutes before using it in salads. When rehydrated, wakame can expand up to seven times its original volume.

Sweeteners

There's no denying that sometimes nothing hits the spot more than something really sweet. Blame it on our genes. Since poisonous plants generally contain bitter alkaloids, scientists speculate this penchant for sweets may have evolved as a protective mechanism to ensure that our early ancestors ate enough high-calorie but nontoxic foods to survive through times of scarcity. However, in these days of plenty, the challenge is to choose sugars wisely and consume them in moderation to maintain a healthy weight. Because sugars contain so few nutrients in relation to their calories, minimizing their intake also helps ensure your diet is comprised of a high percentage of nourishing foods that contribute optimum health and well-being.

The rate at which sugars are digested and the effects sugar has on the body vary widely depending on the sweetener used and which specific types of sugar it contains and in what proportions. The most nutritious sugars are those that remain in whole food form, in fresh and dried fruits, vegetables, milk (lactose), and grains (especially when sprouted). As a component of a whole food that also contains protein, fat, starchy carbohydrates, dietary fiber, vitamins, and minerals, these natural sugars are broken down more slowly and enter the bloodstream at a steady rate, providing the glucose the body needs for fuel in an optimum manner.

Scientifically speaking, sugars are categorized as monosaccharides (single sugar molecules), which includes glucose, fructose, and galactose, and disaccharides (sugars in which two monosaccharides are linked together), such as sucrose, maltose, and lactose. Because glucose is already in the form used by the body, it's absorbed most quickly, requiring insulin to keep blood sugar levels in balance. In contrast, fructose and galactose must first be transported to the liver to be converted into glucose before they can be used as an energy source for the cells. Not only is the metabolism of fructose slower than that of glucose, but it also doesn't require insulin

241

in the process, so it causes little fluctuation in blood glucose levels.

Sucrose, or table sugar, is hydrolyzed by enzymes in the digestive tract into its equal proportions of glucose and fructose. An enzyme called invertase accomplishes this, and the sugars that result are known as invert sugars. The glucose portion of invert sugars is absorbed quite rapidly, again requiring insulin. Because the primary sugar in maple syrup is sucrose, it affects the body in much the same manner. While fructose tastes more sweet, it metabolizes more slowly than glucose and sucrose do. Grain-based sweeteners, barley malt syrup and brown rice syrup, contain varying proportions of glucose and maltose but because they also contain a high level of more complex glucose chains called polysaccharides which take longer to digest, they have a less pronounced effect on blood sugar levels.

So which sweeteners are the best to use? The first step is to rule out artificial and synthetic sweeteners, which have undergone chemical manipulation to dramatically alter the sweetener's sugar profile or to prevent the body from metabolizing the sweetener. Although considerable time and effort have been devoted to developing synthetic sweeteners, chemists have never succeeded in duplicating important qualities of sugar, such as their complex, nuanced flavors and their wide range of functionality—qualities that cooks and bakers appreciate from experience. In addition, synthetic products can't provide the full range of nutrients found within natural products.

Tried-and-true plant-derived sweeteners, as minimally processed as possible, are the best choice. They have proven to be exceptional in flavor and extremely effective in cooking and baking, not to mention safe and nontoxic. These natural sweeteners include familiar ingredients such as maple syrup, molasses, and natural sugar from sugarcane or beets, as well as some options that may be unfamiliar to you, such as agave nectar and stevia. Choosing among these many options comes down to how the sweetener will be used, as each type has distinctive flavors and functional properties, such as color, texture, and viscosity, that affect cooking and baking outcomes. For example, fructose is hygroscopic, meaning it readily takes up and retains moisture, so it yields baked goods that are softer and more moist.

Organic versions of many sweeteners are widely available. This doesn't imply that they confer any health benefits beyond those usually associated with organic foods; it simply means that they have been produced from certified organically grown ingredients and processed in certified organic manufacturing plants. But because agriculture of crops grown for sugar can have substantial negative environmental impacts, purchasing organic sweeteners is good for the environment and a good way to support sound farming and processing methods. It also helps you avoid potentially toxic chemicals and genetically engineered ingredients.

Highly Processed Nutritive Sweeteners

Sugar consumption has reached epidemic proportions in the United States, and this probably has some bearing on the concurrent epidemic of obesity. Because many of the sugars commonly consumed are the most unhealthful, it will be useful to understand why they are best avoided before we explore healthier choices. Many highly processed sweeteners are technically classified as nutritive because they provide calories. Since they are highly processed, they may be treated significantly beyond the basic procedures needed to concentrate sugar from a food. They may also be specially formulated to reduce effects on blood sugar or be manufactured or isolated from different food sources than those where the sweetening agent would naturally occur. Corn syrup, high-fructose corn syrup, crystalline fructose, and polyols are classic examples.

CORN SYRUP

Although corn syrup is developed from corn, a natural product, the extent to which it is processed puts it in a different realm than natural sweeteners, whose sugars are more simply extracted and concentrated. Corn syrup is produced from cornstarch using enzymes to hydrolyze, or break apart, long-chain starch molecules into shorter lengths. Specific proportions of glucose, maltose, and glucose polysaccharides (the remaining longer chains of glucose that account for corn syrup's thick viscosity) are created to match its intended application. The more cornstarch hydrolyzed, the higher the corn syrup's percentage of glucose in relation to maltose, and the more quickly it metabolizes within the body. Manufacturers like corn syrup not just because it's cheap, but also because it helps retain moisture in baked goods, increase browning of foods, and control crystallization in candies and the formation of ice crystals in ice cream. It also contributes more viscosity to condiments and salad dressings.

Corn syrup for home use is generally made from a blend of ingredients rather than just corn syrup. Light corn syrup has some high-fructose syrup to increase sweetness and to reduce viscosity so it's easier to use. Salt and vanilla are also added to enhance flavor. Dark corn syrup typically contains golden syrup (also known as refiner's syrup), caramel flavor and color, salt, and sodium benzoate (a preservative), creating a product with a stronger flavor and darker color.

HIGH-FRUCTOSE CORN SYRUP

Like regular corn syrup, high-fructose corn syrup is created by treating cornstarch with acids and/or enzymes, a process called hydrolysis, to convert the starch into sugars. In regular corn syrup, which is only moderately sweet, hydrolysis ends when a particular proportion of glucose and maltose is achieved. But in high-fructose corn syrup, production starts with a version of corn syrup that is quite high in glucose. From there, additional enzymes are used to transform some of the corn's glucose molecules into the sweeter basic sugar, fructose—a sugar not naturally found in corn. Two varieties of high-fructose corn syrup (HFCS) are manufactured: HFCS-42 (42% fructose and 53% glucose) and HFCS-55 (53% fructose and 42% glucose). Complex sugars called oligosaccharides make up the remaining percentage of sugars to add up to 100%.

Although HFCS has the same relative sweetness level as refined sugar, composed of 50% glucose and 50% fructose, there is a very important difference between the two. The simple sugars in refined sugar are chemically bonded to each other in the disaccharide sucrose molecule, whereas in HFCS, the sugars exist as free, unbound monosaccharides. Therefore, despite what its name may imply, high-fructose corn syrup requires more insulin for its metabolism than fructose does. This difference is especially important for those with diabetes or who have difficulties with metabolizing sugars.

Food manufacturers like high-fructose corn syrup because it is much less expensive than refined sugar and extends shelf life. It also provides better browning in baked goods and softer textures in cookies and snack bars, and it's easier to blend into beverages. As a result, it is ubiquitous, making an appearance in a long list of foods: breakfast cereals, soft drinks, fruit drinks and juices, jams, jellies, soups, sauces, salad dressings, marinades, crackers, potato chips, pretzels, granola bars, energy bars, syrups, dessert toppings, meat products (bacon, ham, deli meats), peanut butter, condiments (ketchup, mustard, mayonnaise, pickles, and pickle relish), and dairy products (ice cream, yogurt, and cheese spreads). HFCS-55 is used to sweeten carbonated soft drinks, and HFCS-42 is used in sports drinks, noncarbonated fruit-flavored beverages, and food products.

When it comes to health, HFCS is often blamed for the current epidemic of obesity and diabetes, as rates of both began increasing at just about the time HFCS appeared on the market. Some health experts also contribute its use to many other health problems, such as high blood pressure and higher uric acid levels in the blood. Others, however, believe there are few differences, if any, between the metabolism of HFCS and sucrose, as both contain similar proportions of glucose and fructose.

Those who are sensitive to HFCS may experience digestive disturbances, including cramps, bloating, gas, and diarrhea. However, other sugars can cause similar problems depending on one's degree of digestive sensitivity, as well as the quantity eaten. The primary culprits are products high in fructose, such as crystalline fructose, agave nectar, honey, dried fruit, apple or pear juice, and whole fruits containing a higher proportion of fructose, such as apples, mangos, melons, and pears. Still, given that HFCS is increasingly used in commonly consumed foods, this sets the stage for people who eat a lot of these foods to experience more digestive disturbances than they otherwise would.

CRYSTALLINE FRUCTOSE

Crystalline fructose is commercially produced from cornstarch that is treated with enzymes to create corn syrup with a minimum of 99.5% fructose and then allowed to crystallize. Since crystalline fructose is about 60% sweeter than sugar, only one-half to two-thirds as much is needed to achieve the same sweetening power, which means fewer calories are needed to achieve the same level of sweetness, especially in cold foods. Fructose also has many beneficial functional properties in food processing, including boosting fruit and chocolate flavors, keeping foods softer and more pliable, and enhancing colors and flavors in baked goods due to increased browning.

For many years crystalline fructose was though to be nutritionally superior because it is metabolized in the body more slowly than glucose and sucrose are. First absorbed in the small intestine,

it is transported to the liver, where it is converted into glucose. As no insulin is needed in the process, little fluctuation in blood sugar levels occurs.

Now, however, pure fructose has lost some of its luster. Research has shown that too much fructose in the diet may lead to elevated triglyceride levels in the blood, increasing the risk of arteriosclerosis, or hardening of the arteries. It may also contribute to being overweight. The secretion of leptin, a hormone that suppresses appetite, is regulated by insulin-mediated glucose metabolism. Since fructose does not stimulate insulin secretion, diets high in fructose may result in reduced blood concentrations of leptin and thus increased sensation of hunger. The American Diabetes Association now recommends that people with diabetes avoid fructose unless it is naturally occurring in fruits, vegetables, and other whole foods. In other words, their advice is to avoid crystalline fructose. This is good advice for all of us. Foods naturally high in fructose contain other important nutrients not found in crystalline fructose, and they'll also have less impact on your blood sugar level than foods high in glucose. Stick with fructose as found naturally in fruits and other minimally processed natural sweeteners such as agave nectar, fruit-based sweeteners, and honey.

POLYOLS

Polyols, or sugar alcohols, are a class of carbohydrates that include erythritol, hydrogenated starch hydrolysates, isomalt, lactitol, maltitol, mannitol, sorbitol, and xylitol. Although their chemical structure is partially similar to that of sugar and partially similar to that of alcohol, they don't actually contain alcohol as we typically think of it in beer, wine, and other alcoholic beverages. In comparison to white sugar, polyols can be anywhere from 50% to 90% as sweet.

Polyols are especially recognized for certain health-associated characteristics. Because polyols are metabolized differently than true sugars, they don't raise blood sugar and insulin levels to the same degree. Nor do they promote tooth decay, since they aren't as readily metabolized by bacteria in the mouth. They typically provide about half the amount of calories as other sugars, with the exact amount depending on the specific polyol.

Sorbitol, one of the first polyols used commercially, often appears as an ingredient in candies for people with diabetes. Currently, however, the American Diabetes Association says that, while polyols are safe, they don't necessarily advocate them over other sugars because there's no evidence that they can have significant positive impacts on blood sugar fluctuations given the amounts in which they're usually consumed. Plus, people who need to manage their blood sugar levels must still factor in polyols as containing at least some carbohydrates.

Polyols are currently marketed to the general public as reduced-calorie sweeteners and promoted to manufacturers for their beneficial properties in food production. Polyols often make an appearance in foods labeled as "lower carbohydrate," "low glycemic," "low calorie," and "sugar-free," including chewing gum, candies, baked goods, jams, and preserves. When used as an ingredient, they can help extend shelf life, promote product stability, boost moisture retention, and help reduce caramelization and browning of foods.

On the other hand, since intestinal microbes metabolize a portion of the polyols a person consumes, these sugar alcohols have the potential to cause diarrhea, gas, or nausea in sensitive individuals or when polyols are consumed in large quantities. It is an effect similar to that of prunes, which, interestingly, have the highest amount of sorbitol of any kind of fruit.

Although sorbitol is naturally found in prunes and other foods, for commercial use, sorbitol and other polyols are extracted from substances where they wouldn't be found in nature. For example, erythritol, hydrogenated starch hydrolysates, malt-itol, and mannitol are all obtained from cornstarch. Isomalt is obtained from sugar, and xylitol from corncobs, birch wood waste, and sugar bagasse (the plant residues remaining after sugar is extracted). An exception is lactitol, which is made by hydrogenating lactose obtained from whey.

OTHER HIGHLY PROCESSED NUTRITIVE SWEETENERS

Other highly processed sweeteners derived from foods will no doubt continue to flood the market, given all the research energy expended on trying to find the perfect "natural" sugar substitute in terms of both flavor and functionality. When it comes down to it, highly processed, nonnutritive sweeteners are considered safe, though not necessarily healthful. And they are certainly better alternatives than artificial sweeteners. However, for optimum flavor and digestibility, minimally processed natural sugars remain the better option.

Artificial, Nonnutritive Sweeteners

Artificial sweeteners are not the answer to appeasing the desire for sugar or keeping blood sugar levels balanced. These purely synthetic compounds are produced through complex chemical processes, and because they have no counterparts in nature, our bodies are ill-equipped to deal with them.

The artificial sugar craze started with saccharin, and since then a variety of sugar substitutes have been developed, including cyclamates, aspartame, acesulfame-K, sucralose, and neotame, each taking the spotlight for a while before being surrounded by controversy and concerns about negative health impacts. Although research results have been mixed, some studies do support these concerns, as do consumer reports of adverse effects.

Since artificial sweeteners are many magnitudes sweeter than table sugar, only a tiny amount is needed to sweeten foods, which means they contribute virtually no calories. As such, they are classified as nonnutritive sweeteners. They also don't affect blood sugar levels. Because such a small amount of artificial sweetener is needed to provide a sweetening effect, they are typically combined with dextrose or maltodextrin, which serve as carriers and also provide some bulk, making them easier to use.

Unlike other sugars, artificial sweeteners are devoid of functional properties that contribute flavor, texture, and other attributes to the foods they're combined with. The only thing they deliver on their own is a sweet flavor, and even that isn't done very well. Their sweetness doesn't have the clean taste found in granulated sugar and other natural sweeteners, and they often have a disagree-able aftertaste. Many of them aren't stable at a wide range of temperatures, which can also contribute to off flavors.

Even the weight-loss claims associated with artificial sweeteners are dubious. Artificial sweeteners perpetuate the myth that people can eat all the sweet foods they want and still lose weight. However, products made with artificial, nonnutritive sweeteners still contain calories from the other ingredients, and some of these products contain just as many calories as those made with natural sweeteners. Even when they contain fewer calories, people are likely to eat more of them, with the end result that they're consuming just as many calories overall, if not even more.

Exploring Natural Sweeteners

Agave Nectar

Agave nectar is derived from sap extracted from the pineapple-shaped core of the agave plant, a desert succulent that is native to Mexico. Although agave is well known as the source from which tequila is made, the juice expressed from the plant can also be used to make a delicious, sweet syrup. Only minimal processing is required to transform the sap into agave nectar. The sap is filtered then heated to break down bonds in its complex carbohydrates and yield a high-fructose liquid. The liquid is then concentrated into the sweet syrup sold commercially.

Being extremely high in fructose, consisting of 90% fructose and 10% glucose, it has minimal effects on blood sugar. Its high fructose content also makes it a good natural alternative to crystalline fructose processed from cornstarch. On the other hand, those who have difficulty digesting fructose may have problems with agave nectar.

Both light and dark varieties of agave nectar are available. Because it's unfiltered, dark agave nectar is amber colored and has a slightly maple-like flavor due to its higher mineral content. Use it as a sweetener for baking and in sauces, and as a syrup or topping. Lighter-colored agave nectar is filtered to provide a more neutral flavor, allowing it to provide sweetness without adding extra flavor of its own. Light agave nectar can be used similarly to dark agave nectar. It's also a good choice for sweetening beverages (both hot and cold) and fruit salads where a sweetener is desired.

Storage and Cooking Guidelines

Store agave nectar in a cool, dry area. Unlike honey, it won't crystallize or solidify when cold.

Although agave nectar is less viscous than honey, it can be used in most recipes that call for honey and thus provides an alternative acceptable to vegans. Substitute it for honey on a one-to-one basis. Also akin to honey, agave nectar contributes a moist texture to baked goods due to its high fructose content. Agave nectar is therefore most suitable for recipes designed to create soft cookies and baked goods, rather than crispy ones. When using agave nectar to replace conventional sugar, for each cup of sugar use ¾ cup agave nectar and reduce the liquid by ⅓ cup. Lower the oven temperature by 25°F.

Amasake

Amasake (ah-mah-ZAH-key), sometimes spelled amazake, is a creamy, rich beverage that, if left undiluted, doubles as a sweetener. A cultured food hailing from Japan, amasake is traditionally made by inoculating cooked sweet rice with koji, rice that has been inoculated with spores of the mold *Aspergillus oryzae*. In fact, its name, *amasake*, means "sweet sake" in Japanese, and if the sake-making process were halted after its first fermentation stage, amasake would be the result. After an incubation period of six to ten hours, the koji starter transforms the grain's starch into maltose and glucose.

Because it is a fermented food and based on whole grains, amasake is easy to digest. Artisan amasake producers continue to make amasake by the traditional koji method and sell it fresh in stores or as a concentrate in shelf-stable pouches. Dried rice koji starter is readily available online or through mail order, so you can easily make amasake at home, too; it's not unlike making yogurt. Either way, the wholesomeness, flavor, and thick, puddinglike texture of traditionally made amasake is unsurpassed.

Enzyme-cultured amasake is also available, made by replacing part or all of the koji with enzymes made from sprouted grain, specially grown and isolated to create a specific sugar profile, flavor, and texture. This kind of amasake is milder in flavor and smoother in texture, characteristics that make it useful as a thick, ready-to-drink malt-like beverage or a milk substitute to pour over breakfast cereals. The different brands of amasake vary in sweetness as well as consistency, with some resembling a thin gruel and others skim milk. To create a smoother texture, some are thickened with xanthan gum.

Storage and Cooking Guidelines

Fresh, undiluted amasake can keep for up to ten days refrigerated. Diluted, enzyme-cultured amasake should be used within a week or by the date indicated on the product.

When using amasake in a recipe that specifically includes it as an ingredient, be sure to check whether the recipe calls for a traditional, thick type of amasake or the diluted variety made with enzymes. When using thick amasake in a recipe, process it in a blender if you prefer a smoother texture.

Traditional amasake can be eaten as is, like a pudding. Diluted with at least an equal amount of water, it can be chilled to drink as a smoothie or warmed for a hot, satisfying drink that is typically served with a pinch of grated ginger. In baked goods, it's a subtle sweetener that will also contribute some degree of leavening and moistness. Because enzyme-cultured amasake is already diluted, it can be substituted for some or all of the liquid in a sweet bread, muffin, or dessert recipe. Or you can thicken it with old-fashioned tapioca or agar flakes and serve it as a pudding or use it as a pie filling.

Barley Malt Syrup

Barley malt is a thick, sticky, dark-colored sweetener with a distinctively malty, molasses-like flavor. It is made from sprouted barley that is dried and mixed with water and cooked grains, such as barley, rice, or wheat. The natural enzymes in the sprouted barley digest the cooked grain to create a sweet, thick mixture. Additional water is added to the slurry and the liquid is then cooked slowly to produce a concentrated syrup.

Barley malt is considered one of the best whole-food-based sweeteners around. The sprouting process naturally transforms the grain's starch into a sweetener, creating a sugar profile with a high percentage of maltose, along with lesser amounts of glucose and polysaccharides, longer chains of sugars that are digested more slowly. This allows for a more steady release of glucose into the blood and thus less fluctuation in blood sugar levels.

In contrast, malt extract is made without added cooked grains, which creates a stronger flavor. Malt extract with active enzymes (diastatic malt) is often used as an ingredient when baking bread, as it provides alpha-amylase enzymes that enhance the dough's fermentation rate. Products labeled as "nondiastatic barley malt" have been dried at high temperatures to retain the malt flavor but inactivate the enzymes.

Storage and Cooking Guidelines

Refrigerate barley malt syrup during warmer months to prevent fermentation.

Barley malt syrup is less sweet than sugar or honey and has a lighter, milder flavor than molasses. It can be substituted for cane syrup or sorghum syrup using equal measures. It also helps retain moisture in baked goods and contributes a dark, rich color. It's best in foods that take well to stronger flavors, such as baked beans, cookies, muffins, and some cakes. It is particularly good combined with ginger, chocolate, or carob. When using it to replace conventional sugar, for each cup of sugar substitute 1⅓ cups of barley malt syrup and reduce the liquid by ¼ cup. Add ¼ teaspoon of baking soda for a lighter texture in baked goods.

Birch Syrup

Birch syrup, a sweetener concentrated from the sap of birch trees, has a caramel-like, slightly spicy flavor. In comparison to maple syrup, birch syrup is richer and more complex. The predominant sugars in birch syrup are fructose and glucose, whereas maple syrup is high in sucrose.

The flavor and color of birch syrup depends on the variety of birch tree, the minerals in the soil, and production methods. Most commercial birch syrup comes from Alaska, where three varieties of

paper birch (*Betula papyrifera*) are used for sugar making, each conferring distinctive flavor and color characteristics. These qualities are further differentiated by the skill of the producer and the year the trees are tapped.

Although birch syrup is produced generally in the same manner as maple syrup, there are several factors that account for the higher cost of birch syrup. Time is the first factor. While the sap run from maple trees usually lasts four to six weeks, with birch trees it is typically only two to three weeks. The sugar content of birch sap is also much lower. It takes about 100 gallons of birch sap to make 1 gallon of birch syrup, in contrast to the 40 gallons of maple sap needed, on average, to make 1 gallon of maple syrup. This means there is a significantly higher percentage of liquid to solids in birch syrup, and as a result, 99% of the water content of the birch sap must be removed. To save time and fuel, most commercial birch syrup producers begin processing by using a reverse osmosis machine to remove about 70% of the water, rather than just boiling down the sap as is done with maple syrup. The resulting liquid is further concentrated using a low-temperature evaporator designed to help prevent scorching, an increased risk with birch syrup due to its high fructose content.

The color of birch syrup can range from light amber to deep reddish brown depending on when the sap was tapped, the pH of the sap (which varies depending on the type of birch tree), and the temperature and time of cooking down the sap. Lighter syrups, from sap early in the season, are more subtle in flavor. They are a good choice as a table sweetener to top pancakes, waffles, oatmeal, yogurt, and ice cream, as well as for cooking and baking when a more delicate flavor is desired. The darker colored syrups have a more full-bodied, caramel-like taste that works well in all-purpose cooking and baking, including barbeque sauces, breads, granola, and cookies. It can also be used at the table as a more robust-flavored topping.

Products labeled "Alaskan birch syrup" are required to be made and produced in Alaska from Alaska paper birch sap. To use the term "pure birch syrup," the syrup must be from 100% Alaska paper birch sap concentrated to at least 66% but not more than 78% dissolved solids by weight (this is known as the Brix value) and free of any additional nutrients, additives, or chemicals, whether added intentionally or inadvertently.

Products labeled as "birch syrup," sometimes called breakfast-style birch syrup, are less expensive, milder, and sweeter because they're stabilized with added fructose. Labeling requirements stipulate that these syrups must contain a majority (51% by weight) of condensed Alaska paper birch sap, and no additives beyond fructose are allowed.

Storage and Cooking Guidelines

Store birch syrup in the refrigerator and use it within six months.

Birch syrup works best in recipes that call for liquid sweeteners with a high fructose content, such as agave nectar, concentrated fruit juice, and honey. When using it to replace conventional sugar, use an equal amount of birch syrup and decrease liquids by ¼ cup per each cup of birch syrup. Because of the high fructose content of birch syrup, baked goods will be moister, so cookies made with birch syrup will turn out soft rather than crisp. Baked goods will also be darker in color, as fructose-rich birch syrup caramelizes at a lower temperature than do sweeteners that consist primarily of sucrose. For a milder flavor or to extend its use, blend birch syrup with other sweeteners in recipes.

Brown Rice Syrup

Brown rice syrup, like barley malt, is relatively rich in complex carbohydrates, so its sugars are released into the bloodstream more slowly. Based on whole or partially polished brown rice, its finished consistency is also similar to that of barley malt syrup.

The flavor of brown rice syrup is caramel-like, with the intensity depending on how it's produced.

The traditional way to make brown rice syrup is to add a small amount of sprouted barley (or occasionally sprouted rice) to cooked brown rice. The diastatic enzymes from the sprouted barley break down the starches of the rice into about 45% maltose, 3% glucose, and 50% complex carbohydrates. It is then strained and cooked to yield a mildly sweet, golden syrup. Traditionally made rice syrup can be identified by the term "sprouted barley," "malted barley," "sprouted rice," or "malted rice" on the ingredient label. It is less sweet than table sugar or honey.

However, many varieties of brown rice syrup now on the market are made by using enzymes isolated from sprouted barley rather than sprouted barley itself. This allows manufacturers to control the amount and varieties of enzymes, so as with corn syrup, different types of rice syrup can be created depending on the intended use. In general, rice syrup made using isolated enzymes is sweeter than varieties made using traditional methods. While the extent of processing and the proportion of sugars will not be indicated on a label, these varieties generally contain 20% to 40% maltose, 20% to 35% glucose, and 30% to 40% complex carbohydrates. This type of rice syrup can be identified by the term "cereal enzymes" on the ingredient label, or they may simply say "brown rice, barley, water" or "brown rice, water."

The differences between traditional malted rice syrup and enzyme-treated rice syrup are apparent when baking. Enzyme-treated rice syrup will be higher in invert sugar (sucrose broken down into its glucose and fructose components) than traditional malted rice syrup, which means crystallization of sugars during baking will be hampered, making enzyme-treated rice syrup inappropriate for some applications. For example, cakes and muffins that are leavened with baking powder or baking soda should always be sweetened with traditional malted rice syrup. Those made with enzyme-treated rice syrups will tend to remain fairly flat and be goopy on the inside. Likewise, sweet-and-sour sauces or puddings thickened with arrowroot or kudzu are best sweetened with malted rice syrup.

On the other hand, because cookies have a low moisture content and aren't expected to rise to a large extent, they can be sweetened with either malted rice syrup or enzyme-treated rice syrup; they'll develop a crisp texture in either case. Marinades, salad dressings, toppings, and spreads that don't depend on added starch to create their texture or consistency can also be made with either malted rice syrup or enzyme-treated rice syrup.

Storage and Cooking Guidelines

Brown rice syrup can be stored at room temperature, but keeping it cool will reduce the tendency for mold to grow on the surface if condensation takes place in the jar.

When using rice syrup to replace conventional sugar, for each cup of sugar use 1 to 1¼ cups rice syrup, reduce the liquid by 3 tablespoons, and add about ⅛ to ¼ teaspoon of baking soda. Even though rice syrup is much less sweet than honey or corn syrup, experiment with using equal proportions of rice syrup when substituting for any of these more intense sweeteners. With time, you may find you prefer foods that are less sweet.

Cane Syrup

Cane syrup is a traditional sweetener that was commonly made right on the farm in many rural areas of the southern United States. Although production of cane syrup declined as the number of family farms declined and other sweeteners became more inexpensive, now there's a resurgence of interest in cane syrup, in part due to the increased appreciation of local and regional foods. It is made from sugarcane, which is crushed to extract the juice. In a process not unlike cooking down sap to make maple syrup, the juice is boiled down and impurities that rise to the top are skimmed off. After the juice has evaporated into a thickened syrup, it is strained and bottled. It takes 7 to 10 gallons of cane juice to make 1 gallon of cane syrup.

About half of the sugars in cane syrup are invert sugars (fructose and glucose), which help keep the cane syrup from crystallizing, along with about 25% to 30% sucrose. The long cooking time involved in the traditional method naturally caused some of the sucrose to convert to fructose and glucose. These days, some producers add an acid or invertase enzyme so they have better control of the process. In addition to reducing cooking time, this helps mellow out the flavor.

Storage and Cooking Guidelines

Unopened cane syrup can be stored up to two years. Once it's opened, refrigerate it to retard mold growth and use it within one year. Any crystals that form during storage can be dissolved by placing the container in warm water.

Golden to medium-brown in color, cane syrup has a mild but rich flavor with hints of butterscotch and a thick consistency. Drizzle it over hot biscuits or pancakes or use it as a sweetener for baked goods and general cooking. Substitute cane syrup for light molasses or sorghum syrup using equal measures. When using cane syrup to replace conventional sugar, for each cup of sugar use 1⅓ cups cane syrup and decrease the amount of liquid by ⅓ cup.

Date Sugar

Date sugar is made from dates first dehydrated to a 35% moisture level and then ground into a coarse, granular sugar. Its delicious, mild date flavor works well in recipes, contributing flavor and color somewhat similar to those of brown sugar. Compared to conventional sugar, date sugar is about two-thirds as sweet.

In addition to its natural sugars, date sugar retains many of the nutrients found in dried dates, most notably fiber and minerals. The specific proportions of sucrose, glucose, and fructose depends on the type of date, but the variety of date used to make the sugar is rarely revealed on the package. In general, glucose and fructose are the primary sugars found in most dates at the stage at which they're consumed, the result of action by the natural enzyme invertase, which breaks down much of the sucrose in the dates into its constituents, glucose and fructose. Known technically as invert sugars, these help enhance flavors and resist crystallization. As a result, they accelerate browning, help retain moisture, and contribute to a chewier, rather than crispy, texture.

The deglet noor variety of date is an exception, as the inversion process in this kind of date will be only partially complete at commercial maturity, leaving its sugar profile at nearly 50% sucrose and 25% each of glucose and fructose. Therefore, sugar made from deglet noor dates is higher in sucrose, which means it will perform more like conventional sugar in baked goods and yield somewhat crispier cookies.

Storage and Cooking Guidelines

Store date sugar tightly wrapped in the refrigerator or freezer to help prevent it from hardening. Many brands of date sugar contain a bit of oat flour to help prevent clumping.

Use date sugar as you would brown sugar, both as a sweetener on hot cereals and yogurt. It can be used for streusel-like toppings, but to prevent burning, this should be done near the end of the baking time. Brush the top of the baked good with oil or melted butter, sprinkle on the date sugar, and return it the oven for just 2 or 3 minutes. Date sugar can substituted for either brown or white sugar on a one-to-one basis in recipes for pancakes, cookies, breads, and muffins. Take a hint from the relative moisture inherent in brown sugar and emulate this characteristic when baking with date sugar by moistening it with some of the oil, melted but-

ter, or other liquid ingredients in a recipe. When substituting for honey, use ½ cup date sugar to equal ⅓ cup honey. Trial and error will determine whether you need to add an extra couple of tablespoons of liquid to compensate for the reduced liquid in the recipe.

Fruit-Based Sweeteners

I include dried fruit, fruit purees, and fruit juice, including concentrated fruit juice, in this category. Nothing beats the natural sweetness from fresh fruit picked at its peak of flavor. Whether fresh fruit is eaten as a snack, included in a meal, or served as a dessert, it's the pinnacle of the concept "naturally sweetened." Accordingly, it would seem to make sense that fruit would be the optimum choice as an added sweetener. However, its overall nutrient value and impact on metabolism depends on how far removed the fruit-derived sweetener is from fresh fruit. Freshly cut fruit, unsweetened fruit sauces and purees, and cooked dried fruit are the most healthful sweeteners because they retain most of the nutrients and fiber naturally found within the fruit. When used to sweeten a recipe, they can also replace some or all of the liquid ingredients. Additional concentrated sweetness can be achieved with uncooked dried fruit, which helps account for the frequent use of dried fruit in all kinds of baking and cooking.

Using these forms of whole fruits as sweetening agents contributes functional benefits beyond sweetening that aren't provided by other fruit-based sweeteners that are more processed. They help maintain freshness and moisture within the final product and also provide extra texture and bulk. Raisin puree will help soften the crumb in baked products. And the pectin in applesauce and plum or prune puree emulates some of the qualities of fat, so these fruit sweeteners can also be used to replace some of the fat in a recipe.

The next best kind of fruit-based sweetener is single-strength juices extracted from whole fruit.

To better appreciate how concentrated the sugars are in single-strength juice, keep in mind that few people could eat as much fruit in one sitting as it would take to make the amount of juice typically served. Juice can do an effective job as a subtle sweetener if it's used to replace some or all of the liquid in cooked hot cereals and baked goods. Juice can also be used instead of granulated sugar to create a delicious base and caramelized glaze when baking fresh fruit. However, the sugar content of single-strength fruit juice may be too low to achieve the level of sweetening typically desired in baked goods unless extra dried fruit or a small amount of another sweetener is added.

Concentrated forms of juice, such as juice concentrates (typically in frozen form), can do a better job as a sole sweetening agent. These concentrates are made by simply evaporating most of the water from the juice, concentrating the natural sugars (primarily fructose) but causing only a minimal loss of nutrients. To keep the aroma and flavor of the original fruit, the essence of the fruit is captured from the water vapor during manufacture and restored to the concentrate. Some brands also retain some of the fruit's pulp and fiber. Any flavor of fruit juice concentrate can be used as a sweetener, but apple and pear have the most neutral flavors. As any juice concentrate will also provide some color, lighter-colored versions are appropriate for lighter-colored dishes and baked goods.

The sweetening power of fruit juice concentrate can be further heightened by evaporating even more of its liquid, yielding a syrupy sweetener that is about one and a half times sweeter than white sugar. Although a ready-made extra-reduced fruit juice concentrate made from pear, peach, and pineapple juices is generally available at natural foods stores and specialty grocers, you can easily make a similar product at home using any flavor of juice concentrate. Bring it to a boil, then lower the heat and simmer for 10 minutes until about as thick as honey. This is similar to the process of boiling maple sap to make maple syrup, concentrating the sugars and transforming the concentrate into an intense sweetener high in fructose. This extra-reduced fruit juice concentrate is a very concentrated sweetener on par with both honey and maple syrup and should be used accordingly.

Both fruit juice concentrate and the extra-reduced version are naturally high in fructose, so when either is used as a sweetener or simply as an ingredient, it will help retain moisture in the finished product. For example, cookies will turn out moist and chewy rather than crisp.

But just because an ingredient is made with fruit doesn't make it good. At the other end of the spectrum are highly processed, decharacterized fruit juice concentrates often used by manufacturers to sweeten cookies and other baked goods, as well as jellies, syrups, beverages, and cereals. These specialized fruit juice concentrates are processed to heighten their sweetening power and for a neutral flavor, rather than to retain any characteristics of the original juice. Ultra-clarified through heat, enzyme processing, and filtration to remove all natural color, flavor, fiber, and nutrients from the juice, only the sugars stay behind. As a result, these decharacterized fruit juice concentrates affect the body like high-fructose corn syrup (HFCS) does.

When it comes to sweetening foods with fruit-based ingredients, your best bet is fresh or cooked fruit, dried fruit, single-strength juice, or minimally processed fruit juice concentrates.

Storage and Cooking Guidelines

All thawed frozen juice concentrates should be kept refrigerated and used within two weeks.

Experiment by substituting unsweetened fruit juice or fruit juice concentrates for part or all the liquids called for in a recipe in place of sugar, but avoid fruit juice that is too acidic in yeasted breads, as it can interfere with the action of yeast. Try using up to ½ cup of dried fruit per loaf of bread or muffin recipe to provide added sweetness. When substituting fruit juice concentrate for granulated sugar in recipes, use an equal amount and reduce the amount of liquids by ⅓ cup for each cup of sugar replaced. When substituting extra-reduced fruit juice concentrate for conventional sugar, use ½ to ⅔ cup per cup of granulated sugar and reduce the amount of liquid by approximately ⅓ cup for each cup of sugar replaced. In most recipes, extra-reduced juice concentrate can be substituted for agave nectar on a one-to-one basis. To prevent the acidity of fruit juice or any form of concentrated fruit juice from affecting the leavening process, add ¼ teaspoon baking soda per recipe when making cookies, pancakes, muffins, and quick breads. Whenever substituting fruit juice (in any form) for sugar, lower the oven temperature by 25°F.

Honey

Honey is extracted from honeycombs, where bees store the result of endless hours of labor, starting with bringing nectar from flowers back to the hive. Created through quite an elaborate process, honey comes to us already concentrated and ready to use, with no additional processing required.

The process begins when bees collect flower nectar and put it into their internal storage area, the honey sac, in order to transport it back to the hive. At the hive, house bees take the nectar and work on evaporating water out of the nectar. The nectar is then deposited in the hexagonal cylinders of the honeycomb, which is built from wax secreted from the glands of worker bees inside the hive. In a process called ripening, the honey is further evaporated through the action of bees fanning their wings and concentrated by additional enzymes to the point where it can be stored without crystallizing. When a honeycomb cell is filled to capacity, it is capped with more wax. Considering that one pound of honey represents nectar collected from about two million flowers, it is a very valuable sweetener, indeed. Not only that, but it is relatively inexpensive, is widely available, and tastes great.

When beekeepers are ready to extract the honey, they remove the honeycomb and pack it in one of three ways: in smaller pieces as comb honey; as chunk honey, in which a piece of comb honey is covered with liquid honey; or as straight liquid honey, derived by spinning the honeycomb in a centrifuge to separate out the wax. Liquid honey may undergo an optional heat and pasteurization treatment at temperatures that range from 140°F to 170°F, depending on the method used to delay crystallization and prevent fermentation. Honey is sometimes filtered to remove pollen grains and small air bubbles that could cause cloudiness. However, the many beekeepers who prefer to retain all the natural flavor and nutritional properties of honey intact simply strain it to remove any wax and other extraneous particles, then let it settle to take care of any air bubbles naturally. As heat can adversely affect the finer, more subtle attributes of honey, the less processing, the better.

Creamed or whipped honey has purposely been crystallized, using a controlled process to create a smooth, easily spreadable consistency rather than the coarse, grainy texture that occurs when honey crystallizes spontaneously. In this process, honey is heated twice, once to 120°F and then to 150° F, and then seeded with dried, finely ground honey to start and end the crystallization process under controlled conditions.

Honey can be packed as a varietal, a specific type of honey created by focusing the bees on one kind of flower, or as a combination of two or more kinds of honey selected to create a specific blend. Common varietals include clover, orange blossom, buckwheat, alfalfa, fireweed, and basswood, but there are thousands of other types reflecting the plants that grow or are cultivated in specific regions. The color, aroma, flavor, and composition of honey depend on the flower from which the bees extracted the nectar.

There are an estimated three thousand varietals worldwide, including three hundred in the United

States, each with unique characteristics: colors ranging from white to dark amber, aromas and flavors that can be subtle or bold, and viscosities ranging from very thin to very thick.

The color is associated with the specific flower and the mineral content of the nectar. In general, the darker the color of the honey is, the bolder the flavor. For example, dark honeys such as buckwheat or heather are much stronger in flavor than light-colored orange blossom and clover honeys. Basswood, with its water-white color and strong, somewhat biting flavor, is an exception. Due in part to their higher protein content, darker-colored honey promotes surface browning of products that are baked, cooked, and roasted. Accordingly, choose lighter-colored honey when sweetening foods and beverages, where its golden hue is more appropriate. White honey is ideal when no additional color is desired.

The sugar profile of honey also affects its flavor and function. The predominant sugar in honey is fructose, followed by glucose, some maltose, and only a minute percentage of sucrose. Like other sweeteners high in fructose, honey tastes sweeter than granulated sugar, as much as one and a half times as sweet. There will be some variations in perceived sweetness among the many varieties of honey due to differences in the ratio of fructose to glucose among the floral sources. Honeys higher in fructose, such as tupelo and black button sage, will taste very sweet, while those with a higher percentage of glucose will taste less sweet in comparison. Honeys with a higher fructose content also tend to resist crystallization, whereas those with higher levels of glucose, such as lavender, lehua, and Tasmanian leatherwood, will crystallize quickly.

Beyond Sweetening

Like most highly concentrated sweeteners, honey can act as a preservative. However, it also has antimicrobial and antioxidant properties, both of which are beneficial to human health and a clear indication that there is more to honey than its sweetening powers. Recognized for centuries as an agent that can discourage the growth and persistence of microorganisms, honey was commonly used medicinally when dressing wounds. In fact, the antimicrobial properties of some varieties of honey can actually be so potent as to make them unsuitable for baking, because they can kill yeast and preventing leavening. However, this is the exception rather than the rule, especially as honeys with very high antimicrobial activity would generally be too expensive or too strongly flavored to be used as an ingredient. Nonetheless, to play it safe, some bread bakers stick with milder flavored honey, such as clover honey.

Darker honeys also tend to contain more antioxidants, in the form of the phytonutrients known as polyphenols. Because these compounds can slow oxidation in foods, including rancidity, adding honey to foods serves as a natural alternative to chemical antioxidant preservatives, such as BHT and BHA, which are also phenols. And, since honey supplies dietary antioxidants, it has the potential, even when heated or used in cooking, to help retard chemical reactions within the body that have been linked to many chronic diseases.

Some people also swear by using honey extracted from hives in their region as a way to boost tolerance to local pollens. Though this hasn't been proven by scientific studies, it's a widespread belief, and there's certainly no harm in the practice.

Given all of these potential health benefits, honey may be among the best sweeteners for contributing not just flavor but also well-being. However, it should *never* be given to a child under the age of one in any form, including via pacifiers, as a sweetener in beverages, or in food. Infant botulism is a rare but serious paralytic disease caused by the microorganism *Clostridium botulinum*, which may be present in honey in the form of spores. In infants whose intestinal microflora is still underdeveloped, the spores can germinate and grow in the lower bowel. Symptoms of infant botulism include constipation, lethargy, a weak cry, feeble sucking, and general muscular weakness. If any of these symptoms are present, the infant should be taken to a doctor immediately.

Storage and Cooking Guidelines

Store honey tightly sealed at room temperature. For optimum flavor and to prevent unwanted crystallization, raw honey should be stored at or below 50°F. Honey that has been pasteurized or heat-processed can be stored between 64°F and 75°F. Honey can be held at higher temperatures for brief periods of time, but avoid storing it near heat sources, such as a stove or an oven. Honey that does crystallize can be used as such, or you can restore it to a liquid state by placing the jar in lukewarm water.

As a flavor enhancer, honey not only intensifies sweetness, but also decreases the perception of sourness (think yogurt or sour cream), bitterness (think chocolate or coffee), and saltiness (think cheese or salted nuts), further explaining its wide use in cooking and baking and as a condiment and topping. Since honey typically has higher levels of fructose, it has humectant qualities, so baked goods sweetened with honey retain moisture and stay fresher longer, and cookies made with honey have with a softer, rather than crispy, texture. Likewise, as fructose caramelizes at lower temperatures than sucrose, honey helps enhance browning.

If substituting honey for conventional sugar, use ½ to ¾ cup honey per cup sugar. Reduce the liquid by about ¼ cup for each cup of honey used. For improved volume and color in baked goods, add ¼ teaspoon baking soda per cup of honey to neutralize its acidity. Since honey caramelizes at lower temperatures, reduce oven temperature by 25°F. Honey can be substituted for birch syrup using the same amount as indicated in the recipe. If replacing date sugar in a recipe, use ⅓ cup honey as a substitute for ½ cup date sugar, reducing

dry ingredients as needed to compensate for the increased moisture added to the recipe from the honey.

Maple Syrup and Maple Sugar

Maple syrup is a natural sweetener wrapped in tradition. Native Americans taught early settlers the technique for concentrating the sap that flows from sugar maples in the early spring, and although the process has been updated since that time, festivities associated with the annual ritual of maple sugaring exist to this day.

Of all the varieties of maple, the sugar maple (*Acer saccharum*), also known as hard maple, produces the best sap. Most of the world's maple syrup is produced in eastern Canada, followed by the northeastern United States, where sugar maples are abundant and weather conditions are optimum for maple sap flow. In fact, the maple tree is so significant to Canada that in 1965 they adopted the now-familiar flag, which features the outline of a maple leaf.

Maple sugaring starts as spring approaches and temperatures start to fluctuate, with nights below freezing and warmer days above freezing. The frozen sap, stored in the tree during the previous growing season, begins to thaw, creating internal pressure within the tree and causing the sap to flow out of any wound on the tree. Maple sugar producers capitalize on this phenomenon and purposely create tap holes on the trees to capture the flow. The alternating freeze-thaw process during the four- to six-week tapping window causes the trees to take up water from the soil, which replenishes the sap so it will flow again the next day, when it's warm. The flow stops when the leaf buds begin to emerge and the freeze-thaw weather pattern ends. In the past, some producers put paraformaldehyde pellets into tap holes to boost production, but this is now illegal.

Each day the sap is collected and it must be boiled down as soon as possible that very day to

Guide to Maple Syrup Grades

- U.S. Grade A Light Amber, Vermont Fancy, or Canadian No. 1 Extra Light: These syrups, made from first sap flows of the season, have a delicate maple flavor and are best for table use.
- U.S. and Vermont Grade A Medium Amber or Canadian No. 1 Light Grade A: This is the most popular grade for pancakes. Generally made from the midseason sap run, it has a slightly darker, amber color and a gentle but more pronounced flavor. It's great for table use and good for cooking and baking.

- U.S. and Vermont Grade A Dark Amber or Canadian No. 1 Medium Grade A: Generally made later in the season, this grade is darkly colored and richly flavored. It's great for table use and good for cooking and baking.
- U.S. Grade B, Vermont Grade B, Canadian No. 2 Amber: Even darker in color and stronger in flavor, this grade is generally the last produced in the season. It's best for cooking and baking and good for table use.

ensure good quality and taste. The watery sap only has about 2% sucrose, so it must be evaporated until it's concentrated to about 65% sucrose, with a Brix level (a measure of the density of syrup), between 66% and 67%, high enough to prevent potential fermentation but low enough to avoid crystallization of the sugars.

The traditional method of evaporating the sap is to boil it for many hours, but to save energy and time, reverse osmosis devices are now often used to remove 75% of the water without heat. The evaporation process is then completed by boiling, which develops the characteristic flavors and color of maple syrup. Minute amounts of a fatty substance, usually vegetable oil or a commercial defoamer made from vegetable fat, are sometimes added to help keep excessive foam from boiling over during the procedure. Some smaller producers might still use butter or whole milk, which are more traditional. When used in small quantities, defoamers will evaporate, not leaving a noticeable trace in the syrup. The syrup is then filtered to remove any gritty minerals (referred to as "sugar sand") and any other solids.

Maple Syrup Grading Systems

The grading of maple syrup is based on color and flavor, which are dependent on when during the season the sap was obtained, the weather during the sugaring period, and the skill of the producer. In general, lighter-colored, more delicately flavored syrups are produced in the earlier stages of the sap run. Syrups that are darker and more concentrated are from later in the season. As the weather warms and the tree goes from winter dormancy into springtime mode, the mineral content of the sap increases and other metabolic changes occur that result in syrups with a deeper, more caramelized flavor.

There are three grading systems used for maple syrup intended for retail sale. The grades they denote are roughly equivalent, with the main difference being in the terms used. The U.S. Department of Agriculture standards are a voluntary system developed to allow for standardized inspection and grading system of maple syrup in the United States. Vermont's quality standards, in place before the USDA standards were created, are required for syrup labeled as "Vermont maple syrup." In Canada, federally mandated standards govern strict labeling and grading requirements for all maple syrup produced in and exported from Canada.

Thanks to strict laws in both the United States and Canada, it is easy to distinguish imitation maple products from the real thing. Neither country allows the terms "maple syrup" or "maple sugar" to appear on products that aren't pure. Instead, phrases such as "pancake syrup with artificial maple flavor" or "artificial maple flavor sweetener" are required to ensure consumers are not misled.

Their high sucrose content also means that maple products will metabolize similarly to conventional sugars. However, it is preferable in terms of nutrient content, most notably calcium and potassium, along with smaller amounts of manganese, magnesium, phosphorus, iron, zinc, and the B vitamins pantothenic acid and niacin. That said, maple syrup, like any sweetener, should be used in moderation.

Other Maple Products

Maple cream is made by further boiling maple syrup to remove more moisture, stirring it as it cools so the crystals essentially become undetectable, leaving a creamy consistency. It is always created from U.S. Grade A Light Amber syrup (Vermont Fancy, Canadian No.1 Extra Light), as it has the lowest amount of invert sugars. Because the fructose component of invert sugars is hygroscopic, using maple syrup that contains too much invert sugar could cause excess moisture to be retained, interfering with the level of crystallization needed to create maple cream. Use maple cream as a topping for toast, pancakes, or muffins, or mix it with butter for a frosting.

Granulated maple sugar, the crystallized form of maple syrup, can be used just like conventional granulated sugar. It is made by heating maple syrup to about 252°F to 257°F, which causes it to crystallize as it cools. After it's transferred to a flat pan to quickly cool, the maple syrup is stirred until crystallization occurs and then put through a screen to achieve uniform granule size. Like maple syrup, its sugar is primarily sucrose, although there is some amount of invert sugar as a consequence of the heating process. In a pinch, maple sugar could be cooked back into syrup by combining it with a small amount of water until the desired consistency is achieved.

Storage

Even though maple syrup purchased in metal tins or cans may have a quaint, old-fashioned feel, this can give the syrup a metallic flavor. Your best bet is to buy maple syrup in a glass container or transfer any maple syrup purchased in a can into a sterilized glass container. Maple syrup can be stored in a food-grade plastic container for three to six months, but since plastic is porous, changes in both flavor and color may occur. Nonporous plastic jugs are preferable, as they will keep out oxygen, which can negatively affect the syrup.

The shelf life of unopened containers of maple syrup stored at room temperature is about six to eight months. However, storing it in the freezer will help retain its flavor and quality indefinitely. If properly manufactured, maple syrup will not freeze, and after only an hour at room temperature, it will be of a suitable pouring consistency. It's most practical to store a smaller amount in the refrigerator so it's ready for use. At a minimum, all opened maple syrup should be stored in the refrigerator and used within six months. The cool temperatures will slow fermentation and prevent mold formation. Any crystals that form can be dissolved by gently warming the syrup.

Any syrup that develops an off flavor should be discarded. Technically, any mold that forms on top can be skimmed off; after doing so, reheat the syrup to around 190°F or to a slight boil, filter it, then transfer it to a sterilized container. If the syrup still has an off flavor, it should be discarded.

Granulated maple sugar has a shelf life of ten to twelve months when stored in a cool, dry place.

Maple cream can be kept for up to two weeks in the refrigerator. For longer periods, it should be stored in the freezer and brought to room temperature before use.

Cooking Guidelines

In baking and cooking, the functionality of maple syrup relates to the fact that its predominant sugar is sucrose (88% to 99%). During processing, a small amount of the sucrose may be converted into fructose and glucose, especially in darker syrups. This may explain why different textures, although slight, may occur in baked goods depending on the grade of syrup used. When it comes to baking cookies, maple syrup will produce a crisp texture similar to that produced by other sweeteners that are also high in sucrose, such as conventional sugar. In fact, granulated maple sugar can be substituted for conventional granulated sugar on a one-to-one basis in recipes and give similar results. The only downside is the price.

Besides topping pancakes and hot cereals, maple syrup can be used to sweeten cookies, cakes, muffins, and granola. When using it to replace conventional sugar, for each cup of sugar use ¾ cup maple syrup and decrease the liquid by 3 tablespoons. Add ¼ teaspoon of baking soda per cup of maple syrup to counter its acidity. Maple syrup can be substituted for honey on a one-to-one basis, but it will change the texture of the finished product.

Molasses

Molasses is a thick syrup made from sugarcane juice. It was the primary, all-purpose sweetener in Colonial America for baking, spreading on breads, making candy, and flavoring meat, and it remained popular until just after World War I, when granulated sugar became more affordable and took the lead. Ranging from golden brown and sweet to brownish black and somewhat bitter, the various colors, flavors, and grades of molasses reflect how the molasses was processed, whether as a direct reduction

from the sugarcane juice or as a by-product from one of the stages of the sugar-making process. Sugarcane is always the source for molasses for human consumption. Molasses made from sugar beets has a strong fishy odor due to several inherent mineral salts, so it is added into cattle feed and also used for the production of yeast and citric acid.

Molasses is often touted as a good food source of iron, calcium, potassium, and magnesium, with blackstrap molasses considered the best. In fact, its calcium content explains why molasses is often added to baked bean recipes; it helps the beans retain their shape during the long cooking process. Even though the amounts of these nutrients are fairly small per tablespoon, any extra nutrients in concentrated sugars is always a plus. Still, it is best to treat it as you would any other sweetener, using it in moderation rather than eating it by the spoonful as a dietary supplement.

Although most molasses sold to consumers is unsulfured, look for the term "unsulfured" on the label to be sure that's what you're getting. Molasses processed with sulfur dioxide is significantly inferior in flavor. If manufacturers use mature raw materials and clarify the juice during processing, sulfur dioxide is entirely unnecessary in the refining process.

Varieties of Molasses

Fancy molasses, sometimes referred to as original molasses, is the highest grade of molasses and the best tasting. It's made from sugarcane juice from which the sugar has not been extracted, which is filtered and slowly boiled down into syrup. The term Barbados is still often used to denote this high-quality molasses, originally used in reference to the island of Barbados, which was noted for its exceptional fancy molasses, not to mention its rum. Fancy molasses has a sweet, mild, light flavor and a rich amber color. Use it as a table syrup to top pancakes, biscuits, bread, and hot cereals and as a sweetener for baked goods. It is also good in marinades and sauces.

Molasses produced as a by-product of sugar refining will have a look and taste that reflects the particular stages of the sugar crystallization process from which it is derived. The later in the process the molasses is extracted, the darker, more strongly flavored, and less sweet it will be.

Dark or cooking molasses may be a by-product from the second stage of sugar crystallization or a blend of fancy molasses for sweetness and thinner consistency and blackstrap molasses for robust flavor. Darker in color and having a more pronounced flavor, these types of molasses are best for general cooking, flavoring, and baking rather than as a table syrup. Foods made with dark or cooking molasses will be less sweet and darker in color than those made with fancy molasses.

Blackstrap molasses is the final syrup left after crystallizing the conventional sugar from sugarcane. Its dark color is due to caramelization that occurs during repeated boiling during processing. It is slightly bitter or tart—a combined effect of its concentrated mineral content and the various chemical reactions that occur during the repeated boiling. Blackstrap molasses can be used in baking when a stronger flavor is desired. Alternatively, it could be blended with other types of molasses or other sweeteners to mellow its punch.

The functionality of each type of molasses depends on its sugar profile, which, like color and taste, is also determined by how the molasses was produced. All molasses will contain sucrose from the sugarcane as well as some invert sugars (fructose and glucose) depending on the temperatures and length of time in the evaporation process. Fancy molasses, the least processed, will have the highest sucrose content and lower amounts of both invert sugars and minerals. At the other end of the spectrum, blackstrap molasses will have the least amount of sucrose and more invert sugars and minerals. Dark or cooking molasses will be somewhere in the middle. The higher the level of invert sugars, the more the molasses will help retain moisture in baked goods and the less likely it will be to crystallize.

Storage and Cooking Guidelines

Store molasses in a dry, cool area away from heat and humidity. Both fancy and dark molasses can be kept for one to two years, while three months or less is optimum for blackstrap molasses.

Molasses can be substituted equally for cane syrup and sorghum syrup. When using molasses to replace conventional sugar, for each cup of sugar use 1⅓ cups molasses and decrease the liquid by ⅓ cup. Since baked goods sweetened with molasses tend to darken more quickly, reduce the oven temperature by 25°F. It's a good idea to add ½ teaspoon baking soda per cup of molasses in recipes for baked goods to counteract its acidity; this will result in improved leavening.

Sorghum Syrup

Sorghum syrup is the concentrated juice of the sweet sorghum plant. A plant that looks similar to millet, this grain with sweet juicy stems is grown specifically for the production of syrup, especially in the southeastern United States. Sorghum varieties with a lower sugar content are used primarily as livestock feed, and also as a food grain for humans in some countries. Though it was quite popular in years past, use of sorghum syrup declined as the price of sugar decreased and corn syrup became more widely available. However, it is still produced and is especially appreciated in southern states, where this regional product is traditionally poured on hot biscuits and pancakes or used as a sweetener in breads.

It takes about 6 to 12 gallons of sweet sorghum juice to make 1 gallon of sorghum syrup. After the juice is extracted from the sorghum by crushing the stalks, it is filtered to remove any stalk fragments and other impurities. The juice is then allowed to settle for a few hours to minimize any potential starch development that could cause the syrup to gel. Depending on the season and variety of sweet sorghum grown, the enzyme amylase (also called malt diastase) is occasionally added to help break down excessive starch into sugars.

The sorghum juice is then evaporated by heat in open pans, and skimmed continuously to remove proteins and starches that float to the top. The enzyme invertase may be added at this point to convert some of the sucrose into glucose and fructose so the syrup is easier to cook and less likely to crystallize in the process. The syrup is done when it has been concentrated into a clear, amber-colored, mildly sweet, sometimes tangy syrup that has a Brix level of 78% to 80%. In the process, sorghum syrup's natural mineral content, including potassium, calcium, magnesium, zinc, and iron, is also further concentrated. The finished syrup is quickly cooled to retain as much of its natural color as possible, strained, and then sterilized by boiling before it's packed into containers.

The sugar profile of sorghum syrup is mostly invert sugars (with slightly more glucose than fructose), with about 25% to 30% sucrose and a very small amount of maltose. In addition to helping it resist crystallization, the high levels of invert sugars means it helps retain moisture in baked goods, creates softer textures in cookies, and, in general, functions similarly to other liquid sweeteners, such as molasses, cane syrup, and honey.

Storage and Cooking Guidelines

Unopened sorghum syrup can be stored for up to two years. Once opened, it should be refrigerated to retard mold growth and be used within one year. Discard the syrup if any mold develops. Any crystallization is easily remedied by placing the jar in warm water.

When using sorghum syrup to replace conventional sugar, for each cup of sugar use 1⅓ cups sorghum syrup and decrease the liquids by ⅓ cup. An equal amount of sorghum syrup can be used to replace barley malt syrup, cane syrup, and light molasses in most recipes, with the exception of cookies and cakes that use baking powder. In contrast, recipes that use baking soda rather than baking powder will work well.

Stevia

Stevia rebaudiana, a plant indigenous to Paraguay and Brazil, has been used as a sweetener by the native people in these areas for hundreds of years. Its sweet taste, ranging from two hundred to three hundred times sweeter than sucrose, is from two primary constituents in the leaves, stevioside and rebaudioside, the latter being less bitter and astringent. In contrast to artificial sweeteners marketed as no-calorie alternatives to sugar, stevia has the merit of being a natural, plant-based substance. Because stevia's sweetness is from glycosides that the human body can't completely metabolize, it is also free of calories and, unlike many artificial sweeteners, its sweetness remains stable under heat.

Stevia has a long history of use in South America and has also been used for many years in Japan, China, and Central America without reports of adverse effects. Despite this, stevia still lacks regulatory approval in North American, European, and Australian markets as a sweetener in food, making it illegal to market it as such. Ironically, however, stevia can be sold as a dietary supplement in the United States, Canada, Australia, and New Zealand, generally in a form that retains its sweet-tasting characteristics. Several countries, including Canada, are conducting trials to determine the feasibility of growing it as a crop, indicating that wider regulatory approval as a sweetener may occur in the future.

Sugars: White, Brown, and Specialty Granulations

Although all forms of sweeteners consist of concentrated sugars, when the general term *sugar* is used, it commonly refers to the granulated sweetener extracted from sugarcane or sugar beets. In

Sugar Substitution Guide

Here are some handy guidelines for substituting alternative sweeteners for conventional granulated or brown sugar. For each cup of sugar make the following adjustments to amounts of ingredients:

Type	Substitute per 1 Cup Sugar	Liquids in Recipe	Other Modifications
Agave nectar	¾ cup	Decrease ⅓ cup	Lower oven by 25°F
Barley malt syrup	1⅓ cups	Decrease ¼ cup	Add ¼ tsp. baking soda
Birch syrup	1 cup	Decrease ¼ cup	
Brown rice syrup	1–1¼ cup	Decrease 3 tbsp.	Add ⅛–¼ tsp. baking soda
Cane syrup	1⅓ cups	Decrease ⅓ cup	
Corn syrup	¾ cup	Decrease 3 tbsp.	
Date sugar	1 cup		Substitute for brown sugar
Fruit juice concentrate (thawed)	1 cup	Decrease ⅓ cup	Add ¼ tsp. baking soda. Lower oven by 25°
Fruit juice concentrate (extra reduced)	½–¾ cup	Decrease ⅓ cup	Add ¼ tsp. baking soda. Lower oven by 25°F
Honey	½–¾ cup	Decrease 2–3 tbsp.	Add ¼ tsp. baking soda
Maple sugar	1 cup		
Maple Syrup	¾ cup	Decrease 3 tbsp.	Add ¼ tsp. baking soda
Molasses	1⅓ cup	Decrease ⅓ cup	Add scant ½ tsp. baking soda. Lower oven by 25°F
Sorghum syrup	1⅓ cup	Decrease ⅓ cup	

addition to adding sweetness and enhancing flavor, as all sweeteners do, the high sucrose content of granulated sugar provides unique texture and other characteristics when used in baking and cooking. Most cookies made with granular sugar have a crisp, almost crystalline texture upon cooling. The more molasses retained in the sugar during processing, the softer the baked goods made with it will be. Sugar's contribution to the color of baked goods also often depends on the level of refinement: the less refined the sugar, the darker the baked good. When granulated sugar and fat are creamed together, it incorporates air into the batter, producing exceptionally light and tender baked goods, a quality that's accentuated by sugar's tendency to inhibit gluten formation.

Despite praise for both its sweetness and its functional attributes in food, sugar has also been maligned for much of its history because of its degree of refinement and the accompanying reduction in nutrients. Nonetheless, it is, indeed, a naturally derived sweetener, and, as such, will always be a significantly better option than other more highly processed nutritive and artificial sweeteners. And because of the wide range of sugar products representing varying degrees of refinement, there's usually a sugar available that can generally fit most any need

The refining process generally starts with juice pressed from crushed sugarcane or a solution derived from soaking sugar beets in hot water to extract their sugar. In both cases, the liquid is

then put through a series of steps, including purification, filtration, evaporation, crystallization,
and centrifuging, to produce, at the far end of the
process, white crystalline sugar.

Varieties of Refined Sugar

Although evaporated cane juice, milled golden
cane sugar, and golden castor sugar, considered
first-crystallization sugars, don't undergo all of the
stages of refinement because they're finely granulated, they function much like white sugar than
darker first-crystallization sugars, like turbinado
and Demerara. The subtle taste and slight golden
or tan color of evaporated cane juice and milled
golden cane sugar reflect the fact that more molasses was removed during the process of centrifuging
them. Both can be used interchangeably with white
sugar in most recipes.

■ LIGHT, DARK, AND SPECIALTY
BROWN SUGARS

There are many varieties of brown sugar: the common light and dark varieties of soft brown sugar, as
well as specialty brown sugars such as Sucanat, turbinado, amber crystal, Demerara, and muscovado.
Although they could be used interchangeably, each
has a unique level of moisture and different quality
of crystal. Experiment to see which varieties you
prefer for different uses or to figure out how the
recipes should be adjusted for best results.

Sucanat, a registered trademark, is an acronym
for *sugar cane natural*. This type of sugar is also
referred to as "dehydrated cane juice." Its porous,
dark granules are derived before the first crystallization process, resulting in a rich molasses flavor.
Sucanat is good for baking, sauces, and sweetening
beverages.

Turbinado is a light golden brown sugar from
the first crystallization process with a mild molasses flavor and medium-size granules. It's a good
all-purpose brown sugar for baking, sweetening
beverages, sprinkling on hot cereals and fruit, and
using in toppings, rubs, and sauces.

Amber crystal, known as coffee sugar in the
United Kingdom, is a coarsely granulated, light
golden brown sugar from the first crystallization
process. It's especially good in coffee due to its
texture.

Demerara is a crunchy, slightly sticky, coarsely
granulated, light golden brown sugar from the first
crystallization process. It has a mild molasses flavor
and is good for sweetening beverages, sprinkling
on hot cereals and fruits, and using in crunchy toppings on cookies, cakes, muffins, and desserts.

Light muscovado is a moist, fine-grained, light
brown sugar with a butterscotch flavor. It's good
for cookies, cakes, puddings, and sauces.

Dark muscovado is an extra-moist, sticky,
fine-grained dark brown sugar with a rich toffee
flavor and more molasses than is in light muscovado sugar. (Molasses sugar is dark muscovado
sugar that contains extra molasses.) It is good for
cookies, chocolate cakes, fruit cakes, puddings,
and sauces.

Bibliography

INTRODUCTION
Articles and Reports

Guigliano, D., and K. Esposito. "Mediterranean Diet and Cardiovascular Health." *Annals of the New York Academy of Sciences* (November 2005).

Knoops, K. T., L. C. de Groot, D. Kromhout, et al. "Mediterranean Diet, Lifestyle Factors, and 10-Year Mortality in Elderly European Men and Women: The HALE Project." *Journal of the American Medical Association* (September 22, 2004).

Willet, W. C. "The Mediterranean Diet: Science and Practice." *Public Health Nutrition* (February 2006).

Willett, W. C., F. Sacks, A. Trichopoulou, et al. "Mediterranean Diet Pyramid: A Cultural Model for Healthy Eating." *American Journal of Clinical Nutrition* (June 1995).

World Health Organization and Food and Agricultural Organization Joint Expert Consultation. "Diet, Nutrition, and the Prevention of Chronic Diseases." *WHO Technical Report Series* 916 (2003).

FRUITS AND VEGETABLES
Books

Brennan, G., I. Cronin, and C. Glenn. *The New American Vegetable Cookbook*. Berkeley, CA: Aris Books, 1985.

Creasy, R. *The Edible Flower Garden*. Singapore: Periplus, 1999.

Creasy, R. *The Edible Herb Garden*. Singapore: Periplus, 1999.

Green, A. *Field Guide to Produce*. Philadelphia: Quirk Books, 2004.

Heaton, D. D. *A Produce Reference Guide to Fruits and Vegetables from Around the World*. Binghamton, NY: Food Products Press, 1997.

Schneider, E. *The Essential Reference: Vegetables from Amaranth to Zucchini*. New York: William Morrow, 2001.

Schneider, E. *Uncommon Fruits and Vegetables: A Commonsense Guide*. New York: William Morrow, 1986.

Smith, M. *Your Backyard Herb Garden*. Emmaus, PA: Rodale Press, 1997.

Weil, A. *Eating Well for Optimum Health*. New York: Alfred A. Knopf, 2000.

Willett, W. C. *Eat, Drink, and Be Healthy*. New York: Free Press, 2001.

Articles and Reports

Cho, E., J. M. Seddon, B. Rosner, et al. "Prospective Study of Intake of Fruits, Vegetables, Vitamins, and Carotenoids and Age-Related Maculopathy." *Archives of Ophthalmology* (June 2004).

De Lorgeril, M., P. Salen, J. L. Martin, et al. "Mediterranean Dietary Pattern in a Randomized Trial: Prolonged Survival and Possible Reduced Cancer Rate." *Archives of Internal Medicine* (June 8, 1998).

DeMuth, S. "Vegetables and Fruits: A Guide to Heirloom Varieties and Community-Based Stewardship." www.nal.usda.gov/afsic/AFSIC_pubs/heirloom/heirloom.htm (March 1999).

DeWitt, D. "The Chiles in Chili." www.fiery-foods.com/dave/chiliconcarne3.asp.

Diver, S. "Biodynamic Farming and Compost Preparation." http://attra.ncat.org/attra-pub/biodynamic.html (1999).

Djousse, L., D. K. Arnett, H. Coon, et al. "Fruit and Vegetable Consumption and LDL Cholesterol: The National Heart, Lung, and Blood Institute Family Heart Study." *American Journal of Clinical Nutrition* (February 2004).

Dufour, R. "Biointensive Integrated Pest Management." www.attra.ncat.org/attra-pub/ipm.html (2001).

Giovannucci, E. "Tomato Products, Lycopene, and Prostate Cancer: A Review of the Epidemiological Literature." *Journal of Nutrition* (August 2005).

Giugliano, D., and K. Esposito. "Mediterranean Diet and Cardiovascular Health." *Annals of the New York Academy of Science* (November 2005).

Harvard School of Public Health. "Fruits and Vegetables." www.hsph.harvard.edu/nutritionsource/fruits.html (2007).

Hung, H. C., K. J. Joshhipura, R. Jiang, et al. "Fruit and Vegetable Intake and Risk of Major Chronic Disease." *Journal of the National Cancer Institute* (November 3, 2004).

Lu, C., K. Toepel, R. Irish, et al. "Organic Diets Significantly Lower Children's Dietary Exposure to Organophosphorous Pesticides." *Environmental Health Perspectives* (September 1, 2005).

Mares-Perlman, J. A., A. I. Fisher, R. Klein, et al. "Lutein and Zeaxanthin in the Diet and Serum and Their Relation to Age-Related Maculopathy in the Third National Health and Nutrition Examination Survey." *American Journal of Epidemiology* (March 1, 2001).

Maynard, M., D. Gunnell, P. Emmett, et al. "Fruit, Vegetables, and Antioxidants in Childhood and Risk of Adult Cancer: The Boyd Orr Cohort." *Journal of Epidemiology and Community Health* (March 2003).

Rentschler, K. "Harvesting, Using, and Storing Fresh Herbs." *Cook's Illustrated* (July/August 2000).

University of Minnesota Division of Epidemiology and Community Health. "The Seven Countries Study in Brief." www.epi.umn.edu/about/7countries/overview.shtm (July 9, 2003).

U.S. Department of Agriculture Agricultural Research Service. "Phytonutrient FAQs." www.ars.usda.gov/Aboutus/docs.htm?docid=4142 (April 8, 2005).

U.S. Food and Drug Administration Center for Food Safety and Applied Nutrition. "Note to Firms That Grow, Condition, Store, or Distribute Seed for Sprouting and to Firms That Produce, Pack, or Ship Fresh Sprouts." www.cfsan.fda.gov/~dms/sproltr.html (August 19, 2004).

U.S. Food and Drug Administration Center for Food Safety and Applied Nutrition. "Safe Handling of Raw Produce and Fresh-Squeezed Fruit and Vegetable Juices." www.cfsan.fda.gov/~dms/prodsafe.html (July 12, 2006).

Willett, W. C. "Diet and Health: What Should We Eat?" *Science* (April 22, 1994).

Willett, W. C. "The Mediterranean Diet: Science and Practice." *Public Health Nutrition* (February 2006).

GRAINS
Books

Bastianich, L. M. *Lidia's Italian Table.* New York: William Morrow, 1998.

Cook's Illustrated editors. *The Complete Book of Pasta and Noodles.* New York: Clarkson Potter Publishers, 2000.

Corriher, S. *CookWise: The Secrets of Cooking Revealed.* New York: William Morrow, 1997.

Divina, F., and M. Divina. *Foods of the Americas: Native Recipes and Traditions.* Berkeley, CA: Ten Speed Press, 2004.

Dominé, A., ed. *Organic and Whole Foods: Naturally Delicious Cuisine.* Cologne, Germany: Könemann, 1997.

Greene, B. *The Grains Cookbook.* New York: Workman Publishing, 1988.

Hensperger, B., and J. Kaufmann. *Not Your Mother's Slow Cooker Cookbook.* Boston: Harvard Common Press, 2005.

Hensperger, B., and J. Kaufmann. *The Ultimate Rice Cooker Cookbook.* Boston: Harvard Common Press, 2002.

Hughes, H. *The Spelt Cookbook: Cooking with Nature's Grain for Life.* Garden City Park, NY: Avery Publishing Group, 1995.

Janick, J., and J. E. Simon. *Advances in New Crops.* Portland, OR: Timber Press, 1990.

Janick, J., and J. E. Simon. *New Crops.* New York: Wiley, 1993.

Lang, J. H. *Tastings: The Best from Ketchup to Caviar.* New York: Crown Publishers, 1986.

Loha-Unchit, K. *Dancing Shrimp: Favorite Thai Recipes for Seafood.* New York: Simon and Schuster, 2000.

Loha-Unchit, K. *It Rains Fishes.* Rohnert Park, CA: Pomegranate Communications, 1995.

London, S., and M. London. *The Versatile Grain and the Elegant Bean.* New York: Simon and Schuster, 1992.

McGee, H. *On Food and Cooking: The Science and Lore of the Kitchen.* New York: Scribner, 2004.

Pitchford, P. *Healing with Whole Foods.* Berkeley, CA: North Atlantic Books, 2002.

Robertson, R. *Fresh from the Vegetarian Slow Cooker.* Boston: Harvard Common Press, 2004.

Rögnvaldardóttir, N. *Cool Cuisine.* Reykjavik, Iceland: Vaka-Helgafell, 2004.

Rögnvaldardóttir, N. *Icelandic Food and Cookery.* New York: Hippocrene Books, 2002.

Saltman, J. *Amazing Grains.* Tiburon, CA: H. J. Kramer, 1990.

Sass, L. J. *Great Vegetarian Cooking Under Pressure.* New York: William Morrow, 1994.

Sass, L. J. *Pressure Perfect.* New York: William Morrow, 2004.

Weinzweig, A. *Zingerman's Guide to Good Eating.* New York: Houghton Mifflin, 2003.

Wood, R. *The Splendid Grain*. New York: William Morrow, 1997.

Articles and Reports

Baker, R. D. "Millet Production." *New Mexico State University Cooperative Extension Service Guide* A-414 (2005).

Behall, K. M., D. J. Scholfield, and J. Hallfrisch. "Diets Containing Barley Significantly Reduce Lipids in Mildly Hypercholesterolemic Men and Women." *American Journal of Clinical Nutrition* (November 2004).

Celiac Sprue Association. "Sorghum, Milo of the Midwest." *Lifeline* (Fall 1995).

Dickerson, G. W. "Nutritional Analysis of New Mexico Blue Corn and Dent Corn Kernels." *New Mexico State University Cooperative Extension Service Guide* H-233 (February 2003).

Environmental Nutrition editors. "Oats May Now Be Okay for People with Gluten Sensitivity." *Environmental Nutrition* (July 2002).

Fletcher, J. "Risotto Revelation." *San Francisco Chronicle* (November 26, 2003).

Gifford, K. D. "The Vast Galaxy of Whole Grains." Presentation at the Whole Grains Go Mainstream Conference, New Orleans, November 14–16, 2004.

Gugino, S. "Rediscovering Rice." *Wine Spectator* (September 15, 2002).

Gugino, S. "A Stirring Account." *Wine Spectator* (August 31, 1998).

Holmes, L. "Ancient Waves of Rice and Grains." *Plate Coverage* (Summer 2002).

Jorge, N. "Paella: Rice at Its Best." *Fine Cooking* (June/ July 1999).

Kujala, T., ed. "Rye and Health." http://rye.vtt.fi/ (2006).

Lane, K. "Israeli Couscous." *National Culinary Review* (October 2001).

Loha-Unchit, K. "All about Thai Jasmine Rice." www.thaifoodandtravel.com/features/jasrice.html (1998).

Mendel, J. "More Than Paella." *Solbank Prestige Club Magazine* (Summer 2002).

National Grain Sorghum Producers. "Sorghum 101." www.sorghumgrowers.com/Sorghum+101 (2007).

Niemi, J. "Wild about Ricing." *Minnesota Conservation Volunteer* (July/August 2004).

Noakes, G., and L. C. Noakes. "Couscous: The Measure of the Maghrib." *Saudi Aramco World* (November/December 1998).

North American Millers' Association. "Oat Milling." www.namamillers.org/prd_o_mill.html (2006).

Oelke, E. A., D. H. Putnam, T. M. Teynor, et al. "Quinoa." In *Alternative Field Crops Manual* (Madison, WI: University of Wisconsin–Extension, Cooperative Extension, 1992). Available at www.hort.purdue.edu/newcrop/afcm/quinoa.html (2000).

Oelke, E. A., T. M. Teynor, P. R. Carter, et al. "Wild Rice." In *Alternative Field Crops Manual* (1992). Available at www.hort.purdue.edu/newcrop/afcm/wildrice.html (1997).

Purdue University Center for New Crops and Plant Products. "Proso Millet." www.hort.purdue.edu/newcrop/Crops/Proso_millet.html (1996).

Small, E. "New Crops for Canadian Agriculture." In J. Janick, ed., *Perspectives on New Crops and New Uses*. Alexandria, VA: ASHS Press, 1999. Available at www.hort.purdue.edu/newcrop/proceedings1999/v4-015a.html.

Stallknect, G. F., K. M Gilbertson, and J. E. Ranney. "Alternative Wheat Cereals as Food Grains: Einkorn, Emmer, Spelt, Kamut, and Triticale." In J. Janick, ed., *Progress in New Crops*. Alexandria, VA: ASHS Press (1996). Available at www.hort.purdue.edu/newcrop/proceedings1996/v3-156.html.

U.S. Grains Council. "Sorghum Handbook: All about White Sorghum." www.grains.org/galleries/default-file/Sorghum%20Handbook.pdf (2004).

Vaasan and Vaasan Group. "Rye Know-How." www.vaasan.com/public/en/03_rye_knowhow/index.jsp (2005).

Wood, R. T. "Tale of a Food Survivor: Quinoa." *East West Journal* (April 1985). Available at www.quinoa.net/Survivor/survivor.html.

WHOLE GRAIN AND SPECIALTY FLOURS
Books

Beranbaum, R. L. *The Bread Bible*. New York: W. W. Norton, 2003.

Cheney, S. J. *Breadtime*. Berkeley, CA: Ten Speed Press, 1998.

Cook's Illustrated editors. *The Complete Book of Pasta and Noodles*. New York: Clarkson Potter Publishers, 2000.

Divina, F., and M. Divina. *Foods of the Americas: Native Recipes and Traditions*. Berkeley, CA: Ten Speed Press, 2004.

Fenster, C. *Gluten-Free Baking*. Centennial, CO: Savory Palate, 2004.

Fenster, C. *Gluten-Free 101: Easy, Basic Dishes without Wheat,* 4th edition. Centennial, CO: Savory Palate, 2003.

Gerras, C., ed. *Rodale's Basic Natural Foods Cookbook.* Emmaus, PA: Rodale Press, 1984.

Hagman, B. *The Gluten-Free Gourmet Bakes Bread.* New York: Henry Holt, 1999.

King Arthur Flour. *King Arthur Flour Baker's Companion.* Woodstock, VT: Countryman Press, 2003.

Leader, D., and J. Blahnik. *Bread Alone.* New York: William Morrow, 1993.

Lebovitz, D. *The Great Book of Chocolate.* Berkeley, CA: Ten Speed Press, 2004.

McGee, H. *On Food and Cooking: The Science and Lore of the Kitchen.* New York: Scribner, 2004.

Reinhart, P. *The Bread Baker's Apprentice.* Berkeley, CA: Ten Speed Press, 2001.

Wood, R. *The New Whole Foods Encyclopedia.* New York: Penguin Compass, 1999.

Wood, R. *The Splendid Grain.* New York: William Morrow, 1997.

Articles and Reports

Baking 911.com "The Pantry: Flour, Grains and Meals." www.baking911.com/pantry/flour,grains.htm (2001–2005).

Berger, J. "Baking Substitution Solutions." *Living Without* (Fall 1999).

Berry, D. "Grains Galore." *Food Product Design* (November 2002).

Campbell, J., M. Hauser, and S. Hill. "Nutritional Characteristics of Organic, Freshly Stone-Ground, Sourdough and Conventional Breads." *Ecological Agriculture Projects* Publication #35. Ste-Anne-de-Bellevue, Quebec: McGill University (1991).

Casa de Fruta. "What Is Mesquite?" www.casadefruta.com/mesquite.aspx (2007).

Celiac Sprue Association. "Sorghum, Milo of the Midwest." *Lifeline* (Fall 1995).

DesertUSA.com. "Mesquite as Food." www.desertusa.com/lil/mesquite.html (1996–2007).

Dickerson, G. W. "Nutritional Analysis of New Mexico Blue Corn and Dent Corn Kernels." *New Mexico State University Cooperative Extension Service Guide* H-233 (February 2003).

Empire Chestnut Company. "Cooking with Chestnuts." www.empirechestnut.com/recipe.htm (January 2005).

Flagstaff's Wild Foraging Newsletter editors. "Mesquite Flour." *Flagstaff's Community Supported Wild Foraging Newsletter* (October 16, 2003).

Katz, F. "You Don't Know Beans about Legume Flours." www.foodprocessing.com/articles/2005/400.html (2005).

Oregon State University. "Cereals, Grains, Seeds: Rye." http://food.oregonstate.edu/g/rye.html (July 20, 2005).

Reilly, R. "The Mystique of Mesquite." *Living Without* (Spring 2005).

Stallknecht, G. F. "New Crop Factsheet: Teff." www.hort.purdue.edu/newcrop/cropfactsheets/teff.html (1998).

Stallknecht, G. F., K. M Gilbertson, and J. E. Ranney. "Alternative Wheat Cereals as Food Grains: Einkorn, Emmer, Spelt, Kamut, and Triticale." In J. Janick, ed. *Progress in New Crops.* Alexandria, VA: ASHS Press (1996). Available at www.hort.purdue.edu/newcrop/proceedings1996/v3-156.html.

Stromnes, J. "Specialty Flour on the Rise." *The Missoulian* (November 16, 2003).

Vaasan and Vaasan Group. "Rye Know-How." www.vaasan.com/public/en/03_rye_knowhow/index.jsp (2005).

BREADS
Books

Beranbaum, R. L. *The Bread Bible.* New York: W. W. Norton, 2003.

Brand-Miller, J., T. Wolever, K. Foster-Powell, et al. *The New Glucose Revolution.* New York: Marlow, 2003.

Brown, A. *I'm Just Here for More Food.* New York: Stewart, Tabori, and Chang, 2004.

Brown, E. E. *The Tassajara Bread Book.* Boston, MA: Shambhala Publications, 1995.

Cheney, S. J. *Breadtime.* Berkeley, CA: Ten Speed Press, 1998.

Cooperative Whole Grain Educational Association. *Uprisings: The Whole Grain Baker's Book.* Hendersonville, NC: Mother Earth News, 1983.

Corriher, S. *CookWise: The Secrets of Cooking Revealed.* New York: William Morrow, 1997.

Divina, F., and M. Divina. *Foods of the Americas: Native Recipes and Traditions.* Berkeley, CA: Ten Speed Press, 2004.

Fenster, C. *Gluten-Free 101: Easy, Basic Dishes without Wheat,* 4th edition. Centennial, CO: Savory Palate, 2003.

Fenster, C. *Special Diet Solutions.* Littleton, CO: Savory Palate, 2003.

Goldman, M., and Y. Huneault. *The Best of Betterbaking.com.* Berkeley, CA: Ten Speed Press, 2002.

Greenstein, G. *Secrets of a Jewish Baker.* Freedom, CA: Crossing Press, 1993.

Hagman, B. *The Gluten-Free Gourmet Bakes Bread.* New York: Henry Holt, 1999.

Herbst, S. T. *Food Lover's Companion.* Hauppauge, NY: Barron's Educational Services, 1995.

PASTA AND NOODLES
Books

Bastianich, L. M. *Lidia's Italian-American Kitchen.* New York: Alfred A. Knopf, 2004.

Bastianich, L. M. *Lidia's Italian Table.* New York: William Morrow, 1998.

Belleme, J., and J. Belleme. *Cooking with Japanese Foods.* Garden City Park, NY: Avery Publishing Group, 1993.

Cook's Illustrated editors. *The Complete Book of Pasta and Noodles.* New York: Clarkson Potter, 2000.

Kushi, A., with A. Jack. *Aveline Kushi's Complete Guide to Macrobiotic Cooking.* New York: Warner Books, 1985.

McGee, H. *On Food and Cooking: The Science and Lore of the Kitchen.* New York: Scribner, 2004.

Solomon, C. *Encyclopedia of Asian Food.* Hong Kong: Periplus Editions, 1998.

Wood, R. *The Splendid Grain.* New York: William Morrow, 1997.

Wright, J. *Pasta.* London: Lorenz Books, 2003.

Igoe, R. S., and Y. H. Hui. *Dictionary of Food Ingredients,* 4th edition. Gaithersburg, MD: Aspen Publishers, 2001.

Katz, S. E. *Wild Fermentation: The Flavor, Nutrition, and Craft of Live-Culture Foods.* White River Junction, VT: Chelsea Green Publishing, 2003.

King Arthur Flour. *King Arthur Flour Baker's Companion.* Woodstock, VT: Countryman Press, 2003.

Lawrence, F. *Not on the Label.* London: Penguin Books, 2004.

Leader, D., and J. Blahnik. *Bread Alone.* New York: William Morrow, 1993.

Lewis, R. J., Sr. *Food Additives Handbook.* New York: Van Nostrand Reinhold, 1989.

McGee, H. *On Food and Cooking: The Science and Lore of the Kitchen.* New York: Scribner, 2004.

Ortiz, J. *The Village Baker.* Berkeley, CA: Ten Speed Press, 1993.

Pitchford, P. *Healing with Whole Foods,* 3rd edition. Berkeley, CA: North Atlantic Books, 2002.

Reinhart, P. *The Bread Baker's Apprentice.* Berkeley, CA: Ten Speed Press, 2001.

Reinhart, P. *Crust and Crumb.* Berkeley, CA: Ten Speed Press, 1998.

Robertson, L., with C. Flinders and B. Godfrey. *The Laurel's Kitchen Bread Book.* New York: Random House, 2003.

Rögnvaldardóttir, N. *Cool Cuisine.* Reykjavik, Iceland: Vaka-Helgafell, 2004.

Rögnvaldardóttir, N. *Icelandic Food and Cookery.* New York: Hippocrene Books, 2002.

Wood, E. *Classic Sourdoughs.* Berkeley, CA: Ten Speed Press, 2001.

Articles and Reports

Agency for Toxic Substances and Disease Registry, Division of Toxicology. "Public Health Statement for Aluminum." www.atsdr.cdc.gov/toxprofiles/phs22.html (September 2006).

Stallknecht, G. F., K. M. Gilbertson, and J. E. Ranney. "Alternative Wheat Cereals as Food Grains: Einkorn, Emmer, Spelt, Kamut, and Triticale." www.hort.purdue.edu/newcrop/proceedings1996/V3-156.html (1996).

Articles and Reports

Decker, K. "The Long and Short of Noodles in Asia." *Food Product Design* (October 2002).

Fletcher, J. "Sardinia's Best-Kept Secret Comes Out." *San Francisco Chronicle* (January 14, 2004).

Hazan, G. "Making Machine-Rolled Pasta." *Fine Cooking* (June/July 1996).

Katz, F. "You Don't Know Beans about Legume Flours." www.foodprocessing.com/articles/2005/400.html (2005).

Michigan State University. "MSU Research Contributes to Launch of New Bean Products." College of Agriculture and Natural Resources press release (January 28, 2005).

BEANS, PEAS, AND LENTILS
Books

Berry, E., and F. Fabricant. *The Great Bean Book.* Berkeley, CA: Ten Speed Press, 1999.

Dominé, A. *Organic and Wholefoods: Naturally Delicious Cuisine.* Cologne, Germany: Könemann, 1997.

McGee, H. *On Food and Cooking.* New York: Scribner, 2004.

Robertson, R. *Fresh from the Vegetarian Slow Cooker.* Boston, MA: Harvard Common Press, 2004.

Shurtleff, W., and A. Aoyagi. *Tofu and Soymilk Production: The Book of Tofu,* vol. 2, 2nd edition. Lafayette, CA: Soyfoods Center, 1990.

Solomon, C. *Encyclopedia of Asian Food.* Hong Kong: Periplus Editions, 1998.

Wood, R. *The New Whole Foods Encyclopedia.* New York: Penguin Compass, 1999.

Articles and Reports

Art Culinaire editors. "3 Sisters." *Art Culinaire* (Fall 2003).

British Nutrition Foundation. "Resistant Starch—Questions and Answers." www.nutrition.org.uk/upload/Resistant%20Starch(1).pdf (2005).

Higdon, J. "Fiber." http://lpi.oregonstate.edu/infocenter/phytochemicals/fiber/index.html (December 22, 2005).

Higdon, J. "Legumes." http://lpi.oregonstate.edu/infocenter/foods/legumes/index.html (December 19, 2005).

Higdon, J. "Lignans." http://lpi.oregonstate.edu/infocenter/phytochemicals/lignans/ (December 30, 2005).

Higdon, J. "Phytosterols." http://lpi.oregonstate.edu/infocenter/phytochemicals/sterols/ (August 11, 2005).

Hymowitz, T., and W. R. Shurtleff. "Debunking Soybean Myths and Legends in the Historical and Popular Literature." *Crop Science* (March/April 2005).

Ingegno, C. "A Lesson in Lentils." *Food Product Design* (February 2000).

Keuth, S., and B. Bisping. "Vitamin B_{12} Production by *Citrobacter freundii* or *Klebsiella pneumoniae* during Tempeh Fermentation and Proof of Enterotoxin Absence by PCR." *Applied and Environmental Microbiology* (May 1994).

Nugent, A. P. "Health Properties of Resistant Starch." *British Nutrition Foundation Nutrition Bulletin* (March 2005).

Parsons, R. "The Long History of the Mysterious Fava Bean." *Los Angeles Times* (May 29, 1996).

Sacks, F. M., A. Lichtenstein, L. Van Horn, et al. "Soy Protein, Isoflavones, and Cardiovascular Health." *Circulation* (February 21, 2006).

U.S. Food and Drug Administration Center for Food Safety and Applied Nutrition. "Phytohaemagglutinin." www.cfsan.fda.gov/~mow/chap43.html (June 14, 2006).

NUTS AND SEEDS
Books

Belitz, H. D., W. Grosch, and P. Schieberle. *Food Chemistry,* 3rd revised edition. Berlin: Springer, 2004.

Edwards, K. A. "Daily Life in Medieval Europe." In *Medieval Europe, 814–1350,* ed. J. Hackett. Farmington Hills, MI: Thomson Gale, 2001.

Kiple, K. F., and K. C. Ornelas, eds. *The Cambridge World History of Food.* Cambridge, UK: Cambridge University Press, 2000.

Loha-Unchit, K. *Dancing Shrimp: Favorite Thai Recipes for Seafood.* New York: Simon and Schuster, 2000.

Matterer, J. L. *A Boke of Gode Cookery,* vol. 1. Princes Risborough, Buckinghamshire, UK: Shire Publications, 2000.

McGee, H. *On Food and Cooking.* New York: Scribner, 2004.

National Academy of Sciences Food and Nutrition Board. *Dietary Reference Intakes for Energy, Carbohydrate, Fiber, Fat, Fatty Acids, Cholesterol, Protein, and Amino Acids (Macronutrients).* Washington, DC: National Academies Press, 2005.

Weil, A. *Eating Well for Optimum Health.* New York: Alfred A. Knopf, 2000.

Articles and Reports

Ahmedna, M., J. Yu, and I. Goktepe. "Peanut Skin Procyanidins: Composition and Antioxidant Activity as Affected by Processing." http://ift.confex.com/ift/2005/techprogram/paper_32062.htm (2005).

Albert, C. M., J. M. Gaziano, Walter C. Willett, et al. "Nut Consumption and Decreased Risk of Sudden Cardiac Death in the Physicians' Health Study." *Archives of Internal Medicine* (June 24, 2002).

Andreoni, N. "Separation of Walnut Kernel Polyphenols." *International Society for Horticultural Science: Fifth International Walnut Symposium* (March 2005).

Coulman, K. D., Z. Liu, W. Q. Hum, et al. "Whole Sesame Seed Is as Rich a Source of Mammalian Lignan Precursors as Whole Flaxseed." *Nutrition and Cancer* (vol. 52, no. 2, 2005).

Davis, B. C., and P. M. Kris-Etherton. "Achieving Optimal Essential Fatty Acid Status in Vegetarians: Current Knowledge and Practical Implications." *American Journal of Clinical Nutrition* (September 2003).

Hu, F. B., M. J. Stampfer, J. E. Manson, et al. "Frequent Nut Consumption and Risk of Coronary Heart Disease in Women: Prospective Cohort Study." *British Medical Journal* (November 14, 1998).

Hyson, D. A., B. O. Schneeman, and P. A. Davis. "Almonds and Almond Oil Have Similar Effects on Plasma Lipids and LDL Oxidation in Healthy Men and Women." *Journal of Nutrition* (April 2002).

Jiang, R., D. R. Jacobs Jr., E. Mayer-Davis, et al. "Nut and Seed Consumption and Inflammatory Markers in the Multi-ethnic Study of Atherosclerosis." *American Journal of Epidemiology* (February 1, 2006).

Jiang, R., J. E. Manson, M. J. Stampfer, et al. "Nut and Peanut Butter Consumption and Risk of Type 2 Diabetes in Women." *Journal of the American Medical Association* (November 27, 2002).

Kiso, Y. "Antioxidative Roles of Sesamin, a Functional Lignan in Sesame Seed, and Its Effect on Lipid and Alcohol Metabolism in the Liver: A DNA Microarray Study." *Biofactors* (vol. 21, 2004).

Kris-Etherton, P. M., W. S. Harris, and L. J. Appel. "Fish Consumption, Fish Oil, Omega-3 Fatty Acids, and Cardiovascular Disease." *Circulation* (2002).

Kris-Etherton, P. M., D. S. Taylor, S. Yu-Poth, et al. "Polyunsaturated Fatty Acids in the Food Chain in the United States." *American Journal of Clinical Nutrition* (January 2000).

Kummer, C. "A New Chestnut." *Atlantic Monthly* (June 2003).

Liu, Z., N. M. Saarinen, and L. U. Thompson. "Sesamin Is One of the Major Precursors of Mammalian Lignans in Sesame Seed (*Sesamum indicum*) as Observed in Vitro and in Rats." *Journal of Nutrition* (April 2006).

Lockette, T. "Peanuts Rival Fruit as Source of Health-Promoting Antioxidants." *University of Florida News* (December 21, 2004).

Morris, J. B. "Food, Industrial, Nutraceutical, and Pharmaceutical Uses of Sesame Genetic Resources." In *Trends in New Crops and New Uses.* Alexandra, VA: ASHS Press, 2002. Available at www.hort .purdue.edu/newcrop/ncnu02/pdf/morris.pdf.

Peñalvo, J. L., S. M. Heinonen, A. M. Aura, et al. "Dietary Sesamin Is Converted to Enterolactone in Humans." *Journal of Nutrition* (May 2005).

Phillips, K. M., D. M. Ruggio, and M. Ashraf-Khorassani. "Phytosterol Composition of Nuts and Seeds Commonly Consumed in the United States." *Journal of Agricultural and Food Chemistry* (November 2005).

Reiter, R. J., L. C. Manchester, and D. Tan. "Melatonin in Walnuts: Influence on Levels of Melatonin and Total Antioxidant Capacity of Blood." *International Journal of Applied and Basic Nutritional Sciences* (September 2005).

Seddon, J. M., J. Cote, and B. Rosner. "Progression of Age-Related Macular Degeneration Association with Dietary Fat, Trans-unsaturated Fat, Nuts, and Fish Intake." *Archives of Ophthalmology* (December 2003).

Simopoulos, A. P. "Omega-3 Fatty Acids in Inflammation and Autoimmune Diseases." *Journal of the American College of Nutrition* (December 2002).

Simopoulos, A. P., A. Leaf, and N. Salem. "Workshop on the Essentiality of and Recommended Dietary Intakes for Omega-6 and Omega-3 Fatty Acids." *Journal of the American College of Nutrition* (October 1999).

Smith, D. T., W. J. Grichar, and A. A. McCallum. "Crop Profile for Sesame in United States." www .ipmcenters.org/cropprofiles/docs/ussesame.html (April 2000).

Talcott, S. T., S. Passeretti, C. E. Duncan, et al. "Polyphenolic Content and Sensory Properties of Normal and High Oleic Acid Peanuts." *Food Chemistry* (May 2005).

Ternus, M., K. McMahon, K. Lapsley, et al. "Qualified Health Claim for Nuts and Heart Disease Prevention: Development of Consumer-Friendly Language." *Nutrition Today* (March/April 2006).

University of Florida. "Peanuts Rival Fruit as Source of Health-Promoting Antioxidants, Researchers Say." www.sciencedaily.com/releases/2005/01/050110120557.htm (January 15, 2005).

U.S. Department of Agriculture Nutrient Data Laboratory. "USDA Database for the Proanthocyanidin Content of Selected Foods." www.ars.usda.gov/research/publications/publications.htm?SEQ_NO_115=169022 (April 21, 2007).

U.S. Food and Drug Administration. "Tree Nut and Peanut Products." www.cfsan.fda.gov/~lrd/FCF164.html (March 24, 1998 amendment).

Vossen, P. "Chestnut Culture in California." http://anrcatalog.ucdavis.edu/pdf/8010.pdf (2000).

Williams, C. M., and G. Burdge. "Long-Chain n-3 PUFA: Plant versus Marine Sources." *Proceedings of the Nutrition Society* (February 2006).

Wu, X., G. R. Beecher, J. M. Holden, et al. "Lipophilic and Hydrophilic Antioxidant Capacities of Common Foods in the United States." *Journal of Agricultural and Food Chemistry* (June 2004).

CULINARY OILS
Books

Belitz, H. D., W. Grosch, and P. Schieberle. *Food Chemistry,* 3rd revised edition. Berlin: Springer, 2004.

Corriher, S. *CookWise: The Secrets of Cooking Revealed.* New York: William Morrow, 1997.

Davis, B., and V. Melina. *Becoming Vegan.* Summertown, TN: Book Publishing Company, 2000.

Freeland-Graves, J. H., and G. C. Peckham. *Foundations of Food Preparation,* 6th edition. Englewood Cliffs, NJ: Prentice-Hall, 1996.

Kiple, K. F., and K. C. Ornelas, eds. *The Cambridge World History of Food.* Cambridge, UK: Cambridge University Press, 2000.

National Academy of Sciences Food and Nutrition Board. *Dietary Reference Intakes for Energy, Carbohydrate, Fiber, Fat, Fatty Acids, Cholesterol, Protein, and Amino Acids (Macronutrients).* Washington, DC: National Academies Press, 2005.

Nestle, M. *What to Eat.* New York: North Point Press, 2006.

Weinzweig, A. *Zingerman's Guide to Good Eating.* Boston: Houghton Mifflin, 2003.

Articles and Reports

Alarcon de la Lastra, C., M. D. Barranco, V. Motilva, et al. "Mediterranean Diet and Health: Biological Importance of Olive Oil." *Current Pharmaceutical Design* (July 2001).

American Journal of Medicine Editorial. "A Symposium: Dietary Fat Consensus Statements." *American Journal of Medicine* (December 30, 2002).

Atinmo, T., and A. T. Bakre. "Palm Fruit in Traditional African Food Culture." *Asia Pacific Journal of Clinical Nutrition* (September 2003).

Brown, M. J., M. G. Ferruzzi, M. L. Nguyen, et al. "Carotenoid Bioavailability Is Higher from Salads Ingested with Full-Fat Than with Fat-Reduced Salad Dressings as Measured with Electrochemical Detection." *American Journal of Clinical Nutrition* (August 2004).

Choudbhury, N., L. Tan, and A. S. Truswell. "Comparison of Palmolein and Olive Oil: Effects on Plasma Lipids and Vitamin E in Young Adults." *American Journal of Clinical Nutrition* (May 1995).

Cordain, L., S. B. Eaton, A. Sebastian, et al. "Origins and Evolution of the Western Diet: Health Implications for the 21st Century." *American Journal of Clinical Nutrition* (February 2005).

De Lorgeril, M., S. Renaud, N. Mamelle, et al. "Mediterranean Alpha-linolenic Acid-Rich Diet in Secondary Prevention of Coronary Heart Disease." *Lancet* (June 1994).

De Lorgeril, M., and P. Salen. "The Mediterranean-Style Diet for the Prevention of Cardiovascular Diseases." *Public Health Nutrition* (February 2006).

Elson, C. E. "Tropical Oils: Nutritional and Scientific Issues." *Critical Reviews in Food Science and Nutrition* (vol. 31, no. 1–2, 1992).

Fielding, J. M., K. G. Rowley, P. Cooper, et al. "Increases in Plasma Lycopene Concentration after Consumption of Tomatoes Cooked with Olive Oil." *Asia Pacific Journal of Clinical Nutrition* (vol. 14, no. 2, 2005).

Giugliano, D., and K. Esposito. "Mediterranean Diet and Cardiovascular Health." *Annals of the New York Academy of Sciences* (November 2005).

Harper, C. R., M. J. Edwards, A. P. DeFilipis, et al. "Flaxseed Oil Increases the Plasma Concentrations of Cardioprotective (n-3) Fatty Acids in Humans." *Journal of Nutrition* (January 2006).

Hedron, E., G. Mulokozi, and U. Svanberg. "In Vitro Accessibility of Carotenes from Green Leafy Vegetables Cooked with Sunflower Oil or Red Palm Oil." *International Journal of Food Sciences and Nutrition* (November 2002).

Hyson, D. A., B. O. Schneeman, and P. A. Davis. "Almonds and Almond Oil Have Similar Effects on Plasma Lipids and LDL Oxidation in Healthy Men and Women." *Journal of Nutrition* (April 2002).

Kris-Etherton, P. M., W. S. Harris, and L. J. Appel. "Fish Consumption, Fish Oil, Omega-3 Fatty Acids, and Cardiovascular Disease." *Circulation* (November 2002).

Kris-Etherton, P. M., D. S. Taylor, S. Yu-Poth, et al. "Polyunsaturated Fatty Acids in the Food Chain in the United States." *American Journal of Clinical Nutrition* (January 2000).

Lee, J., K. Kim, and E. Choe. "Antioxidant Activity of Lignan Compounds in Sesame Oil on the Oxidation of Sunflower Oil During Heating." Paper presented a the Institute of Food Technologists Annual Meeting Food Chemistry Antioxidant Session #18B-23 (July 17, 2005).

National Academy of Sciences Food and Nutrition Board. "Letter Report on Dietary Reference Intakes for Trans-Fatty Acids Drawn from the Report on Dietary Reference Intakes for Energy, Carbohydrate, Fiber, Fat, Fatty Acids, Cholesterol, Protein, and Amino Acids." www.iom.edu/Object.File/Master/13/083/TransFattyAcids.pdf (2002).

Nevin, K. G., and T. Rajamohan. "Beneficial Effects of Virgin Coconut Oil on Lipid Parameters and in Vitro LDL Oxidation." *Clinical Biochemistry* (September 2004).

Ong, A. S., and S. H. Goh. "Palm Oil: A Healthful and Cost-Effective Dietary Component." *Food Nutrition Bulletin* (March 2002).

Ostlund, R. E., S. B. Racette, A. Okeke, et al. "Phytosterols That Are Naturally Present in Commercial Corn Oil Significantly Reduce Cholesterol Absorption in Humans." *American Journal of Clinical Nutrition* (June 2002).

Owen, R. W., A. Giacosa, W. E. Hull, et al. "Olive-Oil Consumption and Health: The Possible Role of Antioxidants." *Lancet Oncology* (October 2000).

Phillips, K. M., D. M. Ruggio, and M. Ashraf-Khorassani. "Phytosterol Composition of Nuts and Seeds Commonly Consumed in the United States." *Journal of Agricultural and Food Chemistry* (November 2005).

Simopoulos, A. P. "Omega-3 Fatty Acids in Inflammation and Autoimmune Diseases." *Journal of the American College of Nutrition* (December 2002).

Simopoulos, A. P., A. Leaf, and N. Salem Jr. "Workshop on the Essentiality of and Recommended Dietary Intakes for Omega-6 and Omega-3 Fatty Acids." *Journal of the American College of Nutrition* (October 1999).

Spilla, G. A., D. J. Jenkins, L. N. Cragen, et al. "Effect of a Diet High in Monounsaturated Fat from Almonds on Plasma Cholesterol and Lipoproteins." *Journal of the American College of Nutrition* (April 1992).

St-Onge, M. P., and P. J. Jones. "Physiological Effects of Medium-Chain Triglycerides: Potential Agents in the Prevention of Obesity." *Journal of Nutrition* (March 2002).

St-Onge, M. P., R. Ross, W. D. Parsons, et al. "Medium-Chain Triglycerides Increase Energy Expenditure and Decrease Adiposity in Overweight Men." *Obesity Research* (March 2003).

Sundram, K., R. Sambanthamurthi, and Y. Tan. "Palm Fruit Chemistry and Nutrition." *Asia Pacific Journal of Clinical Nutrition* (September 2003).

Tuck, K. L., and P. J. Hayball. "Major Phenolic Compounds in Olive Oil: Metabolism and Health Effects." *The Journal of Nutritional Biochemistry* (November 2002).

Unlu, N. Z., T. Bohn, S. K. Clinton, et al. "Carotenoid Absorption from Salad and Salsa by Humans Is Enhanced by the Addition of Avocado or Avocado Oil." *Journal of Nutrition* (March 2005).

U.S. Environmental Protection Agency. "Fact Sheet: Final Air Toxics Rule for Solvent Extraction in Vegetable Oil Production." www.epa.gov/ttn/oarpg/t3/fact_sheets/vegoil_fs.pdf (April 3, 2001).

U.S. Environmental Protection Agency Office of Air Quality Planning and Standards. "Vegetable Oil Processing." www.epa.gov/ttn/chief/ap42/ch09/final/c9s11-1.pdf (November 1995).

Vossen, P. "International Olive Oil Council (IOOC) Trade Standard for Olive Oil." http://cesonoma.ucdavis.edu/hortic/pdf/iocc_standards_purity_grade.pdf (2003).

Wahle, K. W., D. Caruso, J. J. Ochoa, et al. "Olive Oil and Modulation of Cell Signaling in Disease Prevention." *Lipids* (December 2004).

Wanten, G. J., and A. H. Naber. "Cellular and Physiological Effects of Medium-Chain Triglycerides." *Mini Review in Medicinal Chemistry* (October 2004).

Washington University in St. Louis, University Communications. "Corn Oil Reduces Cholesterol Absorption." http://news-info.wustl.edu/tips/2002/medical-health/corn.html (July/August 2002).

Wattanapenpaiboon, N., and M. W. Wahlqvist. "Phytonutrient Deficiency: The Place of Palm Fruit." *Asia Pacific Journal of Clinical Nutrition* (September 2003).

Willet, W. C. "The Mediterranean Diet: Science and Practice." *Public Health Nutrition* (February 2006).

Willet, W. C., F. Sacks, A. Trichopoulou, et al. "Mediterranean Diet Pyramid: A Cultural Model for Healthy Eating." *American Journal of Clinical Nutrition* (June 1995).

Williams, C. M., and G. Burdge. "Long-Chain n-3 PUFA: Plant versus Marine Sources." *Proceedings of the Nutrition Society* (February 2006).

MEAT, POULTRY, AND EGGS
Books

Appleby, M. C., J. A. Mench, and B. O. Hughes. *Poultry Behavior and Welfare.* Cambridge, MA: CABI Publishing, 2004.

Grandin, T., and C. Johnson. *Animals in Translation.* New York: Scribner, 2004.

National Research Council. *Carcinogens and Anticarcinogens in the Human Diet.* Washington, DC: National Academy Press, 1996.

Niman, B., and J. Fletcher. *The Niman Ranch Cookbook.* Berkeley, CA: Ten Speed Press, 2005.

Articles and Reports

Bauman, D. E., L. H. Baumgard, B. A. Corl, et al. "Biosynthesis of Conjugated Linoleic Acid in Ruminants." *Proceedings of the American Society of Animal Science* (1999).

Catry, B., H. Laevens, L. A. Devriese, et al. "Antimicrobial Resistance in Livestock." *Journal of Veterinary Pharmacology and Therapeutics* (April 2003).

Clancy, K. "Greener Pastures." *Union of Concerned Scientists* (March 2006). www.ucsusa.org/food_and_environment/sustainable_food/greener-pastures.html (March 2006).

Collignon, P. "A Review: The Use of Antibiotics in Food Production Animals—Does This Cause Problems in Human Health?" In *Manipulating Pig Production.* Werribee, Australia: Australasian Pig Science Association (2003).

Cordain, L., S. B. Eaton, A. Sebastian, et al. "Origins and Evolution of the Western Diet: Health Implications for the 21st Century." *American Journal of Clinical Nutrition* (February 2005).

Epley, Richard J. "Aging Beef." www.extension.umn.edu/distribution/nutrition/DJ5968.html (2007).

Europa European Commision. "Hormones in Meat." http://ec.europa.eu/food/food/chemicalsafety/contaminants/hormones/index_en.htm (2005).

Kimball, J. W. "Symbiosis." http://users.rcn.com/jkimball.ma.ultranet/BiologyPages/S/Symbiosis.html (April 3, 2007).

Mead, J. F., and J. C. Nevenzel. "The Question of Biohydrogenation of Fatty Acids." *Journal of Lipid Research* (July 1960).

Meyer, J. "Symbiotic Relationships." www.cals.ncsu.edu/course/ent591k/symbiosis.html (January 3, 1998).

National Academy of Sciences. "Letter Report on Dietary Reference Intakes for Trans-Fatty Acids." www.iom.edu/CMS/5410.aspx (July 10, 2002).

Sonon, R. N., Jr., D. C. Beitz, and A. H. Trenkle. "Improving Health Benefits of Beef and Milk: A Field Study." www.iowabeefcenter.org/pdfs/BRR/R1864.pdf (2004).

U.S. Department of Agriculture Animal and Plant Health Inspection Service. "Bovine Spongiform Encephalopathy." www.aphis.usda.gov/publications/animal_health/content/printable_version/BSEbrochure12-2006.pdf (December 2006).

U.S. Department of Agriculture Food Safety and Inspection Service. "Food Labeling: Meat and Poultry Labeling Terms." www.fsis.usda.gov/Fact_Sheets/Meat_&_Poultry_Labeling_Terms/index.asp (August 24, 2006).

U.S. Department of Agriculture Foreign Agricultural Service. "European Union Trade Policy Monitoring: EU Presentation on Hormone Ban Directive." www.fas.usda.gov/gainfiles/200311/145986807.pdf (November 13, 2003).

U.S. Department of Agriculture Foreign Agricultural Service. "European Union Trade Policy Monitoring: Historic Overview and Chronology of EU's Hormone Ban." *Global Agriculture Information Network Report* E23206 (November 7, 2003).

U.S. Department of Agriculture Foreign Agricultural Service, U.S. Mission to the European Union. "WTO Hormone Case." http://useu.usmission.gov/agri/ban.html (January 17, 2007).

U.S. Food and Drug Administration. "Animal Cloning: A Draft Risk Assessment." www.fda.gov/cvm/Documents/Cloning_Risk_Assessment.pdf (December 28, 2006).

U.S. Food and Drug Administration. "Animal Cloning: Proposed Risk Management Plan for Clones and Their Progeny." www.fda.gov/cvm/CloningRA_ProposedPlan.htm (December 28, 2006).

U.S. Food and Drug Administration. "Guidance for Industry: Use of Edible Products from Animal Clones or Their Progeny for Human Food or Animal Feed." www.fda.gov/cvm/Guidance/guideline179.htm (December 28, 2006).

DAIRY PRODUCTS
Books

Cheese Board Collective. *The Cheese Board Collective Works*. Berkeley, CA: Ten Speed Press, 2003.

Fallon, S., with M. G. Enig. *Nourishing Traditions*, revised 2nd edition. Washington, DC: New Trends Publishing, 2001.

Jenkins, S. *Cheese Primer*. New York: Workman Publishing, 1996.

Kiple, K. F., and K. C. Ornelas, eds. *The Cambridge World History of Food*. Cambridge, UK: Cambridge University Press, 2000.

McCalman, M., and D. Gibbons. *The Cheese Plate*. New York: Clarkson Potter, 2002.

McGee, H. *On Food and Cooking*. New York: Scribner, 2004.

Werlin, L. *The New American Cheese*. New York: Stewart, Tabori, and Chang, 2000.

Articles and Reports

American Veterinary Medical Association. "Welfare Implications of Tail Docking of Dairy Cattle." www.avma.org/issues/animal_welfare/tail_docking_cattle_bgnd.asp (April 25, 2006).

Bren, L. "Got Milk? Make Sure It's Pasteurized." *FDA Consumer Magazine* (September/October 2004).

Clancy, K. "Greener Pastures." *Union of Concerned Scientists* (March 2006). www.ucsusa.org/food_and_environment/sustainable_food/greener-pastures.html (March 2006).

Clark, S. "Comparing Milk: Human, Cow, Goat, and Commercial Infant Formula." www.saanendoah.com/compare.html (April 6, 2007).

Cordain, L., S. B. Eaton, A. Sebastian, et al. "Origins and Evolution of the Western Diet: Health Implications for the 21st Century." *American Journal of Clinical Nutrition* (February 2005).

Food and Agricultural Organization. "Water Buffalo: An Asset Undervalued." www.aphca.org/publications/files/w_buffalo.pdf (October 2000).

Haenlein, G. F. W. "Why Goat Milk?" http://goatconnection.com/articles/publish/article_77.shtml (October 2002).

Kennedy, P. "Summary of Raw Milk Statutes and Administrative Codes." www.westonaprice.org/federalupdate/aa2005/infoalert_032205.html (December 1, 2004).

Monsanto. "Prosilac" (product leaflet). www.monsantodairy.com/about/882006AUGUSTAleaflet.pdf (2006).

National Agricultural Library. "Early Developments in the American Dairy Industry." www.nal.usda.gov/speccoll/images1/dairy.htm (September 3, 2002).

National Center for Complementary and Alternative Medicine. "Getting to Know 'Friendly Bacteria.'" *CAM at the NIH* (Summer 2006).

Scott, D. L. "bST Fact Sheet." http://vm.cfsan.fda.gov/~ear/CORbST.html (June 9, 1995).

Tikofsky, L. L. "Pasture and Animal Health." Presentation at the U.S. Department of Agriculture/National Organic Standards Board Dairy Pasture Symposium (April 18, 2003).

Tucker, C. B., and D. M. Weary. "Tail Docking in Dairy Cattle." *United States Department of Agriculture Animal Welfare Information Center Bulletin* (Winter 2001/Spring 2002).

U.S. Public Health Service and the U.S. Food and Drug Administration. "Grade 'A' Pasteurized Milk Ordinance, 2003 Revision." www.cfsan.fda.gov/~ear/pmo03toc.html (March 2, 2004).

Wells, A. "Animal Health, Herd Management, and Organic Pasture." Presentation at the U.S. Department of Agriculture/National Organic Standards Board Dairy Pasture Symposium (April 18, 2003).

SEAFOOD
Books

Clay, J. *World Agriculture and the Environment.* Washington, DC: Island Press, 2004.

Corriher, S. *CookWise: The Secrets of Cooking Revealed.* New York: William Morrow, 1997.

Fraioli, J. O. *Ocean Friendly Cuisine.* Minocqua, WI: Willow Creek Press, 2005.

Gouldthorpe, K. *Ray's Boathouse.* Seattle: Documentary Media, 2003.

Grigson, S., and W. Black. *Fish.* London: Headline Book Publishing, 1998.

Harlow, J. *West Coast Seafood.* Seattle: Sasquatch Books, 1999.

Institute of Medicine of the National Academies. *Seafood Choices: Balancing Benefits and Risks.* Washington, DC: National Academies Press, 2007.

Kiple, K. F., and K. C. Ornelas, eds. *The Cambridge World History of Food.* Cambridge, UK: Cambridge University Press, 2000.

Kurlansky, M. *Cod: A Biography of the Fish That Changed the World.* New York: Penguin Books, 1997.

Articles and Reports

Chandroo, K. P., S. Yue, and R. D. Moccia. "An Evaluation of Current Perspectives on Consciousness and Pain in Fishes." *Fish and Fisheries* (December 2004).

Cohen, J. T., D. C. Bellinger, W. E. Connor, et al. "A Quantitative Risk-Benefit Analysis of Changes in Population Fish Consumption." *American Journal of Preventative Medicine* (November 2005).

European Food Safety Authority, Animal Health and Welfare Panel. "Opinion of the Scientific Panel AHAW Related to the Aspects of the Biology and Welfare of Animals Used for Experimental and Other Scientific Purposes." *Annex to EFSA Journal* (December 22, 2005). Available at www.efsa.europa.eu/en/science/ahaw/ahaw_opinions/1286.html.

European Food Safety Authority, Animal Health and Welfare Panel. "Opinion of the Scientific Panel on Animal Health and Welfare on a Request from the Commission Related to Welfare Aspects of the Main Systems of Stunning and Killing the Main Commercial Species of Animals." *EFSA Journal* (July 6, 2004). Available at www.efsa.europa.eu/en/science/ahaw/ahaw_opinions/495.html.

Hu, F. B., L. Bronner, W. C. Willett, et al. "Fish and Omega-3 Fatty Acid Intake and Risk of Coronary Heart Disease in Women." *Journal of the American Medical Association* (April 2002).

Huntingford, F. A., C. Adams, V. A. Braithwaite, et al. "Current Issues in Fish Welfare." *Journal of Fish Biology* (February 2006).

Kris-Etherton, P. M., W. S. Harris, and L. J. Appel. "Fish Consumption, Fish Oil, Omega-3 Fatty Acids, and Cardiovascular Disease." *Circulation* (November 2002).

Lymbery, P. "In Too Deep: The Welfare of Intensively Farmed Fish." www.ciwf.org/publications/reports/in_too_deep_2001.pdf (2002).

Mozaffarian, D., and E. B. Rimm. "Fish Intake, Contaminants, and Human Health: Evaluating the Risks and the Benefits." *Journal of the American Medical Association* (October 18, 2006).

National Resources Defense Council. "Consumer Guide to Mercury in Fish." www.nrdc.org/health/effects/mercury/guide.asp (2006).

Oken, E., K. P. Kleinman, W. E. Berland, et al. "Decline in Fish Consumption among Pregnant Women after a National Mercury Advisory." *American College of Obstetricians and Gynocologists* (August 2003).

Simopoulos, A. P. "Omega-3 Fatty Acids in Inflammation and Autoimmune Diseases." *Journal of the American College of Nutrition* (December 2002).

Stokstad, E. "Global Loss of Biodiversity Harming Ocean Bounty." *Science* (November 3, 2006).

U.S. Department of Agriculture Food Safety and Inspection Service and U.S. Food and Drug Administration Center for Food Safety and Applied Nutrition. "Cold Storage Chart." www.foodsafety.gov/~fsg/f01chart.html (2002).

U.S. Department of Agriculture Foreign Agricultural Service. "Fishery Products: New EC Proposal on Animal Welfare for Farmed Fish." www.fas.usda.gov/gainfiles/200508/146130719.pdf (August 30, 2005).

U.S. Department of Health and Human Services and U.S. Environmental Protection Agency. "Mercury Levels in Commercial Fish and Shellfish." www.cfsan.fda.gov/~frf/sea-mehg.html (February 2006).

U.S. Department of Health and Human Services and U.S. Environmental Protection Agency. "What You Need to Know about Mercury in Fish and Shellfish." http://vm.cfsan.fda.gov/~dms/admehg3.html (March 2004).

Van de Vis, H., S. Kestin, D. Robb, et al. "Is Humane Slaughter of Fish Possible for Industry?" *Agriculture Research* (February 2003).

Vidal, J. "When the Boat Comes In." *The Guardian* (November 6, 2006).

Willett, W. C. "Fish: Balancing Health Risks and Benefits." *American Journal of Preventative Medicine* (November 2005).

Williams, C. M., and G. Burdge. "Long-Chain n-3 PUFA: Plant versus Marine Sources." *Proceedings of the Nutrition Society* (February 2006).

Worm, B., E. B. Barbier, N. Beaumon, et al. "Impacts of Biodiversity Loss on Ocean Ecosystem Services." *Science* (November 3, 2006).

ESSENTIAL SEASONINGS
Books

Belleme, J., and J. Belleme. *Cooking with Japanese Foods.* Garden City Park, NY: Avery, 1993.

Colbin, A. *Food and Healing.* New York: Ballantine Books, 1996.

Corriher, S. *CookWise: The Secrets of Cooking Revealed.* New York: William Morrow, 1997.

Kiple, K. F., and K. C. Ornelas, eds. *The Cambridge World History of Food.* Cambridge, UK: Cambridge University Press, 2000.

Kurlansky, M. *Salt: A World History.* New York: Penguin Books, 2002.

Kushi, A., with A. Jack. *Aveline Kushi's Complete Guide to Macrobiotic Cooking.* New York: Warner Books, 1985.

McGee, H. *On Food and Cooking.* New York: Scribner, 2004.

Pitchford, P. *Healing with Whole Foods.* Berkeley, CA: North Atlantic Books, 2002.

Articles and Reports

Allen, G. "Laver Bread: Welsh Sea Biscuits." www.leitesculinaria.com/writings/food_history/laver.html (2002–2006).

Bond, A. "Working Alchemy: The Miracle of Miso." www.organicanews.com/news/article.cfm?story_id=187 (Summer 2002).

Canadian Food Inspection Agency. "Inorganic Arsenic and Hijiki Seaweed Consumption." www.inspection.gc.ca/english/fssa/concen/specif/arsenice.shtml (October 2001).

Food and Environmental Hygiene Department (The Government of the Hong Kong Special Administrative Region). "Hijiki and Arsenic." *Safe Food and Public Health Risk in Brief* (January 20, 2005).

Funahashi, H., T. Imai, T. Mase, et al. "Seaweed Prevents Breast Cancer?" *Japanese Journal of Cancer Research* (May 2001).

Gong, Y. F., Z. J. Huang, M. Y. Qiang, et al. "Suppression of Radioactive Strontium Absorption by Sodium Alginate in Animals and Human Subjects." *Biomedical and Environmental Sciences* (September 1991).

Hernandez, B. Y., K. McDuffie, A. A. Franke, et al. "Reports: Plasma and Dietary Phytoestrogens and Risk of Premalignant Lesions of the Cervix." *Nutrition and Cancer* (vol. 49, no. 2, 2004).

Higdon, J. "Iodine." http://lpi.oregonstate.edu/infocenter/minerals/iodine/index.html (April 11, 2003).

Jacobi, D. "Miso." *Natural Health* (May/June 1995).

Klahorst, S. "Soy Sauce Poetics: Flavor That Speaks of Umami." *Food Product Design* (May 2002).

Lindemann, B. "A Taste for Umami." *Nature Neuroscience* (February 2000).

Logeart, D., S. Prigent-Richard, C. Boisson-Vidal, et al. "Fucans, Sulfated Polysaccharides Extracted from Brown Seaweeds, Inhibit Vascular Smooth Muscle Cell Proliferation." *European Journal of Cellular Biology* (December 1997).

Mourao, P. A. "Use of Sulfated Fucans as Anticoagulant and Antithrombotic Agents: Future Perspectives." *Current Pharmacological Design* (vol. 10, no. 9, 2004).

National Center for Complementary and Alternative Medicine. "Getting to Know 'Friendly Bacteria.'" *CAM at the NIH* (Summer 2006).

Ohara, M., H. Lu, K. Shiraki, et al. "Inhibition by Long-Term Fermented Miso of Induction of Gastric Tumors by N-methyl-N'-nitrosoguanidine in CD (SD) Rats." *Oncology Reports* (May/June 2002).

Ohara, M., H. Lu, K. Shiraki, et al. "Radioprotective Effects of Miso against Radiation in B6C3F1 Mice: Increased Small Intestine Crypt Survival, Crypt Lengths and Prolongation of Average Time to Death." *Hiroshima Journal of Medical Science* (December 2001).

Pereira, M. S., B. Mulloy, and P. A. S. Mourão. "Structure and Anticoagulant Activity of Sulfated Fucans." *Journal of Biological Chemistry* (March 19, 1999).

Rosenfeld, L. "Discovery and Early Uses of Iodine." *Journal of Chemical Education* (August 2000).

Shurtleff, W., and A. Aoyagi. "The History of Soy Pioneers Around the World." Unpublished manuscript available at www.thesoydailyclub.com/DisplayArchive.cfm?ArchiveID=784 (2006).

Tang, H., M. Inoue, Y. Uzawa, et al. "Anti-tumorigenic Components of a Sea Weed, *Eeteromorpha clathrata*." *Biofactors* (vol. 22, 2004).

Teas, J., S. Pino, A. Critchley, et al. "Variability of Iodine Content in Common Commercially Available Edible Seaweeds." *Thyroid* (October 2004).

Thompson, L. U., P. Robb, M. Serraino, et al. "Mammalian Lignan Production from Various Foods." *Nutrition and Cancer* (vol. 16, no. 1, 1991).

Tokui, N., T. Yoshimura, Y. Fujino, et al. "Dietary Habits and Stomach Cancer Risk in the JACC Study." *Journal of Epidemiology* (June 2005, supplement 2).

UK Food Standards Agency. "Agency Advises against Eating Hijiki Seaweed." www.food.gov.uk/news/pressreleases/2004/jul/hijikipr (July 28, 2004).

Yamamoto, S., T. Sobue, M. Kobayashi, et al. "Soy, Isoflavones, and Breast Cancer Risk in Japan." *Journal of the National Cancer Institute* (June 18, 2003).

Yuan, Y. V., M. F. Carrington, and N. A. Walsh. "Extracts from Dulse (*Palmaria palmata*) Are Effective Antioxidants and Inhibitors of Cell Proliferation in Vitro." *Food and Chemical Toxicology* (July 2005).

Yuan, Y. V., and N. A. Walsh. "Antioxidant and Antiproliferative Activities of Extracts from a Variety of Edible Seaweeds." *Food and Chemical Toxicology* (July 2006).

SWEETENERS
Books

Belleme, J., and J. Belleme. *Cooking with Japanese Foods.* Garden City Park, NY: Avery, 1993.

Beranbaum, R. L. *The Bread Bible.* New York: W. W. Norton, 2003.

Buhmann, S., with B. Repplier. *Letters from the Hive.* New York: Bantam Book, 2005.

Cheney, S. J. *Breadtime.* Berkeley, CA: Ten Speed Press, 1998.

Corriher, S. *CookWise: The Secrets of Cooking Revealed.* New York: William Morrow, 1997.

Critser, G. *Fat Land.* New York: Houghton Mifflin, 2003.

Fenster, C. *Special Diet Solutions.* Littleton, CO: Savory Palate, 2003.

Feuer, J. *Fruit-Sweet and Sugar-Free: Prize-Winning Pies, Cakes, Pastries, Muffins, and Breads from the Ranch Kitchen Bakery.* Rochester, VT: Healing Arts Press, 1992.

Kushi, A., with A. Jack. *Complete Guide to Macrobiotic Cooking.* New York: Warner Books, 1985.

McGee, H. *On Food and Cooking.* New York: Scribner, 2004.

Nestle, M. *What to Eat.* New York: North Point Press, 2006.

Opton, G. H., and N. Hughes. *Honey: A Connoisseur's Guide with Recipes.* Berkeley, CA: Ten Speed Press, 2000.

Pitchford, P. *Healing with Whole Foods.* Berkeley, CA: North Atlantic Books, 2002.

Robertson, L., C. Flinders, and B. Godfrey. *The Laurel's Kitchen Bread Book.* New York: Random House Trade Paperbacks (2003).

Wood, R. *The New Whole Foods Encyclopedia.* New York: Penguin Compass, 1999.

Articles and Reports

Abdelouahhab, Z., and E. J. Arias-Jimenez. "Date Palm Cultivation." *FAO Plant Production and Protection Paper* 156. Available at www.fao.org/docrep/006/Y4360E/y4360e00.htm (2002).

Agriculture and Agri-Food Canada. "Canada's Agriculture, Food and Beverage Industry: Canada's Maple Syrup Industry." http://ats.agr.ca/supply/factsheets/3310_e.pdf (2003).

American Diabetes Association. "Evidence-Based Nutrition Principles and Recommendations for the Treatment and Prevention of Diabetes and Related Complications." *Diabetes Care* (January 2002).

Bantle, J. P., S. K. Raatz, W. Thomas, et al. "Effects of Dietary Fructose on Plasma Lipids in Healthy Subjects." *American Journal of Clinical Nutrition* (November 2000).

Barreveld, W. H. "Date Palm Products." *FAO Agricultural Services Bulletin* 101. Available at www.fao.org/docrep/t0681E/t0681E00.htm (1993).

Bitzer, M. J., and J. D. Fox. "Processing Sweet Sorghum for Syrup." *University of Kentucky Cooperative Extension Service Publications* AGR-123. Available at www.ca.uky.edu/agc/pubs/agr/agr123/agr123.htm (2004).

Blumenthal, M. "FDA Lifts Import Alert on Stevia: Herb Can Be Imported Only as Dietary Supplement; Future Use as a Sweetener Is Still Unclear." *HerbalGram* (Issue 35, 1995).

Brandle, J. "Stevia Rebaudiana: Its Biological, Chemical, and Agricultural Properties." http://sci.agr.ca/london/faq/stevia_rev_e.htm (2004).

Cantor, S. "Juicing-Up Products with Fruit-Based Ingredients." *Food Product Design* (December 1996).

Chytka, J. "The Life and Times of a Sugar Beet." *Business Farmer* (January 30, 2004).

Department of Justice Canada. "Canada Agricultural Products Act C.R.C., c.289: Maple Products Regulations." http://laws.justice.gc.ca/en/showtdm/cr/C.R.C.-c.289//?showtoc=&instrumentnumber=C.R.C.-c.289 (2006).

Food Standards Agency. "Stevia and Stevioside." www.food.gov.uk/multimedia/webpage/stevia (March 2002).

Hegenbart, S. "Harvesting the Benefits of Fruit-Containing Ingredients." *Food Product Design* (December 1994).

Helfferich, D. "Birch: White Gold in the Boreal Forest." www.uaf.edu/snras/afes/pubs/misc/MP_04_02.pdf (2002).

Illinois Agricultural Experiment Station. "Honey Has Potential as Dietary Antioxidant." *College of Agricultural, Consumer, and Environmental Sciences Biennial Report* (2006).

Keiger, D. "Sweet Persistence." *John Hopkins Magazine* (November 2002).

Keim, N. L. "Why Are Dieters So Hungry?" *Agricultural Research* (August 2001).

Knehr, E. "Carbohydrate Sweeteners." *Food Product Design* (May 2005).

Koelling, M. R., and R. B. Heiligmann. "North American Maple Syrup Producers Manual." *Ohio State University Extension Bulletin* 856 (1996).

Mask, P. L. "Sweet Sorghum Culture and Syrup Production." *Alabama Cooperative Extension Systen Publications* ANR-625 (1991).

Mayes, P. A. "Intermediary Metabolism of Fructose." *American Journal of Clinical Nutrition* (November 1993).

Miraglio, A. M. "Sweetening the Sweetener Pot." *Food Product Design* (August 2003).

National Sweet Sorghum Producers and Processors Association. "Sweet Sorghum FAQs." www.ca.uky.edu/nssppa/sorghumfaqs.html (2005).

Niness, K. R. "Inulin and Oligofructose: What Are They?" *Journal of Nutrition* (July 1999, supplement 7).

Pyevich, C. "Sugar and Other Sweeteners: Do They Contain Animal Products?" *Vegetarian Journal* (March/April 1997).

Raloff, J. "The Color of Honey: A Sweetener That Bee-Devils Food Spoilage." *Science News* (September 12, 1998).

Shimek, J., and J. Kim. "Corn Sugars and DE Values." *University of California Davis Teaching Center Food Science and Technology 100A Discussion Slides*. http://trc.ucdavis.edu/srdungan/fst100a/disc2cornsyrup/ (2003).

Slow Food USA. "Alaskan Birch Syrup." www.slowfoodusa.org/ark/birch_syrup.html (2006).

Southern Minnesota Sugar Cooperative. "Facts about Sugarbeets and Beet Sugar." www.sbreb.org/brochures/SugarCoop/ (2006).

Squires, S. "Sweet but Not So Innocent?" *Washington Post* (March 11, 2003).

State of Vermont. "Title 6 V.S.A., Chapter 32-Vermont Maple Products Law." www.vermontagriculture.com/mapleregs.PDF (1989).

Teff, K. L., S. S. Elliott, M. Tschop, et al. "Dietary Fructose Reduces Circulating Insulin and Leptin, Attenuates Postprandial Suppression of Ghrelin, and Increases Triglycerides in Women." *Journal of Clinical Endocrinology and Metabolism* (June 2004).

University of Iowa News Release. "UI Expert: Fructose Intolerance Is On the Rise." www.news-releases.uiowa.edu/2003/august/082503fructose.html (August 25, 2003).

University of Iowa News Release. "UI Study: Fructose-Reduced Diet Helps People with IBS Symptoms." www.news-releases.uiowa.edu/2003/october/101303fructose.html (October 13, 2003).

University of Maine Cooperative Extension. "Maple Quality Control Manual." www.umaine.edu/umext/maplesyrupproduction (2006).

U.S. Department of Agriculture. "United States Standards for Grades of Maple Sirup." www.ams.usda.gov/standards/mplesirp.pdf (1979).

U.S. Environmental Protection Agency Office of Air Quality Planning and Standards. "Sugar Processing." www.epa.gov/ttn/chief/ap42/ch09/index.html (June 1997).

Index

A

Acorn squash, 28
Adzuki beans, 124–25
Agar, 235
Agave nectar, 246–47
Alaria, 235
All-purpose flour, 94
Almonds, 147–48
oil, 174
Alpha-galactosidase, 120
Amaranth, 36–37
flour, 74, 77
Amasake, 247
Amber crystal sugar, 262
Anasazi beans, 124
Animal welfare
dairy products and, 203
meat and, 192–93
seafood and, 215
Antibiotics, 190, 203–5
Appaloosa beans, 124
Apricot kernel oil, 174
Aquaculture, 214–15
Arame, 235–36
Arborio rice, 55
Argan oil, 174–75
Armenian cracker bread, 100
Arrowroot, 74, 77–78
Arugula, 14
Asian pears, 10
Aspartame, 245–46
Avocado oil, 175
Azuki beans, 124–25

B

Bagels, 98
Baking powder, 97–98
Baking soda, 97
Baldo rice, 55
Banana squash, 28

Barley, 37–39
flour, 74, 78
malt syrup, 247–48
Basil, Thai sweet, 17
Basmati rice, 51–52
Beans
buying, 120–21
digestion of, 118–20
flours, 78
in Native American lore, 119
nutrition and, 118
pastas, 109
preparing, 121–23
role of, in meals, 117
storing, 121
varieties of, 124–36
Bear's head mushrooms, 24
Beef
dry-aged, 193
grass-fed, 193–94
organic, 192–93
Beets, 25–26
Begonias, 18
Bhutanese red rice, 53
Bialy, 98
Biodynamic farming, 2
Birch syrup, 248–49
Black beans, 125
Black Calypso beans, 125
Black-eyed peas, 125
Black forbidden rice, 53–54
Black turtle beans, 125
Bluefoot mushrooms, 23
Blue Hubbard squash, 28
Bok choy, 14
Bolillo, 98
Bolita beans, 125
Borage, 18
Bovine growth hormones, 204–5
Bovine spongiform encephalopathy (BSE), 189
Brazil nuts, 148
Bread flour, 93

Breads
gluten-free, 102
leavening agents for, 96–99
sourdough, 95–96
storing, 104
varieties of, 98–104
Brioche, 98
Broccoflower, 14–15
Broccoli raab, 15
Broccoli Romanesco, 15
Brown rice syrup, 249–50
Buckwheat, 39–40
flour, 74, 78–79
Bulgur, 63
Burdock, 26
Buttercup squash, 28
Butternut squash, 28

C

Cabbage, 15
Cake flour, 94
Calendula, 18
Calrose rice, 54
Camargue red rice, 54
Cane syrup, 250
Cannellini beans, 125–26
Canola oil, 175–76
Carambolas, 10
Carnaroli rice, 55
Carob flour, 74, 79
Cashews, 149
Celery root (celeriac), 26
Cellophane noodles, 112
Cèpes, 24–25
Challah, 98–99
Chanterelles, 23–24
Chayote, 27
Cheese
artisanal, 205–6
making, 200–201
raw milk, 202
sodium in, 201

storing, 208
types of, 206–7
Cherimoyas, 10–11
Chervil, 16
Chestnuts, 149–51
  flour, 74, 79
Chicken. *See* Poultry
Chickpeas. *See* Garbanzo beans
Chicory, 14
Chiles, 19–22
Chinese cabbage, 15
Chinese egg noodles, 111–12
Chinese wheat noodles, 112
Chive blossoms, 18
Chocolate mint, 16–17
Christmas lima beans, 126
Chrysanthemums, 18
Ciabatta, 99
CLAs (conjugated fatty acids), 203
Cloning, 191–92
Cocoa powder, 74, 79–80
Coconut, 151–52
  milk, 146
  oil, 176–77
Collard greens, 15
Corn, 40–42, 119
  flour, 81
  oil, 177
  pasta, 110
  syrup, 243–44
Cornmeal, 74, 80–81
Cornstarch, 74, 81–82
Couscous, 64–66
Cow's milk, 197
Cranberry beans, 126
Crimini mushrooms, 24
Croissants, 99
Cruciferous vegetables, 14–15
Crumpets, 99
Cucumbers, 27
Cured meats, 193
Curry leaves, 16

D

Daikon, 26
Dairy products. *See also* Cheese;
  Milk
  animal welfare and, 203

without antibiotics or growth
    hormones, 203–5
  cultured, 199–200
  lactose intolerance and, 199
Dandelion greens, 15
Dangmyun, 115
Date sugar, 250–51
Delicata squash, 28
Demerara sugar, 262
DHA (docosahexaenoic acid),
    209–10
Dinosaur kale, 15
Duck. *See* Poultry
Dulse, 236
Durum flour, 92

E

Ecologically grown produce, 2–3
Eggs
  cage-free, 195–96
  fertile, 195–96
  grading, 195
  mutualistic approach to, 187–88
  nutrition and, 188–89
  organic, 192–93
Elephant garlic, 26
Endive, 14
English muffins, 99
Enoki mushrooms, 24
EPA (eicosapentaenoic acid),
    209–10
Epazote, 120
Erythritol, 244, 245
Escarole, 14

F

Farina, 64
Farro, 42–43
Fats
  hydrogenated, 172–73
  monounsaturated, 142, 167, 168
  polyunsaturated, 142, 167, 168
  saturated, 167, 168
Fava beans, 126–27
Fennel, 16, 26
Filberts. *See* Hazelnuts
Fish. *See* Seafood
Flageolets, 127

Flavors, five, 221
Flaxseeds, 152–54
  oil, 153, 178
Fleur de sel/flor de sal, 225
Flours
  baking with nonwheat, 73, 76
  enrichment of, 71–72
  grinding methods for, 69–70
  labeling for, 93
  organic, 76
  processing methods for, 70–71
  storing, 72
  varieties of, 74–75, 77–94
Flowers, edible, 17–18
Focaccia, 99
Fougasse, 99
Fregola, 65
French navy beans, 127
Fructose
  crystalline, 244
  metabolism of, 241
Fruits. *See also individual fruits*
  biodynamic, 2
  colors of, 6, 7–9
  dried, 6
  ecologically grown, 2–3
  frozen, 6
  heirloom, 3–4
  juices, 6
  labels for, 2–5
  locally grown, 4
  nutrition and, 1–2, 6
  organically grown, 4–5
  peak seasons for, 7–9
  pesticides and, 5
  ripening, 6, 10
  serving size of, 5
  storing, 6, 10
  sweeteners based on, 251–53

G

Galactose, 241
Game meat, 195
Garbanzo beans, 127–28
  flour, 74, 82–83
Genetic engineering, viii–ix, 192
Geraniums, 18
Gigande beans, 128

Ginger mint, 17
Glucose, 241
Glutamic acid, 221
Gluten, 35, 72–73, 102
Gluten flour, 74, 83
Goat's milk, 198
Golden Hubbard squash, 28
Golden nugget squash, 28
Gomasio, 162, 226
Goose. *See* Poultry
Graham flour, 93
Grains, whole. *See also* Flours
  buying, 31
  components of, 30
  cooking, 31–34
  definition of, 29
  gluten-free and wheat-free, 35–36
  nutrition and, 30
  quick-cooking, 32
  refined vs., 30–31
  seasoning, 35
  sprouting, 34
  storing, 31
  uses of, 31
  varieties of, 36–67
Grano, 43
Grapeseed oil, 178–79
Grass-fed beef, 193–94
Great Northern beans, 128
Greens, 14, 15
Grissini, 99
Grits, 41–42
Guavas, 11

H

Harusame, 112
Hazelnuts, 154–55
  oil, 179
Hedgehog mushrooms, 24
Heirloom varieties, 3–4
Hen-of-the-woods, 24
Herbs
  cooking with, 16
  fresh vs. dried, 16
  nutrition and, 16
  storing, 10
  varieties of, 16–17
Heritage meat, 194

HFCS (high-fructose corn syrup),
    243–44
Hija beans, 128
Hijiki, 236–37
Hiyamugi, 112
Hominy, 41
Homogenization, 202
Honey, 253–55
Hydrogenated fats, 172–73

I

Injera bread, 102
Integrated pest management (IPM),
    2–3
International Federation of
    Organic Agriculture
    Movements (IFOAM), 4–5
Iodine, 223, 233–34
Irish moss, 237
Isomalt, 244
Israeli couscous, 65–66

J

Jacob's cattle beans, 128
Jasmine rice, 52
Jerusalem artichokes, 26
  pasta, 110
Jicama, 26
Job's tears, 43–44
Johnny-jump-ups, 18
Juices, 6

K

Kaffir lime leaves, 16
Kaiser rolls, 99–100
Kale, 15
Kalijira rice, 52
Kamut, 44–45
  bread, 102
  flour, 74, 84
  pasta, 110
Kasha, 40
Kelp, 237–38
Kidney beans, 128
King boletes, 24–25
Kiwifruits, 11
Kobocha squash, 28
Kombu, 238

Kosher salt, 226
Kudzu, 74, 84–85
Kumquats, 11
Kuzukiri, 112–13

L

Labels
  for flour, 93
  for fruits and vegetables, 2–5
  for meat, 192–93
Lactitol, 244, 245
Lactose intolerance, 199
Lahvosh, 100
Lavender, 18
Laver, 238–39
Lavosh, 100
Leavening agents, 96–99
Lebanese couscous, 66
Lemongrass, 16
Lentils, 117, 128–30
Lima beans, 130–31
Lion's mane mushrooms, 24
Locally grown produce, 4
Lotus root, 26
Lupini beans, 131
Lychees, 11

M

Macadamia nuts, 155
Mâche, 14
Mad cow disease, 189
Madeira beans, 131
Maitake, 24
Maltitol, 244
Mangoes, 11
Mannitol, 244
Maple syrup and maple sugar,
    255–58
Marigolds, 18
Marrow beans, 131
Masa, 42
Masa harina, 81
MCTs (medium-chain fatty acids),
    198
Meat
  animal welfare and, 192–93
  antibiotics in, 190
  beef, 193–94

buying, per person, 194
from cloned and genetically engineered animals, 191–92
cured, 193
game, 195
heritage, 194
hormones in, 191
labeling, 192–93
mutualistic approach to, 187–88
nutrition and, 188–89
organic, 192–93
veal, 194–95
Mercury, 210–12
Mesquite flour, 74, 85
Milk
  animal welfare and, 203
  without antibiotics or growth hormones, 203–5
  color of, 197
  cow's, 197
  goat's, 198
  homogenization of, 202
  lactose intolerance and, 199
  nut and seed, 145–46
  pasteurization of, 201–2
  sheep's, 198
  water buffalo's, 198
Millet, 45–46
  flour, 74, 85
Mint, 16–17
Miso, 227–29
Mizuna, 15
Molasses, 258–59
Monounsaturated fats, 142, 167, 168
Montina flour, 74, 86
Morels, 24
Moroccan couscous, 64–65
MSG (monosodium glutamate), 221–22
Mung beans, 131–32
Muscovado sugar, 262
Mushrooms, 23–25
Mustard greens, 15

N

Naan, 100
Nasturtiums, 18
Navy beans, 132

Nitrites, 193
Nixtamal, 42
Nori, 239
Nutrition
  beans and, 118
  eggs and, 188–89
  fruits and, 1–2, 6
  herbs and, 16
  meat and, 188–89
  nuts and, 142–43
  oils and, 167, 168, 172–73
  poultry and, 188–89
  salt and, 222–23
  seafood and, 209–10
  sea vegetables and, 233–34
  seeds and, 142–43
  vegetables and, 1–2, 6
  whole grains and, 30
Nuts. *See also individual nuts*
  blanching, 144–45
  butters, 145
  buying, 143, 144
  definition of, 142–43
  milks, 145–46
  nutrition and, 142–43
  roasting, 144
  storing, 143–44

O

Oats, 46–48
  flour, 75, 86
Oils
  choosing, 167–68, 170
  health and, 167, 168, 172–73
  production of, 167, 168–71
  role of, 167
  smoke point of, 170, 171–72
  storing, 172
  varieties of, 174–86
Olive oil, 179–81
Open pollination, 3
Organic agriculture, 4–5
Oyster mushrooms, 24

P

Pagnotta, 100
Pain au levain, 100
Pain de campagne, 100

Pain paysan, 100
Palm fruit oil, 181–82
Panettone, 100
Panini, 101
Pansies, 18
Papayas, 12
Parsnips, 26–27
Passion fruits, 12
Pasta and noodles
  Asian, 107, 111–16
  cooking, 108
  dried, 108–16
  flours for, 105, 107
  fresh, 107–8
  Italian-style, 107, 108–11
  nutrition and, 105, 107
  shapes of, 106
Pasteurization, 201–2
Pastry flour, 94
Pattypan squash, 27
PCBs (polychlorinated biphenyls), 212
Peanuts, 155–58
  butter, 157–58
  oil, 182–83
Peas, 117, 132
Pecans, 158
Peppers, 19–22
Persimmons, 12
Pesticides, 5
Phytonutrients, ix, 6
Phytosterol, 143
Pigeon peas, 132
Pineapple mint, 17
Pine nuts, 158–59
Pink beans, 132
Pinto beans, 132
Pistachios, 159–60
Pita bread, 101
Plantains, 12
Plums, umeboshi, 231–32
Polyols, 244–45
Polyunsaturated fats, 142, 167, 168
Pomegranates, 12–13
Pom-pom mushrooms, 24
Popcorn, 41
Porcini mushrooms, 24–25
Portobello mushrooms, 25

Posole, 41
Potatoes
　flour, 75, 86
　starch, 75, 86–87
Poultry
　buying, per person, 194
　mutualistic approach to, 187–88
　nutrition and, 188–89
Pretzels, 101
Pugliese bread, 101
Pumpernickel bread, 103
Pumpkins, 28
　seed oil, 183
　seeds, 160–61

Q

Quinces, 13
Quinoa, 48–49
　flour, 75, 87
　pasta, 110

R

Radicchio, 15
Ramen noodles, 113
Rattlesnake beans, 133
Rau ram, 17
rBST, 204–5
Red beans, 133
Red kuri squash, 28
Rennet, 200–201
Rice
　bread, 103
　flour, 75, 87–88
　noodles, 113
　paper wrappers, 113
　pasta, 110
　sticks, 113–14
　varieties of, 49–57
Rice beans, 133
Rice cookers, 33
Rock salt, 224
Rose petals, 18
Russian red kale, 15
Rutabagas, 27
Rye, 57–58
　bread, 103
　crispbread, 103

flour, 75, 88–89
pasta, 110

S

Saccharin, 245–46
Safflower oil, 183–84
Salt
　crystal size of, 226
　importance of, 222
　iodized, 223
　measuring, 227
　nutrition and, 222–23
　storing, 227
　varieties of, 223–26
Sapotes, white, 13
Saturated fats, 167, 168
Savoy cabbage, 15
Scallopini squash, 27
Scarlet runner beans, 133
Schiacciata, 101
Sea beans, 239
Seafood
　buying, by flavor and texture, 217
　buying, per person, 218
　contaminants in, 210–12
　cooking methods for, 218–19
　fresh, 216
　frozen, 216
　humane treatment and, 215
　nutrition and, 209–10
　smoked, 216, 218
　sustainability and, 212–15
　wild vs. farmed, 212–15
Sea lettuce, 239
Sea palm, 239–40
Sea salt, 224–26
Seasonings
　five flavors and, 221–22
　miso, 227–29
　salt, 222–26
　sea vegetables, 232–40
　shoyu, 229–31
　tamari, 229–31
　umeboshi plums, 231–32
Sea vegetables
　classification of, 232
　colors of, 232

cooking, 234, 235–40
nutrition and, 233–34
storing, 234
types of, 235–40
uses for, 232
Seeds. See also individual seeds
　butters, 145
　buying, 143, 144
　milks, 145–46
　nutrition and, 142–43
　roasting, 144
　storing, 143–44
Self-rising flour, 94
Sel gris, 225
Semolina, 92
　bread, 101–2
Sesame seeds, 161–63
　butter, 162–63
　oil, 184
Sheep's milk, 198
Shiitake mushrooms, 25
Shoyu, 229–31
Shrimp. See Seafood
Soba, 114–15
Sodium, 98, 222, 231
Soldier beans, 133
Somen, 115
Sorbitol, 244–45
Sorghum, 58–59
　flour, 75, 89
　syrup, 259–60
Sorrel, 14
Sourdough breads, 95–96
Soybeans, 133–35. See also
　　individual soybean products
Soy flour, 75, 89
Soy oil, 184–85
Soy sauce, 229–31
Spaghetti squash, 28
Spanish tolosana beans, 135
Spelt, 59–60
　bread, 103–4
　flour, 75, 89–90
　pasta, 111
Sprouts, 18–19, 34
Squash
　blossoms, 18
　in Native American lore, 119

summer, 27–28
winter, 27, 28
Steiner, Rudolf, 2
Steuben yellow-eye beans, 135
Stevia, 260
Sticky rice, 51, 57
STP (sodium tripolyphosphate), 216
Straw mushrooms, 25
Sucanat, 262
Sucrose, 242
Sugar alcohols, 244–45
Sugars. *See also* Sweeteners
  classification of, 241–42
  digestion of, 241
  refining of, 260–61
  substitution guide for, 261
  varieties of, 262
Sulfites, 6, 216
Summer savory, 17
Sunflowers
  oil, 185–86
  seeds, 163–64
Sushi rice, 57
Swedish brown beans, 135
Sweeteners. *See also* Sugars
  artificial, nonnutritive, 245–46
  choosing, 242
  highly processed, nutritive, 242–45
  natural, 246–62

T

Tahini, 162–63
Tamari, 229–31
Tamarinds, 13
Tangmyon, 115
Tapioca flour, 75, 90

Taro root, 27
Tarragon, 17
Teff flour, 75, 90–91
Tempeh, 136–37
Texmati rice, 52–53
Thai sweet basil, 17
Three Sisters, 119
Thyme, 17
Tofu, 137–39
Tongues of fire beans, 135
Trans fats, 172–73
Triticale, 61–62
  flour, 71, 75
Tulip petals, 18
Turbinado sugar, 262
Turkey. *See* Poultry
Tuscan kale, 15

U

Udon, 115–16
Ugli fruits, 13
Umami, 221–22, 232
Umeboshi plums, 231–32

V

Veal, 194–95
Vegetables. *See also individual vegetables*
  biodynamic, 2
  colors of, 6, 7–9
  cruciferous, 14–15
  ecologically grown, 2–3
  frozen, 6
  heirloom, 3–4
  juices, 6
  labels for, 2–5
  locally grown, 4
  nutrition and, 1–2, 6

  organically grown, 4–5
  peak seasons for, 7–9
  pesticides and, 5
  serving size of, 5
  storing, 6, 10
Vialone Nano rice, 55
Vietnamese coriander, 17
Violets, 18
Vital wheat gluten, 83

W

Wakame, 240
Walnuts, 164–65
  oil, 186
Water buffalo's milk, 198
Wheat
  allergies to, 35–36
  flour, 75, 91–94
  forms of, 62–66
White button mushrooms, 25
White emergo beans, 135–36
Wild pecan rice, 53
Wild rice, 67
  flour, 75, 94
Wood ear mushrooms, 25

X

Xylitol, 244

Y

Yeast, 96–97
Yellow squash, 27
Yogurt, 199–200

Z

Zucchini, 28